Prediction Statistics FOR Psychological Assessment

Prediction Statistics FOR Psychological Assessment

R. KARL HANSON

AMERICAN PSYCHOLOGICAL ASSOCIATION

Published by
American Psychological Association
750 First Street, NE
Washington, DC 20002
https://www.apa.org

Order Department
https://www.apa.org/pubs/books
order@apa.org

In the U.K., Europe, Africa, and the Middle East, copies may be ordered from Eurospan
https://www.eurospanbookstore.com/apa
info@eurospangroup.com

Typeset in Meridien and Ortodoxa by Circle Graphics, Inc., Reisterstown, MD

Printer: Sheridan Books, Chelsea, MI
Cover Designer: Beth Schlenoff Design, Bethesda, MD

Library of Congress Cataloging-in-Publication Data

Names: Hanson, R. Karl (Robert Karl), 1957- author. | American Psychological Association.
Title: Prediction statistics for psychological assessment / by R. Karl Hanson.
Description: Washington, DC : American Psychological Association, [2022] | Includes bibliographical references and index.
Identifiers: LCCN 2021021482 (print) | LCCN 2021021483 (ebook) | ISBN 9781433836411 (paperback) | ISBN 9781433838453 (ebook)
Subjects: LCSH: Psychological tests—Statistical methods. | Risk assessment. | BISAC: PSYCHOLOGY / Statistics | PSYCHOLOGY / Assessment, Testing & Measurement
Classification: LCC BF176 .H38 2022 (print) | LCC BF176 (ebook) | DDC 150.28/7—dc23
LC record available at https://lccn.loc.gov/2021021482
LC ebook record available at https://lccn.loc.gov/2021021483

https://doi.org/10.1037/0000275-000

Printed in the United States of America

10 9 8 7 6 5 4 3 2 1

To my mother, who was told in 1945 that it was impossible to concurrently study psychology and mathematics.
And my father, for his unwavering confidence in rational problem-solving.

CONTENTS

PREFACE

I wish I had had this book many years ago. Much of my professional career has been as a researcher concerned with recidivism risk assessment. When I was starting out, I struggled with how to analyze recidivism data sets. This book would have set me in the right direction. During my clinical psychology training, I had been taught a little about longitudinal data analysis, and nothing about prediction tools. This was not unusual for those times (1980s), but times change. In my practice area of corrections and forensic mental health, prediction tools are now widely used for routine case management as well as for high-stakes legal decisions. Prediction tools use group data from research studies to inform inferences about the future behavior of specific individuals. To appreciate how risk tools can be used well—or used badly—for such case-specific purposes requires some familiarity with the topics addressed in this book.

Another motivation for writing this book was the need to train trainers of risk tools. Inspired by Meehl (1954) and Jim Bonta (1996; Bonta & Andrews, 2016),[1] I developed a series of actuarial risk tools for sexual recidivism. Some of these measures became widely used, creating a demand for trainers. Actuarial risk tools are based on research findings and should be updated and revised as the research advances. If trainers are going to keep up with these changes, they need to understand research findings. Evidence-based practice requires practitioners who understand evidence.

Outside of my own practice areas, I expect that prediction tools will increasingly be used. The combination of cheap computing power and massive data sets makes the development and use of prediction tools almost inevitable. How many of you were directed to this book by a search history algorithm? There

[1]For many years, Jim Bonta was my direct supervisor at Public Safety Canada.

are many applied questions in education, business, and general clinical psychology that hinge on the likelihood of individuals doing certain things at some future date. Will this student obtain a degree on time if admitted into this program? Will this injured worker return to active duty within 3 months? What is the likelihood that a hospitalized patient will develop a chronic psychotic disorder after a first psychotic episode? Different types of prediction tasks benefit from different approaches to prediction. The prediction tools used by search engines are poorly suited to psychological assessment. There are, however, prediction tools that could helpfully inform decision making in many of the areas in which psychologists aspire for expertise. Most of the examples in this book are drawn from correctional and forensic psychology (the fields which with I am most familiar). Other examples address topics of concern to clinical and educational psychologists. My hope is that readers will find new, productive applications for the material in diverse areas of human service and law.

This book was written for practitioners, who may have selected career paths that minimized their exposure to mathematics and statistics. My expectation is that the typical reader will have, at one time, understood basic mathematical operations and functions and completed an undergraduate statistics course in psychology, criminology, or social work. I do not expect readers to remember all that they once knew. Familiarity with some basic statistical concepts, however, is assumed (e.g., means, medians, standard deviation, correlation, sample, population). If such concepts seem completely foreign, sections of this book may be hard to follow. Readers interested in refreshing their statistical knowledge are encouraged to dust off their old introductory statistics textbook, consult the internet, and refer to the Glossary and Appendix at the end of this book.

Compared with many statistics textbooks, this book has more words and fewer formulas. There are two types of chapters: those that teach specific statistics and those that discuss the role of prediction and prediction statistics in psychological assessment. The chapters that teach specific statistics are chatty, containing stories, anecdotes, and jokes, along with explanations of how and why these statistics could be used to advance applied practice. Readers are expected to skip between chapters, lingering in the sections that appeal to them most. Casual readers can get the main points by skimming the first page (or first sentence) of the statistics chapters. Readers who want mastery of particular statistics are encouraged to work all the way through the relevant chapter(s), including the exercises at the end. Most of the exercises can be completed with a hand calculator. For those interested in the computer exercises, the data sets are available at https://www.apa.org/pubs/books/prediction-statistics-for-psychological-assessment, along with the corresponding syntax (R Statistics and IBM/SPSS).

Although I have worked with these statistics for many years, I have learned much during the process of writing this book. Consequently, I expect that the book will be of interest to other applied researchers. The basic statistical framework assumes that null hypothesis statistical testing helps protect against the overinterpretation of chance findings; however, the focus is on effect sizes, replication, and meta-analysis (what G. Cumming, 2013, called *the new statistics*). The book presents certain materials that may be new to even experienced researchers. I am not aware, for example, of any other text that teaches how to evaluate the calibration of a prediction tool through meta-analysis of logistic regression intercept coefficients (Chapter 14). This is a valuable technique that deserves widespread use. The book also includes considerable practical advice for researchers on how to design and analyze prediction studies in psychology, education, and criminology.

ACKNOWLEDGMENTS

Before thanking my close colleagues and those who explicitly helped me with this book, I would like to thank my critics and professional adversaries. Scientific progress requires sustained criticism to weed out vague, incorrect, and incoherent positions, and I have been fortunate to have had my share of talented critics. Grant Harris and Marnie Rice did much to shape my views, and, from a totally different perspective, so did Stephen Hart and Christopher Webster. It never feels good to be told you are wrong, but it is worse for your mistakes to be left unchecked.

Many of the statistics and arguments in this book were explored and tested with an exceptional group of colleagues and students at Public Safety Canada, including Kelly Babchishin, Andrew Brankley, Andrew J. R. Harris, L. Maaike Helmus, and Seung Chan Lee, as well as international colleagues David Thornton, Amy Phenix, and Ruth Mann. I am particularly grateful to the leadership of Mary Campbell, Bob Cormier, and Jim Bonta of Public Safety Canada, who created the environment that made this work possible.

For helpful comments on specific chapters, thanks are due to Jim Bonta, Martina Faitakis, L. Maaike Helmus, Andrew J. R. Harris, Zoe Hilton, Daryl Kroner, Vernon Quinsey, Kailey Roche, and Skye Stephens. I am also grateful to Linda McCarter, Krissy Jones, and the rest of the editorial team at the American Psychological Association for their skillful support and guidance. Thanks to Vernon Quinsey, David Thornton, and Daryl Kroner for their informal quotes and stories and to Seung Chan Lee, John Hunsley, and Jodi Viljoen for their cameo appearances in my fictional case studies. Leslie Yonce-Meehl very generously provided the photo of her late husband, Paul Meehl.

One highlight of my professional career was reading a paper by Paul Meehl that included a sophisticated criticism of my early work on risk assessment (Janus & Meehl, 1997). A quiet afternoon in a sunlit corner of the Boston Public Library, locking horns with one of my intellectual heroes: It does not get any better than that.

I

BACKGROUND AND OVERVIEW

INTRODUCTION: BACKGROUND AND OVERVIEW

The first two chapters provide an intellectual framework that motivates learning prediction statistics. That numbers can help professionals manage the inherent uncertainty of the world is not obvious, nor is it universally accepted. It is a perspective that requires justification. This book is a teaching text, and before readers dedicate themselves to the study and practice of estimating base rates, risk ratios, and related statistics, it is useful to know the benefits of learning this material now. As stated in Chapter 1, the theory and evidence motivating the use of prediction tools in psychology are not new. What is new is a growing recognition of their value in applied practice. If your professional activities have not yet involved algorithms, they will soon.

Chapter 2 considers different perspectives on probability, with a particular focus on the statements we routinely make concerning the likelihood of specific outcomes for specific people (e.g., Joan is unlikely to succeed in college; Mohammed will excel in his new job). One global criticism of actuarial prediction schemes is that they only concern group data, not individuals. This criticism is misguided, and Chapter 2 explains why.

The last chapter of this section, Chapter 3, is an overview of the statistics chapters. It is intended to orient readers toward the content most aligned with their current concerns.

1

Introduction to Prediction Statistics in Psychology

This introduction contains three main sections. The first part situates this work in the recent history of theory and practice of psychological assessment. It addresses why you may not already know this material and why it is important to learn it now. The second section describes the distinct features of statistical prediction tools and how they are different from other psychological measures. The final section of the Introduction provides of an overview of the types of information provided by statistical prediction tools, which are the core topics of this work.

A BRIEF HISTORY OF STATISTICAL PREDICTION IN PSYCHOLOGICAL ASSESSMENT

In 1954, Paul Meehl published his disturbing little book titled *Clinical Versus Statistical Prediction* (Meehl, 1954, 1986). His conclusion, that statistical prediction was as good as or better than the opinions of respected experts in psychology, was unsettling to those who relied on experts for guidance. It was even more disturbing to the experts. Can we all be replaced by a formula? Should we be?

Meehl's book sparked a generation of research and analysis on the conditions under which professional judgment adds value beyond the opinions of otherwise intelligent laypersons and when the experts can be outdone by a formula. This work showed that, in general, statistical risk tools outperform

https://doi.org/10.1037/0000275-001
Prediction Statistics for Psychological Assessment, by R. K. Hanson

professional judgment when (a) the number of relevant predictor variables is large, (b) the effect of any particular variable is small, and (c) we do not receive rapid feedback concerning the accuracy of our decisions (see Kahneman & Klein, 2009). Most often, when we make predictions about people, all three of these factors apply. Will an individual with a history of criminal behavior reoffend? Will my client relapse if we end treatment today? Will this marriage last? Does this athlete have what it takes to excel in the big leagues? Human existence is complex. Rarely is a single factor determinant of any course of action, and outcomes may not be known for years after the decisions have been made. Under such conditions, we cannot expect to develop intuitive expertise (so-called professional judgment) concerning the likelihood of future behavior. We can, however, increase our predictive accuracy by using statistics.

The use of statistics to predict outcomes for individuals is a relatively recent practice, having gained traction only in the latter part of the 20th century. Since the 1800s, actuaries have routinely used statistical models to estimate life expectancies and insurance risks—for example, how your car insurance premium is calculated. The application of statistical models to human behavior and disease outcomes came much later. Even for ancient, basic problems related to games of chance, there was no mathematic analysis of probability before 1650, despite the obvious incentives. To quote the historian of ideas Ian Hacking (1975), "Someone with only a modest knowledge of probability mathematics could have won himself the whole of Gaul in a week" (p. 3). We have been adding, subtracting, and multiplying numbers for millennia, but we only began to think in terms of statistical probabilities within the past few centuries. At first the practice was restricted to a few members of the intellectual elites; now statistical probabilities are taught in elementary school.

Using statistical probabilities to make decisions does not come naturally; it requires commitment, training, and practice. In his later years, Meehl frequently bemoaned the lack of influence his book had on the routine activities of psychologists. When I was trained in clinical psychology in the 1980s, we read Meehl and his critics. We were not, however, trained on any actuarial risk tools. Few were available. Instead, we were taught that assessing the likelihood of future outcomes for individuals, such as the likelihood of violent recidivism, was beyond the scientific expertise of the profession.

Much has happened since then. I like to think that Meehl's ghost is resting more easily given developments since his passing in 2003. In contemporary correctional psychology and forensic mental health (my areas of practice), statistical prediction tools are ubiquitous. After sporadic use in the 1990s, empirically derived risk tools are now widely used and routinely inform decisions with significant consequences. Dozens of empirically derived risk assessment tools have been introduced during the past 20 years, including tools for general criminal recidivism, violent recidivism, sexual recidivism, intimate partner violence, and arson. Almost all U.S. correctional systems have risk tools for institutional placement, release decisions, and community supervision

FIGURE 1.1. Paul Meehl (1920–2003)

Note. A strong voice for statistical prediction in psychology. Used with permission from Leslie Yonce-Meehl.

(Desmarais & Singh, 2013). Recent trainees in forensic psychology are expected to know how to select, score, and interpret a number of crime and violence risk tools.

From Risk Prediction to Risk Management

The increased use of prediction tools for crime and violence was, in part, motivated by new and better risk tools. In particular, the emerging risk tools responded to evaluators' responsibility to facilitate risk management. Writing in the 1990s, Jim Bonta (1996) described three generations of risk assessment tools in corrections. The first generation was unstructured professional judgment. Before the widespread use of prediction tools, decisions concerning the likelihood of recidivism were based on case analysis and evaluators' implicit theories concerning the causes and correlates of antisocial behavior. For example, I remember case conferences where each of the team members were asked, in turn, "Do you think he is dangerous?" The ensuing, open discussion guided the ultimate decision by the team leader. The problem with this process was not that the decisions were unrelated to the outcome. They were, if weakly. Nor was there a problem with unstructured risk assessment not being accepted by decision makers. The courts in both the United States and Canada have had a wide tolerance for what qualifies as expert opinion concerning risk assessment. The major problem was that the opinions formed by designated experts were no different from those made by otherwise intelligent laypeople (Quinsey & Ambtman, 1979). Individuals who repeatedly reoffended were considered high risk; individuals who committed an isolated offense at an advanced age were considered low risk. A further difficulty with unstructured professional judgment was its lack of transparency. If Johnny Knuckles was designated high risk, he did not know why he was considered dangerous. Disagreements between opposing experts were often decided based on which expert had the most impressive credentials.

Bonta's (1996) second generation of risk tools were actuarial measures based on static, historical risk markers, such as criminal history and age. The risk tools specified, in advance, the risk factors to consider, and how these factors were to be combined into an overall evaluation of risk (often by counting the number of risk factors present). Well-designed second-generation risk tools were more accurate than unstructured professional judgment. Furthermore, Mr. Knuckles could now see why he was deemed high risk. Unfortunately, he still had no idea what he could do about it. Neither did his therapists or case managers. The items on second-generation risk tools documented risk-relevant history without illuminating the psychological and social problems responsible for risk.

Bonta's third generation of risk tools were actuarial risk tools that included dynamic risk factors. Dynamic risk factors can be changed through deliberate intervention, and when the number and severity of such risk factors decrease, so does the likelihood of the outcome. In the context of corrections, dynamic risk factors are often called *criminogenic needs*. Examples of criminogenic needs are negative attitudes toward authority, association with criminal peers, aimless use of leisure time, substance abuse, and lifestyle impulsivity. The risk levels assigned by third-generation risk tools came with explanations. Evaluators using risk tools with dynamic risk factors can easily identify what needs to change to reduce risk and tailor their interventions accordingly.

Although second-generation risk tools are still widely used in corrections and forensic mental health, since the 1990s, there has been increased attention to risk tools that support case formulation and intervention. These tools include an expanding set of validated third-generation risk tools. These tools also include structured professional judgment (SPJ) measures, which are widely used. With SPJ measures, the risk and protective factors are specified in advance, but there is no explicit method of combining the factors into an overall evaluation of risk. Instead, the factors identified inform a case formulation, which is then used to infer overall risk levels. The case formulations and risk levels in the commonly used SPJ measures are primarily intended to inform risk management decisions and only secondarily speak to the likelihood of recidivism. The ideal risk tool, of course, would do both well (see Chapter 17).

The Steady Rise of Prediction Tools in Psychology

The rising influence of statistical prediction tools has been striking in the assessment of risk for crime and violence, but it is far from absent in other areas of applied psychology. Educational psychologists have long been concerned with predicting school success using IQ tests. The University of Waterloo screens potential students using an algorithm that includes empirically derived weights for discounting student grades given by specific high schools (Cain, 2018). Given the widespread availability of high-quality data and cheap data processing, we should expect a steady increase in statistical prediction tools relevant to the concerns of psychologists.

COMMON CRITICISMS OF PREDICTION TOOLS

Even though actuarial risk tools are widely used and many have gained general acceptance in the professional, scientific, and legal communities, they are not without their critics. The following are some common concerns expressed about the use of prediction tools in psychology.

Prediction Tools Are Unnecessary

When we can trust self-report, prediction tools add little and are rarely used. In many contexts, conscious intentions are a good indicator of future behavior (Fishbein & Ajzen, 2010, Chapter 2). Prediction tools in psychology have value only when there are strong situational demands to say the right things (job interviews, parole board hearings) or when individuals lack the insight, knowledge, and judgment to make reliable self-assessments. In such contexts, prediction tools can effectively summarize a wide range of small contributing factors, the influence of which would be otherwise difficult to weight appropriately.

Individuals Are Not Statistics

Some critics challenge the fundamental assumption that statistics can and should be used to predict the behavior of individuals. There are several forms of this argument, some of which are addressed in more detail in subsequent chapters. A common form was expressed by Sherlock Holmes:

> While the individual man is an insoluble puzzle, in the aggregate he becomes a mathematical certainty. You can, for example, never foretell what any one man will do, but you can say with precision what an average number will be up to. Individuals vary, but the percentages remain constant. So says the statistician. (Doyle, 1890/2000, p. 37)

And to this day, it is easy to find statisticians and other contemporary experts who concur. I don't. Although there are academic traditions that support Holmes's view, I doubt that many adherents arrived at this conclusion after a study of the philosophy of probability, such as I review in Chapter 2. Instead, many people are attracted to such views because of deeply held beliefs in the independence, autonomy, and dignity of the individual. We sense that statistics have deep roots in governments' attempts at regulation and social control of the untrustworthy (the colonies) and the undesirable (*Les misérables*; see Hacking, 1990).

Statistical prediction has inherent limitations. Human behavior is not fully determined by any set of conditions. One of my teachers said that a prediction scheme that accounted for more than 50% of the variance was probably misspecified (e.g., the outcome was somehow included in the predictors). Most risk and protective factors in psychology are small things that nudge people in certain directions. Some of these influences are external, such as peers, disease, job requirements, the laws of the land, and social and cultural identities. Some of these influences are the habits, memories, and expectations that we all carry with us. Nobody, however, seriously questions whether there are genuine differences in how individuals behave. And no psychologist would question that these differences can be quantified.

Prediction Tools Can Be Biased

This criticism accepts the premise of statistical prediction for individuals but finds fault with its application. In particular, assessment tools in education and criminal justice have been criticized as biased toward already marginalized ethnic and racialized groups. One form of this argument is that the same indicators mean different things based on different sociocultural histories. Having unstable employment, transient housing, and negative attitudes toward authority may be valid indicators of psychopathy for White males in Canada. For the Indigenous peoples of Canada, however, these are predictable consequences of colonization, systemic discrimination, and intergenerational trauma. Similarly, risk indicators can mean different things for members of the dominant socioeconomic classes compared with individuals who have been marginalized based on race, religion, or gender identification. Assessment tools that aim to promote transparent and equitable decision making can be unintentionally reinforcing the prejudices that these measures were intended to protect against. Such concerns were sufficient for the Supreme Court of Canada to stop the Correctional Service of Canada from using any actuarial risk tools for Indigenous inmates until the tools have been specifically validated for this racial group (*Ewert v. Canada*, 2015, 2018).

NUMERACY IS NEEDED

Regardless of one's position on the preceding issues, serious participation in these debates requires understanding the statistics used to create prediction schemes. Psychologists are expected to understand the measures they use. This requires numeracy in prediction statistics. If a credible research study finds that the area under the curve (discussed in Chapter 8) for Indigenous males was .68 for Risk Tool X, should we be reassured or alarmed? Most actuarial risk tools can be scored without specialized training in prediction statistics; however, scoring an actuarial risk tool is not a complete risk assessment. Scores need to be interpreted. This requires understanding the quantitative information implied by risk scores, such as percentile ranks, recidivism rates, and risk ratios. It also requires understanding what research says about the strengths and weaknesses of any specific prediction tool. Expertise in prediction statistics will never be evenly distributed in the population. It is my conviction, however, that raising the level of numeracy of the users and consumers of statistical prediction tools is both possible and desirable.

Stanislav Andreski (1972) told of a debate about the existence of God between the great Swiss mathematician Euler (on the side of God) and members of the court of Catherine II of Russia (on the side of Voltaire, the skeptic). After going on for some time, Euler got a blackboard and wrote the following: $(x + y)^2 = x^2 + 2xy + y^2$, therefore God exists. As Euler expected, the members of the court did not understand the formula, and because they did not want to look stupid, they conceded the argument to Euler. This is a bad way of making decisions.

The importance of statistical numeracy is not limited, of course, to psychology. In his commentary on Gigerenzer et al.'s (2007) review of the importance of statistical literacy for evidence-based medicine, John Monahan (2007) summarized the evidence as follows:

> marshalling one study after another, [Gigerenzer and colleagues (2007)] demonstrate that, across widely varying samples of health professionals, patients, and policymakers, in all countries studied, statistical illiteracy reigns supreme—often with catastrophic consequences for individual and public health. (p. i)

It is not uncommon for individuals to consider a drug with serious side effects in 15 out of 100 cases to be less risky than another drug that had serious side effects in 128 out of 1,000 cases (this is called *denominator neglect*; Yamagishi, 1997). Harsher criminal justice decisions are made when outcomes are presented as two out of 10 individuals like Jack will reoffend compared with presenting the same information as a 20% recidivism rate (Slovic et al., 2000). It doesn't have to be this way. Although there is considerable variation across fields, there is increasing recognition of the value of using statistics to make predictions about individuals' outcomes in medicine, business, and sports. Thanks to Michael Lewis (2003), *moneyballing* is now a verb.

THE DISTINCTIVE FEATURES OF PREDICTION TOOLS

There is no shortage of books and articles concerned with developing prediction equations in psychology. A very common approach is to designate one variable as the variable of interest (i.e., the dependent variable) and then use the remaining variables (the independent variables) to predict the dependent variable using multiple regression. The primary intent of such studies, however, is either theory development or the description of groups (e.g., are males better at mental rotations than females, after controlling for education?). Some of these studies include longitudinal data, but, again, the primary interest is rarely on predicting the outcome for individuals. The literature on how to use a preexisting prediction scheme for applied decision making is even smaller.

The Conceptual Foundations of Prediction Tools

Prediction tools are created to address questions concerning the likelihood of a future event, behavior, or outcome. The basic assumptions supporting prediction tools are relatively straightforward:

1. Prediction tasks are ubiquitous in psychology. The constructs we use to describe people frequently carry implications for future actions. People who score high on conscientiousness, for example, would be expected to keep their promises.

2. We routinely make judgments about the expected conduct of specific individuals. Not only do we assert that conscientious people are apt to keep their promises, we also assert that *Mary* is likely to keep *her* promise because she is conscientious. This is a prediction for a specific case. In certain contexts, the outcome is of sufficient consequence that there is value in quantifying its likelihood as a probability or rate. There are no conceptual barriers to assigning numeric values to likelihoods for individual cases, any more than there are barriers to using numbers to describe any other feature or characteristic of anybody (see Chapter 2).

3. Group data are extremely useful when forming professional judgments concerning likelihoods for individual cases. Statements concerning likelihoods for individual cases have increased accuracy when informed by the base rate of the outcome in the reference group that the case most closely resembles.

4. Along with the base rate, risk assessments need to consider case-specific features that increase or decrease the likelihood of the outcome. Strong evidence that a characteristic is a risk or protective factor is provided by empirical associations observed in follow-up studies.

5. Given that they are a large number of potentially risk-relevant factors for most outcomes of interest, comprehensive evaluations should consider a range of risk factors, hence the need for risk prediction tools. Risk assessment tools identify, in advance, the risk factors to consider and how they should be organized into an overall evaluation of risk.

Creating useful prediction schemes is both science and art. It requires evidence, but it also requires matching the prediction scheme to the applied decisions and to the decision makers. Research is required to establish a tool's scientific credentials. Statistical prediction tools will not be used, however, unless the decision makers perceive them as improvements over the alternatives. Prediction schemes increase in value when they are easy to learn, easy to use, and provide valuable information that is more difficult or costly to obtain in other ways.

Identifying Risk and Protective Factors

Credible prediction schemes are rarely developed by a single study. All samples, no matter how large and representative, have unique features that do not generalize to other samples and settings. Consequently, prediction equations developed on any specific sample will generally work best on that sample. Single-sample equations are vulnerable to overfitting (i.e., mistaking random features of a data set for basic reality). In other words, don't put too much trust in the results of any single study. Effects that are significant at $p < .05$ or even $p < .001$ may not be found in any other samples. Conversely, the lack of a significant effect in one data set does not mean that it will not be found in others. The reason for the between-study variability is often difficult to determine. Some of the variation will be related to random sampling; however, arbitrary features of the study design can have hidden consequences, which may never be fully understood.

The most generalizable risk tools are based on programs of research that identify factors that are related to the outcome from multiple independent samples and cull factors that seem like they should be related to the outcome but are not. A strong conceptual model that explains why these factors are related to the outcome is desirable but not always necessary (see Chapter 17). A thorough and informed search for valid risk factors minimizes the likelihood of missing major factors.

Combining Predictive Factors

Once a sufficient pool of predictive factors has been identified, the next step is combining them into an overall score. The best way of combining risk factors remains a topic of debate in scientific and professional communities. There are currently three broad approaches guiding research and practice: (a) actuarial risk tools based on relatively simple additive models (e.g., Violence Risk Appraisal Guide—Revised; Harris, Rice, et al., 2015); (b) SPJ tools in which the items are specified in advance but the overall evaluation is based on a unique, case-specific formulation (e.g., HCR-20[v3]; Douglas et al., 2013); and (c) complex statistical prediction tools (e.g., Classification of Violence Risk; Monahan, 2021). Although certain measures do better in certain studies, none of these three broad approaches have demonstrated overall superior predictive accuracy, at least not in the area of crime and violence where risk tools are routinely used (Brennan, 2017; Campbell et al., 2009; Tully et al., 2013; Yang et al., 2010). Consequently, evaluators' decisions concerning the type of prediction tool to use must be based on other considerations.

My own research and professional practice have privileged measures based on relatively simple additive predictive models. My work has focused on sexual recidivism risk assessment; however, simple additive models are likely to work well in many areas of psychological assessment because the causal constructs of interest are correlated with each other and are measured with error. Under such conditions, statistical interactions, which add incremental predictive power to complex statistical models, are rarely observed (Busemeyer & Jones, 1983; McClelland & Judd, 1993). I have also not been convinced that integrating risk factors using professional judgment is more accurate than simpler, mechanical methods (Hanson & Morton-Bourgon, 2009).

Overall, the way of combining predictive factors appears less important than ensuring that relevant factors are considered. In his 1979 article "The Robust Beauty of Improperly Specified Regression Equations," Robin Dawes reviewed research demonstrating that prediction schemes with simple weights do as well as schemes with complex weights. For example, a simple count of the risk factors present (yes = 1, no = 0) usually works as well as fractional weights developed through regression (e.g., score = –1.04 [age in years] + 2.34 [prior failure] + 1.54 [lack of social support] + 1.15 [negative peer influences] + 1.87 [negative attitudes]). Canadian researchers Daryl Kroner, Jeremy Mills, and John Reddon (2005) even found that randomly selecting items (with their original weights) from a diverse set of validated criminal recidivism risk tools did as well as any of the original prediction tools. Although it is almost always possible to improve prediction by refining the item weights, the incremental gains are small. In contrast, meaningful gains can be achieved by considering new, risk-relevant information.

DIAGNOSIS AND PROGNOSIS

Another concern with much of the discourse on prediction in psychology is the blurring of the tasks of diagnosis and prognosis. In *diagnosis*, the task is estimating the likelihood that the individual currently has a specific condition. In *prognosis*, or true prediction, the evaluator wants to know whether an individual who does not currently have the condition will develop it at some future date. For example, a simple test can determine whether a woman is currently pregnant (diagnosis), whereas a completely different set of factors need to be considered to assess the likelihood that she will become pregnant in the next 5 years. Although certain statistics are useful for both, they are interpreted differently. For example, logistic regression can be used to estimate the likelihood of brain cancer given neuroimaging results. Decision thresholds can be set and tested by comparing the decisions implied by the diagnostic measure to a highly credible measure of the true state of affairs for this patient (e.g., biopsy). The diagnostic decisions implied by regression equations can either be correct or incorrect for a specific individual. Using aggregated cases, a diagnostic procedure based on logistic regression can be evaluated in terms such as hits, false positives, positive predictive value, and negative predictive value.[1]

Logistic regression can also be used to create a prediction scheme; however, there is no gold standard against which to evaluate a prognosis for a specific individual. The outcome of interest is not present and may never occur. At the time of assessment, it is impossible to determine whether the assessment is correct or incorrect. Nobody has the outcome of interest at that time. More

[1]For a definition of these terms, see Chapter 7 (Dichotomous Predictors) or the Glossary.

than that, the actual outcome for any individual will never indicate that the prediction was wrong, except in the very unusual case where the prediction was zero or 100%. The validity of a prediction scheme can only be evaluated in aggregate data.

Prediction Schemes Assess the Likelihood of the Outcome

Instead of saying whether the outcome will be present or not, prediction schemes assess its likelihood. These likelihoods can range from very small to very large and are often expressed as probabilities between zero and one (various ways of expressing likelihoods are covered in Chapter 4). When weather forecasters announce that the likelihood of rain today is 50%, they are not expressing ignorance. Instead, they are communicating that they expect it to rain on 5 out of 10 days like today. Similarly, criminal recidivism risk tools distinguish between groups of individuals whose expected recidivism rates can range from less than 5% to well over 80%, with many gradations in between.

The language of hits and false alarms is well suited to diagnostic tests but poorly aligned with the information provided by prediction tools. At the time of assessment, all statements that the individual will have the outcome are necessarily false (the outcome is not present in anybody). Using diagnostic language, everybody in the high-risk groups are "false alarms" at the start of follow-up. Over time, some proportion of the sample will turn into hits, that is, individuals with the outcome who are correctly identified as having the outcome by some decision rule. However, the proportion of hits depends more on the length of follow-up and the base rate of the outcome than on the accuracy of the prediction scheme.

Consider a prediction tool that perfectly ranks employees on the likelihood of advancing within the organization, and assume that the top 200 (20%) of 1,000 employees are designated as high-flyers, that is, those likely to advance. If 150 (15%) of employees advance in any 1 year, then 150 of the 200 high-flyers would advance in the first year of follow-up, which corresponds to a hit rate of 75%. There would be, however, 50 high-flyers who did not advance, which corresponds to a false alarm rate of 25%. When follow-up is extended another year, an additional 150 individuals advance, bringing the total to 300 out of 1,000 (30% base rate). Now the hit rate would be 100% (all the high-flyers have advanced), and there are no false alarms. However, there is another problem: The decision rule failed to identify 100 individuals who did advance (see *specificity* in the Glossary). The point is that diagnostic statistics say little about the accuracy of prediction tools because they are heavily influenced by the decision threshold and the absolute frequency of the outcome.

The Causal Order Is Different for Diagnostic Versus Prognostic Indicators

Diagnostic indicators are typically the results of the disorder (e.g., the fever is caused by the infection). When the disease abates, so do the symptoms. The relationship between the symptoms and the disorder is usually probabilistic (not every symptom is present in every positive case, and sometimes the symptom is present without the disorder), so there may be uncertainty in diagnoses. The strength of the relationship between the disorder and the indicators (or symptom) is often expressed as a statistic called a likelihood ratio (see the Glossary; Akobeng, 2007b). In the context of diagnosis, the probabilistic relationship between the disorder and the indicator is expected to remain constant across samples and settings (e.g., the chances of observing fever when a patient has malaria is roughly the same for patients in Toronto and Mozambique, even though the rates of malaria would be drastically different).

In the context of prediction, the causal order is reversed: the indicators are intended to influence the likelihood of the outcome, not the other way around. The outcome does not influence the indicators because it does not exist at the time of assessment. For example, poor instruction precedes and increases the likelihood of school failure. Humans are goal-oriented creatures, however, so the distinction between predictor and outcome is not 100% pure (e.g., teachers can teach poorly because they expect certain students to fail). Nevertheless, the logic of prediction schemes is that they are using information at Time 1 to predict outcomes at Time 2. What happens at Time 2 cannot change what has already happened at Time 1. Whether a student succeeds cannot change the fact that the student previously received a good or a poor education. Unlike the context of diagnosis, individuals will acquire the outcome without any change in their initial status on the indicator and predictor variables. The consequence is that evaluating prediction tools requires a different point of view and different statistics than those used to evaluate diagnostic schemes. Even when the same statistics are used appropriately in the context of diagnosis and of prognosis, they mean different things and need to be interpreted accordingly.

For applied prediction, however, the distinction between diagnosis and prediction is rarely absolute. In practice, evaluators use historical or current conditions to predict future events. Identifying individuals' past and current functioning is a diagnostic task (i.e., what risk-relevant characteristics apply in this case?). For example, a prediction scheme that uses intelligence to predict school success (a prediction task) must first assess intelligence (a diagnostic task). Notice that a variable such as prior grades is both a diagnostic indicator of intelligence and a predictor of school success. Even when risk factors are identified purely on the basis of their empirical relationship with the outcome, they must also be indicators of risk-relevant latent constructs, even if the nature of these latent construct is unknown. Consequently, in psychological assessment, risk factors typically function as both diagnostic and prognostic indicators. What is being assessed in risk assessment is discussed further in Chapter 2 and Chapter 17.

THE NUMERIC INFORMATION PROVIDED BY PREDICTION TOOLS

Just as different statistics are appropriate for evaluating an assessment measure as a prediction tool rather than as a norm-referenced measure, so too are the inferences that can be made from scores. The quantitative inferences from norm-referenced measures typically concern relative placement in some normative groups (e.g., top 5% of graduate students). In contrast, the quantitative inferences from prediction tools concern the likelihood of the outcome of interest (e.g., 85% chance of successfully completing a doctoral degree). Notice that certain measures can function both as norm-referenced measures and as prediction tools (e.g., academic aptitude tests).

Discrimination and Calibration

Prediction schemes provide two main types of quantitative information: whether certain classes of individuals are more likely to have the outcome than others (relative risk) and the expected rate of the outcome (absolute risk) for individuals "like this." Consequently, statistical prediction schemes are properly judged against these two general criteria. The relative risk information is also called *discrimination*, or the extent to which the individuals who eventually have the outcome look different from individuals who do not have the outcome. The second criterion is often referred to as *calibration*, or the extent to which the observed rates in replication studies match the rates expected by the prediction tool. In other words, if 15 out of 100 individuals like Fred are expected to fail graduate school within 2 years, how stable are these rates against samples and settings?

The most accurate prediction tools are high on both discrimination and calibration. It is possible, however, for measures to still be useful if their calibration is poor. For example, imagine a measure that accurately ranks students in their potential to graduate on time (good discrimination); however, the actual graduation rates vary considerably across universities and programs (poor calibration). In this case, administrators may still want to use the tool to select those most likely to succeed in a timely manner (keeping in mind the local graduation rates). The measure would not provide accurate information about the proportion of students who will graduate (that is determined by the programs); it would, nevertheless, correctly identify who is more likely to graduate.

Quantifying Likelihoods

As previously stated, numeracy is needed to evaluate research findings and integrate new knowledge into practice. For users of statistical prediction tools, numeracy is essential because much of the information provided by these tools is numeric. Although it is possible to talk of likelihoods in words (e.g., low, moderate, high), actuarial prediction tools have the benefit of *quantifying* likelihoods, for example, expressing a low likelihood of rain as a 10% chance. The following section reviews the central numeric information provided by statistical prediction tools.

Dichotomous Outcomes

This book focuses on outcomes that are either present or absent, that is, dichotomous outcomes. Examples of dichotomous outcomes include passing a test, quitting a job, being arrested for a crime, or recovering from depression. Much of the material can be generalized to other types of outcomes, such as annual income, degree of happiness, and the number of criminal convictions. The focus, however, is on socially valued, clearly defined, dichotomous outcomes. Quantifying dichotomous outcomes may seem straightforward but several options are available and widely used (see Chapter 4). It is best not to confuse them. As well, because nobody has the outcome at the time of assessment, all estimates of likelihood must consider time: likelihoods only make sense when paired with a follow-up period (graduate within 5 years, recover from depression within 3 months, quit before the end of basic training).

Relative and Absolute Risk

In addition to quantitative estimates of the likelihood of the outcome, prediction tools also provide information about how risky individuals are compared with others (an aspect of discrimination). It is quite possible to quantify relative risk while having no firm opinion about the absolute likelihoods (see Part III of this volume). For example, the Centers for Disease Control and Prevention (2020) stated that the risk of lung cancer is 25 times greater for men who smoke compared with nonsmokers. This tells you that smoking is bad for your health, but other information is also relevant to judging the health risks.

I have a personal example of the importance of considering both relative risk and absolute risk. When my eldest son was 2, he had a febrile seizure. For those of you who have never seen one in a loved one, this is terrifying. We took him to a neurologist, who, after some basic developmental tests (all normal), asked us whether we wanted to send him for further diagnostic testing. The further tests involved electrodes and sleep deprivation and were not considered particularly informative at this age (poor discrimination). I then asked if febrile seizures increase the likelihood of epilepsy in adulthood. The doctor replied that they double the chances. Notice that he replied in terms of relative risk (a risk ratio, an indicator of discrimination). I then asked about the base rate of epilepsy in adults. He replied that it was about 1% to 2%. In our situation, the base rate information (calibration) was much more important than the discrimination accuracy of the diagnostic indicator. We decided on no further tests.

Percentile Ranks

Another quantitative indicator provided by statistical predictions tools is the percentile rank: compared with some normative group, how unusual is this score? For example, the results of a university entrance exam may be in the 97th percentile, indicating that it is unusually high. This indicates that the candidate is among the top 3% most likely to succeed in university (if the exam is valid), and, for universities using this exam, it is also a good indicator that the candidate could be admitted. In contrast, a candidate whose scores correspond to a percentile rank of 48 (near the middle of the pack) would be less likely to be admitted to the university and less likely to succeed if admitted.

Percentile ranks and related scores (e.g., *Z*-scores, *T*-scores) are probably the most common method of reporting the results of psychological tests. Even though percentile ranks are not unique to prediction tools, they are included in this book because they are a quantitative indicator that is easily calculated, easily understood, and has the potential of enhancing risk communication (see Chapter 16).

PREDICTION TOOLS MAY OR MAY NOT MEASURE LATENT CONSTRUCTS

In most psychological testing, percentile ranks are used to indicate where an individual should be placed, compared with other individuals, on the psychological feature of interest (e.g., impulsivity, neuroticism). These features are considered latent constructs because they are not directly observed. Instead, they are inferred from indicators. For example, the latent construct of neuroticism may be inferred from self-reports of worry, distressed facial expressions, and high autonomic reactivity. The items in most psychological measures are all intended to be indicators of the same construct. Individuals for whom more of the items apply are considered to rank higher on the underlying, latent dimension.

In contrast, the most accurate risk tools consider multiple risk-relevant constructs measured by diverse sources of information. Consequently, percentile ranks on prediction tools rarely lend themselves to easy psychological interpretation, nor do prediction tools aspire to high internal consistency (e.g., omega > .80). Instead, the most accurate prediction tools aim to comprehensively sample all the risk-relevant domains, with no major contributors neglected.

It is sometimes possible, however, to use prediction tools to infer psychological constructs: Specifically, when the construct is dimensional and includes the propensity for the outcome as a core feature, there will be strong overlap between the items in a prediction tool and the items in a measure of the corresponding psychological construct. Chronic rule violation and callous disregard for others are both indicators of antisocial personality disorder as well as efficient indicators of future criminal behavior. Measures designed to predict success in school (past grades) will also assess intelligence (a latent construct). Consequently, relative placement on the risk tool can inform relative placement on some latent psychological constructs.

Even when a risk tool is used purely for prediction purposes, evaluators need some understanding of what is being assessed (Joint Committee, 2014, p. 13). Credible causal theories minimize the likelihood that the observed associations between the indicators and the outcome are confounded by variables that are not appropriate for the assessment task. For example, few evaluators would consider it appropriate to ask about parents' income on a college admissions assessment, even if it is correlated with educational achievement. Further discussion of what should be assessed by prediction tools can be found in Chapter 17.

META-ANALYTIC PERSPECTIVE

This book approaches statistics from the perspective of effect sizes and meta-analysis (Cumming, 2013). Null hypothesis significance tests are occasionally presented but deemphasized. The assumption is that evaluators want to know more than whether a prediction tool works better than chance (a very low threshold). Instead, they want to know the strength of the relationship between the predictor and the outcome, and the plausible range of the size of that relationship (i.e., confidence intervals for effect sizes). The meta-analytic framework is privileged because it is rare for any single prediction study to have sufficient credibility to justify changes in applied practice. Confidence in findings increases when substantively similar effects are found in diverse samples and setting. Meta-analysis provides the framework for estimating average effects across studies and for examining the extent to which the variation across studies is more than would be expected by chance alone.

OVERVIEW OF THE CHAPTERS

This book provides a broad conceptual model supporting the use of prediction tools in psychological assessment. At its heart, however, it is a statistics textbook, accompanied by the requisite explanations, equations, and exercises. The core chapters cover the essential statistics used for evaluating and interpreting prediction tools: proportions and likelihoods (Part II), discrimination (Part III), and calibration (Part IV). Part V (Chapter 16) addresses percentile ranks, which are a useful quantitative indicator for diverse assessment measures. The statistics chapters are followed by a discussion of other, largely nonnumeric, indicators of the quality of prediction tools (Chapter 17) and some suggestions on advancing risk communication (Chapter 18). Because many readers will be unfamiliar with the technical terms used in the book, I have included a Glossary and an Appendix with a brief refresher on formulas and graphs.

As a teaching text, the statistics chapters start easy and get harder. The beginning of the chapters should be accessible to almost everybody interested in the topic; the latter sections assume increased numeracy. Do not be discouraged if you stop reading partway through certain chapters. The book is not intended to be read cover to cover (except, of course, by my students for whom it is required reading). For some of you, it will be light reading, almost conversational. For the statistically minded reader, this would be an introductory text. For all readers, I hope that it increases your confidence with prediction statistics and your motivation to go further.

FIGURE 1.2

"Are you just pissing and moaning, or can you verify what you're saying with data?"

Note. By Edward Koren. From The Cartoon Bank of The New Yorker Collection. Copyright 1999 by Condé Nast. Reprinted with permission.

I do not expect readers to permanently master the material the first time they learn it. I have learned and forgotten this material many times. I was taught logarithms and exponents in high school, then had to relearn them again during my BA, during my PhD, and several more times during my professional career as a researcher. Our brains are finite networks, and we regularly decommission pathways to make room for current concerns. Logits fade away if not frequently revisited.

The working knowledge of communities of practitioners is similarly impermanent. The founding motivation for the first modern university in 1088 in Bologna was to revive the lost learning of the Romans. The great achievements of our civilizations cannot be sustained without continual education of the next generation. Even mundane achievements, such as buttons or hopscotch, need support to survive. One of the recurrent themes in science fiction are worlds filled with advanced technology that nobody understands. These stories resonate with anybody who has marvelled at airplanes, electric lights, and plastic toothbrushes. One contemporary variation on the lost knowledge theme is the Dr. Stone manga series, which chronicles the struggles of a young genius to recreate basic science and technology after waking up in a primitive, dystopian future. How many of us would know how to make paper from scratch, let alone a computer monitor?

Empirical probabilities and statistical prediction are valuable innovations, and their application to the problems of human affairs is a relatively recent development. When used appropriately, they have considerable potential to improve decision making. These innovations can only achieve their potential, however, if they are part of the working knowledge of practitioners. May this book increase the number of people who could create risk tools from scratch.

2

The Nature of Probability

This chapter alerts readers to the existence of multiple perspectives on probability. These perspectives are important because they provide the link between research evidence and practice. Research evidence in psychology rarely identifies direct, one-to-one connections between causes and effects. Instead, almost all the variables of interest to psychologists have probabilistic (stochastic) relationships to each other, such that the presence of one variable tends to increase or decrease the likelihood of another variable. This chapter focuses on how our theories of probability inform the prediction task most commonly faced by psychologists—that is, estimating the likelihood of a particular outcome for a particular person. The link between group frequency data and the individual case is not obvious. Nobody seriously considered how to quantify any type of probability until around 1660 (Courgeau, 2004; Hacking, 1975; Hald, 2003). Debates about how numeric probabilities should inform case-specific decisions continue to this day.

Many of us who completed statistics in psychology left graduate school with the impression that the only truly scientific probabilities were those that could be calculated by formulas. Just as the circumference of a circle can be calculated by $2\pi r$, the probability of events can be similarly calculated with the correct formula. This impression is reinforced by the ubiquitous use of $p < .05$ and asterisks indicating the degree of significance. My graduate school training, however, provided only a limited view of probability. I was unaware that there were other models that may be more helpful for applied risk assessment. I was forced to consider these models by Hart et al.'s (2007) assertion that it

https://doi.org/10.1037/0000275-002
Prediction Statistics for Psychological Assessment, by R. K. Hanson

was both conceptually and empirically impossible to ascribe empirical probabilities to individuals with an acceptable level of precision (see also Cooke & Michie, 2010; Hart & Cooke, 2013); instead, they argued that the best that evaluators could aspire to was broad categories of relative risk, such as the low, moderate, and high risk levels privileged by structured professional judgment (SPJ) risk tools. Although I ended up disagreeing with both their arguments and their conclusions (Hanson & Howard, 2010), their papers inspired reflection on the conceptual foundations of actuarial prediction (i.e., structured prediction with numeric likelihoods). This led me outside psychology to conceptual territory more familiar to students of philosophy and the history of science. This literature provided new and useful perspectives on the applied task of assessing the likelihood of outcomes for individuals.

We are continually making judgments under conditions of uncertainty. Some of these judgments concern the past (e.g., was this individual sexually abused?), the present (e.g., does this person have posttraumatic stress disorder?), and the future (e.g., will this individual respond to cognitive behavior therapy?). Like the rest of this book, this chapter focuses on judgments about the future—that is, prognosis, not diagnosis (i.e., whether a specific condition is currently present). Prognosis presents special challenges because, by definition, the outcome cannot be observed at the time of assessment, and may never occur.

IDIOGRAPHIC AND NOMOTHETIC RISK ANALYSES

There are two general sources of information used to assess the likelihood of future events for individuals, which I will call the *idiographic* and *nomothetic* approaches (following the terms popularized by Gordon Allport, 1937). The idiographic (or anamnestic) approach considers the individual's personal history; the nomothetic approach examines patterns in group data. If Johnny Knuckles frequently gets into fights, then an idiographic analysis could conclude that he is likely to do so again. The nomothetic approach concerns itself with the extent to which individuals with characteristics similar to Johnny's are likely to get into fights.

The idiographic–nomothetic distinction overlaps with the unstructured–structured classification of risk assessment procedures (Heilbrun et al., 2021; Skeem & Monahan, 2011). Unstructured risk assessments are those in which the risk or protective factors (or both) are not specified in advance, and evaluators combine the factors using their own professional judgment. Unstructured evaluations may use a combination of idiographic case information and general findings from the research literature (i.e., nomothetic information). In structured risk assessments, the factors to be considered are specified in advance, which requires reference to nomothetic data. Risk factors are included in checklists if there is prior evidence that they are risk-relevant for at least some people.

There is professional consensus that structured risk assessments are more accurate than unstructured professional judgment; however, there is ongoing debate concerning the relative merits of the two most common forms of structured risk assessment: SPJ and empirical actuarial approaches (Hanson, 2009; Heilbrun et al., 2021; Skeem & Monahan, 2011). The debate does not concern the relevance of nomothetic groups data, which is accepted by evaluators in both camps; instead, the debate concerns the utility of the numeric information provided and the extent to which factors not explicitly mentioned in the risk tools, including idiographic case history factors, should inform the overall evaluation of risk.

Idiographic, case history information works reasonably well for predicting high frequency events, such as angry outbursts, school grades, and conflicts with peers. People are reasonably consistent in their daily or weekly patterns (Epstein, 1979). The idiographic approach works poorly for predicting consequential, low-frequency events, such as criminal recidivism, falling in love, or recovery from depression. It does not work at all for outcomes that happen once (e.g., high school graduation, suicide). In the idiographic approach, evaluators look for factors that precede the outcome for that individual. It is difficult to document such patterns, however, if the outcome has never occurred or happened only rarely.

For low-frequency outcomes, prediction must rely on indicators that are not the outcome itself. For example, evaluators interested in predicting criminal recidivism may look at risk factors such as negative attitudes toward authority, lifestyle impulsivity, aimless use of leisure time, and substance abuse. Andrews and Bonta (2010) considered these to be empirically validated risk factors because individuals who have these factors are more likely to return to crime than those who do not. Like most psychologists, Andrews and Bonta rely on nomothetic group data to guide evidence-based practice. Although certain evaluators assess risk using idiographic case formulations, nobody seriously questions the relevance of nomothetic data for identifying potentially relevant risk factors.

Nomothetic risk factors can be supported or refuted using the normal rules of scientific evidence. If Dr. Viljoen says that Mr. Knuckles is at increased risk for recidivism because he has facial tattoos, this statement can be tested using group data. Researchers can identify groups of individuals with and without facial tattoos, and then observe which group has the highest recidivism rate. If individuals with tattoos reoffend more often than those without, then Dr. Viljoen's decision rule is supported. If the recidivism rate is not higher for those with tattoos than those without, Mr. Knuckles has grounds to complain about his risk assessment.

HART, COOKE, AND MICHIE'S REJECTION OF CASE-SPECIFIC LIKELIHOODS

Expert witnesses who introduce new prediction tools in high-stakes court decisions are accustomed to scrutiny. Most of the challenges concern specific features of the prediction tool, as well as the evidence used to justify its use for the case at hand. In a series of papers, Hart, Cooke, and Michie, challenged the very possibility of numeric estimates of recidivism risk for an individual case. Their primary criticism concerned the lack of precision of the recidivism risk estimates as applied to individual cases. They accepted that it is reasonable to estimate rates for groups (e.g., 20% of males will have criminal conviction in their lifetime). They reject that group data can inform the likelihood of events for individual cases.

Their conclusions are based on three types of statistical analyses. In their first paper, Hart and colleagues (2007) proposed an original way of estimating confidence intervals for the likelihoods associated with individual cases. Specifically, they used Wilson's (1927) formula for the confidence interval of a proportion (see Chapter 4, this volume) and inserted the value "1" in place of the sample size. As was quickly pointed out, however, "with '1' in place of 'n', the formulae just do not mean anything" (Mossman & Sellke, 2007, p. 561). Hart and colleagues acknowledged their error of their analysis but continued to assert that the margins of error for actuarial predictions are large, unknown, or unknowable. Cooke and Michie (2010) then advanced a second original approach to estimating prediction intervals for individuals. Following the logic of prediction intervals for linear regression (continuous outcome variable), Cooke and Michie added an estimate of individual variability to the error term of logistic regression estimates. The resulting confidence intervals, however, are similarly without foundation because the added variability parameter has "no meaning in this context" (Imrey & Dawid, 2015). Unlike linear regression, there is no residual error term in logistic regression (Hosmer et al., 2013, p. 7). Logistic regression parameters can be estimated with more or less precision, and predictor variables may have weaker or stronger relationships with the outcome; however, for dichotomous outcome variables, the variability of the individual observations from the mean value is fully determined by the size of the mean value (see Chapters 4 and 11).

Their third analysis used traditional logistic regression and, again, found large confidence intervals for the predicted values (Hart & Cooke, 2013). They interpreted their results as further confirmation that the margin of error for actuarial predictions was too large to be of practical value. Although their statistical analyses were, in this instance, correct, they did not appreciate the extent to which the width of the confidence intervals depend on the sample size. In general, stable logistic regression results are only expected when there are at least 100 events and 100 nonevents (Vergouwe et al., 2005). As well, it is good practice to have at least 10 events per predictor variable (Hosmer et al., 2013, p. 407). In Hart and Cooke's (2013) study, there were only 16 recidivists and 74 nonrecidivists. With this sample size and four predictor variables, narrow confidence intervals should not be expected. Recidivism prediction studies using logistic regression with adequately large samples routinely find narrow confidence intervals for the predicted values (i.e., ± 2%; Hanson, Thornton et al., 2016; Harris, Rice, et al., 2015).

Although Hart et al.'s (2007) statistical analyses are uninformative, the core argument of their papers remains popular among forensic evaluators.

Just before writing this chapter, I read a risk-assessment report by a competent psychiatrist in which she generally accepted nomothetic research findings as case relevant, except when the research findings concerned recidivism rates. Like most reports, she identified certain characteristics of the case that increased risk (e.g., atypical sexual interests) as well as factors that decreased risk (e.g., advanced age, cooperation with treatment). She also presented the raw scores for several actuarial risk tools, along with their associated nominal risk levels (e.g., above average risk). She also presented the expected recidivism rates associated with these scores. She then stated that the recidivism rates apply only to groups and cannot be applied to the individual in question. As justification, she referenced Hart, Cooke, and Michie. She did not similarly distance herself from the other nomothetic information. She might have said something like the following: "My client has pedophilia. Research has shown that sexual interest in children increases the risk for sexual recidivism; however, that research was based on group data and cannot be used to infer that this individual's risk is increased." She did not. Why did she distance the case from certain nomothetic findings and not others? What is so special about probabilities?

NATURE IS INHERENTLY UNCERTAIN

We cannot avoid uncertainty, but we rarely like it. It interrupts our plans and undermines our defense against the hazards of the world. We employ diverse tactics to minimize uncertainty, including cognitive distortions that assert more order onto our worlds than really exists (e.g., just world hypothesis, racial stereotypes). When individuals do things that are disruptive and appear threatening, we may hire professionals to conduct risk assessments. In the business world, risk is often defined as the "effect of uncertainty on objectives" (International Organization for Standardization, ISO 31000; Gjerdrum & Peter, 2011). Proponents of the SPJ approach to violence risk assessment share a similar perspective. For example, the user guide for the Historical-Clinical-Risk Management–20—Version 3 (HCR-20^{V3}) defines risk as "a threat or hazard that is incompletely understood, and thus whose occurrence can be forecast only with uncertainty" (Douglas et al., 2013, p. 4). If risk is uncertainty, then estimating empirical likelihoods is less important than resolving uncertainty through improved understanding or by employing protective measures.

But what if the outcome is inherently uncertain? On a practical level, many important life events are well beyond our ability to predict with certainty (e.g., falling in love, onset of cancer, global pandemics). Do not expect this to change any time soon. There is no shortage of physical processes in which miniscule differences in the initial conditions lead to major differences in the outcome (i.e., chaotic processes, weather being a well-known example). It may be that even complete knowledge of initial conditions does not allow us to predict the future with certainty. The physicist A. Zeilinger, writing in *Nature*, stated: "The discovery that individual events are irreducibly random is probably one of the most significant findings of the twentieth century" (quoted in Aalen et al., 2008, p. 347).

QUANTIFYING LIKELIHOODS

The idea that chance could be quantified appeared independently in the writings of diverse individuals at the end of the 1600s (Courgeau, 2004; Hacking, 1975). The reasons for the sudden interest in quantifying uncertainty are not known. Perhaps the philosophical acceptance of randomness in human affairs followed disappointment in other ways of knowing, such as arguments from authority, logical certainty, or the fruitless search for immutable laws of human nature. Perhaps problem solvers of that time resigned themselves to the fact that probabilistic knowledge was better than no knowledge at all. Regardless of the reasons, stochastic models soon demonstrated their worth. By the early 1700s, statistical models were providing new and better solutions to diverse practical problems related to government finances (life expectancies are required to fairly evaluate annuities) and public health (Hacking, 1975). Stochastic statistical models also provided the conceptual foundations for empirical research in the social sciences. Unlike physics, the social sciences have never been dominated by the assumption of strict determinism. The relationships between initial conditions and psychologically meaningful outcomes have always been assumed to include some degree of random variation. Documenting probabilistic (stochastic) relationships has been the main activity of research psychologists for the past 100 years.

Classical Probabilities

As the story is told, probability began in 1654 when Blaise Pascal (in Paris) wrote to Pierre de Fermat (in Toulouse) with numeric solutions to problems concerning certain games of chance (Haigh, 2012). This established the field of classical probabilities. Classical probabilities (also called logical or objective probabilities) start with a clearly defined random process (e.g., roll of a dice, poker hand) and then calculate the expected frequencies of outcomes of interest (e.g., two sixes, a pair of aces). Classical probabilities are defined as the frequency of the outcome of interest divided by all possible outcomes. For example, if a deck is known to contain equal size suits of 13 cards each, the likelihood of drawing a spade would be calculated by the number of spades (13) divided by total number of cards in the deck (52): 13/52 = .25. If the rules of the game were "win if the first card drawn is a spade; lose otherwise," then fair odds would be 1 to 3.

Stable Frequencies in Nature

Around the same time, Graunt created the first statistical tables of birth and death rates for London, thereby starting the new field of demography

(Hacking, 1990). When similar numbers were tabulated in other countries, many were surprised to find stable frequencies in human affairs for outcomes that had previously been considered completely unpredictable. The rates of birth, death, crime, and suicide turn out to be remarkably consistent. In 1662, Graunt estimated the ratio of male to female births in London to be 14 to 13 (Hald, 2003), which is not far off the current global estimate of 21 to 20 (World Health Organization, 2019). This opened up new fields of scientific inquiry. Why were more males born than females? Why was the crime and suicide rates so similar year after year? What can we do to reduce them?

Pascal and Fermat's classical probabilities for games of chance were important because they demonstrated that chance could be quantified. In the 1600s, gamblers were already aware of certain empirical probabilities based on their playing experience. Pascal and Fermat's calculus of chances was able to anticipate the empirically observed odds from the rules of the game. In contrast, demography identifies stable frequencies without any clearly defined game, let alone a game with known rules. For the religiously inclined, the surprising consistency in male-to-female birth ratio was considered evidence for the existence of God. The scientifically minded were inspired to unravel the (stochastic) laws of nature.

Frequentist Inferential Statistics

An important step in social scientific reasoning was considering the stable frequencies in nature as if they were the results of games of chance. Most introductory statistics textbooks include a thought experiment involving an urn and an unknown mix of red and white balls. This setup (urn and balls) is a game of chance. The field of inferential statistics allows us to guess the rules of the game. Inferential statistics assumes that observed frequencies arise from unobserved stochastic processes. The gender of babies, for example, could be considered a Bernoulli trial (after Jacob Bernoulli, 1654–1705). Each birth could be considered an independent random event with two possible outcomes. This is a rather simple game, involving a single parameter (the ratio of male to female births). Inferential statistics reduces nature to simple models and then estimates the credibility of these models. Unlike classical probabilities that are calculated in advance based on a set of rules, empirical probabilities are estimated from observations.

Discussions soon turned to the question of how many observations are necessary to obtain the true proportion? The outcome for a single event obviously tells us little, other than the likelihood is neither 0 nor 1. By 1713, Jacob Bernoulli had formulated the Law of Large Numbers, which remains a fundamental tenet of inferential statistics. This law states that as the number of observations increases, the average of these observations will approach the true value. Imagine flipping a coin to determine whether it is biased. The first three flips say little. After 1,000 flips, the average will be close to the true value. The true value, however, is never observed; it is only obtained from an infinite number of repetitions.

This perspective is now called the *frequentist* approach to probability: Each observation is considered an independent trial, and the true probability value is approximated by the average of an increasingly large series of trials. The frequentist approach provided solutions to many previously vexing problems. In particular, it led to the development of a theory of measurement error, which is crucial to all applied psychological assessment. It is important to notice, however, that in the frequentist approach, probabilities for individual events are not defined and have no substantive meaning. Probabilities are only mathematical abstractions, defined as the limits of an infinite series (Greenland, 1998). We need to go further before we can say that Mr. Smith has an 80% chance of recovering from depression within 3 months.

Probabilities as Propensities

Although frequentist logic is canon in most introductory statistics courses, it is not the only way to conceptualize probabilities. Karl Popper, a giant in the philosophy of science, proposed that the problem of assigning likelihoods to individual events can be addressed by a modest adjustment to the frequentist model (Gillies, 2000; Popper, 1959). Specifically, rather than defining probabilities as the limit of an infinite series, as in the frequentist approach, probabilities are considered properties of things. Specifically, probabilities are the *propensities* of things to do something. Most of Popper's examples concerned physical phenomena, such as random emissions during radioactive decay. It is easy, however, to apply a propensity model to individuals; for example, John has the propensity to become violent when drinking. In Popper's model, the stable proportions observed in human affairs (e.g., suicide, divorce) arise because individuals have stable propensities to behave in certain ways, which may or may not actualize. When 20% of a homogenous group of individuals have the outcome, the propensity interpretation indicates that the likelihood of the outcome for each individual is also 20%.

All inferences from group rates to individuals, however, require that the members of the group are all the same. This is never true. No two things are completely alike, and the same thing changes over time ("One cannot step into the same river twice," Heraclitus, cited in Jones, 1970, p. 16). It is, however, approximately true. We continuously relate to the world in terms of concepts and categories. When our categories concern risk-relevant variables, then it is possible to evaluate the likelihood of the outcome for the category as a whole. The important question is not whether differences within the members of the category exist; the question is whether these differences make a difference. As Vernon Quinsey[1] is fond of saying, people are all different in uninteresting ways.

[1]Vernon Quinsey is a strong advocate for actuarial prediction and one of my early influences.

Reference Class Problem

Some differences, however, will influence the likelihood of the outcome, which leads to the reference class problem (Hájek, 2007). The reference class problem concerns the difficulty of identifying a reference class when individuals differ on multiple risk-relevant variables. Assume that previous research has identified that cheating on university entrance exams is more likely for males than females, more likely for Whites than racial minorities, and more likely for students from affluent families than students from nonaffluent families. If a student is a White female from an affluent family, is her likelihood of cheating similar to those of Whites, females, or students from affluent families? Researchers may be tempted to produce frequencies for all possible combinations, for example, White–female–affluent, White–female–nonaffluent, White–male–affluent, White–male–nonaffluent, and so on. If there are three predictor variables, as in the current example, then there are eight possible references groups. This is doable if the sample size is large enough. It is not an option, however, when the number of risk factors is large. If there are 20 relevant predictor variables, there are 1,048,576 possible combinations of risk factors, or distinct risk profiles[2] Given that we will never study each of these one million groups, evaluators seeking evidence-based rates must decide how to combine risk factors into an overall evaluation of risk. In practice, multiple risk factors are not used to create unique risk groups. Instead, simplifying assumptions are used.

Cumulative Stochastic Models

One of the common simplifying assumptions is that each risk factor contributes incrementally to the overall likelihood of the outcome. This is a cumulative stochastic model. *Cumulative* because each factor contributes something to the overall risk; *stochastic* because risk factors have a probabilistic relationship to the outcome. The cumulative stochastic model makes the (testable) assumption that there is relatively little information provided by interactions between predictors. Other, more complicated models are discussed in Chapter 17. The more complicated models allow for certain unique combinations of factors to have extra influence in the overall assessment of risk. Nevertheless, the cumulative stochastic model works well (Dawes, 1979), particularly when the outcome variable is transformed into logits (see Chapter 11).

Combining risk factors into scales or prediction algorithms does not, however, eliminate the reference class problem articulated by Hájek (2007).

---

[2]In R Statistics, the ***choose (n, x)*** command calculates the number of ways of selecting x items out of n possible items, where n is the total possible number of items, and x is the number of items selected (x can be a vector or integer). For example, the number of ways of selecting two risk factors out of three possible risk factors is > ***choose (3, 2)***, which yields three ways. The sum of all possible ways of selecting (or not) 20 items is > ***sum (choose(20, 0:20))***, which yields 1,048,576. Combination functions are also available on many handheld scientific calculators.

No structured risk assessment can consider all risk-relevant factors. Consequently, it is not uncommon for the case at hand to differ from the normative reference group on risk-relevant characteristics that are neither included in structured prediction schemes nor sufficiently researched on their own. Research is ongoing, and, if successful, new risk factors are identified. When this happens, evaluators will know that their structured assessment is incomplete but not know how the excluded variables should influence their overall evaluation of risk.

Probability as Degree of Belief

The models of probability reviewed so far do not speak directly to the likelihood of the outcome for an individual. Classical probabilities require knowing the rules of the game in advance. The frequentist model lacks a concept of likelihoods for individual events. The propensity model has a concept of likelihoods for individual events but requires that all members of the reference class are identical. Identity of class members can be argued for certain material conditions (e.g., pure uranium-238), but it is never the case in human affairs. To make statements about the likelihood of a specific outcome for a specific individual requires *subjective* probabilities.

From its beginnings, probability has had two meanings. One meaning concerns the existence of stable proportions in nature, as exemplified by classical and empirical probabilities discussed earlier. The other meaning of probability, the *subjectivist* or *Bayesian* meaning, concerns the degree of certainty of belief. We can ask questions concerning the likelihood that there will be a significant terrorism incident in the United States next year, and the likelihood that the 9/11 attack could have been prevented if current security practices had been in place. Pundits may answer these questions by saying that there is a 5% chance of terrorist attack next year, and an 80% chance that 9/11 could have been avoided using current security measures. These are conceptually coherent probabilities, but they are neither classical probabilities computed from known rules nor empirical probabilities observed in nature. They are subjective evaluations of the degree to which theory and evidence support specific conclusions. Although credible subjective probabilities should align with empirical evidence, subjective probabilities are not features of the world; instead, they index the certainty of our beliefs (Greenland, 1998).

Within the framework of subjective probability, it is possible to assign probabilities to individual events (Haigh, 2012). We can decide that Ms. Singh's likelihood of recovering from cancer is 70%, that there is a 40% chance of Mr. Knuckles going back to jail, and virtually no likelihood (less than 2%) of Al Pacino getting married. The validity of each of these specific judgments cannot be directly evaluated because no outcome would contradict our estimates (except in the rare case where our estimates are either zero or one).

The overall decision process, however, can be evaluated by group data. When a weather forecaster says that there is a 30% chance of rain today, it means that on 3 out of 10 days like today, it will rain. This is verifiable. Although subjective, professional judgment is required to make predictions about individual cases, these subjective judgments are most accurate when they align with the likelihoods estimated by group data (Dawes et al., 1989; Hanson & Morton-Bourgon, 2009).

CONCLUSION

My brief tour of the history and philosophy of probability was not intended to resolve long-standing debates or convince readers of any one model of probability. My more modest goal was to open up discussion among psychologists concerning the meaning of probability as applied to individual cases. I will, however, articulate where I currently stand on these issues.

First, I believe that all prediction tasks of consequence benefit from knowledge of base rates, which are empirical probabilities calculated for similar outcomes in similar groups. It matters whether the base rate is 1% or 50%. To quote Jacob Bernoulli,

> The Art of Conjecturing or the Stochastic Art is therefore defined as the art of measuring as exactly as possible the probabilities of things so that in our judgments and actions we can always choose or follow that which seems to be better, more satisfactory, safer and more considered. In this alone consists all the wisdom of the Philosopher and the prudence of the Statesman. (from *Ars Conjectandi*, 1713, quoted in Hald, 2003, p. 220)

The empirical probabilities computed using large samples usually provide the best estimates of the probabilities of things. Frequentist statistics, such as those I was taught in graduate school, are an excellent guide to estimating likelihoods and their sampling error. Unlike the frequentist model, however, I believe that probabilities can apply not only to groups (say, women over 40) but also to a specific woman over 40 (Joan). In agreement with Popper's propensity model, it is reasonable to use numeric probabilities to express the propensity for certain individuals to do certain things. Ascribing such likelihoods to individuals, however, requires subjective judgment. There is nothing in a research report, test manual, or data set that compels an evaluator to assign any specific numeric probability to any specific individual. Evaluators must decide how the evidence informs decisions about the case at hand. But in this regard, likelihoods are no different from any other attribute. Professional judgment is required whenever nomothetic research is applied to a specific case (Faigman et al., 2014).

Psychologists who are hired to conduct risk assessments on individuals are expected to know the relevant research evidence. They are not being asked, however, to write a research review. Instead, they are being asked to provide an opinion concerning a specific case. That means that they are being asked to exercise their professional judgment. As previously stated, these subjective judgments are most accurate when they tightly conform to the research evidence. Consequently, it is good practice for psychological assessments to report the rates of the outcome in reference groups similar to the case at hand. It is not good practice to then automatically dismiss these rates simply because they are based on group data. More helpful would be a reasoned analysis of the similarities between the characteristics and circumstances of the case at hand and those of the reference group studied. This analysis would conclude with a judgment of the extent to which the group-based rates accurately describe the risk of the case being evaluated.

The foregoing approach should resonate with readers who have been trained in standardized psychological testing. When administering the Wechsler Adult Intelligence Scale, for example, evaluators are expected to follow explicit procedures for asking and scoring the questions and for calculating the total scores. Test norms depend on standardized administration. Nevertheless, the evaluation report should be more than a test score. Good evaluations make inferences from the test score in the context of the individual's personal and cultural history and of what happened during testing (e.g., the individual had a panic attack during *block design*). Similarly, the plausibility and relevance of the probabilities generated by actuarial risk tools need to be considered with reference to the features of the case at hand and the evidence base for the prediction tool.

GOING FURTHER

This book is built on the premise that empirical probabilities should guide decisions about the likelihood of outcome for individuals. As should be evident from this chapter, judgment is, nonetheless, required to apply research findings to individuals. The numbers do not speak for themselves. For psychologists trained in the scientist–practitioner (Boulder) model, the integration of research and practice is familiar terrain (e.g., Belar, 2000). In some practice settings, however, organizations centralize policies concerning the interpretation of risk prediction tools. Many child welfare organizations, for example, specify a score on a risk tool below which families are considered low priority for further services. Such centralized policies are typically developed by a small committee of managers and content experts. The line staff, who are the end users of the risk tools, are then given practice standards, which they deviate from at their peril. My hope that this book will increase the number of individuals who can meaningfully contribute to decisions concerning the application and interpretation of risk tools. I would also hope that it would deepen the understanding of individuals already engaged in such discussions.

Recommended Readings

Hacking, I. (1975). *The emergence of probability: A philosophical study of early ideas about probability, induction and statistical inference*. Cambridge University Press.

Hacking explores recurrent perspectives on probability and scientific evidence through an analysis of the early contributors. Brilliant and witty. Assumes some background in the history and philosophy of science.

Haigh, J. (2012). *Probability: A very short introduction*. Oxford University Press.

An accessible, nontechnical introduction. No background required.

3

Overview of the Statistics Chapters

Parts II, III, and IV are the heart of this book. They present statistics for describing likelihoods (Part II), differences in likelihoods (i.e., discrimination, Part III), and the match between expected and observed probabilities (i.e., calibration, Part IV). The core chapters are followed by a chapter on percentiles (Part V). Although percentiles are not a prediction statistic, they are useful for describing the results of psychological assessment measures, including risk assessment tools. Each of the major parts contain separate chapters for specific statistics. The statistics chapters share the same general structure. They begin with a one sentence description, followed by a one paragraph description. The one sentence descriptions can also be found in the Glossary. The one-paragraph descriptions are slightly longer versions of the descriptions that are commonly found in the method sections of research studies in psychology and education.

The statistics included in this book have been curated from a large number of potentially relevant ones. Each chapter has a section explaining why these statistics were selected. These sections are chatty, with stories and detailed examples showing the benefits of knowing and using this statistic. This is followed, predictably, by a section describing the statistic's limitations. All statistics have a range of convenience (à la George Kelly, 1963), meaning that they are best suited for certain types of questions and certain types of data. The limitations sections also point out potential alternatives.

The Nuts and Bolts sections specify the data requirements and how to calculate the statistic from typical data. Each chapter also provides directions

https://doi.org/10.1037/0000275-003
Prediction Statistics for Psychological Assessment, by R. K. Hanson

for calculating standard errors. All observations contain a certain amount of random error, and the standard errors provide some guidance as to how much. A useful way of displaying sampling error is through confidence intervals, often 95% confidence intervals. Confidence intervals provide a range of values that could plausibly be used for interpretation (Cumming & Finch, 2005). Standard errors and confidence intervals are also useful for comparing the observed value to other values (e.g., calibration with norms). The size of the confidence intervals is primarily determined by the sample size. Large confidence intervals typically indicate that more research is necessary or that the current findings should be combined with other studies through meta-analysis (see Chapter 14). The Nuts and Bolts sections also provide alternate approaches for determining whether the difference between two findings is more than would be expected by chance.

The next major section, labeled Going Further, is intended for those who seek mastery. It includes computer code, exercises, and recommended readings. The readings are mostly accessible overviews, although occasionally I have listed authoritative works that have shaped my thinking on the topic.

Computer code is provided as a guide for individuals who already have some familiarity with either R Statistics (R Core Team, 2020; version 4.0.3) or IBM/SPSS (IBM Corp., 2020; Version 27). R Statistics is privileged because it is flexible, sophisticated, and free. It has a wide selection of programs and a helpful community of users. More than once, I have had the pleasant experience of requesting edits or additions to R programs and finding that the updated versions were available within a week. When statisticians create new statistical methods, the code to conduct these analyses are frequently first disseminated in R. The major limitation of R Statistics is that it has a less intuitive command structure than IBM/SPSS.

IBM/SPSS is probably the most commonly used statistical software in psychology. SPSS is user-friendly and has a large number of point-and-click functions for data management, analysis, and presentation. It can be expensive, however, for individuals not affiliated with a research institution. Although most of the statistics in this book are available in both software programs, some are not available in the standard versions of IBM/SPSS. Although SPSS is usually run from a drop-down menu, SPSS commands are presented as syntax to avoid many pages of screen shots. The syntax can be run in a SPSS syntax file; alternately, the syntax can be read as directions concerning what to select from the drop-down menus.

The steps to load and run R Statistics and IBM/SPSS are not covered in this book. Readers wishing to learn these programs are encouraged to take courses, seek mentors, read blogs, watch YouTube videos, and redeem goodwill with statistically minded colleagues. Note that both R Statistics and IBM/SPSS are regularly updated, which can change the options available, the algorithms used, and the syntax for running the programs. When using updated versions, do not be surprised by minor changes from the results generated by earlier versions (typically only in the second or third decimal points).

Each of the statistics chapters concludes with exercises. Many of these exercises can be completed with a decent pocket calculator (such as the one preloaded on your smartphone); others require statistical software programs. Although the exercises reference R and IBM/SPSS, readers can complete most of the exercises using almost any statistical software.

Readers are expected to use the statistics chapters to advance their individual learning needs. Chapters can be read in any order, and there is no need to read them through completely. Sometimes all that is needed is the basic summary, as provided by the introductory paragraph. Readers who want a solid overview of the statistic can stop before the Nuts and Bolts section. Those seeking an in-depth understanding will want to work through both the Nuts and Bolts section and the exercises. The Going Further sections are addressed to individuals considering using these statistics in research studies and to expert witnesses called to critique studies in court.

WHERE TO START?

Although the chapters can be read in any order, in the following section, I recommend statistics for the most common forms of prediction research. The chapters that describe these statistics may be a good place for students and other new researchers to start. My primary consideration when recommending statistics was that they were well suited to the question of interest—that is, they address the core questions of the prediction research. This contrasts with statistics that were designed for other purposes (such as analysis of variance or correlations) but can be repurposed for prediction studies. My recommendations also considered popularity and simplicity, which facilitate use and knowledge dissemination. The recommended statistics are not the only choices available; they are, however, solid choices. Routine use of these statistics would do much to advance the overall quality of prediction research in psychology, education, social work, and related fields.

The recommendations address three of the most common types of prediction studies: (a) developmental studies, (b) studies that establish quantitative norms for risk tools, and (c) replication and validation studies of existing tools (see Table 3.1). The risk tools under investigation are assumed to provide output expressed as ordered levels, such as low, moderate, or high, scores from zero to 10 or predicted rates of the outcome (e.g., 73% likelihood of graduating with a BA during the next 5 years). The other assumption is that the length of the follow-up is set by convention or convenience. In other words, the end of follow-up is not firmly set in nature, such as follow-up until death. The preceding assumptions apply to most prediction research in psychology; however, if they do not apply to your research context, you may find statistics that are better suited to your research needs by scanning the first page of the various statistics chapters.

TABLE 3.1. Recommended Statistics for Common Types of Prediction Research

	Coding of follow-up time	
Purpose of study	**Fixed**	**Variable**
Developmental		
Base rate	Proportions	Kaplan–Meier survival analysis
Predictors		
Dichotomous	Odds ratios	Cox regression hazard ratios
Ordered levels	AUC	Cox regression concordance
Creating norms for risk tools		
Relative risk	Logistic regression slope coefficients (B_1)	Cox regression hazard ratios
Absolute risk	Logistic regression predicted values	(not recommended)
Replication/validation of an existing risk tool		
Relative risk	AUC	Cox regression concordance
	Logistic regression slope coefficients (B_1)	
Calibration	E/O index	E/O index with Kaplan–Meier survival analysis
	Meta-analysis of logistic regression intercept coefficients (B_0)	(not recommended)
Percentile ranks	(not needed)	(not needed)

Note. AUC = area under the curve.

The choice of the appropriate prediction statistic depends on how follow-up time is coded: fixed (same for all cases) or variable. Researchers typically have the choice of how to code time at risk. In general, fixed follow-up periods are preferred when developing and evaluating likelihood estimates. Variable follow-up, however, is preferred in developmental research because it has the highest statistical power to detect small effects. In practice, I often code both fixed and variable follow-up and use these different outcome variables for different purposes. Directions for computing fixed follow-up are provided in Chapter 4, and directions for computing survival times for variable follow-up are provided in Chapter 6.

COMMON PREDICTION STUDIES

To motivate the presentation of the recommended statistics (Table 3.1), consider the practical problem of predicting when injured workers will return to work. Actionville is a small company town where most individuals work directly for Mega-Corp. Although Mega-Corp has been steadily improving its safety record, a significant number of employees are still injured each year. Mega-Corp wants to monitor and improve the services provided to injured workers, an initiative that also has the support of the workers' union.

Developmental Studies

One of the first steps in prediction studies is estimating the base rate of the outcome. In the Mega-Corp example, how long are injured employees typically off work? To calculate variable follow-up, the researchers record the date that the individual first was off work, the date that the individual returned to work, or the date that the follow-up ended. Using Kaplan–Meier survival analyses, these dates can then be used to estimate the likelihood of returning to work for any period of time extending up to the longest follow-up period. For fixed follow-up studies, the researchers need to specify in advance one or more follow-up times that have theoretical or practical significance. For example, regular sick-time benefits may expire after 1 month, so it could be useful to know what proportion of injury cases exceed regular sick-time benefits. There would also be considerable practical benefit in knowing the proportion who never return to work due to permanent disability.

Once the base rate is known, the next research task is identifying factors that increase or decrease the recovery time. The list of potential factors can be drawn from theory, other research, or whatever other variables happen to be available to the researchers. If the predictor variable is dichotomous (e.g., cohabiting at time of accident), then the relationship is best expressed as either an odds ratio (for fixed follow-up) or a hazard ratio (for variable follow-up). Descriptions of these statistics can be found in Chapters 7 and 10. When the predictor variable is ordinal or interval (e.g., a three-level rating of the degree of psychological trauma [minimal, moderate, severe]; age), then the relationship with recovery time for fixed follow-up periods is well described by the area under the curve (AUC; Chapter 8). For variable follow-up, I recommend the concordance statistic from Cox regression (also called Harrell's C, Chapter 10).

Creating Norms for Risk Tools

After identifying the base rate and a reliable set of predictors, the research team makes a risk tool for estimating recovery time, with they call HOIPE (Health Of Injured Personnel Estimator). The HOIPE scale has 20 yes–no items that address the seriousness of the injury, the individual's coping strategies and attitudes toward work, and the physical demands of the jobs available. The researchers conduct sufficient validation research that they recommend it for applied use. High scores are associated with a short periods of convalescence and rapid return to work. Now the researchers need norms for interpreting HOIPE scores.

One useful interpretation of risk tools scores is in terms of relative risk. For example, individuals with high HOIPE scores could be described as 4 times as likely to return to work within 1 month compared with individuals with low HOIPE scores. For fixed follow-up studies, the recommended method of computing such relative risk norms is by logistic regression slope coefficients

(B_1, Chapter 11). For variable follow-up studies, similar information is provided by hazard rates from Cox regression (Chapter 10).

For estimating absolute likelihoods (i.e., the proportion of cases expected to return to work within specific time periods), logistic regression estimates using fixed follow-up is recommended. Variable follow-up is not recommended for estimating absolute rates because a number of uncontrolled factors could influence these estimates. These factors include the amount of variation in follow-up times, frailty (see the Glossary), and interactions between risk level and survival time. Although there are some survival models that can address these otherwise uncontrolled factors, these models are not commonly used. Instead, most researchers choose the simpler option of estimating absolute rates from fixed follow-up periods, which provide values that are easier to explain (and to calculate).

Although not a prediction statistic, it is often useful to calculate percentile ranks for risk tools scores (see Part V). Percentile ranks do not require any follow-up period. Instead, calculating percentiles requires a large, representative sample with risk scale scores. Specifically, the sample of individuals used to calculate percentiles should be similar to the population of individuals to whom the risk tool will be applied.

Replication and Validation Studies of an Existing Risk Tool

Mega-Corp has been using the HOIPE risk tool in Actionville for several years, and it appears to be working more or less as intended. They have another company town in France, Ville d'Action, which has a similar concern with injured employees. The managers in Ville d'Action wonder if the HOIPE risk tool would support the same inferences in their setting as it does in Actionville. Consequently, they initiate a validation study of the HOIPE in their community.

The statistics needed for replication and validation studies parallel those used to create norms. If the original norms include percentile ranks, then percentile ranks should be calculated for the new setting. Similarly, it is useful to calculate logistic regression slope coefficients as an indicator of relative risk, if they were provided with the norms. In general, I recommend including at least one global measure of discrimination, such as the AUC for fixed follow-up studies, or the concordance statistic (Harrell's C) from Cox regression for studies with variable follow-up.

Not all risk tools assert expected absolute likelihoods. If they do, then it is possible to test the calibration of these rates in the replication study. The stability of specific likelihoods can be assessed using the E/O index (Chapter 13). Another approach to assessing calibration is by meta-analysis of logistic regression intercept coefficients (B_0; Chapter 14). The meta-analytic approach, of course, requires that the logistic function for the original likelihood norms is known.

The preceding recommendations are provided to orient students and other researchers to the sections of the book of immediate relevance to the most common forms of prediction studies. I do not expect, however, that this book will be read primarily by professional researchers (the base rate of full-time researchers is low). Instead, I expect most readers will be working in applied fields, have passing familiarity with the terms and concepts in this book and want to learn more.

So browse, or study intently, as is your want of the moment. There should be plenty to fulfill diverse, and developing, appetites for learning.

II

STATISTICS FOR DESCRIBING LIKELIHOODS

INTRODUCTION: STATISTICS FOR DESCRIBING LIKELIHOODS

Part II presents useful statistics for describing base rates. Regardless of the approach used, estimates of the likelihood of future outcomes are more accurate when evaluators consider base rates, that is, the frequency of the outcome in general. For example, when considering whether a talented, young baseball player will make the big leagues, the first consideration should be the overall proportion of club players who turn professional (few do). Additional information about the player, such as batting averages and motivation, can then be used to raise or lower this likelihood. The extent to which the overall estimate deviates from the base rate should be informed by the quality and consistency of the indicators (Kahneman et al., 2021).

Although we use numeric likelihoods in natural language (e.g., there is a 50/50 chance that Fred will be on time), there are advantages to using more precise terminology. Specifically, the technical definitions of proportions, odds, and hazards facilitate the identification of stable frequencies in nature. Given that the outcomes of interest are future events, these definitions must consider time. In research studies, there are two general approaches to calculating the time-to-event: (a) fixed follow-up (Chapter 4), and (b) survival analysis (Chapter 5 and Chapter 6). Each approach has its strengths and weaknesses. The chapters in this section also provide considerable detail on how to code raw follow-up data for prediction studies, which should be of particular benefit to researchers conducting their own prediction studies.

4

Proportions

Proportion, probability, and rate are all terms used to describe the same thing: the frequency of the outcome in a particular group. Proportions are calculated by dividing the number of individuals with the outcome by the total number of individuals at risk.

Proportions and rates are the most common ways that likelihoods are communicated in natural language. When a weather forecaster says that there is a 70% chance of rain today, this means that out of 10 days like today, rain is expected on 7 of them. Calculating empirical probabilities requires identifying a group of sufficiently similar members and then counting whether the outcome occurred in each of the members of this group. The characteristics and boundaries of the group is called the *sampling frame*. Calculating empirical probabilities also requires specifying when the outcome could occur (i.e., the follow-up period). The proportion is calculated by dividing the number with the outcome by the total number at risk.

WHY USE PROPORTIONS?

To estimate the likelihood of anything, the starting point should be the base rate. The *base rate* is the expected proportion of possible future events that will contain the outcome of interest. If I want to know whether the Rideau Canal will freeze next January, for example, it is useful to know that it has frozen every January since the canal was built in 1832. People, however, are not that predictable. Consequently, statements about the likelihood of future behaviors

https://doi.org/10.1037/0000275-004
Prediction Statistics for Psychological Assessment, by R. K. Hanson

are better represented by degrees of likelihood (e.g., unlikely, possible, virtually certain) rather than by categorical statements that the behavior will or will not occur. Degrees of likelihood can be expressed by numbers (e.g., 86 out of 100 [86%]). Empirical proportions can range from 0% (nobody has the outcome) to 100% (everybody has the outcome); however, few real circumstances justify predictions of either 0% or 100%.

Proportions are easily understood and have high relevance for many applied assessment questions. The same proportion can be expressed as a decimal between zero and one (e.g., .860), a percentage (e.g., 86.0%), or a number out of a total (e.g., 86 out of 100). When reporting proportions as a number out of a total, it is important to maintain the same denominator (Visschers et al., 2009). When communicating medical risks, for example, patients are likely to focus on the number of events (e.g., 12 vs. 124 deaths) and ignore the denominator. In one study, Yamagishi (1997) found that participants considered a mortality rate of 1,286 out of 10,000 to be worse than a mortality rate of 24.14 out of 100. We misjudge this risk because it is difficult to imagine really large numbers. We have an intuitive sense of 500 to 1,000 people (a typical high school), but we cannot easily imagine 10,000 people. We know that 10,000 is bigger than 100, but unless we engage effortful processing (Kahneman's, 2011, System 2), we are not sure by how much.

Given that it is easier to imagine something happening (e.g., criminal recidivism, relapse into depression) than something not happening, it is often useful to report both the likelihood of the event and the likelihood of not having the event. For example, when asked about the effectiveness of treatment, a clinician may want to say something like the following: The success rate for treating depression at Clinique Guérison is 85%. This means that out of 100 individuals treated for depression at Clinique Guérison, 85 will have recovered and had no further episodes 2 years after starting treatment; conversely, 15 out of 100 who start treatment will either have not recovered or have relapsed within 2 years.

In common language, proportions and odds are often considered synonymous. In statistical language, they mean different things. With proportions (p), the number of events is divided by the total at risk.

$$p = \frac{n_{events}}{n_{total}} \tag{4.1}$$

If 15 out of 100 relapse, the proportion is 15/100 = 0.15. In contrast, the odds is the number of events divided by the number of nonevents.

$$odds = \frac{n_{events}}{n_{nonevents}} = \frac{p}{1-p} = \frac{p}{q} \tag{4.2}$$

The number of nonevents (often called q) is the total minus the number of events. If 15 out of 100 individuals relapse, the number of nonevents is $q = (100 - 15) = 85$. In our example, the odds of relapse would be 15 to 85, that is, for every 15 individuals who relapse, 85 recover successfully. This could also be expressed as a decimal, odds = .176 = 15/85. When base rates are low, the odds are similar to proportions. We will return to odds in Chapter 7 and Chapter 11 because odds have certain statistical properties that facilitate their use in regression analyses. For now, readers should simply be aware that proportions and odds are different and be mindful of their use of these terms in their risk communication.

LIMITATIONS

One common criticism of using group rates to make decisions about individuals is that the case at hand is different from other members of the sampling frame. It is difficult to have confidence in the overall proportion when individuals in the study group are known to vary on risk-relevant characteristics. If sample size permits, then subgroups could be examined separately. If there are a large number of risk-relevant variables, these variables can be combined in prediction tools. The rates associated with the scores or risk levels of the prediction tool would then be estimated. If the goal is simply estimating the likelihood of the outcome, then scales constructed by counting the number of factors present work surprisingly well (Dawes, 1979), as do more complicated statistical procedures. Although it is good practice to report the overall likelihood of the outcome in the complete reference group, case-specific interpretations are often based on the probabilities from risk scale scores (not the overall base rate).

Another limitation with proportions is that base rates are often less stable than relative risk. Academic failure rates, for example, vary with the difficulty of the tests. If the assessment task is to select the 10 best students, then the success rate for each test is less informative than other statistics, such as the percentile rank on an aggregated index of academic ability (Chapter 16). For most outcomes, base rates vary with the length of follow-up (e.g., criminal recidivism, rehospitalization). When there is no natural end to follow-up time, relative risk indicators can be more useful than proportions (e.g., failure to take prescribed medications increases the likelihood of rehospitalization by a factor of 3; see Part III for relative risk statistics).

The analysis and interpretation of proportions is also complicated by an association between the size of the proportion and its variability. The sampling variability of a proportion is highest when the proportion equals .50 and lowest when it is very small (close to zero) or very large (close to 1). Consequently, raw proportions are rarely used in statistical analyses. Instead, comparisons between proportions frequently use transformations of proportions, such as *logits* (Chapter 11), or variance stabilization transformations (Chapter 14).

THE NUTS AND BOLTS

Data Requirements

The following data are required to calculate empirical probabilities:

1. a representative sample,
2. a follow-up time, and
3. an outcome.

The first step in calculating empirical proportions is to define the sampling frame. This is the population of individuals to whom these proportions are intended to apply. The sampling frame can be quite narrow (e.g., clients at a specific clinic) or very large (women over age 40). Researchers then need to identify a sample from this population. Ideally, the sample would be truly random. In practice, researchers set their aspirations lower and instead look for representative samples that are not obviously biased.

One source of bias that is not obvious but is predictable is what has been called the "clinician's illusion" (Cohen & Cohen, 1984; or jailer's illusion, Hanson, 2018). This is the tendency for current users of a service to be more problematic than most users of the service. When I started my practice as a clinical psychologist in community corrections, I felt like a wizard. Most of my initial clients responded well to my short, focused interventions. After resolving their presenting problems, they seldom returned. Soon, however, I was receiving clients with much more serious problems. Some of these individuals required almost continuous interventions simply to remain out of a hospital or prison. Relapses were common. Rather than providing a few sessions to many clients, I was starting to provide many sessions to a few clients. At the end of my first year of practice, my short-term clients had largely disappeared, along with any youthful illusions that I had the magic touch.

Now consider that an evaluator wanted to conduct a recidivism study of the clients on my caseload. If the question is "How many of my clients go on to reoffend?", it would be a mistake for the evaluation to consider only my recent cases. My recent cases would include a disproportionate number of higher risk individuals (Rhodes et al., 2016). A more representative sampling strategy would be to select individuals consecutively from the point of intake assessment (or first treatment session).

Researchers also need to specify the follow-up period. For some outcomes, there is a natural start and end time, for example, what is the proportion of individuals who start university in 2021 that will graduate with a 3-year college degree within 3 years? For many outcomes, however, there is neither a clear starting point nor a clear end to follow-up time; instead, risk is diffusely distributed over time (e.g., depression relapse, criminal recidivism). For such outcomes, researchers must assert for each case a start date and an end date. The preferred start and end points will vary based on the research question and the outcomes studied. In general, the follow-up period (difference between the start and end dates) should be long enough for a reasonable number of outcomes to be observed but short enough to be doable. Birth to death follow-up may be ideal but requires the commitment of a multigenerational research team. It is also good practice to consider the ease with which it can be replicated by others. Excellence can be the enemy of the good.

For all follow-up studies, researchers much decide whether follow-up is fixed (same for all) or variable/ragged (follow-up time varies for each individual). Ragged follow-up is often preferred in prediction studies because it retains more information. With ragged follow-up times, however, the raw proportion is not the ideal statistic. The number of events will be influenced by both the likelihood of the outcome and the length of the follow-up for each case. Survival analysis is the preferred method of estimating base rates from ragged follow-up (see Chapter 5 and Chapter 6). For proportions, fixed follow-up is preferred.

Calculating Fixed Follow-Up Times

The following information is needed to calculate fixed follow-up times:

1. a start date,
2. a follow-up end date,
3. a dichotomous outcome variable, and
4. the date that the outcome occurred.

Individuals who fail after the fixed follow-up period are counted as successes. Individuals who were followed for less than the fixed follow-up period are excluded, regardless of whether the outcome has occurred or not. This latter rule may seem counter intuitive, given that we know that the individual failed during the follow-up period; however, including individuals with insufficient follow-up who failed and not those who succeeded would overestimate the failure rate.

Another research design choice is whether follow-up should be calendar time or at-risk time. In criminal recidivism studies, for example, individuals may be reincarcerated during the follow-up period for reasons other than new criminal behavior (e.g., incarcerated for offenses committed decades ago, violations of release conditions). Researchers may want to subtract these periods of incarceration from calendar time to estimate recidivism probabilities based on street time. Similarly, evaluators of a driver safety program may want to estimate the probability of a bus driver having a traffic accident based on the number of days (or hours) that the driver actually worked (not the number of years that the individual has been employed by the company).

Worked Example

The following is an example of how to compute proportions using fixed follow-up time. This example is based on a certain Dr. Breuer evaluating the recidivism rate of the individuals treated at his forensic clinic in Vienna. Specifically, he wants to calculate the recidivism rate for a fixed 2-year follow-up because that is the time frame routinely reported in Austria. Dr. Breuer decides to use an intent-to-treat sample, involving all individuals who completed intake assessment at his clinic, regardless of how many sessions they attended or whether they were considered to be treated successfully. He asks his new intern, Sigmund, to go through the clinic's files and record the start date of each new case from January 2016 to January 2019. These will be the start dates for the fixed follow-up period.

The end of follow-up was set at the date that recidivism information was obtained from the Austrian Department of Corrections, specifically January 15,

2021. Although follow-up information will stop at a particular date, this may not be the best date to end the follow-up period. Often there is a lag time between when an event occurs and when that event appears in administrative records; consequently, it is often good practice to set the end time for follow-up before the date when the records were received. The length of this gap will depend on the nature of the outcome and the administrative records. Canada, for example, has reasonably reliable records of criminal convictions anywhere in Canada (maintained by the Canadian Police Information Centre [CPIC]); however, it can take up to a year between the date of conviction and the date that the conviction would appear on a records search. To ensure that recent convictions are counted, researchers using CPIC may want to set the end of follow-up 6 months or a year before the date that records were obtained. In the current example, Dr. Breuer trusts that the Austrian records are up-to-date, so he uses the date that the records were received as the end date of follow-up.

Sigmund provides his professor with a table containing 33 cases, of which 16 were known to have reoffended (Table 4.1). As is typical in real-world studies, not all cases will be used in the analysis. In particular, the analyses are restricted to cases that have been followed up for at least 24 months. For most cases, the follow-up end date is January 15, 2021; consequently, to have 24 months of follow-up, they must have started treatment before January 15, 2019. Six cases started treatment after January 15, 2019. When Professor Breuer asks about the late January and February 2019 cases, Sigmund says that he wanted to be thorough and that it is better to oversample at this stage, even if these cases are excluded later. Sigmund also included three additional cases that were treated in 2020 and reoffended. Sigmund is eager to be seen as conscientious and thought his supervisor would be interested in all cases that were known to have reoffended within 2 years.

Professor Breuer appreciates the eagerness of his intern and thinks that he will go far. But he tells Sigmund that he has made a common mistake. To estimate the 2-year recidivism rate, all cases must have at least 24 months of follow-up. This may seem obvious, but it is not. Cases 131, 132, and 133 were known to have reoffended within 2 years; nevertheless, the wise Professor Breuer tells Sigmund to exclude these cases from the study. If they were included, he says, it would bias the estimate upward by some unknown amount. The amount of bias is unknown because we do not know how many individuals were followed for less than 2 years and did not reoffend. Similarly, the 2-year fixed follow-up analyses must also exclude three cases that were started in 2016 but for whom follow-up ended less than 24 months after intake (Cases 106, 107, and 108). For example, these cases could have been deported, died, or missing from the Austrian records. This leaves 24 cases available for analysis.

The next step is determining whether each case was known to have reoffended within 24 months of start date (i.e., the date of intake assessment). Case 101 and Case 102, for example, are straightforward successes, with no new criminal involvement. For the recidivists, add 2 years to the intake date and decide whether this date is earlier or later than the date of

TABLE 4.1. Raw Data Used to Create 2-Year Fixed Follow-Up Study of Criminal Recidivism

ID	Intake date	End of follow-up	2+ years follow-up	Any recid?	New offense date	Recid within 2 years?	Fixed 2-year recid data
101	23-JAN-2016	15-JAN-2021	Yes	No			0
102	01-MAR-2016	15-JAN-2021	Yes	No			0
103	30-APR-2016	15-JAN-2021	Yes	Yes	12-MAR-2017	Yes	1
104	12-JUN-2016	15-JAN-2021	Yes	Yes	04-JUL-2019	No	0
105	15-JUN-2016	15-JAN-2021	Yes	No			0
106	04-SEP-2016	07-OCT-2016	No	No			
107	24-SEP-2016	15-JAN-2017	No	No			
108	12-OCT-2016	15-JAN-2018	No	Yes	24-AUG-2017	Yes	
109	11-NOV-2016	15-JAN-2021	Yes	No			0
110	15-NOV-2016	15-JAN-2021	Yes	Yes	25-DEC-2020	No	0
111	20-DEC-2016	15-JAN-2021	Yes	Yes	01-JAN-2017	Yes	1
112	16-JAN-2017	15-JAN-2021	Yes	No			0
113	25-JAN-2017	15-JAN-2021	Yes	No			0
114	11-FEB-2017	15-JAN-2021	Yes	Yes	23-MAR-2018	Yes	1
115	23-FEB-2017	15-JAN-2021	Yes	Yes	28-APR-2018	Yes	1
116	03-MAR-2017	15-JAN-2021	Yes	Yes	22-MAY-2017	Yes	1
117	20-APR-2017	15-JAN-2021	Yes	No			0
118	13-SEP-2017	15-JAN-2021	Yes	Yes	12-OCT-2018	Yes	1
119	23-NOV-2017	15-JAN-2021	Yes	No			0
120	29-NOV-2017	15-JAN-2021	Yes	Yes	22-OCT-2020	No	0
121	22-FEB-2018	15-JAN-2021	Yes	Yes	12-MAR-2019	Yes	1
122	26-MAR-2018	15-JAN-2021	Yes	No			0
123	22-JUN-2018	12-JAN-2021	Yes	No			0
124	31-OCT-2018	15-JAN-2021	Yes	Yes	12-NOV-2019	Yes	1
125	16-NOV-2018	15-JAN-2021	Yes	No			0
126	27-NOV-2018	15-JAN-2021	Yes	Yes	11-JAN-2019	Yes	1
127	15-DEC-2018	15-JAN-2021	Yes	No			0
128	20-JAN-2019	15-JAN-2021	No	No			
129	01-FEB-2019	15-JAN-2021	No	No			
130	05-FEB-2019	15-JAN-2021	No	No			
131	31-MAR-2020	15-JAN-2021	No	Yes	07-MAY-2020	Yes	
132	22-JUN-2020	15-JAN-2021	No	Yes	24-NOV-2020	Yes	
133	31-OCT-2020	15-JAN-2021	No	Yes	13-JAN-2020	Yes	
	Number of recidivists/*N*			16/33			9/24

Note. Recid = recidivism.

recidivism. Case 103 is a straightforward failure, known to have reoffended after about a year. Case 104 is counted as a success. Even though Case 104, Case 110, and Case 120 were known to have reoffended, they all reoffended more than 2 years after intake. Consequently, these cases are counted as non-recidivists for the purpose of 2-year fixed follow-up estimates.

After applying the rules for fixed follow-up, nine of 24 cases are known to have reoffended. This results in a 2-year fixed follow-up rate of 9 of 24 = 0.375, or 37.5%.

Standard Errors and Confidence Intervals

Standard errors are helpful when comparing proportions. All empirically derived proportions are expected to fluctuate based on random error. The standard error provides a guide to how much fluctuation to expect. Confidence intervals bound the limits of plausible interpretation.

As previously stated, the standard errors of proportions are complicated by their dependence on the observed value. Proportions follow a binomial distribution, such that the variability decreases as the observed value becomes very small (close to 0) or very large (close to 1). There are several ways of estimating standard errors for proportions (Agresti & Coull, 1998; Fleiss et al., 2003). Two are discussed in this chapter, and another is discussed in the chapter on meta-analysis (Chapter 14; a variance stabilization transformation).

In introductory statistics texts, the variance of a proportion is usually given as follows:

$$\text{Variance }(p) = p(1-p)/n \tag{4.3}$$

where p is the observed proportion, and n is the sample size of which it was based. The standard error is the square root of the variance, and the 95% confidence interval is given as

$$p \pm Z\sqrt{p(1-p)/n} \tag{4.4}$$

In Equation 4.4 (called the Wald method), Z sets the width of the confidence interval. Ninety-five percent confidence intervals are commonly used, which correspond to a Z value of 1.96. Equation 4.3 is the same as the definition of the variance of a mean for continuous variables (Equation 4.5) when the only possible values of variable (x) are zero or one.

$$variance\ (x.) = \left(\frac{\sum_1^n [x_i - x.]^2}{n-1} \right) \Big/ n \tag{4.5}$$

In Equation 4.5, $x.$ is the mean value of the x variable.

One problem with the Wald method (Equation 4.4) is that the variance is zero under two quite different conditions: (a) when the sample size is infinitely large and (b) when the sample size is sufficiently small that all the occurrences are of the same type (i.e., everybody or nobody has the outcome). Consequently,

Agresti and Caffo (2000) recommended an alternative method of calculating 95% confidence intervals based on early work by Wilson (1927):

$$\tilde{p} \pm Z\sqrt{\tilde{p}(1-\tilde{p})/\tilde{n}} \tag{4.6}$$

This is the same as Equation 4.4 except p and n are replaced by closely related values, $\tilde{p}$ and $\tilde{n}$. Specifically, $\tilde{n} = n + 4$, and $\tilde{p}$ = ([number with outcome] + 2)/(n + 4). The effect of this adjustment is that the new $\tilde{p}$ is now a weighted average of the observed proportion, p, and ½ (2 out of 4 cases). As the sample size increases, $\tilde{p}$ approaches the usual p. By adding a constant to the numerator and denominator, the estimated value is tilted toward ½ when the sample size is small. The variance of $\tilde{p}$ is similarly a weighted average of the usual variance of the observed p (Equation 4.3) and the variance of the proportion ½ (i.e., ½ * ½ = .25). One desirable feature of Agresti and Caffo's (2000) formula is that the variability estimates are never zero, that is, the formula never indicates that the proportion is estimated without error.

Continuing with our recidivism example, Professor Breuer wants to know how the recidivism rate of the individuals at his clinic (9/24 = .375) compares with the typical rates in Austria. Conveniently, the Austrian correctional service regularly publishes recidivism rates based on the same definition used in the evaluation study (known reoffending within 2 years). The official figure is 52%. To judge whether 37.5% is lower than expected, Dr. Breuer asks Sigmund to calculate the 95% confidence interval, using both the Wald method and that of Agresti and Caffo (2000). The Wald method (Equation 4.4) provides the following value for the 95% confidence interval:

$$0.375 \pm 1.96\sqrt{0.375(1-0.375)/24}$$

This results in a confidence interval of 0.181 to 0.569 (p = 0.375 ± 0.1937). Using the Agresti and Caffo method, $\tilde{n}$ = 24 + 4 = 28, and $\tilde{p}$ = (9 + 2)/(24 + 4) = 0.3929. Inserting these values in Equation 4.6:

$$0.3929 \pm 1.96\sqrt{0.3929(1-0.3929)/28}$$

The resulting value of the Agresti and Caffo 95% confidence interval is 0.212 to 0.574 ($\tilde{p}$ = 0.3929 ± 0.1809).

The confidence intervals calculated by both methods are similar, and both include the expected value, 52%. In other words, the observed recidivism rates for individuals treated at Dr. Breuer's clinic are within the range expected by chance. Dr. Breuer is, nevertheless, encouraged by these results because he believes that his patients are more problematic than average. Without intervention, he believes, the recidivism rates would have been even higher. This is a testable hypothesis; however, evidence for this hypothesis would require a method of estimating risk-adjusted recidivism rates (i.e., a risk prediction tool). It would also require more complicated statistics, such as logistic regression (see Chapters 11, 14, and 15).

When the total sample size is greater than 20 and the number with the outcome is 5 or more, it makes little difference whether the confidence intervals are calculated using the Wald method (Equation 4.4) or the method of Agresti and Caffo (Equation 4.6). When the number of events is close to zero, however, Agresti and Caffo's method is preferred. Consider that Dr. Breuer's clinic specialized in the treatment of individuals with paraphilias and a history of sexual offending. Consequently, the outcome of primary interest would be sexual recidivism, not general criminal recidivism. According to official government statistics, the base rate of sexual recidivism in Austria is 4.0% after 2 years. As it turns out, none of the nine recidivism events (out of 24 at risk) were sexually motivated. Using the Wald method, the observed recidivism rate would be zero, and the standard error would also be zero. In other words, there is complete certainty that recidivism rate is zero. The upper end of the confidence interval is zero, which is lower than the expected base rate (4%). Dr. Breuer is delighted and reports this finding when his contract with the Department of Corrections comes up for renewal.

The contract manager accepts Dr. Breuer's raw data but uses the Agresti and Caffo method for estimating the sexual recidivism rate and its confidence interval. Now $\tilde{p}$ = (recidivists + 2)/(n + 4) = (0 + 2)/(24 + 4) = 2/28 = 7.14%. The variance of this estimate would be (0.0714 ∗ (1 − 0.0714))/(24 + 4) = 0.0023688, and the standard error would be $(0.0023688)^{1/2}$ = 0.04867. Note that "$(x)^{1/2}$" means "the square root of variable x". The 95% confidence interval would be 0.0714 ± 1.96(0.04867), that is, 0.0714 ± 0.09539. Because the lower bound of the confidence interval is below zero, the lower bound is set to zero. The upper end of the confidence interval is 0.0714 + 0.09539 = 0.167. The contract manager concludes that the sexual recidivism rate for Dr. Breuer's clients is unlikely to be more than 17%. This is encouraging but no reason to call Sweden.

Readers should note the difficulty of showing treatment effects when the base rate of the outcome is low. When the expected rate is only 4%, approximately 1,500 observations would be needed for any reasonable chance of detecting a positive effect of a treatment that actually reduced the rate in half (Cohen, 1988, see Table 6.4.1).

Comparing Proportions

Confidence intervals are useful when comparing an observed proportion to an established base rate. In these comparisons, the established base rate is considered to be sufficiently stable as to be essentially measured without error. For example, it is common to compare the rates observed in a study sample to well-established rates based on very large samples (100,000s to millions), or even to complete populations. An inner-city health clinic may, for instance, want to compare the proportion of its patients who are unemployed to the overall unemployment rate in its catchment area. Other methods for comparing observed and expected proportions are presented in Part IV ("Calibration"), such as the chi-square goodness-of-fit test (Chapter 12) and the E/O index (Chapter 13).

When comparing two proportions that are both measured with error, confidence intervals provide a low-powered test (Cumming & Finch, 2005). Instead, researchers should use the statistics described in Chapter 7, such as odds ratios. Comparisons between three or more proportions can be addressed through meta-analysis (Chapter 14).

GOING FURTHER

Readers who have made it this far should have a solid understanding of how to calculate and interpret base rates in prediction studies. The following sections are designed to consolidate learning through further reading and exercises. These sections can be worked with in any order, and it is not necessary to do all (or any) of them.

Recommended Readings

Agresti, A., & Caffo, B. (2000). Simple and effective confidence intervals for proportions and differences of proportions result from adding two successes and two failures. *The American Statistician, 54*(4), 280–288.

Agresti and Caffo (2000) clearly explain the limitations of the commonly recommended Wald method and justify an alternative (the adjustment described in this chapter). They recommend that their adjustment always be applied. My view is that this adjustment is helpful with small samples and extreme base rates, but it adds unnecessary complication when the sample size is large (100+) and the base rates are between 20% and 80%.

Fleiss, J. L., Levin, B., & Paik, M. C. (2003). *Statistical methods for rates and proportions* (3rd ed.). Wiley.

This is a very authoritative text, comprehensive and carefully reasoned. It is not, however, an easy read: Expect lots of formula and mathematical symbols. Nevertheless, their recommendations are sensible, and Fleiss's work is one of my primary sources for the current book.

Computer Code

For simplicity, I have designed the examples and exercises in this section so that they can be easily completed with a handheld calculator and a little mental arithmetic; statistical programs are not necessary. Statistical programs are recommended, however, for calculating fixed follow-up times in large, messy data sets, or when the exact follow-up times are needed (not just whether the time is more or less than 2 years). Directions for using statistical programs to calculate exact follow-up times are provided in the chapter on Kaplan–Meier survival analysis (Chapter 6).

The following computer code is provided to calculate the proportion, its standard error, and 95% confidence intervals using both the Wald method and the Agresti and Caffo adjustment described earlier. The computer code is based on Professor Breuer's imaginary study of recidivism: events/total = p = 9/24 = 0.375

R Code

There are many ways to enter data in R. Here, I use the concatenation function: **object** <- **c(x_1, x_2, . . . x_i)**. R code is presented in Courier New 10 pitch font. In the syntax below, *data, p, n, upperCI,* and *lowerCI* are arbitrary names (set by the user, not by the program).

```
data <-c (1,1,1,1,1,1,1,1,1,0,0,0,0,0,0,0,0,0,0,0,
0,0,0,0)
```

This data set identifies nine cases as failures (1) and 15 cases as successes (0). The next step is to define the values for *p* and *n*.

```
p <- mean (data)
p
[1] 0.375
n <- length (data)
n
[1] 24
```

The following calculates the 95% confidence intervals using the Wald method:

```
upperCI <- p + (1.96)*(sqrt((p)*(1-p)/n))
upperCI
[1] 0.5686895
lowerCI <- p - (1.96)*(sqrt((p)*(1-p)/n))
lowerCI
[1] 0.1813105
```

which gives an observed value of 0.375 with 95% confidence interval of 0.181 to 0.569.

To calculate the Agresti and Caffo confidence intervals, *p* is replaced by *P* = (events + 2)/(*n* + 4), and *n* is replaced by *N* = events + 4. Note that small letter *p* and capital letter *P* are different variables in R.

```
data <- c(1,1,1,1,1,1,1,1,1,0,0,0,0,0,0,0,0,0,0,0,
0,0,0)
events <- sum(data)
n <- length (data)
N = n + 4
P = (events + 2)/N
P
[1] 0.3928571
ACupperCI <- P + (1.96)*(sqrt((P)*(1-P)/N))
ACupperCI
[1] 0.5737577
```

```
AClowerCI <- P - (1.96)*(sqrt((P)*(1-P)/N))
AClowerCI
[1] 0.2119566
```

This gives an adjusted proportion of 0.393 with 95% confidence intervals of .212 to 0.573.

IBM/SPSS Code

Analyses in IBM/SPSS are typically conducted with a predefined data set. In this example, the IBM/SPSS data set contains a single variable, recidivism, coded as 1 for yes (9 cases), and 0 for no (15 cases; total $N = 24$; Chap4_p_example.sav, available at https://www.apa.org/pubs/books/prediction-statistics-for-psychological-assessment). A version of the Wald confidence interval is provided in *T-Test* command. This command is found by following *Analyze, Compare Means,* then *One-Sample T-Test*. You only need to select the outcome variable. Ninety-five percent confidence intervals are provided as the default. The SPSS syntax is as follows:

```
T-TEST
/TESTVAL=0
/MISSING=ANALYSIS
/VARIABLES=recidivism
/CRITERIA=CI(.95).
```

This produces the following output:

One-Sample Test

	Test Value = 0					
					95% CI of the difference	
	t	*df*	Significance (two-tailed)	Mean difference	Lower	Upper
recidivism	3.715	23	.001	.375	.17	.58

Note. CI = confidence interval.

The relevant numbers are the mean difference = .375, which is the proportion, and the 95% confidence interval of the difference, 0.17 to 0.58. When the test value is set to zero (the default), the CI of the difference is the one you want. In this program, the confidence interval is slightly wider than before because it is based on the *t* distribution ($t = 2.069$, $df = 23$, $p = .025$), not the normal distribution ($Z = 1.96$). In most cases, the differences between using *t* or *Z* will be too small to have practical significance. So, take your pick.

IBM/SPSS version 27.0.0.0 does not have a command for calculating Agresti and Caffo adjusted confidence intervals. They can be calculated in SPSS with the COMPUTE function; however, if you are considering this option, it is generally easier to use R Statistics, any commercial spreadsheet (e.g., Excel), or your hand calculator.

EXERCISES

This exercise extends the Dr. Breuer criminal recidivism example presented earlier. For the cases since January 2016, Dr. Breuer observed that nine out of 24 individuals were known to have reoffended after a fixed 2-year follow-up period. He realizes that this is a small sample, so he aims to increase his sample size by including older cases. He again approaches his intern, Sigmund, requesting that he identify cases going back as far as January 1, 2013. He again uses an intent-to-treat sample with the start date set at intake assessment. Criminal recidivism information for the new sample was then collected on June 1, 2021, which was set as the maximum value of the follow-up end date. The intake dates, follow-up end dates, and recidivism dates for the new sample are presented in Table 4.2.

TABLE 4.2. Two-Year Fixed Follow-Up of Criminal Recidivism for Cases Treated Since January 1, 2013

ID	Intake date Start date	End of follow-up End date	2+ years follow-up	Any recid?	New offense date	Recid within 2 years?	Fixed 2-year recid data
(1)	(2)	(3)	(4)	(5)	(6)	(7)	(8)
1	10-JAN-2013	01-JUN-2021		No			
2	15-JAN-2013	01-JUN-2021		Yes	03-JUL-2014		
3	07-FEB-2013	01-JUN-2021		No			
4	23-MAR-2013	11-SEP-2014		Yes	04-JUL-2014		
5	20-APR-2013	01-JUN-2021		No			
6	15-MAY-2013	01-JUN-2021		Yes	29-JUN-2017		
7	30-OCT-2013	01-JUN-2021		Yes	30-APR-2016		
8	25-JAN-2014	01-JUN-2021		No			
9	15-MAR-2014	01-JUN-2021		No			
10	22-APR-2014	01-JUN-2021		Yes	15-JAN-2016		
11	31-MAY-2014	01-JUN-2021		No			
12	12-JUN-2014	15-OCT-2015		No			
13	18-JUL-2014	01-JUN-2021		Yes	25-DEC-2020		
14	10-SEP-2014	01-JUN-2021		No			
15	12-NOV-2014	01-JUN-2021		No			
16	07-DEC-2014	01-JUN-2021		No			
17	03-FEB-2015	01-JUN-2021		Yes	23-MAR-2016		
18	26-MAR-2015	01-JUN-2021		No			
19	25-APR-2015	01-JUN-2021		No			
20	24-MAY-2015	01-JUN-2021		Yes	09-FEB-2017		
21	21-JUN-2015	01-JUN-2021		No			
22	28-JUN-2015	01-JUN-2021		Yes	01-JAN-2021		
23	15-OCT-2015	01-JUN-2021		Yes	20-MAY-2020		
24	18-OCT-2015	01-JUN-2021		No			
25	28-NOV-2015	01-JUN-2021		Yes	15-JAN-2016		
	Number of recidivists/*N*			11/25			

Note. Recid = recidivism.

Question 4.1

Complete Table 4.2 by indicating the following:

(i) whether each case was followed for 2 years (yes–no in Column 4);
(ii) for those who were known to have reoffended, whether it occurred within 2 years after intake (yes–no in Column 7); and
(iii) whether, using a fixed 2-year follow-up, each case should be coded as a failure/recidivist (1), a success (0), or missing (Column 8).

Question 4.2

Based on your coding of Table 4.2,

(i) What is the 2-year criminal recidivism rate in this sample?
(ii) Calculate the 95% confidence intervals for this estimate using the Wald method (Equation 4.4).

Question 4.3

In the combined sample of all cases who started treatment between January 1, 2013, and January 14, 2019 (all usable cases in Table 4.1 and Table 4.2),

(i) What is the criminal recidivism rate for a fixed 2-year follow-up period?
(ii) How does this rate compare to the expected value of 52% in Austria?

Question 4.4

In the combined sample, there were still no individuals who reoffended with a sexually motivated offense.

(i) Using the Agresti and Caffo method (Equation 4.6), what is the upper limit of the 95% confidence interval for the rate of sexual recidivism?
(ii) How does this compare to the expected value of 4% in Austria?

ANSWERS TO EXERCISES

Question 4.1

See Table 4.3 for the completed table. Note that Case 4 (who reoffended within 2 years) is excluded because the total follow-up time for this case (difference between start date and end date) was less than 2 years. Case 5 is also coded as missing because this case was lost to follow-up before 2 years at risk. Cases 6, 7, 13, 22, and 23 are coded as successes. Even though they were known to have reoffended, the offense dates were after 2 years of follow-up. The final tally is five failures and 18 successes out of 23 cases available for analysis.

TABLE 4.3. Two-Year Fixed Follow-Up of Criminal Recidivism for Cases Treated After January 1, 2013

ID	Intake date Start date	End of follow-up End date	2+ years follow-up	Any recid?	New offense date	Recid within 2 years?	Fixed 2-year recid data
(1)	(2)	(3)	(4)	(5)	(6)	(7)	(8)
1	10-JAN-2013	01-JUN-2021	Yes	No			0
2	15-JAN-2013	01-JUN-2021	Yes	Yes	03-JUL-2014	Yes	1
3	07-FEB-2013	01-JUN-2021	Yes	No			0
4	23-MAR-2013	11-SEP-2014	No	Yes	04-JUL-2014	Yes	
5	20-APR-2013	01-JUN-2021	Yes	No			0
6	15-MAY-2013	01-JUN-2021	Yes	Yes	29-JUN-2017	No	0
7	30-OCT-2013	01-JUN-2021	Yes	Yes	30-APR-2016	No	0
8	25-JAN-2014	01-JUN-2021	Yes	No			0
9	15-MAR-2014	01-JUN-2021	Yes	No			0
10	22-APR-2014	01-JUN-2021	Yes	Yes	15-JAN-2016	Yes	1
11	31-MAY-2014	01-JUN-2021	Yes	No			0
12	12-JUN-2014	15-OCT-2015	No	No			
13	18-JUL-2014	01-JUN-2021	Yes	Yes	25-DEC-2020	No	0
14	10-SEP-2014	01-JUN-2021	Yes	No			0
15	12-NOV-2014	01-JUN-2021	Yes	No			0
16	07-DEC-2014	01-JUN-2021	Yes	No			0
17	03-FEB-2015	01-JUN-2021	Yes	Yes	23-MAR-2016	Yes	1
18	26-MAR-2015	01-JUN-2021	Yes	No			0
19	25-APR-2015	01-JUN-2021	Yes	No			0
20	24-MAY-2015	01-JUN-2021	Yes	Yes	09-FEB-2017	Yes	1
21	21-JUN-2015	01-JUN-2021	Yes	No			0
22	28-JUN-2015	01-JUN-2021	Yes	Yes	01-JAN-2021	No	0
23	15-OCT-2015	01-JUN-2021	Yes	Yes	20-MAY-2020	No	0
24	18-OCT-2015	01-JUN-2021	Yes	No			0
25	28-NOV-2015	01-JUN-2021	Yes	Yes	15-JAN-2016	Yes	1
	Number of recidivists/*N*			11/25			5/23

Note. Recid = recidivism.

Question 4.2

(i) The 2-year recidivism rate is $5/23 = 0.2174$ or 21.7%.

(ii) Using $p = 0.2174$, $n = 23$, and $Z = 1.96$ in Equation 4.4, the 95% confidence interval is between 4.9% and 38.6%.

Question 4.3

(i) The easiest way of combining the two samples is with the raw numbers, that is, $9 + 5 = 14$ failures; $24 + 23 = 47$ cases. This gives an overall recidivism rate of $14/47 = 0.2979$, or 29.8%.

(ii) A rate of around 30% is better than the expected rate of around 50%. To determine whether the observed rate is within the range expected by sampling error, it is helpful to calculate confidence intervals. Using the Wald method (Equation 4.4) with $p = .2979$, $n = 47$, and $Z = 1.96$, the 95% confidence interval is between 16.7% and 42.9%. Using the Agresti and Caffo adjustment (Equation 4.6), with $p = .3137$, $n = 51$ and $Z = 1.96$, the 95% confidence interval is between 18.6% and 44.1%. Note that with this rate and sample size, there is little practical difference between the two methods for calculating the confidence intervals. Dr. Breuer is pleased. For the individuals treated at his clinic, the observed 2-year recidivism rates are lower than expected (52%), and the difference is unlikely to be attributable to chance.

Question 4.4

(i) With zero sexual recidivists out of 47 cases, the Agresti and Caffo adjustment (Equation 4.6) estimates the rate as $p = (0 + 2)/(47 + 4) = 2/51 = .03921$, or 3.9% with 95% confidence intervals of zero to 9.2%.

(ii) The confidence interval for the observed proportion contains the expected value of 4%. Even though the observed sexual recidivism rate is as good as it can get (zero), Dr. Breuer would still need a much larger sample to demonstrate that his clinic is making a meaningful impact on the rate of sexual recidivism.

5

Discrete-Time Survival Analysis

Discrete-time survival analysis estimates the likelihood of the outcome when not all cases are followed for the complete follow-up period. The complete follow-up period is divided into time intervals, and the proportion with the outcome (hazards) in each of these time intervals are used to estimate the overall proportion who would have had the outcome if they were followed to the end of the follow-up period.

Discrete-time survival analysis is a workhorse of actuarial prediction. It is widely used in insurance, demography, health economics, and medicine. It is called survival analysis, or life-table analysis, because of its central role in estimating life expectancies. The follow-up time of interest (e.g., 10 years, lifetime) is divided into convenient time intervals (e.g., 1 year). The likelihood of the outcome for each time interval is then calculated by dividing the number of cases with the outcome by the number at risk in that time interval. This probability is called a hazard. The hazards for previous years are combined to estimate the overall likelihood for any follow-up time of interest. It is not necessary (or possible) for the same individuals to contribute to the calculation for the hazard rates for every time interval; consequently, it can be used to estimate likelihoods for follow-up times longer than the shortest observed follow-up time. It is particularly useful when the hazard rates for specific time intervals are of substantive interest (e.g., during which ages are individuals at most risk for depression?).

https://doi.org/10.1037/0000275-005
Prediction Statistics for Psychological Assessment, by R. K. Hanson

WHY USE DISCRETE-TIME SURVIVAL ANALYSIS?

Discrete-time survival analysis was developed to estimate life expectancy. In the 1600s, certain European communities began recording the number of births and death in their jurisdictions. Edmond Halley (1656–1742), the English polymath of Halley's comet fame, demonstrated how such birth and death statistics could inform estimates of life expectancies as well as the overall size of the population (Hald, 2003). Halley used his newly crafted life-table to calculate a number of previously unknowns, such as the expected proportion of men able to bear arms (nine out of 34 of the total population) and the value of an annuity given (a) an interest rate (e.g., 6%) and (b) the age of the annuitant. It turned out that the English government was selling annuities for cheap, particularly if the annuitant was a child. Halley's calculations did not have an immediate effect on English fiscal practices. They did, however, provide the analytic basis for the Scottish Ministers' Widow Fund of 1744, which has operated continuously to this day (Hald, 2003). Currently, versions of Halley's life-table are routinely used by all successful insurance companies, pension funds, and government statistics departments.

Discrete-time survival analyses are particularly useful for estimating very long-term rates, such as lifetime rates. For example, psychologists may be interested in how the annual risk of various mental disorders varies across the lifespan. Hazard rates are closely related to *incidence* rates—that is, the proportion of a population that will develop the disorder over a period of time. When incidence rates are stratified by age, they can be used as hazard rates for the purpose of life-table analysis. The ideal study of lifetime hazard rates would involve yearly assessments of a complete cohort from birth to death. Don't expect such a study any time soon. Life-table analysis, however, provides more practical options for researching risk across the lifespan. The simplest design would ask a representative sample of individuals of various ages to report if and when they experienced any of the disorders of interest (e.g., depression, psychosis). Yearly incidence rate can also be estimated by asking respondents about their symptoms during only the past 12 months (or during the next 12 months). These incidence rates can be transformed into life-table hazard rates by considering the ages of the respondents.

In psychology and education, survival analysis is often used to estimate the likelihood of the outcome for time periods longer than the shortest follow-up time for individuals in the study. This commonly occurs when the individuals enter the sample gradually (e.g., consecutive admissions), but the follow-up time ends abruptly (e.g., when the outcome information is collected). The result of this very practical design is that follow-up times will vary across individuals. If a study used a 10-year recruitment period, the average follow-up would be around 5 years, the maximum would be 10 years, and the minimum could be less than a month. Survival analysis uses all cases to make estimates for time periods up to 10 years. Even if most of the sample is followed for 5 years or less, all cases still contribute to the precision of the 10-year estimates. In contrast, studies with fixed follow-up periods (see

Chapter 4) restrict analyses to a smaller subsample of cases, resulting in less precise estimates for shorter follow-up times.

Compared with the other types of survival analysis discussed in this book (Kaplan–Meier, Chapter 6; Cox regression, Chapter 10), discrete-time survival analysis is recommended when estimating hazard rates for specific, discrete time intervals. Sometimes these time intervals are based on conventions (e.g., yearly incidence rates); sometimes the time intervals are intrinsic to the research questions. For example, educators may be interested in the number of school years completed but have little interest in the exact day that students withdrew from school. Consequently, when estimating school attrition rates, the survival time units would be school years, not calendar time.

In my own research, we used discrete-time survival analysis to estimate time to desistance for individuals with a sexual offending history (Hanson, Harris, et al., 2018). In criminology, there is a well-established pattern that the longer individuals remain crime free, the less likely they are to return to crime (Hanson, 2018; Kurlychek et al., 2012). Our question was when does the yearly hazard rate for sexual recidivism decline to a level where individuals with a sexual offending history no longer present a meaningful risk for new sexual offending. This required defining a threshold for very low risk (Kahn et al., 2017), then calculating the number of years sexual offense free in the community until the yearly hazard dropped below this threshold. For most individuals with a sexual offense history, it took about 10 years, although the time period could be substantially shorter or longer depending on their initial risk levels (Hanson, Harris, et al., 2018).

Once hazard rates are known, it is possible to adjust and revise them as individuals survive the hazards of previous intervals. In Canada, for example, life expectancy at birth is 82 years; however, for individuals who have made it to 82, they can expect to live until 91 (Statistics Canada, 2019). Similarly, the risk of smoking relapse substantially declines for individuals who manage to get through the first months, which is by far the highest risk period (Hughes et al., 2004). The risk of sexual recidivism is cut in half for every 5 years individuals remain sexual offense free in the community (Hanson, Harris, et al., 2014; Thornton et al., 2021).

LIMITATIONS

Survival analysis provides estimates of the likelihood of the outcome. It does not directly observe the full follow-up period; instead, it relies on certain assumptions to estimate what would have been if all cases were followed for the complete follow-up period. One assumption is that the hazard rates for each interval are stable. In other words, if the cases with short follow-up had not been lost to follow-up, they would face the same risk as the risks observed for cases that were followed longer. A related assumption is that the cases that remain at risk are substantially similar for all time periods. This may not be the case when individuals are withdrawn (censored) for reasons that are correlated with the outcome. For example, researchers who are interested in estimating the likelihood of rehospitalization due to psychosis must decide how to code cases that are rehospitalized for other reasons (e.g., suicide risk, depression). Although certain solutions have been proposed (e.g., competing risk/multistate models; Aalen et al., 2008, §1.2.2), it is often difficult to know the extent to which the remaining at-risk sample changes over time. Consequently, it is sometimes preferable to report observed rates for fixed follow-up periods (Chapter 4) rather than estimated rates based on cases with incomplete data.

Compared with other forms of survival analysis, discrete-time survival analysis requires relatively large samples. There should be 20 cases at-risk in all time intervals, and preferably 40 to 50. In practice, this means that follow-up ends when there are fewer than 20 cases left surviving. It is hard to anticipate the length of the follow-up period because the size of the remaining sample depends on the hazard rates, which can only be roughly approximated in advance. When the sample size is not large (less than 100), it may be preferable to use Kaplan–Meier survival analysis (Chapter 6) to estimate the overall survival rate. For all types of survival analyses, it is common for the last segments of follow-up time to yield unstable results that overestimate the hazard rates. When reporting the maximum rate of the outcome (minimum value of the survival rate), be prepared to disregard the end of the survival curve and instead interpret the last region of the curve with adequate sample size.

Discrete-time survival analysis is not well suited to questions concerning the contribution of variables that increase or decrease the likelihood of the outcome (i.e., covariates). Group differences can be examined by creating separate survival curves for separate groups, and it is relatively easy to test whether the various groups' survival curves are different. There is, however, no natural metric for describing the size of these differences. Another concern is that life-table survival analysis becomes awkward when there are multiple predictor variables or when predictor variables are continuous (e.g., age, income). If the primary questions concern the influence of potential predictor variables, Cox regression survival analysis is usually the preferred option (Chapter 10).

Another limitation of survival analysis is that there are two types of processes that contribute to changes in hazard rates. This complicates the interpretation of the shape of all survival curves. One process, known as *frailty*, is that individuals more prone to the outcome are likely to fail before other individuals in the sample. The other process involves changes in individuals' propensities to have the outcome. Consequently, when hazard rates decline over time, it may mean that individuals' risk is declining. It could also mean no change at all at the individual level. All the apparent decline in risk could be attributed the surviving individuals being the least risky. If the goal is simply prediction, then the reasons for the declines in risk can remain unresolved. Many applied decisions, however, are informed by understanding change at the individual level.

THE NUTS AND BOLTS

Data Requirements

The information needed to calculate survival times is the same as for fixed follow-up times:

1. a start date,
2. a follow-up end date,
3. a dichotomous outcome variable, and
4. the date that the outcome occurred.

Survival times start on the at-risk date and end when either (a) the outcome occurs or (b) follow-up ends. Cases without the outcome are referred to as *censored*. Survival times can be either continuous (e.g., 1.2, 2.5, 3.1 years) or discrete (e.g., 1, 2, 3 years). The construction of data sets with continuous survival times is discussed in the next chapter. This chapter considers data that naturally occur in discrete intervals (e.g., school years) or have already been transformed into the units of interest before discrete-time survival analysis. Just as studies using fixed follow-up time must make a yes–no decision concerning whether the follow-up time is sufficient to include the case in the study, constructing discrete-time survival data sets requires a decision whether follow-up time for each case is sufficient to be included in each interval. Not all cases need to be included in each interval.

Researchers must also decide on the length of the discrete-time intervals. In some cases, there is a natural unit of analysis, such as school years. More frequently, time is continuous but divided into intervals as a matter of convenience. Another decision is whether survival time should be based on at-risk time or calendar time. In criminal justice and forensic mental health, for example, it is common for individuals to be institutionalized during part of the follow-up period for reasons other than new offending. Researchers may subtract periods of incarceration from the criminal recidivism at-risk time; alternately, they could calculate survival times based on calendar time. Each approach asks a slightly different question and informs different decisions. If the primary research questions concern individual differences in the likelihood of criminal recidivism, then survival analysis using at-risk time is the preferred approach. If the analyses are being conducted to inform resource allocation questions (how many of the current sample will come back within 2 years?), use survival times based on calendar time.

Calculating Discrete-Time Survival Analyses

Discrete-time survival analyses estimates the likelihood of the outcome based on the hazard rates for each time interval (Allison, 1984; Singer & Willett, 1993, 2003; Willett & Singer, 1993). A *hazard rate* is the proportion of individuals who have the outcome during the interval divided by the number of individuals at risk. Hazards (h_t) can assume values from zero (no outcomes in that time period) to 1.0 (all at-risk individuals had the outcome in that interval). The subscript *t* indicates that there is a hazard rate for each time interval. The proportion surviving a single time interval (s_t) is one minus the hazard rate for that interval ($s_t = 1 - h_t$). The overall rate of the outcome is one minus the cumulative proportion surviving ($1 - S_T$). The cumulative proportion surviving (S_T) is the product of the survival rates for all previous intervals:

$$S_T = \prod_{interval=1}^{t} (1 - h_t) \tag{5.1}$$

In this equation, h_t is the survival rate for each time interval. The symbol Π (Greek capital pi) indicates that the survival rates are multiplied together. Equation 5.1 could also be written as $S_t = (1 - h_1) \times (1 - h_2) \times (1 - h_3) \times (1 - h_3) . . . . (1 - h_t)$, where *t* is the number of discrete time intervals.

When researchers are creating discrete-time hazard rates from continuous time follow-up studies, they must decide what to do with cases that are not followed for the complete interval. For certain research questions, it is prudent to exclude cases from the interval if they were not followed for the complete interval. It is common practice, however, to give partial credit to cases that are followed for only part of an interval. These are referred to as *actuarial* or *life-table* methods (Singer & Willett, 2003, §13.2.3). For example, cases withdrawn during the interval could be given half credit. Consequently, if 100 individuals enter the interval and 10 are withdrawn during the interval, the effective at-risk sample could be given as 100 − 10/2 = 95. If all cases must complete the interval to be included, the effective at-risk sample would be 90. Some actuarial methods also include adjustments for the number of events during the interval. The actuarial adjustments typically result in small increases in the absolute value of the estimates. In relatively small samples that were originally coded using continuous time, giving partial weight to incomplete cases should increase the precision of the estimates. When statistical power is not a concern, using only complete cases may increase confidence in the results because it replaces some inferences with observations.

Worked Example

The following hypothetical example concerns the likelihood of sexual victimization of women attending Vail University. Media reports and surveys at other universities indicated that many female students experience sexual victimization at some point in their lives; however, there was little information concerning the likelihood of sexual victimization while they were students at Vail. The administrators of the university want to know if there were periods of increased risk, which could facilitate communications and community safety planning. They also want to know the overall risk of women being sexually victimized during the course of a 4-year degree at Vail.

To estimate the likelihood of sexual victimization at Vail, a survey study was conducted in 2018. The study was designed and implemented as a collaboration among two psychology professors, Vail's sexual assault support center, the local police, and a consultation group of students with and without lived experience of sexual victimization. The self-report survey asked about whether the student had experienced sexual victimization in each of the previous academic years, that is, first-year students were asked about sexual victimization during their first year, whereas second-, third-, and fourth-year students were asked about their current year and all previous years. For the purpose of the study, however, only incidents of first-time victimization of women during the current (2017–2018) year were included in the discrete-time survival analysis. Males and students who had been victimized in previous years were excluded from the 2018 victimization rates, even if they had also been victimized in the current year.

The results of the 2018 study are presented in Table 5.1. Column 2 is the number of female respondents to the survey in each of the four academic years. Column 3 is the number who reported a first-time sexual victimization incident in that year. The yearly hazard rate (Column 4) is the number of events divided by the number at risk (e.g., 307/2,045 = .1501). The survival rates for each academic year is one minus the hazard for that year. The cumulative survival is the survival rate for the current year multiplied by the survival rates for all previous years. For example, the cumulative survival at the end of the second year is .8157 (the survival rate for Year 2) times .8499 (the survival rate for Year 1) = .6932.

The proportion identified as having been sexually victimized for any specific follow-up period (Column 7) is one minus the cumulative survival rate up to that point. For example, the cumulative victimization rates would be 36.9% at the end of the third academic year (1 – .6313 = .3687) and 42.5% at the end of the fourth year (1 – .5754 = .4246). In other words, the risk of a female student being sexually victimized was 42.5% should she stay at Vail University for all 4 years.

The researchers are pleased with their study, particularly because they were able to obtain an estimate of the 4-year rate based on a data collection period of less than one month. They had some concerns, however, that differential effects of recall may be influencing their results. In particular, salient

TABLE 5.1. Discrete-Time Survival Analysis for Sexual Victimization During 4 Academic Years Based on the Hypothetical 2018 Survey

1	2	3	4	5	6	7
Year	At-risk sample	Events during interval	Hazard (h_t)	Survival for interval ($1 - h_t$)	Cumulative survival	Victimization rate
1	2,045	307	.1501	.8499	.8499	.1501
2	1,329	245	.1843	.8157	.6932	.3068
3	885	79	.0893	.9107	.6313	.3687
4	722	64	.0886	.9114	.5754	.4246
Total	4,981	694	.1395			

emotional events often seem more recent than they actually are, which could result in students reconstructing victimization events as happening this year rather than the year before. Consequently, the research team conducts a new, prospective study starting in September 2019, designed to minimize the effects of recall bias. The 2019 study sample comprised female students at the start of each academic year (four separate cohorts). These students are then followed for one academic year (until April 2020), during which the research team records whether they have had a sexual victimization experience and whether they have remained enrolled as student at Vail. By an uncanny coincidence, the yearly sample sizes and number of victimization experiences in the 2019 study are exactly the same as in their 2018 retrospective survey study. The only difference is that a certain proportion of each cohort is lost to follow-up during the interval. Consequently, to estimate the yearly hazards, the researchers use the life-table method, which gives a weight of ½ to cases that are not followed for the complete interval. The results are presented in Table 5.2.

The first column identifies the interval. The notation [0, 1) means that the interval includes zero (the start of term) and end just before the start of the second year. Although in natural language we speak of first-year students, these students have not yet completed a full year (only months); consequently, they are still in year zero in the language of survival analysis. The second column indicates the number of students who start each academic year; Column 3 indicates the number who are no longer available to the study (e.g., they left the university). Half of the withdrawn cases are subtracted from the initial sample to obtain a revised estimate of the at-risk sample (Column 4). For example, of the 2,045 students who started their first year, 409 did not complete, resulting in an at-risk sample of 2,045 – (409/2) = 1,840.5. The yearly hazard rates in Column 6 are calculated by dividing the number of events (Column 5) by the number at risk (Column 4; e.g., 307/1,840.5 = .1668). The yearly and cumulative survival rates are calculated in the usual way (Equation 5.1). Notice that the overall survival rate is slightly lower (victimization rates are higher) using

TABLE 5.2. Life-Table (Actuarial) Survival Analysis for Sexual Victimization During 4 Academic Years Based on 1-Year Follow-Up of the September 2019 Cohort of Female Students at Vail

1	2	3	4	5	6	7	8
Year	Initial sample	Withdrawn during interval	At-risk sample	Events during interval	Hazard (h_t)	Survival for interval ($1 - h_t$)	Cumulative survival
[0,1)	2,045	409	1,840.5	307	0.1668	0.8332	0.8332
[1,2)	1,329	199	1,229.0	245	0.1993	0.8007	0.6672
[2,3)	885	84	843.0	79	0.0937	0.9063	0.6046
[3,4)	722	60	692.0	64	0.0925	0.9075	0.5487
Total	4,981	752	4,604.5	694			

the life-table actuarial method (.5487/45.1%) than the discrete-time method (.5754/42.5%, from Table 5.1).

The yearly hazard rates appear to vary across the 4 academic years. The highest rates were in the first 2 years, followed by lower rates in the final years. It is difficult to know the extent to which the fluctuations indicated substantive periods of increased risk or whether they were within the range expected by chance variation. Consequently, the administrators ask the researchers to calculate standard errors and confidence intervals for the yearly hazard rates.

Standard Error and Confidence Intervals

The standard errors of the hazard rates are given by

$$SE(h_t) = \sqrt{h_t(1-h_t)/n_t} \tag{5.2}$$

where h_t is the observed hazard rate for the interval and n_t is the sample size at risk. As usual, the 95% confidence interval is given by

$$CI = h_t \pm (Z * SE(h_t)) \tag{5.3}$$

Z sets the width of the confidence interval. Ninety-five percent confidence intervals (95% CI) are commonly used, which correspond to a *Z* value of 1.96. Astute readers will notice that this is the Wald standard error for dichotomous variables discussed in Chapter 4 (Equation 4.4; the Wald method) and comes with all the same strengths and weaknesses.

The standard error of the overall survival rates is complicated by the fact that the survival function is the product of multiple estimates. Nevertheless, it can be reasonably estimated by the Greenwood standard error, provided that there are at least 20 cases in the smallest time interval (Singer & Willett, 2003):

$$SE(S_t) = S_t\sqrt{\frac{h_1}{n_1(1-h_1)} + \frac{h_2}{n_2(1-h_2)} + \frac{h_3}{n_3(1-h_3)} + \cdots + \frac{h_t}{n_t(1-h_t)}} \tag{5.4}$$

In this equation, h_1 is the observed hazard for the first interval (based on n_1 cases at risk), and S_t is the estimated cumulative survival function. In the initial 2018 survey described in our worked example, h_1 is .1501, n_1 is 2045, and cumulative survival value is .8499, which results in an *SE* (S_1) of 0.007899 = $.8499 * (.1501/(2{,}045 * (1 - .1501)))^{1/2}$. As the number of intervals increases, the standard error of the cumulative survival function will also increase. In other words, the estimates for later intervals will be less precise than the estimates for earlier intervals.

Table 5.3 includes the standard errors of the hazards and the cumulative survival rate for the discrete-time survival analysis of the 2018 survey study (Table 5.1). Allowing for sampling error, a reasonable estimate of the proportion of female students who would be sexually victimized after 4 years is between 41% and 46%. Given that the confidence intervals do not overlap,

TABLE 5.3. Discrete-Time Survival Analysis for Sexual Victimization With Standard Errors and Confidence Intervals for the 2018 Survey Study at Vail University

1	2	3	4	5	6	7	8
Year	Sample size	Hazard (h_t)	*SE* (h_t)	95% CI of h_t	Cumulative survival (S_t)	*SE* (S_t)	95% CI of S_t
1	2,045	.1501	0.007899	.135 – .166	.8499	0.00774	0.818 – 0.848
2	1,329	.1843	0.010637	.164 – .205	.6932	0.01088	0.658 – 0.701
3	885	.0893	0.009584	.070 – .108	.6313	0.01186	0.596 – 0.642
4	722	.0886	0.010578	.068 – .109	.5754	0.01264	0.539 – 0.589

Note. CI = confidence interval.

the rates for the final 2 years (3 and 4) appear lower than for the first 2 years. In this example, the confidence intervals are narrow (± .02) because the sample sizes are large and the hazard rates are low.

On the basis of these results, the university administrators conclude that sexual victimization is a common problem and that intervention efforts should be focused on students during their first 2 years.

Comparing Cumulative Survival Rates

It is relatively simple to compare the discrete-time survival rates based on different groups in the same study. For example, researchers may want to know whether the rates vary across faculties. We will not, however, review these procedures here because another type of survival analysis (Cox regression, Chapter 10) is usually the preferred option for identifying predictors or covariates of hazard rates and survival curves. That being said, discrete-time survival analysis can provide excellent opportunities to build and test certain types of complex models—for example, models that include multiple covariates or dynamic predictors that change over time. Readers interested in these types of analyses are encouraged to read Singer and Willett (2003, specifically their Chapters 11 and 12).

In many cases, all the necessary information for comparing survival rates is provided by the estimated likelihood and its standard error. For example, if the administrators at Vail University are interested in comparing their rates to those of other universities, they should first consider the absolute magnitude of the differences, and, if big enough to be meaningful, they should then consider whether the confidence intervals for the estimates overlap (Cumming & Finch, 2005). Meta-analysis (Chapter 14) can also be used to test whether the observed differences in survival rates from independent samples are more than would be expected by chance.

GOING FURTHER

Readers who have made it this far should have a sufficient understanding of discrete-time survival analysis to be educated consumers of studies using this statistical approach. The following sections are designed to deepen this understanding through further reading and exercises. These sections can be worked with in any order, and it is not necessary to do all (or any) of them.

Recommended Readings

Singer, J. D., & Willett, J. B. (1993). It's about time: Using discrete-time survival analysis to study duration and the timing of events. *Journal of Educational Statistics, 18*(2), 155–195. https://doi.org/10.3102/10769986018002155

A readable introduction to why and how to conduct discrete-time survival analyses. The later section discusses complex models, which will primarily be of interest to researchers. This article covers much of the same materials as their book (Singer & Willett, 2003).

Allison, P. D. (1984). *Event history analysis: Regression for longitudinal event data.* Sage Publications.

A short introduction to various forms of event history (survival) analysis. Similar to other teaching texts, Allison presents discrete-time survival analysis as a foundation for understanding other types of event history analysis.

Computer Code

Calculating discrete-time survival analysis (without the actuarial adjustments) is often easiest with generic spreadsheets, such as Excel. Neither R Statistics nor IBM/SPSS have specific algorithms for this purpose. Discrete-time hazard rates can be computed using aggregate data, as in the examples above. With large data sets, the tabulation of hazard rates is easily calculated when the data set is organized in the person-period, or long format. In the long format, there is a new row for each interval for each case. Directions for constructing and analyzing person-period data sets are available in Singer and Willett (1993, 2003) and Willett and Singer (1993).

Both R Statistics and IBM/SPSS have algorithms for calculating actuarial life-tables (with the adjustments for cases withdrawn during an interval). The examples that follow assume the data is in short form, where each case is represented by one and only one row. Two variables are required: one indicating the length of survival time (ordered or continuous) and another indicating whether the event occurred by the end of follow-up. Both programs are able to transform continuous survival times into discrete intervals.

The examples use the data set from the 2019 Vail University victimization study, which followed students for 1 year to estimate 4-year rates (Table 5.2).

Although the actual sample size was 4,981, the cases are aggregated to only 2,045 rows, corresponding to the number of students in the first cohort. Students in subsequent years are coded *as if* they were continuations of the initial cohort. In other words, the cases in Year 2, Year 3, and Year 4 provide estimates of what would have happened to the initial cohort of 2,045 if they had been followed for that long.

R Code

The relevant package in R Statistics is called **discSurv** (Welchowski & Schmid, 2019). This package contains diverse algorithms, including routines for transforming continuous time survival times into discrete time. The **lifeTable** routine computes life-tables that give ½ weight to cases withdrawn during the interval.

If you have not already done so, download the package from the R repository.

```
install.packages("discSurv")
```

This will ask which CRAN site you want to use. Choose one that is geographically close to you.

Next, tell R that you want to use these programs, and where to find the data:

```
library ('discSurv')
labels <-c("Case", "Interval", "Event")
data <-read.csv
(file="c:\\run.files\\Book\\Chap5_DTime_example.csv",
col.names=labels)
```

In this example, my data is an EXCEL.csv file, entitled "Chap5_Surv_example.csv", available at https://www.apa.org/pubs/books/prediction-statistics-for-psychological-assessment. I then confirm the variable names.

```
names (data)
[1] "Case" "Interval" "Event"
```

The general form of the **lifeTable** command is as follows:

```
model <- lifeTable(dataSet=data, timeColumn="Interval",
censColumn="Event")
```

In the example, *model* is an arbitrary name that you give to your results, and *data* is the name you have given to your data set. *Interval* (coded 1 to 5) and *Event* (coded 0 or 1) are the time and the outcome variables, respectively. A quirk of the **lifeTable** routine is that the time variable must start at 1 (not zero). In this data set, there are only four intervals (years) in which events can occur. An additional, fifth year was added to the data set, during which all remaining cases are censored/withdrawn. To see the results, type

```
model
```

which produces the following output:

	n	events	dropouts	atRisk	hazard	seHazard
[0, 1)	2045	307	409	1840.5	0.1668	0.0087
[1, 2)	1329	245	199	1229.5	0.1993	0.0114
[2, 3)	885	79	84	843.0	0.0937	0.0100
[3, 4)	722	64	60	692.0	0.0925	0.0110
[4, 5)	598	0	598	299.0	0.0000	0.0000

	S	seS	cumHazard	seCumHazard	margProb
[0, 1)	0.8332	0.0087	0.1668	0.0095	0.1668
[1, 2)	0.6672	0.0118	0.3661	0.0159	0.1660
[2, 3)	0.6046	0.0126	0.4598	0.0191	0.0625
[3, 4)	0.5487	0.0132	0.5523	0.0223	0.0559
[4, 5)	0.5487	0.0132	0.5523	0.0223	0.0000

R produces a table that is essentially the same as Table 5.2, with a couple of extra columns. The most important columns are labeled "S" for survival and "seS" for standard error of the survival function. The final entries of these columns provide the overall survival rate (0.5487) and its standard error (0.0132). These can be used to obtain an overall likelihood of victimization for female students who remain at Vail for 4 years (1 – .5487 = .4513). Using Equation 5.3, the 95% confidence interval for this estimate is 42.5% to 47.7%.

IBM/SPSS Code

The **Life Table** routine in IBM/SPSS computes discrete-time survival analysis from an existing data set. In this example, the data set (called *Chap5_DTime_example.sav*) includes the 2,045 cases and two variables from the 1-year prospective study of the 2019 students (Table 5.2). The two variables are *Interval* (coded 0 to 4) and *Event* (coded 0 or 1). There are no events in Year 4—all cases are withdrawn/censored during that period. The **Life Table** command is found by following **Analyze**, **Survival**, then **Life Table**. At the **Life Table** screen, you will need to specify the duration of the interval. This is a convenient option when survival times were originally coded as a continuous variable. You will also need to specify which value of the dichotomous outcome variable indicates that the event occurred. An example of the completed syntax is as follows:

```
SURVIVAL TABLE=Interval
/INTERVAL=THRU 4 BY 1
/STATUS=Event(1)
/PRINT=TABLE
/PLOTS (SURVIVAL)=Interval.
```

Table 5.4 is a mildly edited version of the SPSS output. Specifically, I have increased the number of decimal points for reporting of the proportion

TABLE 5.4. An Edited Version of the Output From IBM/SPSS Life Tables for the Hypothetical 1-Year Prospective Vail Victimization Study of the 2019 Students

Interval start time	Number entering interval	Number withdrawing during interval	Number exposed to risk	Number of terminal events	Proportion terminating	Proportion surviving	Cumulative proportion surviving at end of interval	*SE* of cumulative proportion surviving at end of interval
0	2,045	409	1,840.500	307	.167	.833	.833	.00869
1	1,329	199	1,229.500	245	.199	.801	.667	.01177
2	885	84	843.000	79	.094	.906	.605	.01259
3	722	60	692.000	64	.092	.908	.549	.01323
4	598	598	299.000	0	.000	1.000	.549	.01323

Note. The median survival time is 4.00.

surviving and other variables. To change the number of decimal points reported, double click on the table, then right click on the cell, then select **Cell Properties**, then **Format Value**. The output reproduced in Table 5.4 contains the same values as those generated by the **lifeTable** command in R Statistics. IBM/SPSS **Life Table** also calculates a number of other statistics, which I have not copied into the text. These statistics may be useful in certain research contexts. In particular, it distinguishes between the *proportion terminating* and the *hazard rate*. The IBM/SPSS hazard rate has the same substantive interpretation as the proportion terminating (which this chapter and R Statistics refer to as the *hazard rate*); however, the SPSS *hazard rate* reported in **Life Tables** is calculated using an additional actuarial adjustment not included in R Statistics (IBM Corp., 2020). As in R Statistics, the standard errors of the hazards are estimated using the Wald method (Equation 5.2), and standard error of the cumulative survival rates are calculated using Greenwood's approximation (Equation 5.3). The median survival time is when 50% of the sample has the outcome. Given that the overall survival rate was greater than 50%, the median survival time is set to the end of the follow-up period (4 years).

A graph of the life-table survival function is plotted in Figure 5.1 (from IBM/SPSS). The figure starts in the top left-hand corner, at which point nobody has experienced the outcome (everybody is still alive). As individuals experience the outcome, they are removed from the sample and the remainder of the sample is followed into the next interval. Given that the study examined four discrete time intervals, there are four opportunities for the line to decline. The declines are abrupt because all incidents are counted at the end of each interval.

FIGURE 5.1. IBM/SPSS Life-Table Survival Curve for the Hypothetical 1-Year Prospective Vail Victimization Study of the 2019 Students

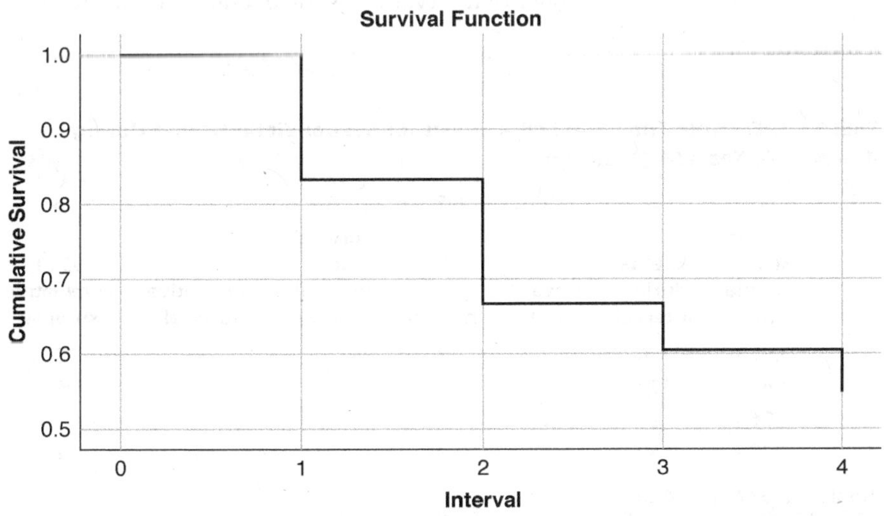

EXERCISES

Concerned with the high victimization rates identified in their 2018 and 2019 studies, Vail University implements a violence prevention program. The program included minimizing high-risk situations (e.g., discouraging drunken parties), public advertisements directed toward potential perpetrators ("Don't be that guy"), peer support for good decision making in high-risk situations (for both males and females), and repeated surveys addressing victimization, attitudes tolerant of sexual assault, and allegiance with negative peer influences. To evaluate program effectiveness, they conducted a victimization study in 2021 using the same method as their 2018 study. The raw data from the new, 2021 study are presented in Table 5.5. Column 2 presents the number of female students for whom data were available, and Column 3 identifies the number of at-risk students known to have experienced sexual victimization for the first time during the past academic year.

Question 5.1

Complete Table 5.5 using discrete-time survival analysis. Do not use adjustments for individuals withdrawn during the time intervals.

Question 5.2

You are an admissions officer at Vail University answering questions from a young woman considering which university to attend. Among her many questions, she asks about the extent of sexual victimization at Vail. What is your best estimate of the likelihood of a female student experiencing sexual victimization at some point should she complete all 4 years at Vail University?

Question 5.3

On the basis of the 95% confidence intervals, was the overall victimization rate lower in 2021 than in 2018?

TABLE 5.5. Discrete-Time Survival Analysis for Sexual Victimization During 4 Academic Years (2021 Study)

1	2	3	4	5	6	7	8
Year	At-risk sample (*n*)	Events during interval	Hazard (h_t)	*SE* of hazard	Survival for interval ($1 - h_t$)	Cumulative survival	*SE* of cumulative survival
1	1,978	150	?	?	?	?	?
2	1,430	134	?	?	?	?	?
3	965	77	?	?	?	?	?
4	704	59	?	?	?	?	?
Total	5,077	420					

ANSWERS TO EXERCISES

Question 5.1

See Table 5.6. All the values can be computed from the raw data using the formula given in this chapter. Because you are not using adjustments for individuals who are not followed for the complete interval, the at-risk sample (Column 2) is the denominator in the calculation of the hazard rates (Column 4). The standard error of the yearly hazards (Column 5) is computed using Equation 5.2. For computing cumulative survival (Column 7), use Equation 5.1, and use Equation 5.4 for the standard error of the cumulative survival (Column 8). It is often easiest to conduct these calculations using a spreadsheet, such as Excel.

Question 5.2

If you are optimistic that the positive effects of the recent policy changes will endure, the best estimate is provided by the 2021 study—that is, 1 − .7061 = .2939, or 29.4%. If you are concerned that victimization rates will slip back to their previous (2018/2019) levels, you could use either of those estimates (42.5% or 45.1%). If you believe all the studies (2018, 2019, and 2021) were influenced by diverse, random factors (e.g., the #MeToo movement in 2017) that may or may not endure, then you could report a range (29.4%–42.5%), or an average (see Chapter 14).

Question 5.3

First, you will need to calculate the confidence intervals for the 2018 and 2021 studies using Equation 5.4 for the standard error of the cumulative survival estimate. For the 2021 study, the standard error is the final entry of Column 7 of Table 5.5. To calculate the 95% confidence interval, multiply the standard error by 1.96, then add to and subtract from the cumulative survival rate. You

TABLE 5.6. Discrete-Time Survival Analysis for Sexual Victimization During 4 Academic Years (2021 Study)

1	2	3	4	5	6	7	8
Year	At-risk sample	Events during interval	Hazard (h_t)	*SE* of hazard	Survival for interval ($1 - h_t$)	Cumulative survival	*SE* of cumulative survival
1	1,978	150	0.0758	0.00595	0.9242	0.9242	0.00595
2	1,430	134	0.0937	0.00771	0.9063	0.8376	0.00893
3	965	77	0.0798	0.00872	0.9202	0.7707	0.01100
4	704	59	0.0838	0.01044	0.9162	0.7061	0.01290
Total	5,077	420					

TABLE 5.7. Summary of Findings From the Hypothetical 2018 and 2021 Victimization Studies

Year	Cumulative survival	Proportion with the outcome (1 − survival)	*SE* of cumulative survival	Plus/minus	Lower bound of CI (%)	Upper bound of CI (%)
2018	.5754	.4246	0.01289	0.02526	39.9	45.0
2021	.7061	.2939	0.01290	0.02528	26.9	31.9

Note. CI = confidence interval.

will similarly need to calculate the standard error of the cumulative survival rate from the 2018 study (Table 5.1) using Equation 5.4. This information is summarized in Table 5.7.

Given that the confidence intervals do not overlap, it is unlikely that the difference is fully attributable to sampling error.

6

Kaplan–Meier Survival Analysis

Kaplan–Meier survival analysis estimates the likelihood of the outcome when not all cases are followed for the complete follow-up period. Follow-up time is considered to be continuous, and the cumulative likelihood is updated with each new outcome.

Kaplan–Meier survival analysis is one of the preferred methods of estimating the likelihood of an outcome over time. Like other forms of survival analysis, not all cases need to be followed for the complete follow-up period. Time is coded as a continuous variable (not aggregated into intervals), and the cumulative survival rate is updated whenever there is a new outcome. For each new outcome, the probability at that time is calculated based on the number of individuals remaining at risk. For example, if there are 20 individuals at risk when one individual has the outcome, the probability of the outcome would be 1/20 (.05), and the probability of surviving at that time would be 1 − .05 (.95). The survival probabilities of all previous events are multiplied together to obtain the cumulative survival probability. Although Kaplan–Meier survival analysis is an excellent method for estimating likelihoods at specific follow-up times, it does not identify periods of increased or decreased risk.

WHY USE KAPLAN–MEIER SURVIVAL ANALYSIS?

Evaluating the likelihood of outcomes requires thinking about time. For some outcomes, there are natural time limits (e.g., graduation from high school). However, for many outcomes of interest to psychologists, the number of individuals

https://doi.org/10.1037/0000275-006
Prediction Statistics for Psychological Assessment, by R. K. Hanson

with the outcome gradually increases over time with no clear time limit (e.g., onset of psychosis, recovery from depression, criminal recidivism, substance use relapse). Furthermore, not all individuals are expected to have the outcome. Consequently, statements about the likelihood of the outcome should also specify *by when*.

Kaplan–Meier survival analysis calculates the likelihoods for every possible time during the follow-up period. Consequently, evaluators can choose the follow-up period that is most relevant for their decision at hand. For example, a patient may ask about the likelihood of full recovery from depression. Reading off a Kaplan–Meier survival table, the therapist may respond that 80% are back to work within 6 months. If the patient then asks what are the chances of recovery by Christmas (2.5 months away), the therapist can find that likelihood by referring back to the same Kaplan–Meier survival table.

Kaplan–Meier survival analysis is useful for program evaluation when the follow-up time varies substantially among cases (Greenhouse et al., 1989). This commonly occurs when the individuals enter the sample gradually but the follow-up time ends abruptly (e.g., when the outcome information is collected). By considering the timing of the outcome, statistical power is increased. Kaplan–Meier survival analysis can be used with relatively small samples (less than 30) containing few events. Whereas having sparse data is a challenge to discrete-time survival analysis (intervals will be weakly populated), Kaplan–Meier survival uses every single outcome at the moment it occurs. The stability of the estimates is primarily determined by the overall sample size, not by the size of the time intervals. Like all survival analyses, the estimates become unstable when the remaining at-risk sample becomes too small (less than 20).

LIMITATIONS

Kaplan–Meier survival analysis is not recommended for identifying periods of increased or decreased risk. If the primary question is when the outcome is most likely or whether risk is above or below a threshold, use discrete-time survival analysis (Chapter 5). Kaplan–Meier survival analysis is also not well suited to questions concerning the contribution of variables that increase or decrease the likelihood of the outcome (i.e., covariates). Group differences can be examined by creating separate Kaplan–Meier survival curves for separate groups. This approach, however, only works for a limited number of groups. Studies concerned with identifying potential predictor variables should consider Cox regression survival analysis (Chapter 10). Both Cox regression and Kaplan–Meier survival analysis use the same type of survival data; consequently, it is relatively easy to switch between different types of survival analyses to answer different questions of interest.

It can also produce too much information. Full Kaplan–Meier survival tables can be very large when the sample size is large (e.g., 500 cases). Depending on the program, the survival tables can either include a row for each event (e.g.,

R Statistics) or a row for each case (e.g., IBM/SPSS). This can result in pages and pages of detailed output, most of which is of little concern. With large data sets, discrete-time survival analysis provides pithier summary statistics.

Other general limitations of survival analysis are discussed in the previous chapter (Chapter 5). These limitations include potentially fallible assumptions concerning the stability of the hazard rates, the consistency of the at-risk group over time, competing risks, and frailty (i.e., selective attrition of the most vulnerable cases).

THE NUTS AND BOLTS

Data Requirements

Calculating survival times requires the following data:

1. a start date,
2. a follow-up end date,
3. a dichotomous outcome variable, and
4. the date that the outcome occurred.

The dates are then recoded into two variables: (a) survival time and (b) a dichotomous variable indicating whether the outcome occurred or not. Survival times start at the at-risk date and end when either (a) the outcome occurs or (b) follow-up ends. The average survival time will be shorter than the average follow-up time because survival time ends when the outcome occurs. Cases without the outcome are referred to as *censored*. For Kaplan–Meier survival analysis (and Cox regression), survival times are continuous (e.g., 1.22 years, 24.34 minutes). Ideally, the precision of measurement should be such that no events happen at the same time. Although equal survival times are common in practice, ties reduce the precision of the estimates. Cases with short follow-up times contribute to the estimates for longer follow-up times. If a case is censored before the first outcome, it is not included in the analysis.

A visual representation of continuous survival times is presented in Figure 6.1. To motivate this example, consider that these cases are from a study of rehospitalization rates for individuals with a *Diagnostic and Statistical Manual of Mental Disorders* (American Psychiatric Association, 2013) bipolar I disorder diagnosis. The individuals were considered to be at risk the day they were discharged from inpatient care and to have been rehospitalized when they returned for an overnight stay. As you can see from Figure 6.1, there was approximately one patient each month matching the study selection criteria. Patient A, the first of this series of 10 patients, was released in January, and the final case, Patient J, was released in October. Given that follow-up ended on December 31, the follow-up times ranged from 2 months (Patient J) to 12 months (Patient A). In addition to the length of follow-up, each case is coded as either having the event (rehospitalization) or not (censored) at the end of follow-up. The most common date of censoring is the follow-up end date (December). However, Patient C was

FIGURE 6.1. Follow-Up Time for 10 Cases (A Through J) Organized by Calendar Time

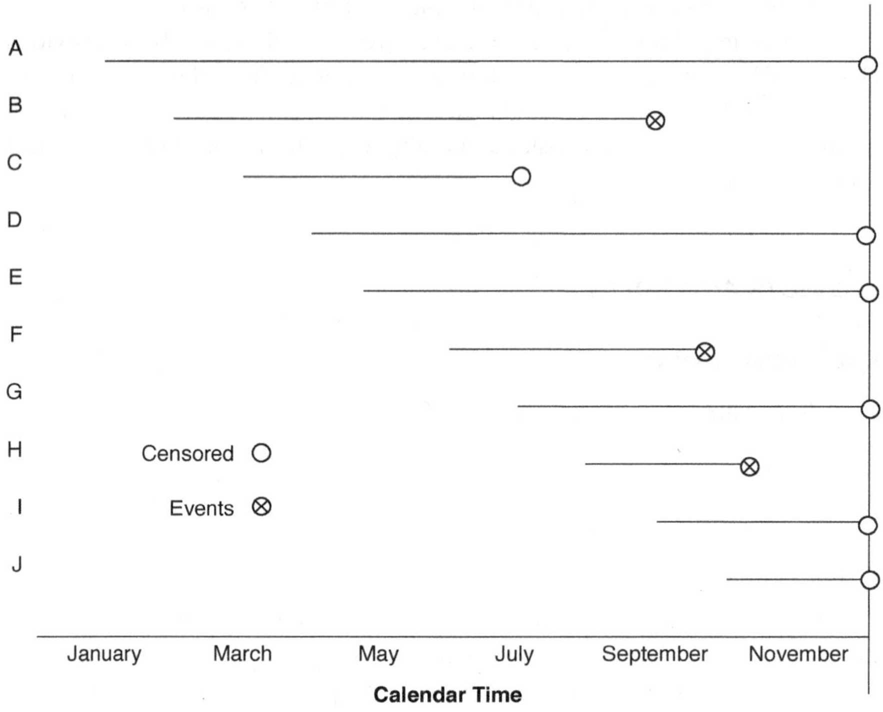

censored in July after moving to a beautiful, remote island off the coast of Belize and was thereby lost to follow-up.

For the purposes of survival analysis, the follow-up times are reorganized as in Figure 6.2. The at-risk date is coded as zero, and the survival time is coded in months until either rehospitalized or follow-up ended for that patient.

Calculating Kaplan–Meier Survival Analyses

In both Kaplan–Meier and discrete-time survival analysis, the basic units of risk are also called hazards, but they are subtly different. In discrete-time survival analysis, the hazard is the proportions who have the outcome during a predefined time interval (e.g., 1 month, 1 year). In Kaplan–Meier survival analysis, the unit of risk is the instantaneous hazard, which expresses the likelihood of having the event during the next instant if the outcome has not already occurred. Given that an instant is vanishingly small, so, too, is the likelihood of having the outcome *in that instant.* To actually have numbers that can be talked about, Kaplan–Meier hazards are defined as the likelihood of having the outcome in the next vanishingly small interval divided by the size of that interval (Aalen et al., 2008, equation 1.2):

$$h(t) = limit\ \Delta t \to 0 \frac{P(t \le T < t + \Delta t | T \ge t)}{\Delta t} \qquad (6.1)$$

FIGURE 6.2. Follow-Up Time for 10 Cases (A Through J) Organized by Survival Time (At-Risk Time Set to Zero)

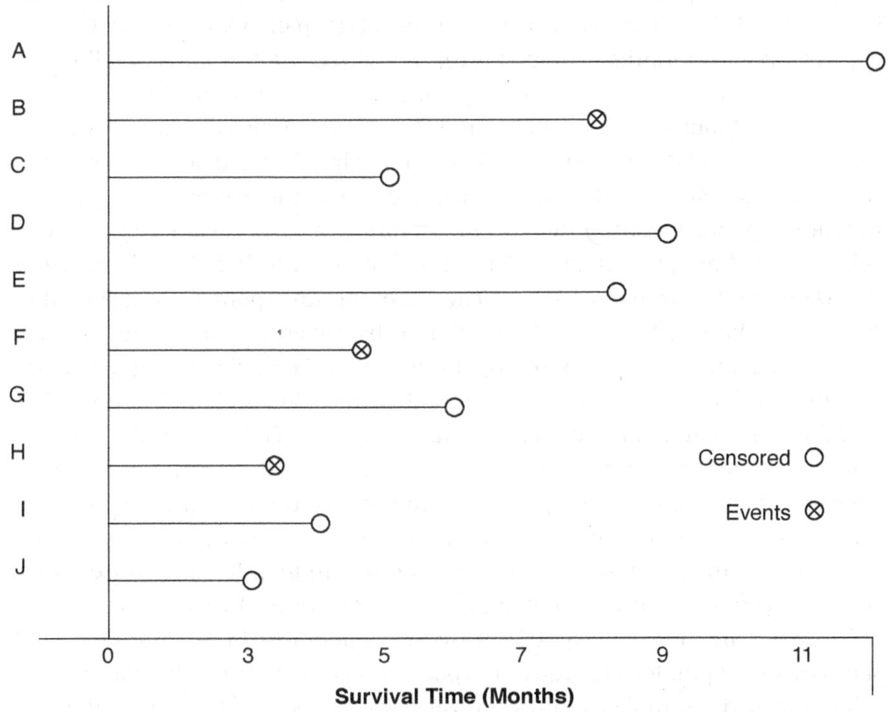

A translation of Equation 6.1 is as follows: the instantaneous hazard for a specific time (*h(t)*) is equal to the probability of the first occurrence of the outcome in that time interval (Δt) divided by the size of that time interval, when the size of the time interval approaches zero (*limit* $\Delta t \rightarrow 0$). This may seem like an odd way of describing risk. However, when formulated in this way, it allows for elegant solutions to estimating likelihoods and for identifying factors that increase or decrease the likelihoods.

Kaplan–Meier survival analysis calculates hazards for each outcome. Specifically, the hazard (h_t) is the number of individuals with the outcome (i.e., one and only one) divided by the total number at risk when the individual has the outcome (i.e., $1/n_t$). The subscript *t* indicates that there is a hazard rate for each time the outcome occurs. The proportion surviving that instant (s_t) is one minus the hazard rate for that instant ($s_t = 1 - h_t$). During time periods where there are no event occurrences, the hazard rate is set at zero. The overall rate of the outcome is one minus the cumulative proportion surviving ($1 - S_T$). The cumulative proportion surviving (S_T) is the product of the survival rates for all previous event occurrences:

$$S_T = \prod\nolimits_{event=1}^{t} (1 - h_t) \tag{6.2}$$

In this equation, h_t is the survival rate for each event occurrence. The symbol Π (Greek capital pi) indicates that the survival rates are multiplied together. The number of events is indicated by *t*, and *event* = 1 indicates the first event.

Worked Example

To illustrate the calculation of Kaplan–Meier survival curves, consider the cases in Figure 6.2. The first event in this group of 10 patients is Patient H. After approximately 4 months Patient H is rehospitalized. At 4 months of follow-up, nine patients are still at risk (including Patient H), so the probability of rehospitalization in Month 4 is 1/9 = .1111, and the survival rate for that event occurrence is (1 − .1111) = .8888. Patient J has already been lost to follow-up (censored), so Patient J does not contribute to the calculation of the survival function. Patient F contributes the next point in the survival curve by being rehospitalized at approximately 5 months when seven individuals are still at risk (1/7 = .1429, survival = .8571). The third and final point is contributed by Patient B, who is rehospitalized after 8 months. Given that there are only four patients remaining in the risk set, the probability is ¼ = .25 of being rehospitalized in Month 8; conversely, the likelihood of surviving is 75% (1 − .25 = .75).

Table 6.1 organizes the data into a survival table. There are three substantive rows, one for each patient rehospitalized. In addition, there is a row for the start of the study ($t = 0$) and a row to indicate the end of the study (i.e., when no cases remain at risk). The hazard rates will always increase during the course of the follow-up period. This is not a finding. It is the consequence of the necessarily diminishing sample size over time. In this example, the hazard rates are unusually large because the sample size is tiny. Although small samples are helpful for illustrative purposes, do not expect reliable hazard rates when the at-risk sample comprises fewer than 20 cases. In this illustration, the cumulative survival rate was 0.5714, indicating the estimated rate of rehospitalization at 12 months was 42.9%. In contrast, the raw rate that did not account for variable follow-up time was .30 (three out of 10 cases were rehospitalized). The estimate from survival analysis indicates what the rate would have been if all cases were followed for the full 12 months.

Standard Errors and Confidence Intervals

The standard errors of the hazards and cumulative survival function are calculated using the same formula as those used for discrete-time survival analysis

TABLE 6.1. Kaplan-Meier Survival Analysis of Hypothetical Rehospitalization Study ($n = 10$)

1	2	3	4	5	6	7
Time (months)	Number at risk	Number of events	Hazard (h_t)	Survival for interval ($1 - h_t$)	Cumulative survival	Cumulative proportion with outcome
0.0	10	0	0	1	1	0
3.5	9	1	0.1111	0.8889	0.8889	0.1111
4.8	7	1	0.1429	0.8571	0.7619	0.2381
8.1	4	1	0.2500	0.7500	0.5714	0.4286
>12	0	0	0	1	0.5714	0.4286
Total	10	3				

(Singer & Willett, 2003, Section 13.3). The standard errors of the instantaneous hazards are rarely of interest because they are fully determined by the number of cases at risk at that time (i.e., the standard error of the instantaneous hazard is approximately $1/n_t$).[1] The standard errors of the cumulative survival rates are reasonably estimated by the Greenwood standard error, provided that there are at least 20 cases remaining:

$$SE(S_t) = S_t\sqrt{\frac{h_1}{n_1(1-h_1)} + \frac{h_2}{n_2(1-h_2)} + \frac{h_3}{n_3(1-h_3)} + \ldots + \frac{h_t}{n_t(1-h_t)}} \qquad (6.3)$$

In this equation, h_1 is the observed hazard for the first event (based on n_1 cases at risk), h_t is the hazard for the last event, and S_t is the estimated cumulative survival function. The standard error of the cumulative survival function increases as the number of events increase. As with discrete-time survival analysis (Chapter 5), the estimates for later intervals will be less precise than the estimates for earlier intervals.

A plot of a Kaplan–Meier survival curve with 95% confidence intervals is provided in Figure 6.3. This survival figure is based on a hypothetical study of rehospitalization for 150 patients, discussed further in the Computer Code section later in the chapter. The curve starts in the upper left-hand corner and descends over time. The curve is jagged, dropping down vertically whenever there is an event. Notice that the drops get bigger over time because there are fewer cases remaining at risk. Also notice that the 95% confidence intervals gradually increase over time.

Comparing Cumulative Survival Rates

There are several procedures available to compare the Kaplan–Meier survival rates based on different groups (see Altman, 1991, Section 13). These procedures will not be reviewed here because another type of survival analysis (Cox regression, Chapter 10) is usually the preferred option for identifying predictors or covariates of hazard rates and survival curves. A versatile approach to comparing cumulative survival rates is by examining their 95% confidence intervals (Cumming & Finch, 2005).

GOING FURTHER

Readers who have made it this far should have a sufficient understanding of Kaplan–Meier survival analysis to be educated consumers of studies using this statistical approach. The following sections are designed to deepen this understanding through further reading and exercises. These sections can be worked with in any order, and it is not necessary to do all (or any) of them.

1

$$SE(h_t) = \sqrt{h_t(1-h_t)/n_t} = \sqrt{\frac{1}{n_t}\left(1-\frac{1}{n_t}\right)\Big/ n_t} = \sqrt{(n_t-1)/n_t^3} \approx 1/n_t$$

FIGURE 6.3. Kaplan-Meier Survival Curve With 95% Confidence Intervals for Hypothetical Study of Rehospitalization

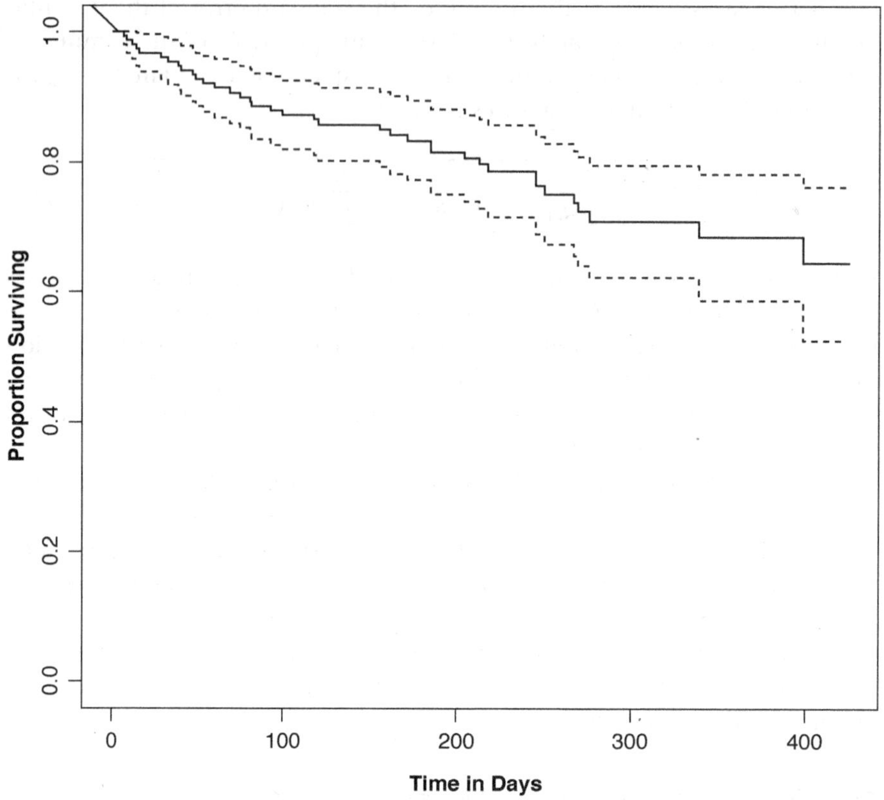

Recommended Readings

Greenhouse, J. B., Stangl, D., & Bromberg, J. (1989). An introduction to survival analysis: Statistical methods for analysis of clinical trial data. *Journal of Consulting and Clinical Psychology*, 57(4), 536–544. https://doi.org/10.1037//0022-006x.57.4.536

A readable, brief introduction to Kaplan–Meier survival analysis. Clear and accurate. The computer code and software examples are outdated.

Aalen, O. O., Borgen, Ø., & Gjessing, H. K. (2008). *Survival and event history analysis: A process point of view*. Springer.

A sophisticated treatment of various forms of survival analysis (including ones developed by the authors). Section 3.2 covers the Kaplan–Meier estimator in depth. For aficionados.

Computer Code

Both R Statistics and IBM/SPSS have Kaplan–Meier survival analysis programs. Both programs calculate survival rates and their standard errors using the formula presented earlier in this chapter (Equations 6.2 and 6.3, respectively). Two variables are required: one indicating the length of survival time, and another indicating whether the event occurred by the end of follow-up.

Although only two variables are required, data sets for survival analysis usually start with more variables; specifically, the dates used to compute survival times: at-risk date, follow-up end date, and date of the outcome (for those who have the outcome). To demonstrate the computation of survival time, the computer code examples start with data sets that contain the outcome variable and the necessary dates.

The example is a scaled-up version of the hypothetical rehospitalization study previously discussed, with 150 cases (instead of 10). The hospital administration was interested in the 12-month readmission rate. Consequently, the researchers used a 1-year recruitment period (January 1 to December 31, 2020), with an end of follow-up 2 months later (March 1, 2021). Four cases were lost to follow-up earlier for other reasons (e.g., leaving the country). The sample was identified with the goal to have at least 20 cases still at-risk at 12 months. The number still at risk is determined by the initial sample (controlled by the researchers) and the survival rate (controlled by nature).

R Code

The R Statistics data set for this example is an EXCEL.csv file called Chap6_KM_example.csv (available at https://www.apa.org/pubs/books/prediction-statistics-for-psychological-assessment). This is a typical format used by researchers to record the raw data for a study involving survival analysis. The data set includes five variables: a case identifier (*case*; coded as 1 to 150), a variable indicating whether the event occurred (*event*, coded 0 for *no* and 1 for *yes*), and the three dates needed to compute survival time: *atrisk.date*, *end.followup*, and *event.date*. Each of these date variables are recorded in a form recognized as a date by Excel (e.g., "01/21/2010"). The *event.date* variable is only coded for the 37 of the 150 cases who were readmitted to the hospital.

The first step is to transform the raw variables *atrisk.date*, *end.followup*, and *event.date* into a single survival time variable. Survival time starts at the at-risk date and continues until either the event occurs, or the end of follow-up.

```
KMdata <-read.csv("c:\\run.files\\Book\\Chap6_KM_
example.csv")
attach (KMdata)
```

The first line in the preceding code creates an R data file called "KMdata" from the Excel.csv file. You will need to specify where the Excel file is stored. In my computer, it is in a subdirectory called *Book* within a directory called *run.files* on my C:\drive. The next command, **attach**, tells R that you want to work with this data set. Because the date formats in Excel are different than those in R, the next three lines tell R how to read the Excel dates, which in this case are in *month/day/year* format.

```
Atrisk.date <- strptime(atrisk.date, format = "%m/%d/%Y")
End.followup <- strptime(end.followup, format = "%m/%d/%Y")
Event.date <- strptime(event.date, format = "%m/%d/%Y")
```

For the purpose of date arithmetic, the dates are then transformed from character variables (e.g., "01/01/2010") into seconds (from 1–Jan–1970, e.g., 1262304000).

```
Atrisk.datep <- as.POSIXlt(Atrisk.date)
End.followupp <- as.POSIXlt(End.followup)
Event.datep <- as.POSIXlt(Event.date)
```

The next few lines calculate follow-up time (in days), and checks the mean.

```
followup.days <- difftime (End.followupp, Atrisk.datep)
mean (followup.days)
Time difference of 253.6397 days
```

To display other properties of the variables, use commands such as **min** (followup.days), **max** (followup.days), and **sd** (followup.days), which produce the values 62, 425, and 104.2.

Now calculate the variable *time.to.event,* which indicates the time between release and readmission. R Statistics does not like missing values. Consequently, the missing values in the *time.to.event* variable must be replaced with a noninformative value, in this case, the value *999.* The value of 999 was selected because it was larger than the longest follow-up time. The survival time variable is *survival.days.*

```
time.to.event <- Event.datep - Atrisk.datep
time.to.event999 <-ifelse(is.na(time.to.event),
999, time.to.event)
survival.days <- pmin (followup.days, time.to.event999)
```

The preceding steps create two useful variables, *followup.days* and *survival.days,* which can be added to initial working data sets, and saved for future analyses.

```
KMdata <- data.frame (KMdata, followup.days, survival.
days)
write.table(KMdata,
"c:\\run.files\\Book\\Chap6_KMoutdata.table")
```

The *follow-up* variable is used only to describe the research method (e.g., the follow-up time ranged from 62 to 425 days, with an average of 254 days and standard deviation of 104 days). Now that the survival time variable has been defined (*survival.days*) and matched with the outcome variable (*event*), you are ready to conduct the survival analysis. Kaplan–Meier survival analysis is included in the *'survival'* package in R Statistics (Therneau, 2020). If you have not used it before, download it using the following command:

```
install.packages ('survival')
```

Once you downloaded the package, tell R that you want to use that set of programs.

```
require ('survival')
```

The next line is the main Kaplan–Meier analysis.

```
KMmodel <- survfit(Surv(survival.days, event) ~ 1,
type = "kaplan-meier")
```

This syntax defines the variables used in the survival analysis. The labels for the variables *KMmodel, survival.days,* and *event* are set by you. Because Kaplan–Meier is the default, you can simply use the following:

```
KMmodel <- survfit(Surv(survival.days, event) ~ 1)
```

The syntax requires a predictor variable, which in this example is "1". The value "1" is noninformative. It simply tells R to fit the survival model without predictors. To see what you have got, type

```
summary (KMmodel)
```

This command displays a survival table with one row for each event (see Table 6.2).

Time is measured in days. The first event is on Day 7, followed by events on Day 9, Day 12, Day 15, and so on. The final event is on Day 398. With only 17 individuals still at risk on Day 398, this estimate is likely to be unstable. The hospital administrators would like a 12-month rate. To find this value, look at the survival rate indicated by the event just before 365 days. This is the event on Day 339 (in **bold**). At that time, there were 28 individuals in the risk set; although not a large number, it is probably enough for a reasonable estimate. At Day 339 the survival rate was 0.684 with 95% confidence intervals from .594 to .788. In other words, this hospital can expect that between 21.2% to 40.6% of individuals released will be rehospitalized within a 1-year period.

Note that the default confidence intervals shown above are calculated on log values. To obtain confidence intervals based on $\pm 1.96(SE(S_t))$, you need to specify "plain" as the option:

```
KMmodel2 <- survfit(Surv(survival.days, event) ~ 1,
conf.type = "plain")
```

Plotting the survival curve provides some indication of the timing of rehospitalization. The following syntax produced Figure 6.3:

```
plot (KMmodel, xlab ="Time in Days", ylab = "Proportion
Surviving", cex.lab = 1.3)
```

Visual inspection of Figure 6.3 suggests a consistent downward slope, with no unusually steep or flat periods. Format tests of changes in slope, however, are most easily conducted using discrete-time survival analysis, not Kaplan–Meier.

IBM/SPSS Code

The SPSS data sets (Chap6_KM_example.sav, https://www.apa.org/pubs/books/prediction-statistics-for-psychological-assessment) contains five variables: *case* (1 to 150), *atrisk.date* (coded as yyyy/mm/dd), *end.followup* (coded

TABLE 6.2. Kaplan-Meier Survival Table From R Statistics Based on Hypothetical Study of Rehospitalization for 150 Cases

Time	n.risk	n.event	Survival	std.err	Lower 95% CI	Upper 95% CI
7	150	1	0.993	0.00664	0.980	1.000
9	149	1	0.987	0.00937	0.968	1.000
12	148	1	0.980	0.01143	0.958	1.000
15	147	1	0.973	0.01315	0.948	0.999
16	146	1	0.967	0.01466	0.938	0.996
29	145	1	0.960	0.01600	0.929	0.992
33	144	1	0.953	0.01722	0.920	0.988
39	143	1	0.947	0.01835	0.911	0.983
41	142	1	0.940	0.01939	0.903	0.979
47	141	1	0.933	0.02037	0.894	0.974
49	140	1	0.927	0.02128	0.886	0.969
53	139	1	0.920	0.02215	0.878	0.964
60	138	1	0.913	0.02297	0.869	0.959
69	136	1	0.907	0.02376	0.861	0.954
75	133	1	0.900	0.02454	0.853	0.949
81	131	1	0.893	0.02530	0.845	0.944
82	130	1	0.886	0.02602	0.837	0.939
93	128	1	0.879	0.02672	0.828	0.933
99	127	1	0.872	0.02739	0.820	0.928
118	121	1	0.865	0.02810	0.812	0.922
120	118	1	0.858	0.02880	0.803	0.916
155	110	1	0.850	0.02958	0.794	0.910
161	106	1	0.842	0.03036	0.784	0.904
171	101	1	0.834	0.03119	0.775	0.897
185	94	1	0.825	0.03209	0.764	0.890
185	93	1	0.816	0.03295	0.754	0.883
204	85	1	0.806	0.03393	0.742	0.876
212	82	1	0.796	0.03491	0.731	0.868
217	79	1	0.786	0.03590	0.719	0.860
245	68	2	0.763	0.03838	0.692	0.842
250	60	1	0.750	0.03980	0.676	0.833
267	57	1	0.737	0.04122	0.661	0.823
269	55	1	0.724	0.04259	0.645	0.812
276	50	1	0.709	0.04413	0.628	0.801
339	**28**	**1**	**0.684**	**0.04930**	**0.594**	**0.788**
398	17	1	0.644	0.06063	0.535	0.774

Note. CI = confidence interval; std.err = standard error.

as yyyy/mm/dd), *event* (coded 0 or 1), and *event.date* (coded as yyyy/mm/dd). The at-risk dates range from the start of the study (2020/01/01) to when the last case was recruited (2020/12/29).

This first step is transforming the dates into follow-up times and survival times. Directions for date arithmetic can be found in the drop-down menus by following **Transform**, then **Compute Variables**. The following syntax calculates the survival time variable (*survival.days*) and the overall follow-up time from the raw dates (*atrisk.date, end.followup,* and *event.date*). The SPSS syntax described below is also available at https://www.apa.org/pubs/books/prediction-statistics-for-psychological-assessment; "Prediction Statistics SPSS syntax.sps."

```
compute survival_end.date=min.1(end.followup, event.
date).
compute survival_days=datediff(survival_end.date,
atrisk.date, "days").
compute followup_days=datediff(end.followup, atrisk.
date, "days").
EXECUTE.
```

The new variables will be automatically added to the active data set. After computing new variables, it is good practice to run **Descriptives** (follow **Analyze, Descriptive Statistics**, then **Descriptives**) to verify that the computes worked as intended.

```
DESCRIPTIVES VARIABLES=followup_days survival_days event
/STATISTICS=MEAN STDDEV RANGE MIN MAX.
```

Descriptives generates the following results:

Descriptive Statistics

	N	Range	Minimum	Maximum	*M*	*SD*
follow-up_days	150	363.00	62.00	425.00	253.6133	104.20616
survival_days	150	418.00	7.00	425.00	225.1133	113.85458
event	150	1	0	1	.25	.433
Valid *N* (listwise)	150					

The means and standard deviations are the same to four significant figures to those produced by R Statistics. The minor differences are due to different methods for how each program counts ties (individuals who were readmitted at the same follow-up time). Ensure that the mean follow-up time is longer than the mean survival time. Without considering follow-up time, the raw proportion with the outcome was .25 = 37/150.

The **KM** routine in IBM/SPSS computes Kaplan–Meier survival analysis. This requires only two variables: *survival_days* (ranging from 7 to 425) and *event* (coded at 0 or 1). The **KM** command is found by following **Analyze, Survival**, then **Kaplan–Meier**. At the **Kaplan–Meier** screen, specify which value of the dichotomous outcome variable indicates that the event occurred (in our case, the value *1*). The **KM** command also provides options for comparing the survival curves across groups (*Factor*) and for aggregating survival curves across groups (*Strata*). These options are not needed when estimating a single proportion, as in the following example syntax:

```
KM survival_days
/STATUS=event(1)
/PRINT TABLE
/PLOT SURVIVAL.
```

This produces a table with one row for each case (150 rows total). An edited version of the output is presented in Table 6.3.

The values in this table are the same (within rounding) as those produced by R Statistics. The confidence intervals, however, are not given and would need to be calculated by using the survival rate and its standard error. For example, the "plain" 95% confidence interval for Day 339 is .684 ± (1.96) * (0.049) = .588 to .780.

TABLE 6.3. A Selection From IBM/SPSS Kaplan-Meier Survival Table for Hypothetical Rehospitalization Study

	Survival table					
			Cumulative proportion surviving at the time			
	Time	Status	Estimate	*SE*	*N* of cumulative events	*N* of remaining cases
1	7.000	1	.993	.007	1	149
2	9.000	1	.987	.009	2	148
3	12.000	1	.980	.011	3	147
4	15.000	1	.973	.013	4	146
5	16.000	1	.967	.015	5	145
6	29.000	1	.960	.016	6	144
7	33.000	1	.953	.017	7	143
8	39.000	1	.947	.018	8	142
9	41.000	1	.940	.019	9	141
10	47.000	1	.933	.020	10	140
...						
122	325.000	0	.	.	35	28
123	339.000	1	.684	.049	36	27
124	351.000	0	.	.	36	26
125	356.000	0	.	.	36	25
126	366.000	0	.	.	36	24
127	366.000	0	.	.	36	23
128	368.000	0	.	.	36	22
129	371.000	0	.	.	36	21
130	380.000	0	.	.	36	20
131	394.000	0	.	.	36	19
132	395.000	0	.	.	36	18
133	396.000	0	.	.	36	17
134	398.000	1	.644	.061	37	16
135	401.000	0	.	.	37	15
...						
149	424.000	0	.	.	37	1
150	425.000	0	.	.	37	0

EXERCISES

Question 6.1

Table 6.4 is another selection from the Kaplan–Meier survival table for the hypothetical rehospitalization study.

(i) What are the hazard, survival, and cumulative survival rates for Day 16? Day 161? Day 162? Day 163?

(ii) What proportion of former patients would be expected to return to the hospital within 6 months?

(iii) What is the 95% confidence interval for this estimate?

TABLE 6.4. Another Selection of the IBM/SPSS Kaplan-Meier Survival Table for Hypothetical Rehospitalization Study

Survival table						
			Cumulative proportion surviving at the time			
	Time	Status	Estimate	*SE*	*N* of cumulative events	*N* of remaining cases
1	7.000	1	.993	.007	1	149
2	9.000	1	.987	.009	2	148
3	12.000	1	.980	.011	3	147
4	15.000	1	.973	.013	4	146
5	16.000	1	.967	.015	5	145
. . .						
44	159.000	0	.	.	22	106
45	161.000	1	.842	.030	23	105
46	162.000	0	.	.	23	104
47	166.000	0	.	.	23	103
48	168.000	0	.	.	23	102
49	168.000	0	.	.	23	101
50	171.000	1	.834	.031	24	100
51	171.000	0	.	.	24	99
52	175.000	0	.	.	24	98
53	176.000	0	.	.	24	97
54	179.000	0	.	.	24	96
55	182.000	0	.	.	24	95
56	183.000	0	.	.	24	94
57	185.000	1	.	.	25	93
58	185.000	1	.816	.033	26	92
59	187.000	0	.	.	26	91
60	188.000	0	.	.	26	90
61	191.000	0	.	.	26	89
62	193.000	0	.	.	26	88

Question 6.2

Using either R Statistics, IBM/SPSS, or any software of your choice, conduct a Kaplan–Meier survival analysis for the 150 cases in the rehospitalization study. Start with either Chap6_KM_example.csv (R Statistics) or Chap6_KM_example.sav (for IBM/SPSS).

(i) Verify your answers by comparing them with Table 6.2, Table 6.3, and Table 6.4.

(ii) For the survival time variable (e.g., *survival_days*), compute the following descriptive statistics: (a) number of cases, (b) mean, (c) minimum, (d) maximum, and (e) standard deviation.

ANSWERS TO EXERCISES

Question 6.1

(i) The hazard rates are 1/(number at risk). The number at risk includes the individual who had the event. Survival is 1 – hazard. The cumulative survival rate is the product of previous survival rates, which is given in Table 6.4. On Day 16, there were 145 + 1 = 146 individuals at risk, of which one experienced the event, resulting in a hazard rate of 1/146 of 0.006849 and a survival rate of 1 – hazard = 1 – 0.006849 = 0.99315. The cumulative survival is the product of previous survival rates, given on the output as .967. On Day 161, there were 105 + 1 = 106 individuals at risk, resulting in a hazard rate of 1/106 = .00943, survival of 0.9906, and cumulative survival of .842 (from the table). On Day 162, one individual was censored, and there were no events. Consequently, the hazard rate for that day was zero and survival was 1.0. Cumulative survival remains unchanged from what it was at the last event (.842). On days when there were neither events nor individuals censored (Day 163), the hazard rate is zero, the survival rate is one, and the cumulative survival remains unchanged (.842).

(ii) The proportion of former patients expected to return to the hospital within 6 months is 16.6%. Six months is between 182 and 183 days (365/2 = 182.5; [365.25]/2 = 182.625). Given that there were no events at either 182 or 183 days, go back to the closest, previous event (Day 171). The cumulative survival rate for that day was .834, suggesting a rehospitalization rate of 1 – .834 = .166, or 16.6%. The value remains constant until there is another event.

(iii) The 95% confidence interval for this estimate is 10.5% to 22.7%. The 95% confidence interval is calculated on the basis of either the survival rate or the event/failure rate. I use the event rate here because the question asks about the rate of rehospitalization. Consequently, the confidence interval is calculated as 0.166 ± (1.96)(.031), which results in an interval from 10.5% to 22.7%. The value 1.96 specifies the size of the confidence intervals as 95%, and the value 0.031 is the standard error of the cumulative survival rate (from the output).

Question 6.2

(i) Ideally, you were able to replicate the tables in this chapter from the data sets and syntax provided. The most common problem is reading the data sets. If it all becomes very frustrating, remember that intense mental effort grows brain cells. You may then want to check the internet for instructional videos, or call a Zoom meeting with that statistically minded colleague who owes you a favor.

(ii) (a) 150 (number of cases), (b) mean of 225.11, (c) 7 (minimum), (d) 425 (maximum), and (e) standard deviation of 113.85.

III

DISCRIMINATION AND RELATIVE RISK

INTRODUCTION: DISCRIMINATION AND RELATIVE RISK

Part III considers useful statistics for describing *discrimination*, or the extent to which individuals with the outcome are different from individuals without the outcome. This is one of two fundamental properties of risk prediction tools, the other being calibration. Statistics for describing *calibration*, or the match between predicted and observed values, are presented in Part IV.

When evaluators are asked why an outcome is more or less likely for specific individuals, they will typically speak about one or more features of the individuals or their life circumstances. Mr. Unalaq is likely to complete his new home this summer because he has drive and ambition. The Parkers' marriage is likely to fail because Mrs. Parker found out about Mr. Parker's extramarital affair. Dr. Brankley is likely to use actuarial risk prediction tools in his next forensic assessment because he has used them in his previous assessments.

Although such statements are applied to specific individuals, they are rooted in general statements about people. People with drive and ambition are likely to complete their personal projects, and Mr. Unalaq has drive and ambition. Known infidelities increase the likelihood of divorce. Past behaviour is a good predictor of future behavior. Each of these statements is a testable hypothesis that can be confirmed or refuted by evidence.

We carry a large number of assumptions about what predicts what. Many of these assumptions are obvious and correct. Some appear obvious but are actually incorrect. The true expertise of experts is not found in their credentials, their long experience, or their confidence; it is their ability to justify their opinions with evidence. The most basic evidence for a risk factors comes from follow-up studies demonstrating that individuals with the characteristic were more likely to have the outcome than were individuals without that characteristic. Although there are ongoing debates about how risk assessments should be conducted, there is no argument that evaluators must consider characteristics that are empirically associated with the outcome of interest.

Chapter 7 considers relative risk statistics for characteristics that are either present or absent—that is, *dichotomous* variables. The remaining sections of Part III consider statistics for predictor variables with ordinal scaling that rank order individuals (e.g., low, moderate, or high hostility) or characteristics that exist along a dimension in nature (e.g., age, income). When the follow-up time is unequal, Cox regression (Chapter 10) is recommended for both dichotomous and dimensional predictors. Evaluators scouring research reports for evidence-based risk factors will see lots of fourfold tables, rate ratios, odds ratios, hazard ratios, and area under the curve (AUC) values. Ideally, after working through Part III, these statistics will become part of your native vocabulary. The statistics in the latter sections of Part III are particularly useful for describing the predictive accuracy (discrimination) of risk prediction tools.

WHAT ABOUT CORRELATIONS?

Notably absent from the list of statistics presented in this book are correlation coefficients. Although correlations are commonly used, I do not recommend their use in prediction research. In all contexts where correlations could be used, there are better alternatives. In prediction research, Pearson correlation coefficients will be either point-biserial correlations (with linear predictors) or phi coefficients (with dichotomous predictors) because the outcome is always dichotomous. With a dichotomous outcome, all forms of correlations are highly influenced by the base rate of the outcome. Consequently, correlations will often indicate that outcomes with higher base rates have stronger associations with the predictor variables than outcomes with lower base rates. Given that base rates increase as the follow-up period increases, the use of correlations can paradoxically make it appear that it is easier to predict long-term than short-term outcomes. Studies that use appropriate statistics consistently find the opposite pattern (e.g., Babchishin & Hanson, 2020; Lloyd et al., 2020). A related limitation is that correlations are also influenced by restriction of range in the predictors, which is often hard to appreciate.

In an informative empirical demonstration of the effects of base rates on the magnitude of correlations, Babchishin and Helmus (2016) examined 109 correlations based on 60,415 individuals. The correlation between the base rate of the outcome and the size of point-biserial correlation was $r = -.81$. As expected, the largest correlations were found when the base rate was close to .50 and smallest when the base rate approached zero or 1. Although there are certain adjustments that can be made to correct for the base rate effects on correlations, the simpler alternative is to use statistics more suited to prediction tasks, such as odds ratios (for dichotomous predictors) or AUCs (for predictors with ordered levels), described in the following section.

7

Dichotomous Predictors

This chapter presents statistics for describing how much the presence or absence of a characteristic influences the likelihood of the outcome. For example, is the likelihood of attending university higher for children born in this country than for those born elsewhere? Does living together before marriage increase or decrease the likelihood of separation? Such variables are called *dichotomous,* meaning having only two values. And, like all the statistics in this book, the outcome is also dichotomous; consequently, the basic empirical findings can be expressed in two by two tables, also called *fourfold* tables.

This chapter has three sections. The first section describes the fourfold table in some detail, with attention to how the four elements of the table can be reorganized to inform different types of decisions. The second and third sections present two ways of describing relative risk differences between individuals with or without the attribute in question: namely, the *rate ratio* and the *odds ratio*.

SECTION 7A: THE FOURFOLD TABLE

The *fourfold table,* also called the two-by-two table, provides the frequencies of all possible outcomes when both the predictor variable and the outcome can take only one of two values.

Fourfold tables contain the complete information on the likelihood of the outcome for individuals with or without a specific predictor variable. As can

https://doi.org/10.1037/0000275-007
Prediction Statistics for Psychological Assessment, by R. K. Hanson

TABLE 7.1. The Fourfold Table

	Outcome		
Predictor	**Has the outcome**	**Does not have the outcome**	
Has the predictor	A	B	A + B
Does not have the predictor	C	D	C + D
	A + C	B + D	N

be seen in Table 7.1, individuals can be placed into one of four cells: (A) those with both the predictor and the outcome, (B) those with the predictor but not the outcome, (C) those with the outcome but not the predictor, and (D) those with neither the predictor nor the outcome. The cells in the fourfold table (A, B, C, and D) can be raw frequencies counts (e.g., 20 individuals had both the predictor and the outcome; Cell A) or proportions of the total (e.g., 20 out of 80 = 0.25, or 25%; Cell A). *N* is the total sample size on which the table is based: A + C and B + D are the column totals and A + B and C + D are the row totals. In Table 7.1, the outcome variable is presented as columns, and the predictor variable is presented as rows. This is an arbitrary choice. In some fourfold tables, the outcome variable defines the rows and the predictor variable defines the columns. Both formats express the same information; however, the content of the cells A, B, C, and D will be different.

Cases in Cell A are often referred to as *hits,* or *true positives.* If there is a strong relationship between the predictor and the outcome, the value of Cell A will be relatively large. Cases in Cell B are called *false alarms,* or *false positives.* Ideally, this number will be small. The cases in Cell C are *misses,* or *false negatives;* again, we want this number to be small because it indicates that we failed to anticipate certain cases who go on to have the outcome. Finally, we want Cell D, *true negatives,* to be large. If the predictor works well, cases without the predictor should also not have the outcome.

WHY USE FOURFOLD TABLES?

Fourfold tables contain the core information about the relationship between a dichotomous predictor variable and an outcome, as well as the base rates of both the predictor and the outcome. In some cases, simple visual inspection of the fourfold table can be sufficient for decision-making. For example, the raw number with the outcome could inform resource allocation decisions. Frequently, however, we understand fourfold tables by comparing relative frequencies for certain subgroups.

There are many ways of reorganizing values in the fourfold table. Each of these approaches emphasizes certain features of the data, and are intended to inform specific types of decision making. In addition to being used in studies of predictive accuracy, fourfold tables are widely used for reporting the effectiveness of interventions, diagnostic accuracy, and group differences in case control studies. The reorganizations of the A, B, C, and D values that are useful for one context may or may not be useful for other contexts.

LIMITATIONS

Fourfold tables require that the predictor variable is represented by only two values (yes–no, present–absent). In some cases, this is a reasonable representation of nature (e.g., comparing two distinct intervention programs); however, many predictor variables are best represented by an ordered dimension (e.g., age, depression, antisocial attitudes, employment status). Dichotomizing constructs that are continuous in nature results in a loss of information and reduced statistical power (Cohen, 1983). When continuous measures of predictor variables are available, researchers are encouraged to use other statistics, such as the area under the curve (AUC) from the receiver operating characteristic (ROC) curve (Chapter 8), Cohen's *d* (Chapter 9), or logistic regression (Chapter 11).

Another limitation of fourfold tables is that they are heavily influenced by the research design on which they were based. These influences are not always obvious, which can lead to arbitrary design choices being misinterpreted as empirical findings. An extreme example are case–control studies, in which cases with the outcome are matched to an equal number of cases without the outcome. It should be obvious that the base rate of the outcome in case–control studies is a feature of the research design, not a finding. It is less obvious, however, that indicators of predictive accuracy (e.g., positive predictive accuracy, negative predictive accuracy) can also be artificially constrained by fixing the base rate of the outcome at 50%. Consequently, some of the simple descriptive statistics described in the first part of this chapter may not be appropriate. Instead, researchers should consider odds ratios, which are relatively robust to arbitrary design features (e.g., length of follow-up).

THE NUTS AND BOLTS

Data Requirements

Fourfold tables from prediction studies require the following data:

1. a dichotomous outcome variable,
2. a dichotomous predictor variable,
3. the predictor variable exists before the outcome, and
4. a defined follow-up time (preferably the same for all cases).

Directions for computing fixed (same for all) follow-up periods are provided in Chapter 4.

This chapter focuses on statistics for describing fourfold tables in two types of prediction studies: those with and those without a natural follow-up period. An example of an outcome with a natural follow-up period is completing high school on time. An example of an outcome without a natural follow-up period is marital separation. Whereas there is a common age at which children are expected to complete high school (usually in their 18th year), there is no schedule for divorce. When there is a natural (nonarbitrary) end to follow-up, the base rate of the outcome is an important empirical finding. In contrast, when the follow-up period is arbitrary, the base rate is a consequence of research design. Researchers can increase or decrease the base rate by extending or shortening the follow-up period. The distinction between natural and arbitrary follow-up is important because many of the statistics used to describe fourfold tables are heavily influenced by base rates.

Worked Example

To illustrate the various statistics describing fourfold tables, consider a hypothetical study of living with both parents to age 16 as a predictor of completing high school by age 18. This is an example of a prediction study with a natural (nonarbitrary) follow-up period. Using archival records from the Geneva school district, Dr. J. Piaget identifies a random sample of 100 students enrolled in Grade 1 in September 1999. He then records whether, up to the age of 16, the students lived at the same address as both parents each school year from Grade 1 to Grade 10. Finally, Dr. Piaget notes who graduated with a high school diploma in 2018, which was the outcome of interest. The raw numbers are presented in Table 7.2.

So what does this table tell us? The first thing to look at is the *base rate* of the outcome—in this case, 80 of the 100 students graduated on time, whereas 20 did not. In the absence of more specific information, the base rate should be the basis for estimating likelihoods. Consequently, if Dr. Piaget was asked whether a typical student in this school district was going to graduate on time, he could respond that there is an 80% chance that this student would graduate on time.

Dr. Piaget wants to know whether living with both parents increases the likelihood of school completion. This requires examining the *conditional probability*

TABLE 7.2. Living With Both Parents as a Predictor of High School Completion

	Education at age 18		
Parents in family of origin	Completed high school	Did not complete high school	
Still together at age 16	Cell A 60	Cell B 5	65
Separated before age 16	Cell C 20	Cell D 15	35
	80	20	100

of completion for those who lived with both parents and those who did not. Note that the labels for the outcome are not fixed in nature and can be changed depending on the question. In our example, the outcome could be either *school completion* or *school noncompletion*. Similarly, the predictor could be *still living with parents* or *separated*. The choice of labeling the values of dichotomous variables does not change the raw numbers; however, it will change some of the statistics used to describe fourfold tables. For example, if the outcome is school completion, the base rate for the outcome is 80%. If the outcome is school noncompletion, the base rate for the outcome is 20%.

In our example, 65 of the 100 students were still living with both parents at age 16, and 35 were not. Among the 35 students who separated, 15 failed to complete high school. This is a noncompletion rate of 15/35 = .429 and a completion rate of 20/35 = .571. Consequently, if Dr. Piaget knows that a child did not live with both parents, a reasonable estimate of the child's likelihood of completing high school would now be only 57% (down from 80%). If the child had lived with both parents, the expected graduation rate would be 60/65 = .923, or 92.3%.

The Geneva school board is considering an intervention program to prevent school noncompletion, and, given financial constraints, wants to provide the program only to students who would not have otherwise completed high school. How effective is parental separation at identifying students who would not complete? As previously stated, 15 of the 35 students with parental separation failed to complete, which translated to a *positive predictive accuracy* (or *positive predictive value)* of 42.9% when parental separation is considered a predictor of school noncompletion. In other words, if parental separation was the only variable used to select 100 new cases for intervention, the intervention would be given to 43 students who needed it; however, it would also be given to 57 students who would have graduated without it.

The Canton of Geneva is also considering a savings scheme for the parents of school-age children to pay for postsecondary education. The contributions to the savings scheme would start in elementary school and would only be available when students completed high school. How effective is living with both parents as a predictor of school completion? Notice that this question reverses the labels such that the outcome is now school completion, whereas in the previous paragraph it was school noncompletion. As previously stated, if the child lived with both parents, the expected graduation rate would be 60/65 = .923, or 92.3%. This would be a *positive predictive accuracy* of 92.3%. Notice that the same predictor variable (parental separation) has a higher positive predictive accuracy for school completion (92.3%) than for school noncompletion (42.9%). There is no magic here. It is simply that you are more likely to be correct if you anticipate a common event than a rare event. Because the base rate of school completion was high (80%), completion is easier to predict than noncompletion.

When the savings scheme was discussed at council, there was an objection from one of the legislators, who just happened to be divorced. The legislator pointed out that even though separation from parents increases the likelihood of noncompletion, most children who experience parental separation nevertheless complete high school (20 completers vs. 15 noncompleters out of 35 students). In statistical language, living with both parents has poor *negative predictive accuracy* for school noncompletion. *Positive predictive accuracy* is the number of cases with the predictor and the outcome (Cell A) divided by the total number with the predictor (sum of Cell A and Cell B). *Negative predictive accuracy* is the number of cases with neither the predictor nor the outcome (Cell D) divided by the total number without the predictor (sum of Cell C and Cell D). In our example, the negative predictive accuracy of living with both parents is 15/(20 +15) = .429 or 42.9%. The legislators decide to advance the scheme to all children, regardless of whether they are living with both parents.

There are two other statistics commonly used to describe fourfold tables: *sensitivity* and *specificity.* These statistics are not intuitive and are seldom directly relevant for applied decision making; however, they are important because they are not influenced by the base rate of the outcome. Sensitivity and specificity describe the relationship between the predictor and the outcome regardless of whether the base rate is 5%, 50%, or 95%. Consequently, they can be used to compare the accuracy of predictors for outcomes with arbitrary follow-up times (e.g., divorce, criminal recidivism, depression relapse). They are the basis of the AUC of the ROC curve discussed in Chapter 8.

Sensitivity is the number of cases with the predictor and the outcome (i.e., hits, Cell A) divided by the total number with the outcome (sum of Cell A and Cell C). In our example, the sensitivity of parental stability as a predictor of school completion was 60/(60 + 20) = .75. Specificity is the number of cases with neither the predictor nor the outcome (true negatives, Cell D) divided by the total number without the outcome (sum of Cell B and Cell D). In our example, specificity was 15/(5 + 15) = .75. That both sensitivity and specificity are the same in this example has no special meaning (a chance feature of how the example was written).

In general, sensitivity can be expected to increase when specificity decreases and vice versa. When extreme features or circumstances are used as predictors, the number of hits will decrease (Cell A), and the number of true negatives will increase (Cell D). For example, if the predictor variable was *3 or more out-of-home placements for aggressive behavior,* this variable would apply to fewer students than the original variable of *any separation from parents before age 16*; however, the students identified by multiple out-of-home placements would have an even lower likelihood of completing high school on time than those identified by the original variable used in this example.

Common terms used to describe fourfold tables for prediction studies are summarized in Table 7.3. Readers interested in additional terms used for diagnostic studies are encouraged to read Akobeng (2007a, 2007b) or Altman (1991, Section 14.4). There are also specialized ways of summarizing fourfold tables from intervention studies, such as the *number needed to treat* (Altman,

TABLE 7.3. Terms for Describing Fourfold Tables

Terms	Descriptions	Calculation
Hits, true positives	Cases with both the predictor and the outcome	Cell A
False alarms, false positives	Cases with the predictor but not the outcome	Cell B
Misses, false negatives	Cases with the outcome but not the predictor	Cell C
True negatives	Cases with neither the predictor nor the outcome	Cell D
Base rate of outcome	The proportion of the total that have the outcome	(A + C)/N
Base rate of predictor	The proportion of the total that have the predictor	(A + B)/N
Positive predictive accuracy	The proportion of cases with the predictor that also have the outcome	A/(A + B)
Negative predictive accuracy	The proportion of cases without the predictor that also do not have the outcome	D/(C + D)
Sensitivity	The proportion of cases with the outcome that also have the predictor	A/(A + C)
Specificity	The proportion of cases without the outcome that do not have the predictor	D/(B + D)

Note. A, B, C, and D are the cells of the fourfold table. *N* is the total sample size.

1998; Cook & Sackett, 1995). When faced with a new or unfamiliar term, it is often helpful to identify how it is constructed from the four basic cells of the fourfold table.

GOING FURTHER

Readers who have made it this far should understand how to create and interpret fourfold tables. The next sections provide opportunities to deepen this understanding through readings, computer code, and exercises. In most situations, understanding of the fourfold table is incomplete without a statistical index of relative risk (i.e., how much riskier is one group compared with another?). Consequently, readers are encouraged to proceed to the next sections of this chapter (rate ratios, odds ratios), even if they skip the exercises provided here.

Recommended Reading

Helmus, L. M., & Babchishin, K. M. (2017). Primer on risk assessment and the statistics used to evaluate its accuracy. *Criminal Justice and Behavior, 44*(1), 8–25. https://doi.org/10.1177/0093854816678898

An overview of the various statistics that have been used (for better or worse) to describe the accuracy of criminal recidivism prediction tools. The authors include a detailed discussion of the fourfold table, and the distinction between statistics for diagnostic accuracy and statistics for predictive accuracy.

Computer Code

Fourfold tables are easily constructed and described with a handheld calculator. Nevertheless, I have provided examples of computer code in R Statistics and IBM/SPSS for those who may find them helpful.

R Code

The R code that follows assumes you have already compiled the frequencies for each quadrant of the fourfold table. These values are set as the variables A, B, C, and D. The syntax then follows the same steps that you would follow if calculating by hand. The # symbol indicates instructions or reminders that are not read by R. This example uses the same values as the previous mock example of Dr. Piaget's examination of the relationship between living with both parents to age 16 and high school graduation.

```
A <- 60 #the number with the predictor and the outcome
(hits)
B <- 5 #the number with the predictor but not the
outcome (false alarms)
C <- 20 #the number with the outcome but not the
predictor (misses, false negatives)
D <- 15 #the number with neither the predictor nor the
outcome (true negatives)
N <- sum(A, B, C, D)
baserate.outcome <- (A + C)/N
baserate.predictor <- (A + B)/N
PosPredAccuracy <- A/(A + B)
NegPredAccuracy <- D/(C + D)
sensitivity <- A/(A + C)
specificity <- D/(B + D)
baserate.outcome
[1] 0.8
baserate.predictor
[1] 0.65
PosPredAccuracy
[1] 0.9230769
NegPredAccuracy
[1] 0.4285714
sensitivity
[1] 0.75
specificity
[1] 0.75
```

IBM/SPSS Code

The IBM/SPSS analysis that follows uses the sample numbers. It starts, however, with a data set of 100 cases that includes two variables: *Graduates*

(Yes = 1/No = 2), and *Lived_Parents* (i.e., lived with both parents: Yes = 1/No = 2; Chap7_Fourfold_example.sav; available from https://www.apa.org/pubs/books/prediction-statistics-for-psychological-assessment). All the requisite statistics can be found using the **CROSSTABS** command; however, to find the terms in Table 7.3 (e.g., sensitivity, positive predictive accuracy), you will need to know what you are looking for because they are not labeled as such. The output will also change based on the values used to define *yes* and *no*. The values in this SPSS file were selected so that the top left quadrant are hits (Cell A, cases with the predictor and the outcome, i.e., lived with both parents and graduated) and the bottom right quadrant are true negatives (Cell D, cases with neither the predictor nor the outcome, i.e., neither lived with both parents nor graduated).

Using the drop-down menus, start with **ANALYZE**, then **DESCRIPTIVE STATISTICS**, then **CROSSTABS**. Select your variables, with the outcome variable as columns, and the predictor variable as rows. In the options for **CELLS**, select **PERCENTAGES** for **ROW** and **COLUMN**. This will provide the following syntax and output:

```
CROSSTABS
/TABLES=Lived_Parents BY Graduates
/FORMAT=AVALUE TABLES
/CELLS=COUNT ROW COLUMN
/COUNT ROUND CELL.
```

Lived With Both Parents * Graduated Crosstabulation

			Graduated		
			Yes	No	Total
Lived with both parents	Yes	Count	60	5	65
		% within lived with both parents	92.3%	7.7%	100.0%
		% within graduated	75.0%	25.0%	65.0%
	No	Count	20	15	35
		% within lived with both parents	57.1%	42.9%	100.0%
		% within graduated	25.0%	75.0%	35.0%
Total		Count	80	20	100
		% within lived with both parents	80.0%	20.0%	100.0%
		% within graduated	100.0%	100.0%	100.0%

The base rate of the outcome is found in the second row from the bottom (80%, 20%). The base rate of the predictor is found in the last column (65%, 35%). Positive predictive accuracy is the percentage who graduated and lived with both parents divided by the total who lived with both parents (60/65 = 92.3%). Negative predictive accuracy is the percentage who did not graduate and did not live with both parents divided by all those who did not live with both parents (15/35 = 42.9%). Sensitivity is the percentage who graduated and lived with both parents divided by all those who graduated (60/80 = 75.0%). Specificity is the percentage who did not graduate and did not live with both parents among those who did graduate (15/20 = 75.0%).

FOURFOLD TABLE EXERCISES

This exercise continues the same example of living with both parents at age 16 as a predictor of high school completion at age 18. After finishing his Geneva report, Dr. Piaget is hired by the Zurich school board to examine whether the same patterns apply there. Dr. Piaget hires an underpaid undergraduate to collect the raw data ($n = 100$), which is presented in Table 7.4.

Question 7.1

Create the fourfold table for living with both parents at age 16 as a predictor of high school graduation. Place the frequency of cases that both lived with parents and graduated in the top left quadrant (Cell A).

TABLE 7.4. Raw Data on Separation From Parents and Graduation for 100 Students in Zurich

ID	Sep	Grad	ID	Sep	Grad	ID	Sep	Grad	ID	Sep	Grad	ID	Sep	Grad
1	Yes	Yes	21	No	Yes	41	No	Yes	61	Yes	Yes	81	Yes	No
2	No	No	22	No	Yes	42	No	Yes	62	No	Yes	82	Yes	No
3	Yes	Yes	23	No	Yes	43	No	Yes	63	No	Yes	83	No	No
4	Yes	Yes	24	No	Yes	44	No	Yes	64	No	Yes	84	No	Yes
5	Yes	Yes	25	No	Yes	45	Yes	Yes	65	No	Yes	85	No	Yes
6	Yes	Yes	26	No	Yes	46	No	Yes	66	No	Yes	86	No	Yes
7	Yes	Yes	27	No	Yes	47	Yes	No	67	No	Yes	87	No	Yes
8	No	No	28	No	Yes	48	No	Yes	68	No	Yes	88	Yes	Yes
9	Yes	Yes	29	No	Yes	49	No	Yes	69	Yes	No	89	Yes	No
10	Yes	Yes	30	No	Yes	50	No	Yes	70	Yes	Yes	90	No	No
11	Yes	Yes	31	Yes	No	51	No	Yes	71	No	Yes	91	No	Yes
12	Yes	Yes	32	No	Yes	52	No	Yes	72	No	Yes	92	No	Yes
13	Yes	Yes	33	No	No	53	Yes	No	73	No	Yes	93	No	Yes
14	No	No	34	No	Yes	54	Yes	Yes	74	No	Yes	94	No	No
15	Yes	Yes	35	No	Yes	55	Yes	Yes	75	Yes	Yes	95	Yes	No
16	Yes	Yes	36	Yes	No	56	No	Yes	76	No	Yes	96	Yes	Yes
17	No	No	37	Yes	Yes	57	No	Yes	77	No	Yes	97	No	Yes
18	Yes	Yes	38	No	Yes	58	No	Yes	78	No	No	98	No	Yes
19	Yes	Yes	39	No	Yes	59	No	Yes	79	Yes	Yes	99	No	No
20	Yes	Yes	40	No	Yes	60	No	No	80	Yes	Yes	100	Yes	No

Note. Grad = graduated from high school by age 18; Sep = separated from both parents prior to age 16.

Question 7.2

Based the table you created in the previous question,

(i) What is the likelihood of the typical student in Zurich graduating from high school?

(ii) What is the likelihood of graduating on time if the child was separated from both parents at or before age 16?

(iii) When *living with both parents* is considered a predictor of school completion: (a) What is its positive predictive accuracy? (b) Negative predictive accuracy? (c) Sensitivity? (d) Specificity?

(iv) Without conducting formal statistical tests, does living with both parents seem as important for school graduation in Zurich as it was in Geneva?

SECTION 7B: RATE RATIOS

The *rate ratio* is a measure of relative risk, or how much a variable is related to the outcome. Specifically, it compares (a) the proportion with the outcome among those with the predictor to (b) the proportion with the outcome among those without the predictor.

Rate ratios, also called *relative risk ratios,* describe how much more at risk individuals are when they have the predictor compared with individuals who do not have the predictor. It is calculated by dividing two proportions: (a) the proportion with the outcome observed for all cases with the predictor by (b) the proportion with the outcome observed for all cases without the predictor. When the predictor increases risk, the rate ratio is greater than one. When the predictor decreases risk, the rate ratio is less than one. A rate ratio of one indicates that the predictor has no relationship to the outcome. The basic elements of rate ratios are the rates, proportions, and probabilities described in Chapter 4 and in the first section of this chapter (fourfold tables). Rate ratios are widely used in risk communication. When used in risk communication, it is important to accompany the rate ratio with information concerning the base rate. Knowing that a predictor doubles the risk, for example, means something different if the base rate is 4% or if it is 40%.

WHY USE RATE RATIOS?

Rate ratios provide a simple, intuitive way of describing the relative risk associated with a predictor variable. Rate ratios do not describe the likelihood of the outcome; instead, they describe the importance of a specific variable for anticipating that outcome. Rate ratios are a stable metric for reporting relative risk that is conceptually independent of the base rate of the outcome. Rate ratios are also easily calculated and widely accepted in both natural language and professional risk communication.

For outcomes that have no natural follow-up periods (e.g., recovery from depression, violent recidivism, falling in love), the raw values in fourfold tables have limited utility because these values are expected to change over time. At the start of follow-up, nobody has the outcome (Cell A is zero), and the proportion with the outcome increases over time. In prediction studies, the base rate increases without changing the proportion of the sample that has the predictor variable (unlike studies of diagnostic accuracy). For example, if gender (male, female) is used to predict the onset of depression, the proportion diagnosed with depression will increase over time without changing the proportion of the sample who are female. Changes in base rates are important because they also change many other features of fourfold tables.

One feature of fourfold tables that may not change is the rate ratio. For many predictors and outcomes, relative risk is consistent even when there is substantial variation in the frequency of the outcome (Babchishin et al., 2012a; Helmus, Hanson, et al., 2012; Weinberger et al., 2010). This inherent stability makes them a useful metric for comparing the results of prediction studies. When considering the importance of two predictor variables, the one with the largest rate ratio deserves the most weight in decision-making. The degree of stability of rate ratios is an empirical question, however, and needs to be established for each predictor–outcome pairing. Nonetheless, in the absence of reasons for variability, it is reasonable to expect similar rate ratios across settings, follow-up times, and different ways of measuring the predictor and the outcome.

Rate ratios are perhaps the most intuitive way of describing relative risk. When base rates are low (less than 20%), rate ratios are similar to other relative risk indicators, such as odds ratios (see the next section) and hazard ratios (see Chapter 10, Cox Regression). These other metrics have valuable statistical properties, which make them useful for complex analyses. They are not, however, used in natural language. Consequently, it is common for researchers to communicate their results using rate ratios, even when the analyses were conducted using more complex metrics. For example, results could be expressed as follows: When both members of a couple have a history of adverse childhood events, the divorce rate is 2.5 times higher than for other couples. This means that if the divorce rate for most couples is 20%, the divorce rate would increase to 50% if both members had a history of adverse childhood events. In this example, the rate for the comparison group would be selected to facilitate communication, not necessarily because it was the actual rate for any specific time period.

LIMITATIONS

The major limitation with risk ratios is that they appear to say more than they actually do. Being told that the risk of lung cancer is 25 times higher for smokers is scary. However, without knowledge of the base rate of lung cancer, it is hard to tell how likely smokers are to have lung cancer. When used in risk communication, it is essential to include base rate information along with relative risk ratios.

Another limitation is that rate ratios only work for relatively infrequent events. When the base rate is high, it is not unusual for risk ratios to imply probabilities greater than one. Imagine a 5-year study of divorce with a 20% base rate. It would not be unreasonable to find a risk ratio of 2.5 for a specific risk factor. For example, a study may observe a relative risk increase of 2.5 in the divorce rate when both members of the couple had a history of adverse childhood events. The researcher then extends the study up to 20 years, and the divorce rate is now 50%. With a base rate this high, a rate ratio of 2.5 would imply an impossible divorce rate of 125%. If the base rate was 80% and a risk factor increased that risk to 100%, the maximum possible rate ratio is now only 1.25.

When the base rate in the reference group is greater than 25%, it is generally better to conduct the analyses using odds ratios (see next section). Odds ratios provide relatively stable estimates across diverse base rates of the outcome and predictor. The results of analyses conducted using the odds ratio metric can then be transformed back into rate ratios for communication with clients and decision makers.

Very infrequent events can be problematic. Proportions are unstable when the absolute number of cases with the outcomes is small (less than 10); ratios of proportions multiply this instability. Sometimes the base rates are so low that relative risk indicators are not even useful. Consider a rare psychological symptom, such as sustained visual distortions in the absence of psychosis. If a follow-up study found that 14 out of 50 heavy LSD users had this problem whereas only one out of 500 cases in the reference group had the problem, there would be little point of calculating a rate ratio. Instead, it would be more informative to present the raw numbers in the fourfold table, supplemented by the conditional probabilities of sustained visual distortions for individuals with (14/50 = .28, 28.0%) and without a history of heavy LSD use (1/500 = .002, 0.2%). For example, these findings could be summarized as follows: 28 out of 100 heavy LSD users develop sustained visual distortions whereas this symptom is almost never found in other groups (one out of 500).

A related concern is rare predictor variables. If only a tiny proportion of the sample has (or does not have) the indicator, the number of cases in certain cells will be too small for reliable estimates. As well, from a practical perspective, rare indicators influence only a small proportion of cases. Consequently, researchers who are identifying risk factors and building risk tools typically privilege variables that describe between 10% and 90% of the sample.

NUTS AND BOLTS

Data Requirements

Risk ratios require the same data as fourfold tables:

1. a dichotomous outcome variable,
2. a dichotomous predictor variable,

3. the predictor variable exists before the outcome, and
4. a defined follow-up time (preferably the same for all cases).

A further consideration is that risk ratios are not the preferred metric when the base rate of the outcome is high. If the base rate is greater than 25%, proceed with caution; if it is greater than 50%, reconsider your choices. Sometimes it makes sense to reverse the outcome measure (e.g., use 20% school dropout rather than 80% completion). Sometimes it is preferable to use another measure of relative risk, such odds ratios (next section) or hazard ratios (Chapter 10).

Calculating Risk Ratios

Rate ratios are defined as the ratio of two proportions (or rates):

$$\text{Rate ratio} = \frac{n_2/N_2}{n_1/N_1} = \frac{p_2}{p_1} = \frac{A/(A+B)}{C/(C+D)} \quad (7.1)$$

In this equation, N_1 and N_2 are the sample sizes of two groups defined by the two levels of the predictor variable, and n_1 and n_2 are the number within each group who have the outcome. Equivalently, p_1 and p_2 refer to probabilities, or proportion with the outcome in each group. The third way of expressing the rate ratio uses the frequencies from the fourfold table (i.e., Cell A = hits, Cell B = false alarms, Cell C = misses, and Cell D = true negatives, see discussion earlier in the chapter).

Worked Example

The worked example again uses the hypothetical study of Dr. Piaget examining the influence of parental stability on high school graduation. Because the graduation rate was high (80%), the outcome and predictor variables were reversed to lower the base rate of the outcome. Consequently, the predictor is now *separation from parents before age 16* and the outcome variable was *did not complete high school by age 18,* which has a base rate of 20% (1 − .80 = .20). The fourfold table is presented in Table 7.5.

TABLE 7.5. Separation From Parents as a Predictor of Failure to Complete High School

	Education at age 18		
Parents in family of origin	**Did not complete high school**	**Completed high school**	
Separated before age 16	Cell A 15	Cell B 20	35
Still together at age 16	Cell C 5	Cell D 60	65
	20	80	100

The proportion that did not complete high school (Cell A) among those who separated from their parents (Cell A + Cell B) was 15/35 = .42857, or 42.9%. The proportion who did not complete high school (Cell C) among those still living with their parents (Cell C + Cell D) was 5/65 = .07692, or 7.7%. Consequently, the rate ratio was (.42857)/(.07692) = 5.5716. In other words, students who did not live with both parents were 5.6 times more likely to not complete high school compared with students who lived with both parents.

Disentangling the causal relationships between variables is a perennial concern of psychological research. In prospective research, the outcome cannot cause the predictor, which rules out one possible confound. However, it is possible, indeed likely, that other variables contributed to the relationship between the predictor and the outcome. We are complex creatures living in complex worlds. Everything we care about is connected to many other things. Inferences concerning causal relationships are theories, and scientific theories are disciplined by evidence. The strong relationship between separation from parents and failure to complete high school, if true, would not establish a causal effect of separating from parents. It would, however, be a fact that would need to fit into any advancing scientific model. It would also be relevant to decision making. Even if the reasons for the relationship are unknown, separation from parents is still an efficient marker for students who may need extra help to graduate on time.

Standard Errors and Confidence Intervals

It is quite difficult to calculate the standard error of rate ratios in their original form. It is much easier to calculate when the rate ratio is transformed into its natural logarithm. Consequently, calculating standard errors and confidence intervals (CIs) for rate ratios requires using logarithms and exponents. These functions are available on most handheld calculators, including the calculator preloaded on your smartphone. For readers who are unfamiliar with these functions, an introduction is provided in the Appendix. Exponents and logarithms have almost magical statistical properties, which have been used to facilitate calculations and solve previously unsolvable problems. They are not, however, intuitive. Do not worry if the idea of an exponential function remains less than completely clear or if you learn and forget logarithms many times. For our purposes, it is sufficient to recognize that a few extra steps are necessary.

The first step for calculating CIs is to transform the observed rate ratio into its natural logarithm (natural log). This is the logarithm to base *e*, often indicated by symbols such as lnX, log_e, or ln. Note that natural logarithms are different from logarithms to base 10, which are often symbolized by log_{10} or log. An additional source of confusion is that *log* can refer to both natural logarithms (to base *e*) as well as logarithms to the base 10. Before committing to a logarithm command, make sure it is the one you want, which will typically be the natural log (base *e*).

If the rate ratio is greater than one, the log of the rate ratio will be a positive number. If the rate ratio is less than one, the log of the rate ratio will be a negative number. If the rate ratio is one, the log of the rate ratio will be zero. The standard error of the natural log of the rate ratio can be calculated from the cells in the fourfold table (Altman, 1991, p. 267):

$$SE(\ln[\textit{rate ratio}]) = \sqrt{\frac{1}{A} - \frac{1}{A+B} + \frac{1}{C} - \frac{1}{C+D}} \quad (7.2)$$

In this formula, A is the number with the predictor and the outcome, (A + B) is the total number with the predictor, C is the number with the outcome but not the predictor, and (C + D) is the total number without the predictor. To create the 95% CI, multiply the standard error by 1.96, then add and subtract it to the log of the rate ratio. This will create a 95% CI in log units. The CI is then transformed back into raw units by taking the exponent of the upper bound and the lower bound. On calculators, this function is indicated by symbols such as *exp(X)*, e^x, and *(INV)lnX*.

Continuing the preceding example, the rate ratio for separation from parents predicting not completing high school was 5.5716, and ln(5.5716) = 1.718. Using the values from Table 7.5, the standard error is calculated as follows:

$$SE(\ln[\textit{rate ratio}]) = \sqrt{\frac{1}{15} - \frac{1}{15+20} + \frac{1}{5} - \frac{1}{5+60}} = 0.4719$$

Consequently, the 95% CI is 1.718 ± (1.96)(0.4719), or 1.718 ± 0.92496, which gives a range of 0.7927 to 2.643 in log units. Taking the exponents of these values provides a range of 2.21 to 14.05 in the original rate ratio units. Consequently, it is reasonable to consider that separation from parents before age 16 is associated with an increase in the risk of not completing high school by age 18, an increase that could be as low as doubling the risk, or as high as 14 times the risk. Given that the CI does not include one, the relationship is statistically significant (unlikely to be observed by chance alone).

GOING FURTHER

If you made it this far, you have sufficient mastery to understand and communicate rate ratios in professional practice. The following sections are intended for those who want to deepen their knowledge, typically because they are using rate ratios in research projects. In most cases, rate ratios are calculated by handheld calculators or generic spreadsheets. Computer code is nonetheless provided for both R Statistics and IBM/SPSS.

Recommended Readings

Crowson, C. S., Therneau, T. M., Matteson, E. L., & Gabriel, S. E. (2007). Primer: Demystifying risk—understanding and communicating medical risks. *Nature Clinical Practice Rheumatology*, *3*(3), 181–187. https://doi.org/10.1038/ncprheum0397

Fleiss, J. L., & Berlin, J. A. (2009). Effect sizes for dichotomous data. In H. Cooper, L. V. Hedges, & J. C. Valentine (Eds.), *The handbook of research synthesis and meta-analysis* (2nd ed., pp. 237–253). Russell Sage Foundation.

Both of these readings discuss rate ratios as one of the ways to describe the relationship between a dichotomous predictor and a dichotomous outcome. Crowson et al. (2007) focus on their utility for medical risk communication; Fleiss and Berlin (2009) focus on research synthesis and comparisons across studies. Both of these articles also provide helpful discussions of relative risk statistics that are not covered in the current book, such as risk differences.

Computer Code

R Code

The R code that follows assumes that you have already compiled the frequencies for each quadrant of the fourfold table. These values are set as the variables A, B, C, and D. The syntax then follows the same steps that you would follow if calculating by hand. The symbol # at the front of the first few lines indicates instructions and reminders that are not read by R. This example uses the same values as the previous mock example of Dr. Piaget's examination of the relationship between living with both parents to age 16 and high school graduation in Geneva. However, the variables are reversed so that the predictor is not living with both parents, and the outcome is failing to complete high school.

```
A <- 15 #the number with the predictor and the outcome
(hits)
B <- 20 #the number with the predictor but not the
outcome (false alarms)
C <- 5 #the number with the outcome but not the
predictor (misses, false negatives)
D <- 60 #the number with neither the predictor nor the
outcome (true negatives)
rate.separate <- A/(A + B)
rate.together <- C/(C + D)
rate.ratio <- rate.separate/rate.together
ln.rate.ratio <- log(rate.ratio) # the log command
calculates the natural logarithm (base e)
SE.rate.ratio <- sqrt ((1/A)-(1/(A + B))+(1/C)-
(1/(C + D)))
lowerCI <- exp(ln.rate.ratio - ((1.96)*SE.rate.ratio))
upperCI <- exp(ln.rate.ratio + ((1.96)*SE.rate.ratio))
rate.ratio
[1] 5.571429
lowerCI
[1] 2.209318
upperCI
[1] 14.04995
```

IBM/SPSS Code

The IBM/SPSS analysis below uses the same numbers. It starts, however, with a data set of 100 cases that includes two variables: *Graduates.Geneva* (1 = yes, 0 = no), and *Separated.Geneva* (0 = yes, 1 = no; Chap7_RR_example.sav; available at https://www.apa.org/pubs/books/prediction-statistics-for-psychological-assessment). The format of the outcome changes based on the values used to define *yes* and *no*. The values in this example were selected so that the top left quadrant are hits (Cell A, cases with the predictor and the outcome, i.e., separated and did not graduate) and the bottom right quadrant are true negatives (Cell D, cases with neither the predictor nor the outcome, i.e., lived with both parents and graduated).

The rate ratio and its CI are found in the **RISK** option under **STATISTICS** in the **CROSSTABS** command:

```
CROSSTABS
/TABLES=Separated.Geneva BY Graduates.Geneva
/FORMAT=AVALUE TABLES
/STATISTICS=RISK
/CELLS=COUNT ROW COLUMN
/COUNT ROUND CELL.
```

This produces the following output:

Risk Estimate

		95% CI	
	Value	Lower	Upper
Odds ratio for Separated.Geneva (Yes/No)	9.000	2.903	27.905
For cohort Graduates.Geneva = No	5.571	2.209	14.050
For cohort Graduates.Geneva = Yes	.619	.461	.832
N of valid cases	100		

Note. CI = confidence interval.

The output includes an odds ratio (to be discussed in the next section) and two risk ratios. The one we are interested in is the risk of not graduating given separation, here labeled "For cohort Graduates.Geneva = No", with values of 5.571 and a 95% CI of 2.209 to 14.050. The other risk estimate is the risk of graduating, here labeled "For cohort Graduates.Geneva = Yes". Notice that this rate ratio is less than one (0.619), indicating that separation decreases the risk of graduating.

Given that rate ratios and their standard errors change based on how the predictor and outcome variables are coded, it is important to verify that the rate ratio calculated by SPSS is actually the one you want. It is good practice to routinely examine the cells in the fourfold table, and spot check the ratios with a hand calculator.

RATE RATIO EXERCISE

This exercise uses the data collected by Dr. Piaget for his examination of the relationship between parent separation and high school graduation in Zurich. These are the same data used to demonstrate the calculation of the fourfold

TABLE 7.6. Living With Both Parents as a Predictor of High School Completion in Zurich

	Education at age 18		
Parents in family of origin	**Did not complete high school**	**Completed high school**	
Separated before age 16	Cell A 10	Cell B 27	37
Still together at age 16	Cell C 11	Cell D 52	63
	21	79	100

table in Exercise Question 1 of the previous section (fourfold tables). Table 7.6 is reproduced subsequently (same numbers as Table 7.4 but in different positions) with the predictor switched to being *separation* and the outcome now being *failing to graduate*:

Question 7.3

(i) What is the likelihood of not graduating for students in Zurich who did not live with both parents to age 16?

(ii) What is the likelihood of not graduating for students in Zurich who did live with both parents to age 16?

(iii) What is the rate ratio for separation from parents as a predictor of not graduating?

(iv) What is the standard error for this rate ratio in log units?

(v) What is the 95% CI for this rate ratio in log units?

(vi) What is the 95% CI for this rate ratio in its original units?

(vii) By comparing the CIs, is the effect of parent separation on failing to graduate weaker in Zurich than in Geneva (rate ratio of 5.57, 95% CI of 2.2 to 14.0)?

SECTION 7C: ODDS RATIOS

The odds ratio is a measure of relative risk. Specifically, it is the odds of the outcome for individuals with the predictor divided by the odds of the outcome for individuals without the predictor.

The odds ratio is a common metric for quantifying relative risk in statistical analyses. It is similar to rate ratio; however, it is a ratio of odds, not of proportions. An *odds* is defined as the proportion with the outcome divided by the proportion without the outcome. If p is the proportion with the outcome (e.g., 10% or .10), the odds of the outcome would be one to nine. This could also be expressed as $p/(1-p)$, or $.10/(1-.10) = .10/.90 = .111$. The odds ratio is the ratio of (a) the odds of the outcome for individuals with the predictor and (b) the odds of the outcome for individuals who do not have the predictor. Odds ratios can be calculated from fourfold tables, including fourfold tables created by pairs of scores or risk levels from prediction tools. Odds and odds ratios have valuable statistical properties that facilitate analyses and comparisons across studies, samples, and settings. They may not, however, be the preferred metric for risk communication. When the base rate is low (< 20%), odds ratios are similar to rate ratios and can be roughly interpreted as such. However, odds ratios and rate ratios provide very different numbers when the base rate of the outcome is high. Using Cohen's (1988) definitions, odds ratios of 1.4, 2.3, and 3.7 could be considered *small, medium,* and *large,* respectively (using Sánchez-Meca et al.'s, 2003, formula for transforming odds ratios to *d* values[1]). When reporting odds ratios, it is important to also report the base rate of the outcome.

WHY USE ODDS RATIOS?

Odds ratios are an excellent metric for comparing results across studies. They are minimally influenced by the base rate of the outcome or the prevalence of the risk factor. I have grown very fond of them. For much of my research career, I scoured government reports, dissertations, and published articles for predictors of sexual offense recidivism. Each study reported the data differently, so I needed some way to compare the results across studies. I tried different metrics and transformations, some more successful than others. Then I tried odds ratios. When other statistics suggested that the findings were inconsistent across studies, the findings were often consistent when expressed as odds ratios. Before my eyes, the noise introduced by arbitrary design features was stripped away revealing stable features of nature. That nature speaks in odds ratios still remains marvelous to me and to others who have thought on these things (Fleiss et al., 2003).

Another advantage of odds ratios is that, unlike rate ratios, they are symmetrical: Reversing the value that is considered to be the outcome (e.g., graduating or not graduating) does not change the magnitude of the odds ratio nor its standard error (only its direction). The odds of graduation, for example, is equal to one divided by the odds of not graduating: odds $(x) = 1/(\text{odds [not } x])$. Consequently, arbitrary choices about which of two state of affairs is that the outcome does not change the calculations or the interpretation of the findings (as it did for rate ratios). Because of this and other desirable statistical property, odds and odds ratios are widely used in statistical analyses. In particular, they form the basis of logistic regression, a key approach to estimating the

[1]Cohen's $d = \ln(\text{odds ratio})/1.65$

likelihood of the outcome when multiple risk factors are considered simultaneously (see Chapter 11).

Although proportions are more commonly used than odds in popular language, odds have deep roots in probability theory (Hald, 2003). When the 16th-century French aristocrats Pascal and Fermat were debating how to divide the money should their gambling games be interrupted (say, by a peasant uprising), they argued about odds. Odds are still the preferred metric of gamblers. When I bet on Mr. Mulligan to win the 1997 Cheltenham Cup horse race, the likelihood of his winning was expressed as an odds of 1 to 20. Luck was with me: Mr. Mulligan won, and I made a few pounds.

When the base rate is low (less than 20%), odds ratios resemble rate ratios and can be interpreted much in the same way. When the base rate is very low (less than 5%), odds ratios and rate ratios are almost identical. Consequently, it is reasonable for researchers to report and directly interpret odds ratios when examining predictors of low frequency events (e.g., suicide, onset of psychosis, qualifying for the Olympics). It is also reasonable to use odds to communicate likelihoods when neither of the two possible outcomes has more intrinsic importance than the other. For example, it is common to report the birth rates of males versus females as an odds, which is about 105 boys to 100 girls, or 21 to 20 (World Health Organization, 2019). Saying that 21 boys are born for every 20 girls is more easily understood than saying that the probability of the next child being a boy is 51.22% (105/(105 + 100) = 0.5122).

LIMITATIONS

Odds ratios are not intuitive and present special challenges for risk communication. For rare events, they can be interpreted as rate ratios; for common events, they cannot. For example, consider two studies that both found an odds ratio of 2.0. In the first study, the rate for those without the predictor was 5% (.05) and the rate for those with the predictor was 9.5% (0.09523). It would be reasonable to say that predictor in this study doubled the relative risk. In the second study, the base rate for those without the predictor was 50%. An odds ratio of 2.0 would indicate a rate of 66.7% (not 100%) among those with the predictor. This may be high, but it is not double the original risk level. Consequently, it is often useful to transform odds ratios into other forms for the purposes of risk communication (Grant, 2014). Like all statistics based on fourfold tables, the interpretation of odds ratios requires knowledge of the base rate.

Another limitation of odds ratios is that their stability is determined by the number of cases in the cell of the fourfold table with the fewest cases. If the overall sample size is large (thousands) but the number in one cell is less than 5, do not expect stable results across studies.

When low numbers are due to the predictor or the outcome being very rare, the odds ratio may be less informative than basic descriptive information, such as the sample size and proportion with and without the outcome.

For example, consider that a diagnosis of bipolar I disorder increases the odds of suicide by 15. It is hard to appreciate the meaning of such as statistic without considering the base rates. Approximately 1% of the total population will ever be diagnosed with bipolar I, and the annual incidence of suicide in the United States is about 20 per 100,000. Consequently, an odds ratio of 15 would correspond to annual suicide rate of 300 out of 100,000 individuals with this diagnosis, or 0.3% per year. In this context, the incidence rates convey more clinically useful information than the odds ratio on its own.

A related problem is when nobody or everybody has the outcome, in which case odds ratios are undefined. One option is to report the raw numbers, or the proportions for each group, with or without Agresti and Caffo's adjustment (2000; Chapter 4, this volume). These basic frequencies often convey sufficient information for applied decision-making. A related option, discussed later in the chapter, is to calculate the odds ratio after adding ½ to each cell; however, adding ½ to the cells is not ideal when the base rate in the population is near zero. Other options for adjusting odds ratios for rare events are discussed by Sweeting et al. (2004).

THE NUTS AND BOLTS

Data Requirements

Odds ratios require the same data as fourfold tables:

1. a dichotomous outcome variable,
2. a dichotomous predictor variable,
3. the predictor variable exists before the outcome, and
4. a defined follow-up time (preferably the same for all cases).

Calculating Odds Ratios

The *odds ratio* is defined as the odds of the outcome for individuals with the predictor divided by the odds of the outcome for individuals without the predictor: odds ratio = $\text{odds}_{\text{predictor}}/\text{odds}_{\text{no.predictor}}$ or the odds for Group 1 divided by the odds for Group 2, that is, $\text{odds}_1/\text{odds}_2$. An odds is the proportion with the outcome divided by the proportion without the outcome: $p/(1-p)$. The proportion without the outcome is sometimes referred to as q, such that $p+q=1$.

$$\text{Odds ratio} = \frac{p_1}{1-p_1} \bigg/ \frac{p_2}{1-p_2} \tag{7.3}$$

For the purpose of calculation, Equation 7.3 can be rearranged to use only the cells of the fourfold table:

$$\text{Odds ratio} = \frac{A * D}{B * C} \tag{7.4}$$

In Equation 7.4, A is the raw number of individuals with both the outcome and the predictor, B is the number of individuals with the predictor but not the outcome, C is the number with the outcome but not the predictor, and D is the number of individuals with neither the predictor nor the outcome.

Equation 7.4 generally works and is the default in many software packages (e.g., IBM/SPSS). It does not work, however, when one of the cells is zero. There are several options for dealing with empty cells (Sweeting et al., 2004), the most common of which is to add ½ to each cell of the fourfold table (also called a continuity correction):

$$\text{odds ratio} = \frac{(A+.5)(D+.5)}{(B+.5)(C+.5)} \tag{7.5}$$

Adding ½ to each cell is not recommended when the base rate is very low overall (< 1%) because it can distort the size and direction of the effects. Under normal circumstances, however, using this continuity correction results in a less biased estimator of the population value than does Equation 7.4 (Fleiss et al., 2003, p. 106). Consequently, in my own research, I follow Fleiss et al.'s (2003) recommendation to routinely add ½ to each cell. When the overall sample size is small ($N < 20$), it is not unusual for odds ratios calculated without the continuity correction to flip from small to large, or even to change direction, based on the results of one or two cases. Adding ½ to each cell reduces such wild fluctuations. When the number of cases in each cell is 10 or more, Equations 7.4 and 7.5 produce equivalent results.

Worked Example

The worked example again uses the hypothetical study of Dr. Piaget examining the influence of parental stability on high school graduation in Geneva. The data are the same as in Table 7.5: Cell A, separated and did not complete high school, n = 15; Cell B, separated and completed high school, n = 20; Cell C, lived with parents and did not complete high school, n = 5; and Cell D, lived with parents and completed high school, n = 60. The odds ratio is calculated with Equation 7.5 (i.e., ½ is added to each cell):

$$\text{odds ratio} = \frac{(15+.5)(60+.5)}{(20+.5)(5+.5)} = 8.32$$

This indicates that the odds of not completing high school was 8 times higher for those who did not live with both parents than for those who did. Notice that the value of the odds ratio is larger than the rate ratio for the same data (rate ratio = 5.6), calculated earlier. Both values, however, indicate a strong relationship between living with both parents and completing high school.

Standard Errors and Confidence Intervals

As with rate ratios, the standard error of the odds ratio is calculated using the natural log of the odds ratio (Equation 6.33 from Fleiss et al., 2003):

$$\text{SE}(\ln \text{OR}) = \sqrt{\frac{1}{(A+0.5)} + \frac{1}{(B+0.5)} + \frac{1}{(C+0.5)} + \frac{1}{(D+0.5)}} \tag{7.6}$$

The 95% CI is calculated by adding or subtracting 1.96 * (SE[ln OR]) to the natural log (base *e*) of the odds ratio (ln OR). For both the odds ratio and its standard error, it is good practice to add ½ to each cell.

Continuing with the example of parental separation and failure to complete high school, the odds ratio was 8.3171, and its natural log (ln OR) was 2.118. The standard error of ln OR is calculated using Equation 7.6:

$$0.5583 = \sqrt{\frac{1}{(15+0.5)} + \frac{1}{(20+0.5)} + \frac{1}{(5+0.5)} + \frac{1}{(60+0.5)}}$$

This leads to a 95% CI in log units of 2.118 – (1.96 * 0.5583); 2.118 + (1.96 * 0.5583), or 2.118 ± 1.0942, which is 1.0238 to 3.2122. Taking the exponent (e^x) of these values provides the 95% CI in the original log units: 2.78 to 24.8. Given that the CI does not include 1, it is statistically significant.

One advantage of using the log of the odds ratio is that it is symmetrical. For positive relationships (predictor increases the likelihood), it has a possible range from zero (no relationships) to plus infinity. For negative relationships (predictor decreases the likelihood), it has a possible range from zero to minus infinity. In comparison, odds ratios can range from 1 (no relationship) to plus infinity for positive relationships but can only range from 1 to zero for negative relationships. For example, if the outcome variable was coded such that the odds ratio was 4.2 (4.2 to 1), changing the coding to the other pole of the outcome variable would result in an odds ratio of 0.238 (1 to 4.2). In log units, the equivalence of the relationship is obvious. The natural log of 4.2 is 1.435, and the natural log of 0.238 is −1.435. The direction of the effect has changed, but the magnitude is the same.

GOING FURTHER

The following are resources for those who want to deepen their knowledge of odds ratios, typically because they plan to use them in research studies. It contains three sections: (a) recommended readings, (b) computer code for calculating odds ratios in R and IBM/SPSS, and (c) exercises.

Recommended Readings

Fleiss, J. L., Levin, B., & Paik, M. C. (2003). *Statistical methods for rates and proportions* (3rd ed.). John Wiley & Sons.

This is a very authoritative text, although not the easiest read. It provides an in-depth discussion of the strengths and weaknesses of odds ratio and alternatives, including a brief history of the development of the odds ratio. The authors share my enthusiasm for odds ratios as a metric for comparing results across studies.

Grant, R. L. (2014). Converting an odds ratio to a range of plausible relative risks for better communication of research findings. *BMJ, 348,* f7450. https://doi.org/10.1136/bmj.f7450

This article provides an accessible introduction to odds ratios and relative risk (rate ratios) for the purpose of risk communication in medicine.

Computer Code

For researchers following the recommendation to add ½ to each cell, odds ratios and their standard errors can be calculated by hand calculation, programmable spreadsheets (e.g., Excel) or the R code given below. IBM/SPSS only calculates odds ratio without the adjustment (i.e., Equation 7.4).

This example uses the same values as the previous worked mock example of Dr. Piaget's examination of the relationship between living with both parents to age 16 and high school graduation in Geneva. The data are organized such that the predictor is *not living with both parents* and the outcome is *failing to complete high school.*

R Code

The R code that follows assumes you have already compiled the frequencies for each quadrant of the fourfold table. These values are set as the variables A, B, C, and D. The syntax then follows the same steps that you would follow if calculating by hand. The symbol # at the front of the first few lines indicates instructions and reminders that are not read by R.

```
A <- 15 #the number with the predictor and the outcome
(hits)
B <- 20 #the number with the predictor but not the
outcome (false alarms)
C <- 5 #the number with the outcome but not the
predictor (misses, false negatives)
D <- 60 #the number with neither the predictor nor the
outcome (true negatives)
odds.ratio <- ((A +.5)*(D + .5))/((B + .5)*(C + .5))
ln.odds.ratio <- log(odds.ratio) #The log command
calculates the natural logarithm (base e)
SE.odds.ratio <- sqrt ( 1/(A+.5) + 1/(B+.5) + 1/(C+.5)
+ 1/(D+.5) )
lowerCI <- exp (ln.odds.ratio - ((1.96)*SE.odds.
ratio))
```

```
upperCI <- exp (ln.odds.ratio + ((1.96)*SE.odds.ratio))
odds.ratio
[1] 8.317073
> lowerCI
[1] 2.784697
> upperCI
[1] 24.84065
```

IBM/SPSS Code

The IBM/SPSS analysis that follows uses the same numbers. It starts, however, with a data set of 100 cases that includes two variables: *Graduates.Geneva* (1 = yes, 0 = no), and *Separated.Geneva* (0 = yes, 1 = 0). The data set is the same as that used in the risk ratio example in the previous section (Chap7_RR_example.sav; available at https://www.apa.org/pubs/books/prediction-statistics-for-psychological-assessment). The format of the outcome changes based on the values used to define *yes* and *no*. The values in this example were selected so that the top left quadrant are hits (Cell A, cases with the predictor and the outcome, i.e., separated and did not graduate) and the bottom right quadrant are true negatives (Cell D, cases with neither the predictor nor the outcome, lived with both parents and graduated).

The odds ratio and its CI are found in the **RISK** option under **STATISTICS** in the **CROSSTABS** command. The data set, commands, and results are the same as in the previous section on rate ratios.

```
CROSSTABS
/TABLES=Separated.Geneva BY Graduates.Geneva
/FORMAT=AVALUE TABLES
/STATISTICS=RISK
/CELLS=COUNT ROW COLUMN
/COUNT ROUND CELL.
```

This produces the following results:

Risk Estimate

		95% CI	
	Value	Lower	Upper
Odds ratio for Separated.Geneva (Yes/No)	9.000	2.903	27.905
For cohort Graduates.Geneva = no	5.571	2.209	14.050
For cohort Graduates.Geneva = yes	.619	.461	.832
N of valid cases	100		

The output includes an odds ratio calculated using Equation 7.4, that is, without ½ added to each cell. Adding ½ is difficult to do within SPSS; if you want to add it, generate the fourfold table than calculate the odds ratio by hand. For this data set, the values are similar with or without the adjustment and would lead to the same substantive conclusion—namely, that there is a strong, statistically significant relationship between not living with both parents at age 16 and not completing high school by age 18.

ODDS RATIO EXERCISES

This exercise uses the data collected by Dr. Piaget for his examination of the relationship between parent separation and high school graduation in Zurich. This is the same data used in the previous section (fourfold tables and rate ratios). The fourfold table is reproduced in Table 7.7 (same as Table 7.6) with the predictor being *separated from parents at age 16* and the outcome being *failing to graduate*:

Question 7.4

(i) What are the odds of not graduating for students in Zurich who did not live with both parents to age 16?
(ii) What are the odds of not graduating for students in Zurich who did live with both parents to age 16?
(iii) What is the odds ratio for separation from parents as a predictor of not graduating?
(iv) What is the standard error for this rate ratio in log units?
(v) What is the 95% CI for this rate ratio in its original units?

Question 7.5

Dr. Piaget is criticized by Dr. Rogers for focusing only on risk factors, not strengths. Dr. Rogers says that people are motivated by positive goals and that it is disrespectful to focus only on negative features. Consequently, Dr. Piaget recodes the variables in his Zurich sample so that *staying with both parents* is the predictor and *graduating from high school* is the outcome.

(i) What are the values of the cells of the fourfold table (i.e., Cell A, Cell B, Cell C, and Cell D)? To help answer this question, you may want to refer back to Tables 7.1 or 7.3.

TABLE 7.7. Living With Both Parents as a Predictor of High School Completion in Zurich

	Education at age 18		
Parents in family of origin	Did not complete high school	Completed high school	
Separated before age 16	Cell A 10	Cell B 27	37
Still together at age 16	Cell C 11	Cell D 52	63
	21	79	100

(ii) What is the odds ratio for living with both parents as a predictor of completing high school (add ½ to each cell)?

(iii) What is the natural log of this odds ratio?

Question 7.6

Dr. Laing considers the institution of the family to be coercive and toxic to the healthy development of children. Consequently, in his model, separation from parents should be associated with greater likelihood of prosocial goals, including completing high school.

(i) In Dr. Laing's model, what are the cells in the fourfold table?
(ii) What is the odds ratio for separating from parents predicting completion of high school (use the ½ adjustment)?
(iii) What is the inverse of this odds ratio (i.e., 1/OR, or, equivalently, OR^{-1})?
(iv) What is the natural log of the odds ratio calculated separation from parents predicting completion of high school (Question ii)?

ANSWERS TO EXERCISES

Section 7a: Fourfold Table Exercises

Question 7.1

The fourfold table for the data in Table 7.4 can be found in Table 7.8.

Question 7.2

(i) The best estimate of the likelihood of the typical student in Zurich graduating from high school is the base rate, which is 79/100 = 79.0%.

(ii) The likelihood of graduating for children who experienced parental separation is 27/37 = 73.0%.

(iii) When *living with both parents* is considered a predictor of school completion: (a) the positive predictive accuracy is A/(A + B) = 52/63 = 82.5%; (b) negative predictive accuracy is D/(C + D) = 10/37 = 27.0%; (c) sensitivity is A/(A + C) = 52/79 = 65.8%; and specificity is D/(B + D) = 10/21 = 47.6%.

(iv) It seems that living with both parents is less important in Zurich than Geneva. There are only modest differences from the base rates 79% for those who lived with both parents (82.5%) or separated (73.0%) in Zurich. In comparison, the rates were 92.3% for those who lived with both parents in Geneva compared with 57.1% for those who separated, against a similar base rate of 80%.

Section 7b: Rate Ratio Exercise

Question 7.3

(i) The rate of not graduating among students who did not live with both parents was A/(A + B) = 10/37 = 0.2703, or 27.0%

(ii) The rate of not graduating among students who did live with both parents was C/(C + D) = 11/63 = 0.1746, or 17.5%

TABLE 7.8. Living With Both Parents as a Predictor of High School Completion in Zurich

	Education at age 18		
Parents in family of origin	Completed high school	Did not complete high school	
Still together at age 16	Cell A 52	Cell B 11	63
Separated before age 16	Cell C 27	Cell D 10	37
	79	21	100

(iii) The rate ratio is the ratio of the rates calculated in the previous two questions: 0.2703/0.1746 = 1.548, or approximately 1.5 times.

(iv) The standard error in log units is calculated using Equation 7.2: *SE*(log of rate.ratio) = sqrt ((1/A) – (1/(A + B)) + (1/C) – (1/(C + D))) = sqrt((1/10) – (1/(10 + 27)) + (1/11) – (1/(11 + 52))) = 0.3847.

(v) The log of the rate ratio is *ln*(1.548) = 0.4370. Add and subtract 1.96 times the *SE*: 0.4370 + (1.96 * 0.3847) = 1.191 for the upper limit in log units; 0.4370 – (1.96 * 0.3847) = –0.3170 for the lower limit in log units.

(vi) Taking the exponent of these values: $e^{(-0.3170)} = 0.728$; $e^{(1.191)} = 3.29$. The 95% CI is from 0.73 to 3.3 in its original units.

(vii) The value of the rate ratio is smaller in Zurich than in Geneva. However, this could be due to sampling error, given that the CIs for the two estimates overlap. Note that examining the overlap in CIs is a low powered test. Other methods are described in Chapter 14 (meta-analysis of rates). For a detailed discussion of the various ways of comparing rates and proportions, see Fleiss et al. (2003).

Section 7c: Odds Ratio Exercises

Question 7.4

(i) The odds of not graduating for students in Zurich who did not live with both parents to age 16 was p/(1 – p), or A/B = 10/27 = 0.37037. When using the ½ adjustment, (A + .5)/(B + .5) = 10.5/27.5 = 0.38182.

(ii) The odds of not graduating for students in Zurich who did live with both parents to age 16 was p/(1 – p), or C/D = 11/52 = 0.2115. When using the ½ adjustment, (C + .5)/(D + .5) = 11.5/52.5 = 0.21904.

(iii) The odds ratio for separation from parents as a predictor of not graduating was AD/BC = 10 * 52/27 * 11 = 1.751 (using Equation 7.4). Using the ½ adjustment (Equation 7.5), (A + .5)(D + .5)/(B + .5)(C + .5) = (10.5 * 52.5)/(27.5 * 11.5) = 1.743.

(iv) With the ½ adjustment (Equation 7.6), the standard error in log units is 0.4874. Without the ½ adjustment (the option used by SPSS), the standard error would be 0.4972.

(v) The 95% CI for this rate ratio in its original units is 0.6705 to 4.532 (with the ½ adjustment). Without the ½ adjustment (the SPSS option), it would be 0.6608 to 4.639.

Question 7.5

(i) Cell A (predictor and outcome) = 52; Cell B (predictor but not the outcome) = 11; Cell C (the outcome without the predictor) = 27; and Cell D (neither the predictor nor the outcome) = 10.

(ii) Using Equation 7.5, (A + .5)(D + .5)/(B + .5)(C + .5) = (52.5 * 10.5)/(11.5 * 27.5) = 1.743. Notice that this is exactly the same odds ratio as when *not being with both parents* is used to predict *not completing high school.* Another way of calculating the odds ratio is to first calculate the odds for each level of the predictor. The odds of completing high school for those who lived with both parents was (A + .5)/(B + .5) = 52.5/11.5 = 4.5652, and the odds of completing high school for those who did not live with both parents was (C + .5)/(D + .5) = 27.5/10.5 = 2.6190. The ratio of these odds is 4.5652/2.6190 = 1.743.

(iii) Ln (1.743) = 0.556.

Question 7.6

(i) Cell A (predictor and outcome) = 27; Cell B (predictor but not the outcome) = 10; Cell C (the outcome without the predictor) = 52; and Cell D (neither the predictor nor the outcome) = 11.

(ii) Using Equation 7.5, (A + .5)(D + .5)/(B + .5)(C + .5) = (27.5 * 11.5)/(10.5 * 52.5) = 0.5737.

(iii) 1/.5737 = 1.743

(iv) Ln (0.5737) = –0.556.

Notice that reversing the coding of both the predictor and the outcome results in the same odds ratio as the original coding. Reversing the coding of either the predictor or the outcome will result in an odds ratio that is the inverse of that computed with the original coding. Reversing the coding of one of the variables will produce a log odds ratio that is the same size but opposite in direction to the log odds ratio computed with the original coding (i.e., positive to negative, or negative to positive).

8

Area Under the Curve

The *area under the curve* (*AUC*) is a measure of the accuracy (discrimination) of prediction tools. Specifically, the value of the AUC is the likelihood that an individual with the outcome will have a higher score than an individual without the outcome.

The curve in question is the receiver operating characteristic curve (ROC; also called the *receiving* operating characteristics curve; Swets et al., 2000). AUC values can vary between 0 and 1, with .50 indicating no difference between the groups. AUC values above .50 indicate that the individuals with the outcome have higher scores than individuals without the outcome. AUC values below .50 indicate that individuals with the outcome have lower scores than individuals without the outcome. An AUC value of .76, for example, would indicate that there is a 76% chance that an individual with the outcome would have a higher score than an individual without the outcome. Although originally designed for signal detection tasks, the AUC statistic is widely used to describe the accuracy of medical diagnostic procedures (e.g., scans for brain cancer) and prediction tools. AUC values are expected to be smaller in prognostic studies than in diagnostic studies because the outcome of interest in prognostic studies does not exist at the time of assessment and may never happen (Helmus & Babchishin, 2017; Royston et al., 2009). Although there are no universal standards for describing effects sizes (for anything), Cohen's (1988) heuristics are widely used in psychology. For AUC values, .56 indicates a small effect, .64 indicates a moderate effect, and .71 indicates a large effect (Rice & Harris, 2005) of a prediction tool. Conversely, for measures scored as

https://doi.org/10.1037/0000275-008
Prediction Statistics for Psychological Assessment, by R. K. Hanson

protective factors, .44 indicates a small effect, .33 indicates a moderate effect, and .29 indicates a large effect. Good diagnostic measures are expected to have AUC values greater than .80, and it is not uncommon for diagnostic measures to have AUC values greater than .95 (e.g., pregnancy tests).

WHY USE AUCs?

When I was an undergraduate in psychology, I read Daniel Kahneman's (1973) *Attention and Effort* and was intrigued by the studies demonstrating that the ability to sustain attention in short, simple laboratory tasks (e.g., dichotic listening tasks) was correlated with success in the real world (e.g., learning to fly a fighter jet). Consequently, I recorded and tested my own dichotic listening task. My task involved a series of variably faint signals played in one side of the headset (e.g., "four") masked by conceptually similar noise in the other side (e.g., "three," "five"). Respondents were asked to raise their hand whenever they heard the signal, of which I had recorded 10 during a 5-minute tape. In pilot testing with family and friends, I came across a finding I did not anticipate. Whereas most of my participants correctly identified between five and nine signals (with a few false alarms), my grandmother, Hazel, raised her hand 14 times. Given that there were only 10 real signals, many of her responses were false alarms (i.e., she frequently indicated that the signal was present when it was not).

Hazel was a gifted storyteller, prone to spinning intriguing and inspiring tales from her family history. She was also prone to confusing fantasy and reality. Although I was tempted to redirect my honors thesis project toward the use of dichotic listening tasks for clinical diagnosis, I had a more pressing research problem: How should I summarize the individuals' responses to my dichotic listening measure into a single number? Identifying a large number of real signals (true positives, or "hits") was obviously good, but what should I do with the false positives? Did a response of six hits and zero false alarms indicate the same accuracy as a response of 14 hits and eight false alarms?

Unknown to me, this type of problem had already been extensively studied in the context of signal detection theory during the 1950s (Swets, 1973). Researchers in psychology have long been interested in quantifying how well individuals perceive certain types of lights and sounds. The solution developed by Swets and his colleagues was the ROC curve. The ROC is a plot of hits (true positives; cases with the predictor and the outcome) and false positives (cases with the predictor but not the outcome) for all possible decision thresholds. The researchers who developed the ROC wanted an index of accuracy that was not unduly influenced by motivation, or the raters' natural tendencies to be bold or cautious when guessing. The ROC approach to quantifying accuracy was not widely known in the 1980s. When I described my measurement problem to my honors thesis advisors, none of them recommended the AUC. Since that time, the use of AUC has caught on in medicine and psychology; currently, it is a standard statistic used to describe the accuracy (discrimination) of both diagnostic and prognostic measures.

AUCs are popular because they provide a simple and effective method of comparing the accuracy of different measures (Swets et al., 2000). The AUC statistic is also an excellent general-purpose effect size statistic for describing the magnitude of differences between two groups (Ruscio, 2008). When comparing different measures, the measure with the highest AUC is almost always "better than" a measure with a lower AUC value (all else being equal). Being an ordinal statistic, the AUC values are not unduly influenced by extreme values. The scaling of the risk tool is also of no concern; all that matters is how the tool orders individuals. Another desirable property is that AUC values are robust to the base rate of the outcome. Consequently, it is possible to compare AUC values across studies even when the base rate of the outcome is substantially different.

Consider the relationship of height to being selected for a school's basketball team. In this example, 40 girls show up for tryouts, of whom 10 will be selected for the A team. The coach starts by lining the girls up from tallest to shortest and assigns each a number between 1 (tallest) and 40 (shortest). Notice that the coach doesn't need to be concerned about inches or centimeters; all the coach needs to decide is whether Susan is taller than Gail. Consequently, height is used as an ordinal, or rank order, measure. If height were the only selection criteria, then the AUC value for height predicting team selection would be 1.0. This would mean that all of the 10 girls selected for the team were taller than the tallest of the 30 girls who were not selected. A more typical selection procedure would consider both height and skill, perhaps resulting in an AUC value of .70 for height alone. An AUC value in this example would mean that there is a 70% chance that a randomly selected girl from the A team is taller than a randomly selected girl who did not make the team.

Now consider that the coach wants to increase the roster from 10 to 20. This would increase the base rate of the outcome (being selected for the A team) from 25% to 50%. If the coach used only height at the selection criterion, then the 20-member team would include the 20 tallest girls, again resulting in an AUC value of 1.0. If the coach used the more typical combination of height and skill to select the additional 10 members, then the AUC value would remain close to .70. In other words, changing the size of the team should not change the AUC values, provided that the same selection criteria are being used. With the 20-member team, there would still be a 70% chance that a randomly selected girl from the A team is taller than a randomly selected girl who did not make the expanded team, even if the average height of the girls was shorter in the 20-member roster than the 10-member roster.

LIMITATIONS

The AUC is a measure of discrimination, not calibration. It says nothing about how likely individuals are to have the outcome, which is often of primary importance in applied decisions. Because the AUC controls for the base rate, the same AUC values across studies could be associated with wildly different recidivism rates per score or risk level.

Another limitation is that AUC values are sensitive to restriction of range in the prediction measure: the smaller the variability of the predictor, the smaller the AUC value (Hanson, 2008; Howard, 2017). For example, if the new coach only considered girls who were at least 5′8″ for the 10 member A team, the pool of potential candidates could be restricted to tall girls. If the new coach then used exactly the same combination of height and skill to select from this restricted sample, the AUC value for height would be smaller than .70, perhaps .60. Consequently, without considering the initial variability, the AUC values may mistakenly imply that the new coach was less concerned with height than the previous coach. For readers interested in discrimination (relative risk) statistics that are less influenced by restriction of range in the predictor, see the chapters on Cox regression (Chapter 10) and logistic regression (Chapter 11).

Another limitation of the AUC is that it does not consider time. For many significant outcomes, the timing of the outcome is as important as whether the outcome occurs or not (e.g., recovery from depression, language acquisition, desistance from crime, death). For such contexts, survival analysis is more informative than ROC analysis. Specifically, Harrell's Concordance (Harrell's C) is an effect size statistic from Cox regression survival analysis (see Chapter 10) that is interpreted much like the AUC. Specifically, given two randomly selected cases, Harrell's C is the probability that the case who had the outcome first also had the higher risk score. With variable follow-up time, Harrell's C is a more sensitive statistic (lower standard error) than the AUC because it uses more of the available information.

THE NUTS AND BOLTS

Data Requirements

The following data are required to calculate the AUC for a prediction study:

1. a dichotomous (present/absent) outcome variable,
2. an ordinal or continuous predictor variable, and
3. the predictor variable exists before the outcome.

AUC values can also be calculated when both the predictor and the outcome variable are dichotomous (two by two tables), but its use with these tables poorly matches the measurement model on which the ROC framework was based. Consequently, it tends to be unstable, being influenced by arbitrary features of the data in two by two tables. If the focus is on two by two tables, then statistics designed for them, such as rate ratios and odds ratios, are preferred over AUC values (see Chapter 7).

Calculating AUC Values

AUC values are calculated in two steps. The first step constructs the ROC curve; the second step calculates the area under that curve. The ROC curve is a plot of the sensitivity and one minus the specificity for each value of the predictor variable. Sensitivity and specificity are calculated from two by two tables constructed by considering every possible cut-point in the predictor variable as a dichotomous predictor variable. In two by two tables, sensitivity is the number with the predictor and the outcome divided by all cases with the outcome (A/[A + C]; see Table 7.1 and Table 7.3 in the previous chapter). Specificity is the number without the predictor who do not have the outcome divided by all cases without the outcome (D/[B + D]). One minus specificity is the number of cases with the predictor but not the outcome divided by the cases without the outcome (B/[B + D]; also called *false positives* or *false alarms*). Because sensitivity only considers cases with the outcome and specificity only considers cases without the outcome, the shape of the ROC curve is conceptually independent of the base rate.

Once the ROC curve is constructed, researchers have two options for calculating the AUC: the fitted curve method or the trapezoidal method. Different computer programs use one or the other, and users can select their preference. In general, the trapezoidal method will provide AUC values slightly smaller than the fitted curve method; however, the differences are negligible when the number of points defining the ROC curve is greater than eight. The fitted curve method, as its name suggests, connects the points in the ROC using a mathematical function and then uses calculus to compute the area under the function. The trapezoidal method uses basic geometry and can be computed with a spreadsheet or the calculator that is preloaded on your phone.

Worked Example

To demonstrate the calculation of the AUC value, we will use a hypothetical example of relapse to substance abuse for men on community supervision (probation or parole) in Aucland (not be to confused with Auckland, the city in New Zealand). There are two substance abuse programs in this community that accept individuals with a criminal conviction: (a) a residential program and (b) a community program. Because there are limited spaces in the residential program (and it is expensive), it is reserved for those most in need of intensive services. To facilitate the referral process, the correctional service developed the Substance Abuse Need Evaluation (SANE). It contains items such as (a) current offense was committed while impaired by drugs or alcohol, (b) self-reports of a substance abuse problem, and (c) substance use has interfered with prosocial goals. The SANE is a structured professional judgment measure, meaning that evaluators do not interpret a total score; instead, they summarize the assessment information into three possible risk levels: *high*, for clients who need intensive residential services; *moderate*, for clients who need intervention but can be adequately managed in the community; and *low*, for clients who do not need specialized substance abuse programming.

Before implementing the risk tool, the correctional service conducted a study that included 100 probation clients, with the outcome criteria being relapse within 2 years postrelease. The basic data from this study are presented in

TABLE 8.1. Two Forms of Raw Data for Area Under the Curve Analysis of a Hypothetical Relapse Study

A. The raw data in words			B. The raw data in numbers		
Case	Risk level	Relapsed within 2 years?	Case	Risk level	Relapsed within 2 years?
RKH	Low	No	1	1	0
AJRH	Moderate	Yes	2	2	1
BH	Moderate	No	3	2	0
LMH	Low	No	4	1	0
VQ	High	Yes	5	3	1
.	.	.	.	.	.
.	.	.	.	.	.
.	.	.	.	.	.
PEM	Low	No	100	1	1

Table 8.1. The upper panel is the findings in words; the lower panel is the same information in numbers. For AUC analysis, the numeric values for the risk levels can be anything, as long as the value for moderate risk is higher than the value for low risk, and the value for high risk is higher than the value for moderate risk. The data format in Table 8.1 is that most commonly used by computer programs to calculate AUC values.

When calculating AUC values by hand, however, it is more convenient to reorganize the data into the form of Table 8.2. In our example, the base rate of relapse was 40% (40 out of 100). Half of the sample (50 out of 100) were rated as low risk, 30% were rated as moderate risk, and 20% were rated as high risk. The observed relapse rates within 2 years for the low-, moderate-, and high-risk groups were 20.0% (10/50), 53.3% (16/30), and 70.0% (14/20), respectively.

The ROC is calculated from the number who relapsed and the number who did not relapse at each level of the risk tool. The ROC can also be considered a summary of decision rules (see Table 8.3). These decision rules are the thresholds where relapse is expected. For example, if only the high-risk group was expected to relapse, all individuals designated as high risk would be expected to relapse. This would correctly identify 14 of the total of 40 individuals who relapsed (hits). As well, it would incorrectly indicate six individuals as relapsing out of the 60 individuals who did not relapse (false positives). Setting the decision threshold low will increase the proportion of hits but also

TABLE 8.2. Summarized Data for a Risk Tool With Three Levels (Substance Abuse Need Evaluation)

Risk level	Sample size	Relapsed	Did not relapse	Relapse rate
Low	50	10	40	.200
Moderate	30	16	14	.533
High	20	14	6	.700
Total	100	40	60	.40

TABLE 8.3. Data Organized for Hand Calculation of Receiver Operating Characteristic Curve

Risk level	Those who relapsed			Those who did not relapse		
	Each level, *n*	This level or higher, *n*	This level or higher, %	Each level, *n*	This level or higher, *n*	This level or higher, %
Low	10	40	1.00	40	60	1.00
Moderate	16	30	.75	14	20	.33
High	14	14	.35	6	6	.10
Higher than high	0	0	0	0	0	0
Total	40			60		

increase the proportion of false positives (reduces the specificity). Setting the decision threshold high decreases false alarms but decreases hits. The ROC is a summary measure of hits and false positives across the full range of possible decision thresholds.

The Lowest Case

As shown in Table 8.3, the lowest possible decision threshold is to say that anybody with a score of low or higher will relapse. This correctly identifies all 40 who relapse (a good thing); however, it also incorrectly identifies all 60 individuals who did not relapse as relapsing (a bad thing). Because this decision threshold necessarily captures all individuals, this decision point provides no information; however, it is required for the calculation of the ROC.

The Moderate Case

The next possible decision threshold (and the first reasonable one) is to say that all those with a moderate rating or higher will relapse. This correctly identifies 75.0% of those who relapse (30/40) and 33.3% of those who do not (20/60).

The High Case

When the threshold is set as high risk, the proportion of hits is 35% (14/40) and the proportion of false positives is now only 10% (6/60).

The Maximum (Highest) Case

The ROC also considers a threshold higher than the maximum possible value (higher than high). Because nobody ever has such a rating (by definition), the proportion of hits and false positives for this decision threshold will always be zero.

As demonstrated in Figure 8.1, the ROC is the plot of the proportion of hits and false positives for every possible decision threshold. The vertical axis is the cumulative proportion of individuals who relapsed that were correctly identified as relapsing (also called *sensitivity*), and the horizontal axis is the cumulative proportion of individuals who did not relapse who were incorrectly expected to relapse (also called *1 – specificity*). In general, the number of line segments in the ROC curve will equal the number of levels, the number of points that define the curve will be one more than the number of lines, and the number of inflection points in the curve will be one less than the number of levels. In the current example, with a three-level rating scheme, the ROC has four points, three line segments, and two informative inflection points (moderate or higher; high only). The two most extreme points in a ROC curve will always be (0, 0) and (1, 1). The AUC is the part of the 1.0 × 1.0 box that is below the line drawn by the ROC curve (cross-hatched with dotted lines). In this example, the AUC is .729, a large effect for a prediction tool. Also indicated on the figure is a diagonal line indicating what the graph would look like if the risk tool provided no information (AUC of .50).

FIGURE 8.1. The Receiver Operating Curve for the Substance Abuse Need Evaluation, a Hypothetical Three-Level Risk Tool

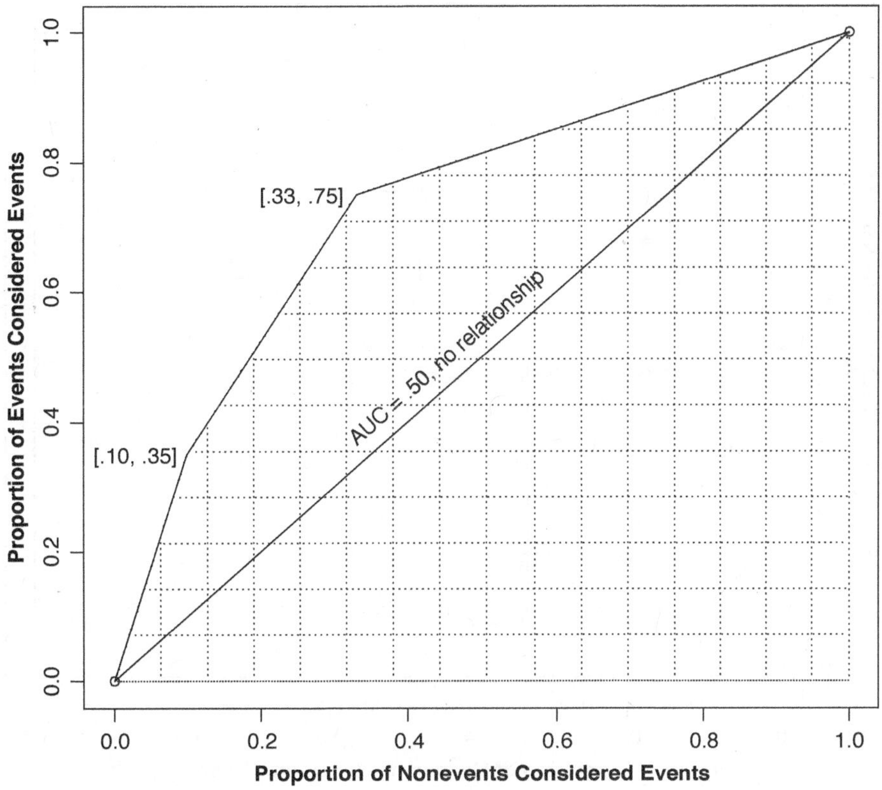

Note. AUC = area under the curve.

As demonstrated by Figure 8.2, the first step in the trapezoidal method is to divide the area into triangles and squares, which are labeled a, b, c, d, and e. The AUC is simply the sum of the areas of a, b, c, d, and e. The calculations are shown in Table 8.4.

Interpreting the Shape of the ROC Curve

Although we are mostly interested in the total area under the ROC curve, the shape of the ROC also can provide useful information. In particular, the shape indicates how well different thresholds discriminate between those with or without the outcome. For example, the shape of a ROC curve may indicate whether a risk tool is better at identifying high-risk individuals (positive predictive accuracy) or low-risk individuals (negative predictive accuracy).

Positive predictive accuracy is important when decision makers want high confidence that the individual in question has the problem before the intervention is applied, typically because the intervention is expensive or aversive. For example, in the Canadian criminal justice system, it is possible to designate an individual as a Dangerous Offender based on, among other criteria, the likelihood that the individual will commit another serious personal injury

FIGURE 8.2. Calculating the Area Under the Curve Using the Trapezoids in the Receiver Operating Characteristic Curve Graph

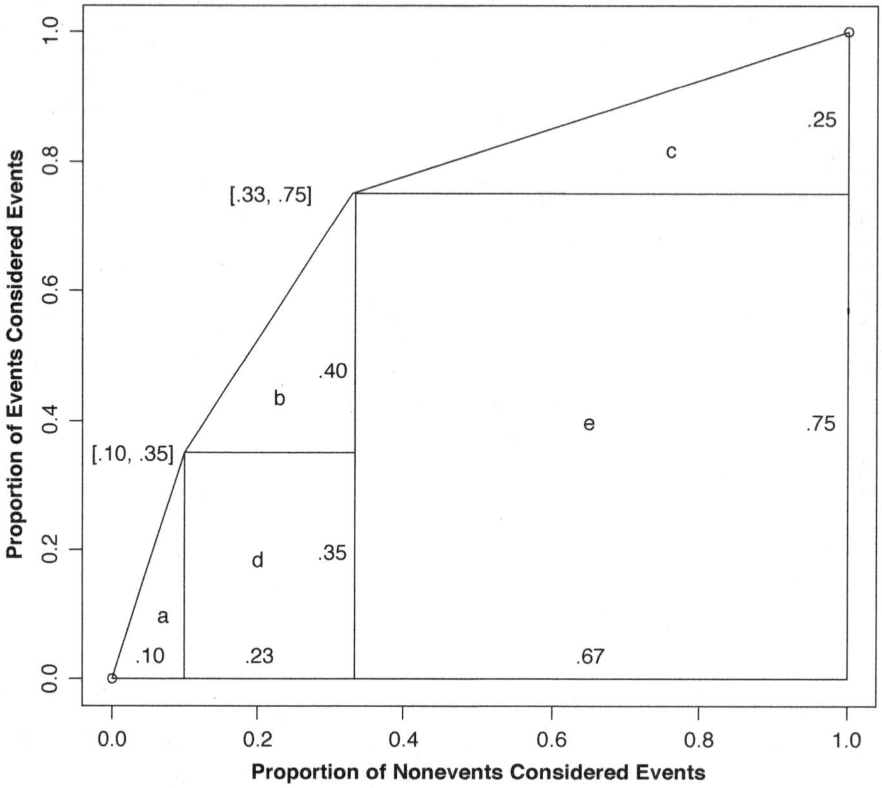

offense. This designation is rare, and individuals so designated are effectively given life sentences with little opportunity for parole. Consequently, judges want assurance that the individual is indeed likely to reoffend before sentencing the case as a Dangerous Offender. Conversely, negative predictive accuracy is important when decision makers desire high confidence that the outcome will not occur. For example, parole board members want to release individuals from incarceration when their risk of criminal recidivism is low. Consequently, one risk tool may be particularly useful for Dangerous Offender evaluations, whereas a different risk tool may work better for parole board release decisions.

TABLE 8.4. The Trapezoidal Method of Calculating the Area Under the Curve From the Receiver Operating Characteristic in Figure 8.2

Section	Dimensions	Area
a	(.10 × .35)/2	.017500
b	(.233333 × .40)/2	.046667
c	(.666666 × .25)/2	.083333
d	.233333 × .35	.081667
e	.666667 × .75	.500000
Total area		**.72917**

In the ROC curve, the risk levels go from lowest in the top right corner to highest in the bottom left corner. A prediction tool works best in the regions (risk scores) where the ROC curve is close to the outside box and far from the middle diagonal line. When the high scores contain mostly those with the outcome (good positive predictive accuracy), the ROC will be close to the bottom left edge of the box, as in Figure 8.3.

In Figure 8.3, close to half of the individuals with the outcome are in the highest risk group (44%), compared with a very small proportion (5%) of those without the outcome. The points in the AUC do not directly translate into rates of the outcome because the base rate is unknown; however, it is apparent that the high-risk category predominantly identified individuals with the outcome. In comparison, membership in the lowest risk group provides relatively little information: 20% of those with the outcome are in lowest risk level, which is similar to the proportion of individuals without the outcome (29%).

When the low risk levels contain mostly individuals without the outcome (good negative predictive accuracy), the ROC curve will be close to the top edge of the box, like Figure 8.4.

In Figure 8.4, the lowest risk group contained a small proportion of the individuals with the outcome (3%) and a much larger proportion (30%) of

FIGURE 8.3. A Prediction Tool With Good Positive Predictive Accuracy

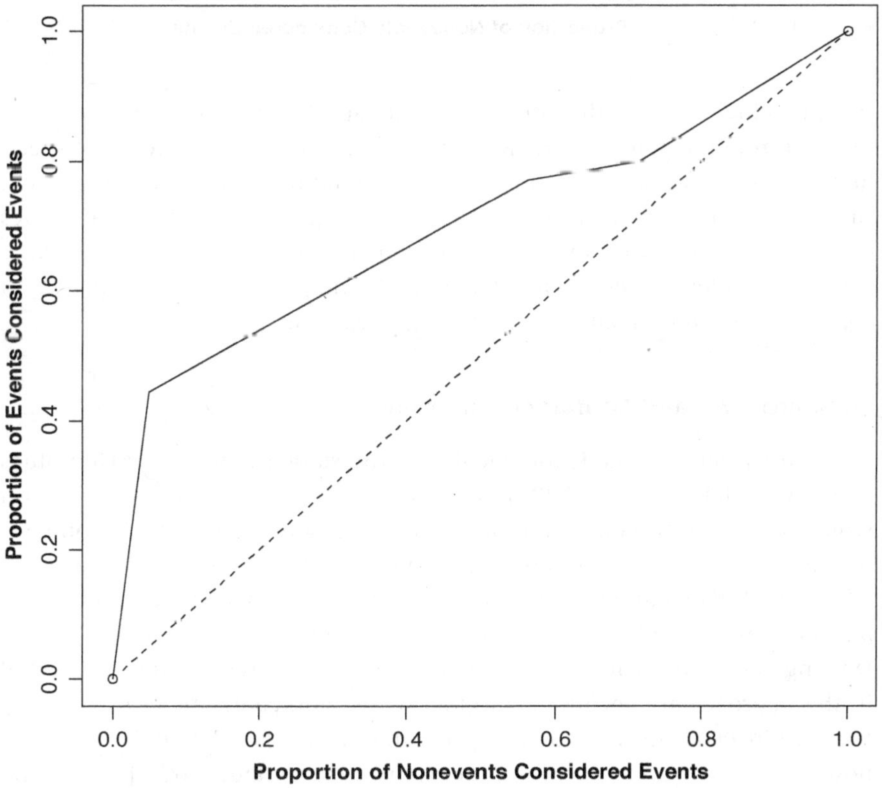

FIGURE 8.4. A Prediction Tool With Good Negative Predictive Accuracy

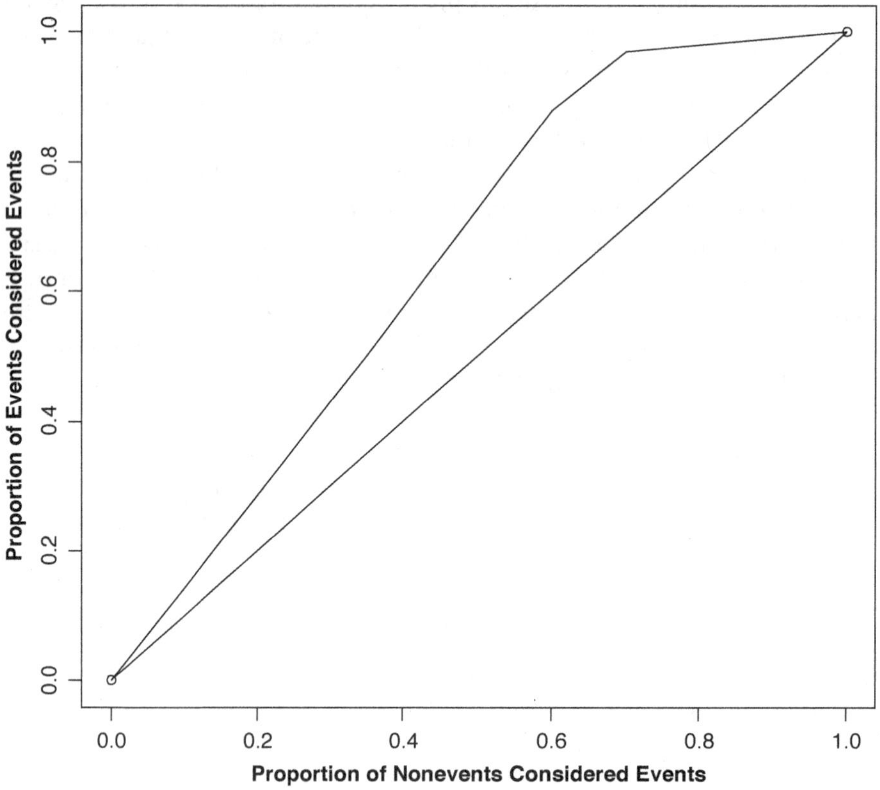

the individuals without the outcome. Again, absolute rates cannot be directly inferred from the points on the ROC curve because the base rate is not specified. Nevertheless, parole board members should prefer the second risk tool (in Figure 8.4) over the previous risk tool (in Figure 8.3) because it provides greater confidence that a low score is actually low. Conversely, judges making Dangerous Offender sentencing decisions should prefer the tool displayed in Figure 8.3, given its ability to identify high risk cases.

Standard Error and Confidence Intervals

There are several methods for calculating the standard error of AUC values (Hanley & Hajian-Tilaki, 1997). The initial selection decision is based on whether the ROC is considered parametric (a smoothed curve) or nonparametric (discrete steps or trapezoids, as in our examples). For nonparametric AUCs, the DeLong and bootstrap methods are recommended, each of which provide similar results (DeLong et al., 1988; Hanley & Hajian-Tilaki, 1997). DeLong standard errors can be calculated by hand; researchers interested in this approach are encouraged to follow the worked examples provided in Babchishin et al. (2012b) and Hanley and Hajian-Tilaki (1997). Typically, however, researchers rely on computer software to compute both the AUC and its standard error. In the ROC program in R Statistics (pROC), the DeLong and bootstrap options are both available, with the default set to the DeLong method (Robin et al., 2011).

Why do you want to know the standard error? The standard error provides information about the precision of the AUC estimate. Typically, the standard error is multiplied by 1.96 to create 95% confidence intervals. This is the range of plausible interpretation. For example, if the 95% confidence interval is .40 to .65, it is possible that the true value is .50, meaning that the risk tool may not be able to predict the outcome any better than chance. It could also mean that the true AUC value is .65, meaning that the risk tool predicts the outcome with moderate accuracy. Large confidence intervals typically indicate that more research is needed, or that the current findings should be combined with the results of previous studies through meta-analysis (see Chapter 14). In our fictitious SANE evaluation, the AUC is .7292, the DeLong standard error is .04858, and the range of the 95% confidence intervals is between .63 and .82.

Comparing AUC Values

Confidence intervals can also be used to compare the predictive accuracy of different risk tools. When the 95% confidence intervals do not overlap, their predictive accuracy can be considered to be different with a statistical significance of $p < .01$ (Cumming & Finch, 2005). This is a conservative approach to comparing AUC values and may be justified when examining multiple measures. If researchers are interested in directly comparing two AUC values, then more statistically powerful approaches are recommended.

Comparing AUC Values From Independent Samples

When the AUCs are computed for two independent samples, they can be compared using the standard formula for the standard error of a difference.

$$SE_{diff} = \sqrt{SE_1^2 + SE_2^2} \tag{8.1}$$

As an example, imagine that the Aucland Correctional Service was not the first to propose a risk tool for predicting relapse. In previous years, other researchers had developed and tested the Individualized Numeric Substance Abuse Need Evaluation (INSANE) on a different sample of 150 individuals. They reported an AUC value of .6000, with a standard error of .0300, resulting in a 95% confidence interval of .54 to .66. The Aucland Correctional Service was not impressed with the INSANE measure, so they commissioned a new measure (the SANE). As noted earlier, our hypothetical SANE measure had an AUC value of .7292, a standard error of .04858, with a 95% confidence interval of .63 to .82. Given that the confidence intervals of the SANE and INSANE overlap, the decision makers may want to go further to determine whether the apparent improvement of the SANE over the INSANE is more than would be expected by chance. The difference between the AUC values is .1292, and the standard error of the difference is $.05710 = ((.0300)^2 + (.04858)^2)^{1/2}$, using Equation 8.1. The 95% CI for the observed difference is the observed difference plus and minus 1.96 times the standard error of the difference (difference ± $1.96(SE_{difference})$), in our example, .1292 ± 1.96(.05710), or from .0173 to .2411. Because the confidence interval for the difference did not include zero, there are reasonable grounds to believe that the SANE is more accurate than the INSANE. Because the confidence interval is still wide, more research would be needed to make any strong statements concerning how much better it is.

Comparing AUC Values From the Same Sample

When two measures are used on the same subjects, the statistical power to detect differences increases. The standard formula for estimating the standard error of a difference between correlated measures is as follows:

$$SE_{dif} = \sqrt{SE_1^2 + SE_2^2 - 2covariance_{1^\circ 2}} \tag{8.2}$$

Notice that this is the same formula for independent groups, with the exception that it is reduced by a factor proportional to the covariance between the two measures. Whenever risk tools are positively correlated, it is more efficient to test them together on the same subjects than to use two samples, one for each measure. There are several methods for estimating the covariance between two prediction tools; among these, the DeLong method is recommended for nonparametric data, and a bootstrap standard error is recommended for parametric data (Hanley & Hajian-Tilaki, 1997; Robin et al., 2011).

The standard error is also required for asking questions about whether a new measure is more accurate than other similar measures. For example, before conducting the study that led to the development of the SANE, the Aucland Correctional Service may have commissioned a review of the accuracy (discrimination) of other measures designed to predict relapse. The average effect size in the previous studies could be summarized by meta-analysis and then compared with effect size for the SANE (see Borenstein et al., 2010; Hanson & Broom, 2005). Readers will find further applications of meta-analysis when it is used to evaluate calibration (Chapter 14).

GOING FURTHER

Readers who have made it this far should have sufficient understanding of AUCs to be educated consumers of research studies using this statistic. The following sections are intended for students and researchers who want further mastery, typically because they are considering using AUCs in their own research projects. The next steps comprise three sections: (a) recommended readings, (b) exercises involving calculating an AUC value by hand, and

(c) computer code for calculating AUC values from data sets. These sections can be worked with in any order, and it is not necessary to do all (or any) of them.

Recommended Readings

Swets, J. A., Dawes, R. M., & Monahan, J. (2000). Psychological science can improve diagnostic decisions. *Psychological Science in the Public Interest, 1*(1), 1–26. https://doi.org/10.1111/1529-1006.001

This is a very readable introduction by John Swets, who was instrumental in developing ROC statistics. His coauthors, Robin Dawes and John Monahan, have been key figures in advancing statistical prediction tools within psychology. This article focuses on AUC in the context of diagnosis (i.e., the outcome is present at the time of assessment); however, the article also discusses some examples of using AUCs with prediction tools (e.g., weather forecasting).

Mossman, D. (1994). Assessing predictions of violence: Being accurate about accuracy. *Journal of Consulting and Clinical Psychology, 62*(4), 783–792. https://doi.org/10.1037/0022-006x.62.4.783

In this article, Douglas Mossman introduces the AUC in the context of evaluating the risk for violence. The focus is evaluating the quality of evidence across studies (i.e., systematic reviews and meta-analyses).

Computer Code

Both R Statistics and IBM/SPSS have routines for calculating AUC values and plotting ROC curves. Their algorithms are similar, although not identical for all analyses.

R Code

If you have not already done so, start by downloading the pROC package (Robin et al., 2011).

```
install.packages ("pROC")
```

The **install.packages** command will ask you to choose a site (CRAN Mirror) from which to download the software. Choose one close to you. Next, indicate that you would like to use that set of programs:

```
library(pROC)
```

The data set used in this example is called Chap8_AUC_example.csv; it is the same data presented in Table 8.2 (SANE, Study 1), reorganized with one row per case. The EXCEL.csv file has three variables: *Case* (1–100), *Level* (1 = *low*, 2 = *moderate*, 3 = *high*), and *Relapse* (0 = *no*; 1 = *yes*). If you would like to run the analyses yourself, the data set is available at https://www.apa.org/pubs/books/prediction-statistics-for-psychological-assessment. The next two lines identify the data set to analyze and tells R that you want to work with that data set. In this example, the data set is on my c:\ drive, in a directory called Book, i.e., c:\run.files\Book\Chap8_AUC_example.csv. You will need to download the Excel file and make note of where it is stored on your computer. The **read.csv** command requires double backslashes.

```
AUCdata <- read.csv("c:\\run.files\\Book\\Chap8_AUC_
example.csv")
attach (AUCdata)
```

Now you are ready to compute the ROC curve.

```
roc(Relapse, Level)
```

The two variables in the **roc** command are the dichotomous outcome variable (in this example, *Relapse*) and the predictor variable (*Level*). The **roc** command will automatically provide the AUC, in the SANE example from the Aucland correctional service, the AUC value calculated by the **roc** command is .7292. If you want the 95% confidence interval, it is useful to create a ROC object; this will save steps later on.

```
exampleROC <- roc(Relapse, Level)
```

Then you can ask R to conduct analyses on the ROC object instead of the raw data. For example, to compute confidence intervals, use **ci.auc**:

```
ci.auc(exampleROC)
```

By default, **ci.auc** produces 95% confidence intervals using the DeLong method:

```
95% CI: 0.634-0.8244 (DeLong)
```

This is a reasonable choice in most situations. If you would like to see what the ROC curve looks like, then type

```
plot (exampleROC)
```

This will produce a plot very much like Figure 8.1.

The **roc.test** command compares two AUC values, using the DeLong method as the default. There are several ways of writing the syntax, of which the following two are the most common:

```
roc.test(first ROC object, second ROC object, . . . )
```

or

```
roc.test (response, first predictor, second predictor,
  . . .)
```

The first option compares two previously defined ROC objects. The second option creates the required ROC objects and the correlation between the predictors from the data set (a set of vectors).

IBM/SPSS Code

The SPSS analyses use the data set called Chap8_AUC_example.sav, which contains three variables for the hypothetical SANE risk tool: *Case*, a case identifier; *Level*, with values of 1, 2, or 3; and *Relapse*, with values of 1 for *yes* or 0 for *no*. The data set is available at https://www.apa.org/pubs/books/prediction-statistics-for-psychological-assessment.

Once the data set is loaded in SPSS, you can run the analyses either through drop-down menus or syntax (see the syntax file called "Prediction Statistics SPSS syntax.sps" also available at https://www.apa.org/pubs/books/prediction-statistics-for-psychological-assessment). Using drop-down menus, click **ANALYZE**, then **CLASSIFY**, then **ROC CURVE**. Select *Level* as the test variable, and *Relapse* as the state variable. The value of the state variable in our example is 1. Select the 95% confidence intervals to be printed. The syntax is as follows:

```
ROC Level BY Relapse (1)
/PLOT=CURVE
/PRINT=SE
/CRITERIA=CUTOFF(INCLUDE) TESTPOS(LARGE)
DISTRIBUTION(FREE) CI(95)
/MISSING=EXCLUDE.
```

This produces the AUC curve plotted using the trapezoidal method (see Figure 8.5) and the following table:

Area Under the Curve

Test result variable(s): level

			Asymptotic 95% CI	
Area	***SE*[a]**	**Asymptotic sig.[b]**	**Lower bound**	**Upper bound**
.729	.052	.000	.626	.832

Note. The test result variable(s): Level has at least one tie between the positive actual state group and the negative actual state group. Statistics may be biased. CI = confidence interval.
[a]Under the nonparametric assumption. [b]Null hypothesis: true area = 0.5.

The AUC value is the same as that calculated using the trapezoidal, nonparametric method (by hand, or by R syntax). The nonparametric standard error and confidence intervals calculated by SPSS version 27 are slightly different from those calculated by R. The AUC standard errors in SPSS version 26 (and higher versions) are also different from those calculated in previous versions of SPSS. Although the differences are not big enough to be practically important, it is good practice to identify the version of the software used when reporting AUCs and their confidence intervals.

IBM/SPSS version 26 (and higher) introduced a program for comparing AUCs. Click **ANALYZE**, then **CLASSIFY**, then **ROC ANALYSIS**. This program uses the DeLong method to compare correlated AUCs. When comparing correlated AUCs value in SPSS, the confidence intervals for the individual

FIGURE 8.5. IBM/SPSS Receiver Operating Characteristic Graph for the Hypothetical Three-Level Substance Abuse Need Evaluation Risk Tool

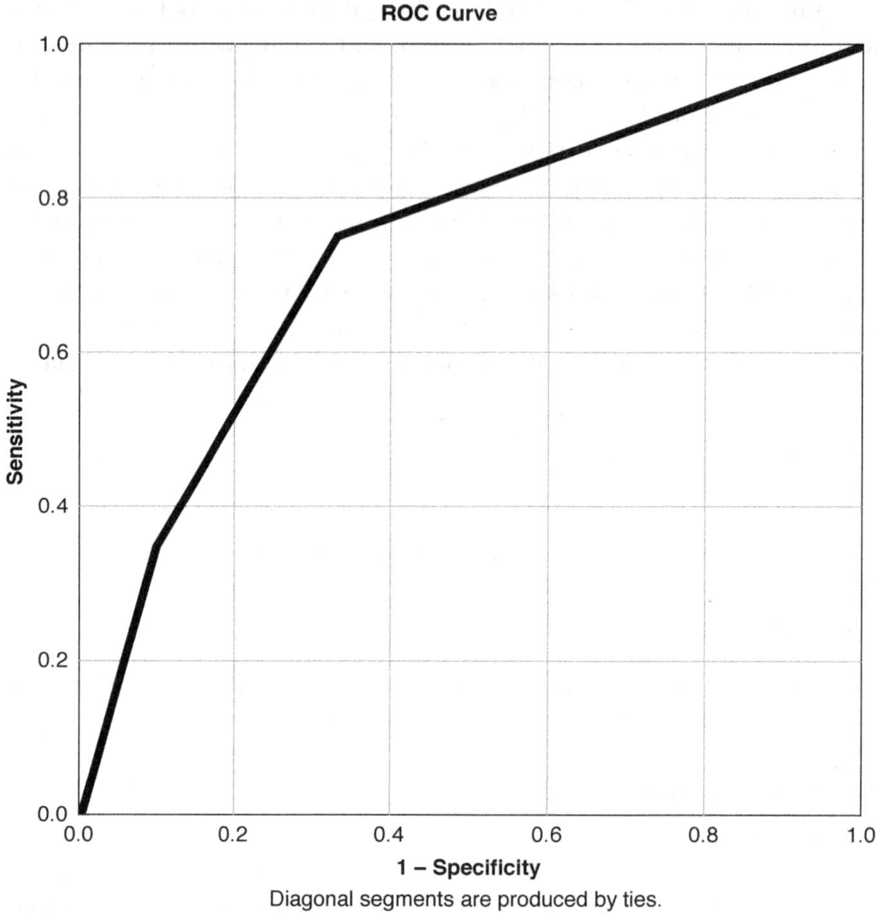

predictors are now also calculated using the DeLong method (the same as in R Statistics). Consequently, if you are using SPSS and want the DeLong standard errors, include the predictor along with other predictors in a **Paired-Sample Design**, and request *Standard error and confidence interval* in the **Display** option.

EXERCISES

The Aucland Correctional Service was encouraged by the results of the initial study of the SANE prediction tool. They are mindful, however, of the need for replication before risk tools are used for applied purposes. Consequently, they conduct another validation study of the SANE, this time using a shorter follow-up time (1 year) and a larger sample (150 participants). They are also concerned that there were too many individuals in the low group who

TABLE 8.5. Summarized Data for a Risk Tool With Four Levels (SANE-R)

Risk level	Sample size	Relapsed	Did not relapse	Relapse rate
Very low	30	0	30	.000
Low	20	4	16	.200
Moderate	60	21	39	.350
High	40	20	20	.500
Total	150	45	105	.300

relapsed. To respond to this concern, the test developers introduced a new category, very low risk, to identify individuals who would be extremely unlikely to have substance abuse problems in the future (e.g., individuals who never had any problems with substances in the past). The test developers label the revised scale the SANE-R. The results of the SANE-R study are displayed in Table 8.5.

Question 8.1

(i) Calculate the coordinates of the ROC curve for the SANE-R. Start by constructing a table similar to Table 8.3.

(ii) Using graph paper (or lined paper and a ruler), plot the points of the ROC curve.

(iii) On the basis of a visual inspection of the graph, is the SANE-R better at identifying individuals who relapse or better at identifying individuals who will not relapse? Justify your answer.

(iv) Using the trapezoidal method, calculate the AUC for the ROC for the SANE-R.

(v) Using R, SPSS, or any other software of your choice (you will need to enter the information in Table 8.5 into a data file that can be read by your program):

- **(a)** Verify that your hand calculation of the AUC for the SANE-R was correct.
- **(b)** Calculate the standard error and 95% confidence intervals for the SANE-R AUC value.

Question 8.2

The researchers want to know how well the SANE (the original three levels) worked in the new study.

(i) Calculate the points in the ROC curve for the SANE by aggregating the values for the low and very low risk levels in Table 8.5.

(ii) Plot the ROC points for both the SANE-R and SANE in the same graph.

(iii) Using the pROC procedure in R Statistics, or the software of your choice,

(a) Calculate the AUC for the SANE along with its 95% confidence interval.

(b) On the basis of the confidence intervals for the SANE and SANE-R in study 2, what could you conclude about their relative predictive accuracy?

(c) Using an analysis that considers the correlation between the SANE and SANE-R (DeLong or bootstrap), is the difference in AUC values statistically significant? What would you now conclude about their relative predictive accuracy?

ANSWERS TO EXERCISES

Question 8.1

(i) Table 8.6 shows the data organized for hand calculation of the SANE-R. The coordinates of the ROC curve are the values in the columns labelled "% this level or higher."

(ii) The ROC plot of Table 8.6 is shown in Figure 8.6. Those who did not relapse are plotted on the x (horizontal axis) and those who relapsed are plotted on the y (vertical axis). Plot from the bottom of the column to the top.

This graph is plotted using R Statistics. Your hand-drawn graph should look similar. The diagonal line from (0,0) to (1,1) is optional.

(iii) On the basis of visual inspection of the graph, the ROC curve for the SANE-R looks more like Figure 8.4 than Figure 8.3, indicating that it does relatively better at identifying those who did not relapse compared with identifying those who relapsed (relatively high negative predictive accuracy).

(iv) The first step to calculating the AUC using the trapezoidal method is dividing the ROC curve into triangles and rectangles, as in Figure 8.7. Note that there are several different ways of dividing it up, so don't worry if they way you did it was not identical to the example shown in Figure 8.7.

Once the trapezoids are identified, the next step is calculating the area of each of the pieces. The sum of these areas is the AUC. In the calculation, retain more significant figures than you plan to report. For example, if you plan to report two significant figures (e.g., .73), conduct the calculations with four or more significant figures. The AUC in this exercise is 0.725 when reported to three significant figures or 0.7254 when reported to four significant figures. Table 8.7 includes up to six significant figures, which is more than is typically required.

(v) Most programs require you to organize the data one row per subject, as in the lower section of Table 8.1. Once the data are cleaned and in a usable format, the analyses are usually straightforward.

(a) AUC = .7254, based on the nonparametric (or trapezoidal) method in the pROC program in R or the nonparametric estimate in SPSS.

(b) *SE* = 0.03818, 95% confidence interval of .6506 to .8002 (DeLong method) in R (and the paired comparison analysis in IBM/SPSS). In SPSS, the default standard error is 0.041 with 95% confidence interval of .645 to .806.

Question 8.2

(i) The points on the ROC curve for the SANE in Study 2 are shown in Table 8.8.

TABLE 8.6. Data Organized for Hand Calculation of Receiver Operating Characteristic for the Four-Level Substance Abuse Need Evaluation—Revised

Risk level	Those who relapsed			Those who did not relapse		
	Each level, *n*	This level or higher, *n*	This level or higher, %	Each level, *n*	This level or higher, *n*	This level or higher, %
Very low	0	45	1.00	30	105	1.00
Low	4	45	1.00	16	75	.714
Moderate	21	41	.911	39	59	.562
High	20	20	.444	20	20	.190
Higher than high	0	0	0	0	0	0
Total	45			105		

FIGURE 8.6. The Receiver Operating Curve for the Substance Abuse Need Evaluation—Revised, a Four-Level Risk Tool

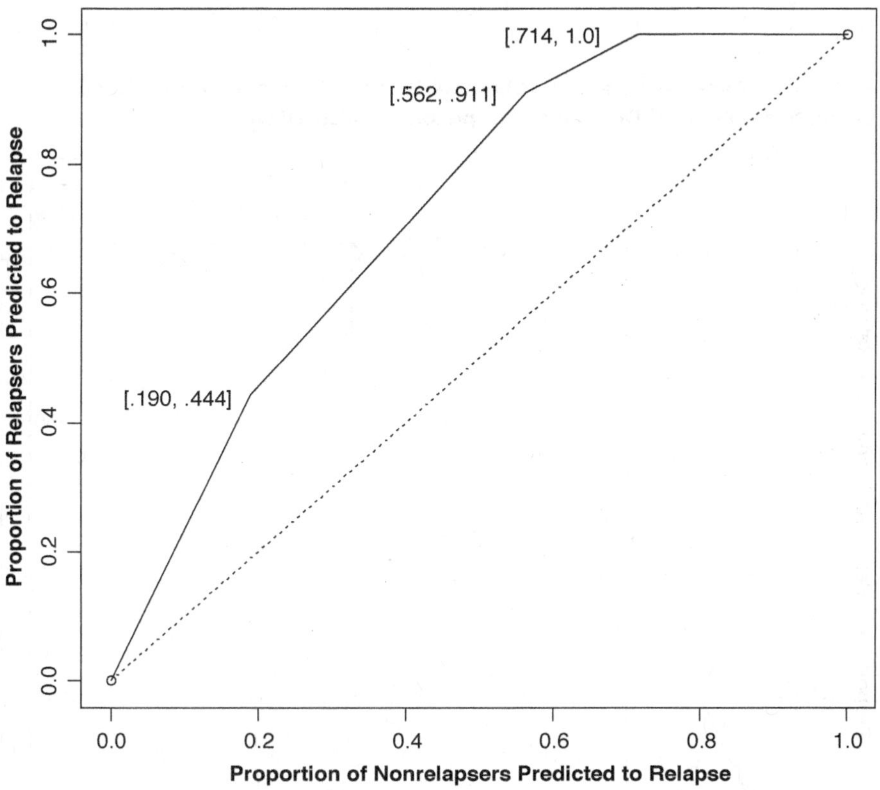

Notice that combining the low- and very low-risk levels eliminates the point associated with very low risk, but all the other coordinates remain the same.

(ii) ROC plot of SANE and SANER is shown in Figure 8.8.

The dashed segment from (.562, .911) to (1.0, 1.0) is where the SANE is different from the SANE-R.

(iii) To conduct these analyses, you will need to create a data set with a row for each participant and three columns: relapse (yes–no), SANE-R score (four levels, e.g., 0, 1, 2, 3), and SANE score (three levels, e.g., 1, 2, 3).

(a) The trapezoidal AUC for the SANE in Study 2 is .7127, with 95% confidence interval of .6333 to .7921 (DeLong) or .626 to .798 (SPSS).

(b) The AUCs and confidence intervals for the SANE-R and SANE were .725 (.65 to .80) and .713 (.63 to .79), respectively. On the basis of wide overlap of the confidence intervals, it is reasonable to conclude that the AUC values were similar for both versions.

(c) Use the DeLong method (from pROC in R or IBM/SPSS **ROC Analysis**). The DeLong method identified that the difference was more than

FIGURE 8.7. Receiver Operating Characteristic for Substance Abuse Need Evaluation—Revised Divided for Trapezoidal Calculation

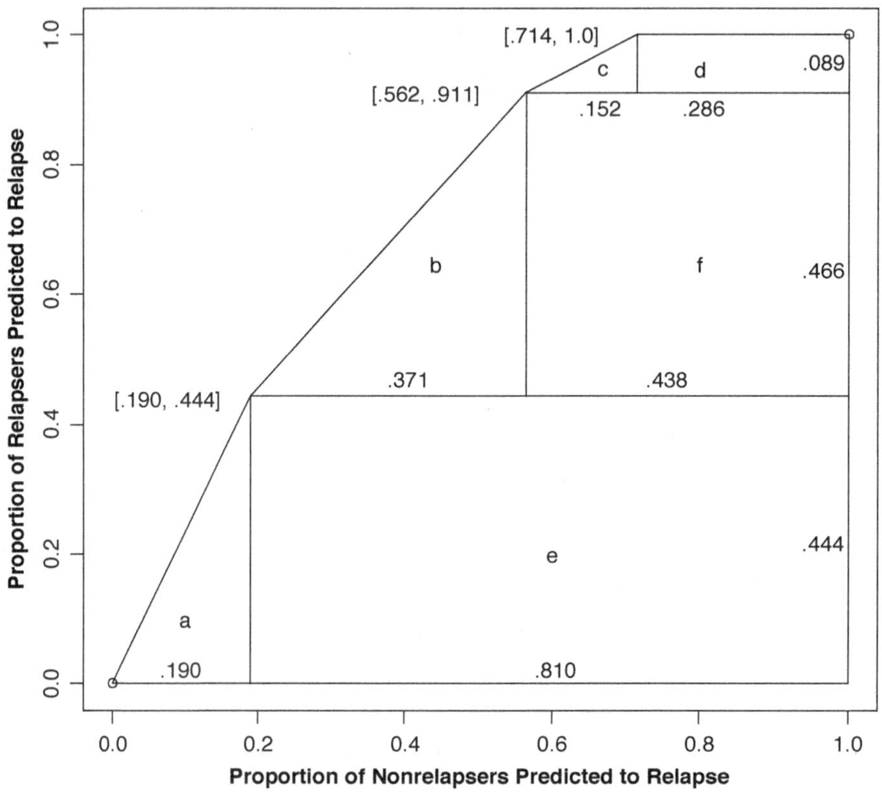

TABLE 8.7. Trapezoidal Method of Calculating the Area Under the Curve From the Receiver Operating Characteristic in Figure 8.7

Section	Dimensions	Area
a	0.190476 × (0.444444)/2	= 0.042328
b	0.371429 × (0.466666)/2	= 0.086667
c	0.152381 × (0.088889)/2	= 0.006772
d	0.285714 × 0.088889	= 0.025397
e	0.809524 × 0.444444	= 0.359788
f	0.438095 × 0.466667	= 0.204444
Total area		0.725397

TABLE 8.8. Data Organized for Hand Calculation of the of Receiver Operating Characteristic Coordinates for the Three-Level Substance Abuse Need Evaluation in Study 2

	Those who relapsed			Those who did not relapse		
Risk level	Each level, *n*	This level or higher, *n*	This level or higher, %	Each level, *n*	This level or higher, *n*	This level or higher, %
Low	4	90	1.000	46	105	1.000
Moderate	21	41	.911	39	59	.562
High	20	20	.444	20	20	.190
Higher than high	0	0	0	0	0	0
Total	45			105		

FIGURE 8.8. The Receiver Operating Characteristic Curves for the Substance Abuse Need Evaluation (SANE) and SANE—Revised in Study 2

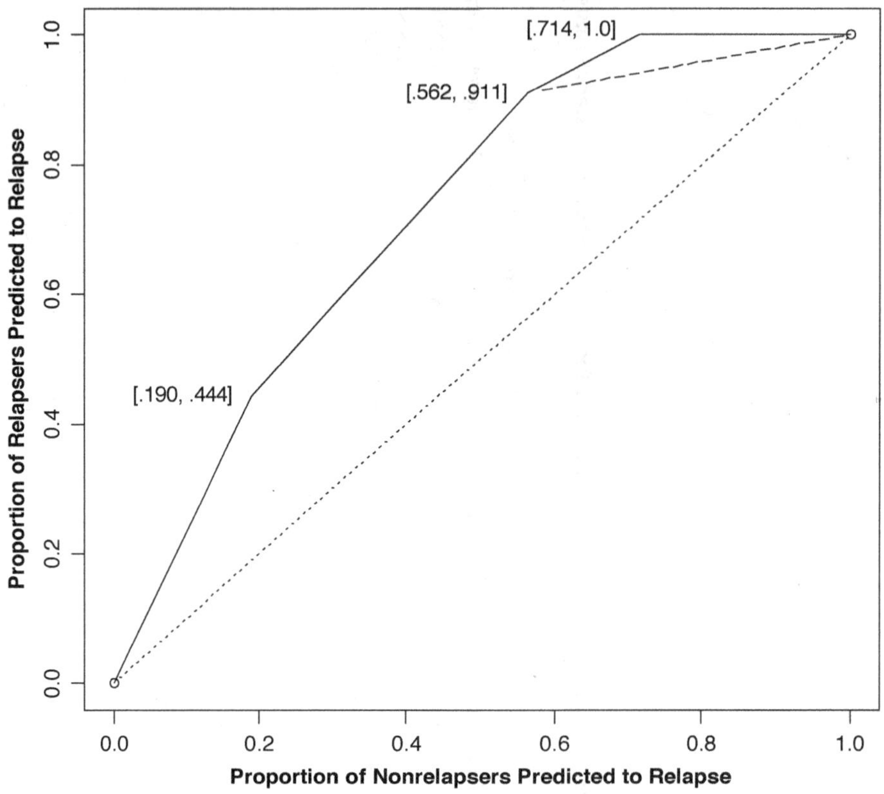

> would be expected by chance ($Z = 1.973$, $p = .0485$). Even though the observed difference was small (0.0127), the very high correlation between the measures ($r = .954$) resulted in a small standard error of the difference and narrow confidence intervals (.00008135 to .0253). In this case, SPSS easily provides the confidence interval for the difference, whereas pROC does not. Both programs use the same default method for comparing AUC values (DeLong). The bootstrap method in pROC also indicated a significant difference between the AUC values at $p = .04637$. The bootstrap values will change slightly with each analysis because they are based on random resampling from the data set, so if you used the bootstrap standard errors, do not be surprised if they are slightly different from the ones reported here.

This exercise demonstrates the increased statistical power of analyses that take into account the correlation between the prediction tools being compared. When measures are highly correlated, it is easy to detect differences in discrimination as measured by their AUCs.

9

Cohen's *d*

Cohen's *d* describes the size of the difference between individuals who have the outcome and those who do not have the outcome.

Cohen's *d* is a measure of discrimination—that is, it expresses the extent to which individuals who have the outcome are different from individuals who do not have the outcome. The difference is calculated by subtracting the mean values for individuals with and without the outcome. Because the units of measurement of predictor variables are usually noninformative, the raw difference is divided by a measure of variability to obtain a *standardized mean difference*. By convention, *d* values of .20, .50, and .80 are considered *small*, *medium*, and *large*, respectively (Cohen, 1988). Cohen's *d* is best suited to continuous predictor variables (e.g., age), although it works reasonably well with the ordered variables commonly used in psychology (e.g., school grades, symptom severity). Cohen's *d* is not the preferred measure of discrimination when the predictor variables are dichotomous (present/absent) or when they contain extreme values (i.e., highly skewed distributions).

WHY USE COHEN'S *d*?

Jacob Cohen (1969, 1988) developed the standardized mean difference, or *d*, as an effect size indicator—that is, a measure of the size of experimental findings. For too long, researchers have been preoccupied with testing null

https://doi.org/10.1037/0000275-009
Prediction Statistics for Psychological Assessment, by R. K. Hanson

hypothesis statistical testing (NHST), which is still emphasized in most introductory statistics books in psychology. When used appropriately, NHST provides protection against overinterpreting findings that could easily be attributed to chance (Nickerson, 2000). In practice, however, $p < .05$ often functions as a type of Go–No Go test. Researchers routinely report and promote statistically significant results and do little or nothing with nonsignificant results. This created a distortion in the research literature, called *publication bias* (Dickersin, 1990). Some authors have gone so far as to suggest that most published research is false because of the selective nonreporting of nonsignificant results (Ioannidis, 2005). There is no question that NHST is often misused.

Cohen's criticism of the null hypothesis paradigm was twofold (Cohen, 1994). First, the null hypothesis is never strictly true. There is always some difference between groups. Second, sample size is the major difference between studies that have statistically significant results and those that do not. Studies with large samples will almost always be statistically significant, whereas studies with small samples will not. The sensible research question is not whether differences exist; instead, research should focus on whether the differences are large enough to matter. For this question, an effect size measure is required. Since the early 1900s, Pearson's correlation coefficient has been used as an effect size indicator for the degree of association between two continuous variables. In the 1960s, however, there were still no commonly used effect size measures for describing the difference between two groups. Consequently, Cohen (1969) promoted the standardized mean difference as a generic measure of the size of the differences between two groups.

The standardized mean difference is the difference in the means between two groups divided by how much members of each group differ from each other. Cohen recommend that the pooled, within-group standard deviation, which is a weighted average of the standard deviations in each group, as the indicator of within-group variability.

To demonstrate this statistic, consider differences in girls' heights during adolescence. If 18-year-old girls are, on average, 1 inch taller than 14-year-old girls, and the standard deviation for both groups is 2 inches, then $d = 1 \div 2 = .50$, or a medium effect size. If the difference between a 15-year-old and 16-year-old girls is 0.5 inches, with a standard deviation of 2.1, then $d = .5/2.1 = .24$, or a small effect size. A 1.6-inch difference between 13- and 18-year-old girls would translate into a large effect size, $.80 = 1.6/2.0$ (assuming a common standard deviation of 2.0). In general, we are likely to perceive medium to large effect sizes in our daily lives; small effect sizes, however, may only be perceptible through systematic measurement and tabulation.

Variations of Cohen's *d* were rapidly adopted by researchers interested in comparing results and summarizing findings across studies (e.g., Borenstein et al., 2021; Smith & Glass, 1977). I have found it a versatile, informative effect size indicator for meta-analyses of prediction studies (Hanson & Morton-Bourgon, 2005, 2009; Helmus, Hanson, et al., 2013). It is also extremely useful for eye-balling data tables. Informal comparisons of the mean and standard deviation of a variable provide a rough guide to how big the raw, unstandardized differences between groups needs to be in order to be of practical significance. Knowing whether an effect size is of practical significance, of course, requires some prior knowledge of the effect sizes commonly found in this practice area. For example, in sexual recidivism research, *d* values of .15 or greater identify variables worthy of consideration in applied risk assessments (Mann et al., 2010).

LIMITATIONS

Cohen's *d* assumes normally distributed scores. As well, the standard deviations should be similar for both groups. If the standard deviations are meaningfully different, then the interpretation of Cohen's *d* is not clear because the *d* value would get bigger or smaller based on which standard deviation is used. One option is to consistently standardize group differences based on one of the groups. In treatment outcome studies, for example, it is common to use the standard deviation of the control group (Smith & Glass, 1977). For prediction studies, however, there is rarely a reason to privilege the standard deviation of either group (i.e., those with or those without the outcome).

Cohen's *d* is sensitive to outliers, that is, extreme values can have a disproportionate influence on the means and standard deviations. For example, income in the general population has a highly skewed distribution such that a small percentage of individuals make as much as the rest of us combined. When income is used to predict the onset of a disorder, a single individual making $2 million per year would greatly raise the mean of whichever group the case was in (disorder or no disorder). Consequently, it is worth checking for extreme values before calculating Cohen's *d*. If the distribution is highly skewed, the variable can be transformed to minimize the effects of extreme values. Another option is to routinely remove the top and bottom 20% of observations (Winsorized variables; Erceg-Hurn & Mirosevich, 2008). Yet another option would be to use an effect size statistic that is robust to outliers, such as the area under the receiver operating characteristic curve (AUC; Ruscio, 2008; Chapter 8).

Standardized mean differences are not recommended when the predictor variable is dichotomous (i.e., present–absent, yes–no). Although it is possible to calculate *d* from fourfold tables, they are not easily interpreted because the means are fully determined by their standard deviations and vice versa. Consequently, the *d* values are influenced not only by the differences between groups but also by the overall base rate of the predictor. For fourfold tables, it is preferable to use rate ratios or odds ratios (Chapter 7).

Another limitation is that Cohen's *d* does not directly consider time. It compares those with and without the outcome at one point during the follow-up period. The members of each group, however, will necessarily change over time as an increasing proportion of cases have the outcome. Consequently, the *d* value that describes the strength of the predictor may depend on when the outcome is measured. For example, depression will lift for most individuals if they are followed long enough. Given an effective treatment for depression, differences between the treatment and control groups may be large during short to medium follow-up time but become negligible if both groups were followed for many years. When group differences are expected to wax and wane over time, survival analysis can be helpful in identifying changes in relative risk over time.

A related limitation is that Cohen's *d* does not indicate the likelihood of the outcome. For many decisions, the primary concern is whether the case at hand will have the outcome, not whether the case is more or less likely than other cases to have the outcome. For example, an employer may want to know if a job applicant will succeed in a particular post. If almost anybody could do the job (high base rate), there is little value in administering an aptitude test. Consequently, for applied decision making, indicators of relative risk (such as Cohen's *d*, AUCs, and odds ratio) should be considered, along with information concerning the base rate of the outcome of interest (Chapter 4).

When the sample sizes are small (less than 20 per group), Cohen's *d* slightly overestimates the population value. This bias can be corrected by an adjustment based on the inverse of the sample size (Borenstein et al., 2021, Equation 4.22). Once corrected, the resulting statistic is called Hedges's *g*. Hedges's *g* is recommended when conducting meta-analyses of small samples (Goulet-Pelletier & Cousineau, 2018). For most research questions, however, the differences between Cohen's *d* and Hedges's *g* are not large enough to matter.

THE NUTS AND BOLTS

Data Requirements

Standardized mean differences in prediction studies require the following data:

1. a dichotomous outcome variable,
2. a continuous predictor variable, and
3. the predictor variable exists prior to the outcome variable.

The predictor variable ideally would have strong interval measurement (e.g., age, body mass); however, *d* works reasonably well with the ordered variables common in psychology (e.g., Psychopathy Checklist—Revised scores; a five-level clinician rating of symptom severity). In prediction studies, *d* values are most easily interpreted when they are based on a fixed follow-up time (i.e., all cases are followed for the complete follow-up time).

Calculating Cohen's *d*

First, separate the sample into those with and without the outcome. Next, calculate the mean and standard deviation for each group, using the standard formula:

$$Mean = \frac{\sum_{i=1}^{n} y_i}{n} \tag{9.1}$$

The mean is the sum of all the observed values divided by the sample size. In this formula, y_i indicates each value of the predictor, and n is the sample size. The standard deviation is the square root of the variance. The variance is the sum of the squared deviations from the mean divided by one less than the sample size.

$$SD = \sqrt{\frac{\sum(mean - y_i)^2}{n-1}} \tag{9.2}$$

The following is the formula for Cohen's *d*:

$$d = \frac{M_o - M_{no}}{SD_{within}} \tag{9.3}$$

M_o and M_{no} indicate the means for the groups with and without the outcome, respectively, and SD_{within} is the pooled, within-group standard deviation calculated as follows (Borenstein et al., 2021, equation 4.19):

$$SD_{within} = \sqrt{\frac{(n_o - 1)SD_o^2 + (n_{no} - 1)SD_{no}^2}{n_o + n_{no} - 2}} \tag{9.4}$$

SD_o and n_o indicate the standard deviation and sample size for cases with the outcome, and SD_{no} and n_{no} indicate the standard deviation and sample size for cases without the outcome. Note that researchers can choose whether d is defined as $(M_o - M_{no})/SD_{within}$ or $(M_{no} - M_o)/SD_{within}$. The choice will determine whether d is positive (e.g., 1.2) or negative (e.g., −1.2).

Worked Example

A residential drug treatment program is concerned about their rate of substance abuse relapse. Their records indicate that approximately half of their clients are using again within 6 months. To identify the factors associated with relapse, the program collaborates with a local academic, Professor T. Leary, to design and conduct a study. The study uses a fixed 12-month follow-up of 100 individuals from the date of admission to the program (i.e., individuals who relapse during treatment are considered failures). A large number of predictor variables are coded from the extensive records available for each case, including the key variable of whether they had any illegal or problematic substance use after starting treatment. The results for four of the variables are reported in Table 9.1. The difference between the means, as well as the pooled, within-sample standard deviations, are presented to demonstrate how the *d* values are calculated.

In this mock study, substance abuse severity was coded by the research assistants based on the degree of interference in prosocial functioning (e.g., lost job, health concerns, relationship problems). The scores are the number of problems present (up to a maximum of 10). The Self-Control Questionnaire is a 40-item self-report measure inspired by the writings of the Stoic philosopher Epictetus, whose philosophy inspired the center's treatment model. The questionnaire is completed by clients after about 4 weeks in the program. The raw scores of the Self-Control Questionnaire are standardized so that the expected mean is zero with a standard deviation of 1.0. Positive scores indicate high levels of self-control. Shame is rated by clinicians at intake using a 5-point scale, from 1—*little or no shame* to 5—*high levels of shame across multiple life domains* (e.g., substance use, relationships, body image). During the 12-month fixed follow-up period, 59 of the 100 cases were known to have relapsed. The number available for analysis varied somewhat based on missing data.

As can be seen in Table 9.1, the absolute differences in the raw scores ranged from 0.2 to 2.5. These differences are difficult to interpret without considering how much scores vary within each group. The age difference between groups, for example, was 2.5 years, whereas the variability in age within each group was much higher. Although a precise calculation of the pooled, within-group standard deviation can be obtained from Equation 9.4, it is often helpful to obtain a rough estimate by choosing a value between the values of the standard deviations for each group. In our example, the standard deviations were 14.4 and 16.8; consequently, a rough estimate of the pooled standard deviation would be about 15. With a standard deviation of 15, a moderate effect ($d = .50$) would require a raw difference between groups of 7 or 8. The raw difference in age was only 2.5 years, indicating a small effect. Using Equation 9.4, the pooled, within-group standard deviation of 15.4 years, resulting in a *d* value for age of $-0.162 = -2.5/15.425$. The negative sign indicates that those who relapsed were slightly younger than those who did not.

The *d* values in the final column of Table 9.1 provide an indication of the relative importance of each variable. The strongest predictor of relapse was the Self-Control Questionnaire, with $d = -1.019$. The negative sign indicates that individuals who reported less self-control were more likely to relapse. Substance abuse severity showed a moderate effect ($d = .474$), indicating increased risk based on a history of problems in multiple domains. The effect sizes for age ($d = -0.162$) and shame ($d = -.135$) were both sufficiently small that it is unlikely they would be of practical significance.

The program was pleased with these results because the study supported their model of treatment, which emphasizes the development of self-control.

TABLE 9.1. A Selection of Variables Considered as Predictors of Relapse Among 100 Individuals Treated at a Residential Drug Treatment Center (Hypothetical Data)

Variables	Relapse			No relapse					
	n	M	SD	n	M	SD	$M_o - M_{no}$	SD_{within}	d
Age	59	39.2	14.4	41	41.7	16.8	−2.5	15.425	−0.162
Substance abuse severity (0–10)	55	7.3	2.4	38	6.2	2.2	1.1	2.321	0.474
Self-Control Questionnaire (*Z* scores)	58	−0.486	0.845	40	0.525	1.27	1.011	1.039	−0.974
Shame (1–5)	53	2.9	1.4	35	3.1	1.6	−0.2	1.482	−0.135

Further research is needed, however, before they can be confident that self-control is a dynamic risk factor (i.e., changes in self-control align with changes in the likelihood of the outcome; Kraemer et al., 1997). Ultimately, they would like to know whether self-control is a *causal* risk factor, which would require a program of research that rules out alternate explanations for the association between low self-control and relapse. For now, however, the program has evidence that low self-control identifies individuals at increased risk for relapse, individuals who may benefit from additional services.

Standard Errors and Confidence Intervals

The standard error of d is influenced by the total sample size, the base rate of the outcome, and the size of the d value. Of these three factors, the total sample size has the greatest influence. The other factors only gain influence when the sample size is small (less than 20 per group). There are a number of different, but closely related, formulas for calculating the standard error of d (SE_d; Goulet-Pelletier & Cousineau, 2018). My preference is the following:

$$SE_d = \sqrt{\frac{n_o + n_{no}}{n_o n_{no}} + \frac{d^2}{2(n_o + n_{no})}} \tag{9.5}$$

This version is also recommended by Borenstein et al. (2021; equation 4.20) because it is simpler than some of the alternatives while providing a very good estimate. In this formula, N_o and N_{no} are the sample sizes of the groups with and without the outcome, respectively. The R package **effsize** (Torchiano, 2020) uses a somewhat more complicated version:

$$SE_d = \sqrt{\left(\frac{n_o + n_{no}}{n_o n_{no}} + \frac{d^2}{2(n_o + n_{no} - 2)}\right)\left(\frac{n_o + n_{no}}{n_o + n_{no} - 2}\right)} \tag{9.6}$$

The differences between these versions is unlikely to be of practical significance.

The 95% confidence interval for the estimated d value can be reasonably estimated by the usual formula: $d \pm (1.96) * SE_d$. The Z value 1.96 corresponds to the upper 0.025% of the normal curve. With small sample sizes, slightly more accurate confidence intervals can be obtained by using the t distribution or an asymmetric t distribution (Cumming & Finch, 2001). For simplicity, I have used the (symmetrical) Z value of 1.96 to calculate the 95% confidence intervals in Table 9.2. Confidence intervals that do not include zero are indicated in bold. Table 9.2 is a useful way to present the results of multiple variables simultaneously.

This table indicates that the strongest predictors of relapse were the Self-Control Questionnaire and Substance Abuse Severity, both of which were statistically significant (their confidence intervals did not include zero). Both

TABLE 9.2. Predictors of Relapse With 95% CIs (Hypothetical Data From Table 9.1)

Variables	Relapse			No relapse				95% CI	
	n	*M*	*SD*	*n*	*M*	*SD*	*d*	Low	High
Age	59	39.2	14.4	41	41.7	16.8	–0.162	–0.561	0.237
Substance abuse severity (0–10)	55	7.3	2.4	38	6.2	2.2	**0.474**	**0.055**	**0.893**
Self-Control Questionnaire (*Z* scores)	58	–0.486	0.845	40	0.525	1.27	**–0.974**	**–1.400**	**–0.548**
Shame (1–5)	53	2.9	1.4	35	3.1	1.6	–0.135	–0.562	0.292

Note. Confidence intervals that do not include zero are indicated in bold. CI = confidence interval.

Age and Shame demonstrated small effects, neither of which were statistically significant (their confidence intervals included zero).

Comparing *d* Values

Standardized mean differences are primarily used to describe individual findings or to summarize findings across studies using meta-analysis. Fixed-effect meta-analysis (Chapter 14) provides a general method of comparing *d* values from different samples. Researchers rarely employ format tests to compare *d* values from the same study. When formal tests of the relative importance of predictor variables are desired, most researchers switch to other metrics, such as the area under the receiver operating characteristic curve (AUC; Chapter 8).

As with other statistics, a versatile approach to comparing *d* values is by examining their 95% confidence intervals (Cumming & Finch, 2005). This is a low-powered test, meaning that if differences are found, they are likely to be real. Unless the sample size is very large, it is also common for sample statistics to have overlapping confidence intervals when the population values are genuinely different.

GOING FURTHER

Readers who have made it this far should have a sufficient understanding of Cohen's *d* to be educated consumers of studies using this statistical approach. The following sections are designed to deepen this understanding through further reading and exercises. These sections can be worked with in any order, and it is not necessary to do all (or any) of them.

Recommended Readings

Grissom, R. J., & Kim, J. J. (2005). *Effect sizes for research: A broad practical approach.* Lawrence Erlbaum Associates.

Chapter 3 provides a nontechnical discussion of Cohen's *d* and other versions of the standardized mean difference, such as Hedges's *g* and Glass's *d*.

Goulet-Pelletier, J. C., & Cousineau, D. (2018). A review of effect sizes and their confidence intervals, part I: The Cohen's *d* family. *The Quantitative Methods for Psychology, 14*(4), 242–265. https://doi.org/10.20982/tqmp.14.4.p242

A more detailed coverage, with simulations demonstrating the statistical properties of the various members of Cohen's *d* family.

Computer Code

R has a convenient package for calculating *d* values (Torchiano, 2020), as does IBM/SPSS Version 27.0.0.0.

R Code

Cohen's *d* is available in the **effsize** package. If this is your first time using this package, you will need to install it.

```
install.packages ('effsize')
```

Choose a CRAN site geographically close to you. Next, tell R that you want to use this package.

```
library ('effsize')
```

The data can be read into **cohen.d** in several ways. The simplest option is to have two separate vectors: one for those with the outcome and another for those without. This example uses the Self-Control Questionnaire as a predictor of relapse (Table 9.2). The vector called *relapse* has values for 58 cases, whereas the vector called *no.relapse* has values for 40 cases. The raw data was entered in EXCEL.csv files called *Chap9_relapse.csv* and *Chap9_no_relapse.csv*.

```
V1 <- read.csv ("c:\\run.files\\Book\\Chap9_relapse.
csv")
relapse <- (V1$x)
V2 <- read.csv ("c:\\run.files\\Book\\Chap9_no_
relapse.csv")
no.relapse <- (V2$x)
```

The Self-Control Questionnaire is coded as *Z* scores with an expected mean of zero and standard deviation of one. The following commands verify that the means, standard deviations, and sample sizes are the same as those in Table 9.1.

```
mean (relapse)
[1] -0.4863265
sd (relapse)
[1] 0.845246
length (relapse)
[1] 58
mean (no.relapse)
[1] 0.5254158
sd (no.relapse)
[1] 1.267407
length (no.relapse)
[1] 40
```

Now type the following command:

```
cohen.d (no.relapse, relapse)
```

which produces the following output:

```
Cohen's d
d estimate: 0.9750101 (large)
```

```
95 percent confidence interval:
   lower      upper
0.5442566   1.4057636
```

When the confidence intervals from **cohen.d** [.544, 1.406] are compared with those in Table 9.2 [.548, 1.400] there are slight differences due to the formula used. Table 9.2 used Equation 9.5 and $Z = 1.96$, whereas **cohen.d** used Equation 9.6 and the (symmetrical) t distribution. The d values are not identical (.975 and .974) due to rounding.

You can also compute Cohen's d from a datafile with 98 cases and two variables: *self.control* (Z score) and *outcome* (0, 1). The data set is called *Chap9_example.table*, available at https://www.apa.org/pubs/books/prediction-statistics-for-psychological-assessment. In this syntax, *outcome* is considered a factor with two levels.

```
Chap9 <- read.table (file =
"c:\\run.files\\Book\\Chap9_example.table")
attach(Chap9)
outcome <- factor (outcome)
cohen.d (self.control ~ outcome)
```

This produces the same output as above (Cohen's $d = 0.975$ with a 95% confidence interval of 0.544 to 1.406). If you want to change from positive to negative, change the order of entry of the vectors in the **cohen.d** command. If you want Hedges's g or the noncentral t estimates of the confidence intervals, use the following commands:

```
cohen.d (self.control ~ outcome, hedges.correction =
TRUE, noncentral = TRUE)
```

This produces the following:

```
Hedges's g
g estimate: 0.9673729 (large)
95 percent confidence interval:
   lower      upper
0.5470061   1.3984471
```

As expected, Hedges's g is slightly smaller (0.967) than Cohen's d (0.975) calculated from the same data, although the difference, in this case, would have no practical significance.

IBM/SPSS Code

IBM/SPSS introduced Cohen's d in Version 27.0.0.0. The SPSS example data set contains 98 cases with three variables: *Case, self.control,* and *outcome* (https://www.apa.org/pubs/books/prediction-statistics-for-psychological-assessment). Effect size statistics can be found by clicking on **ANALYZE**, then **COMPARE MEANS**, then **INDEPENDENT-SAMPLES T-TEST**. At this screen, designate *self.control* as the test variable, and *outcome* as the grouping variable. Then check the box requesting effect sizes. Alternately, use the following syntax:

```
T-TEST GROUPS=outcome(0 1)
/MISSING=ANALYSIS
/VARIABLES=self.control
/ES DISPLAY(TRUE)
/CRITERIA=CI(.95).
```

This produces the following output:

Independent Samples Effect Sizes

				95% CI	
		Standardizer[a]	Point estimate	Lower	Upper
self.control	Cohen's *d*	1.0376737	.975	.547	1.398
	Hedges's correction	1.0458694	.967	.543	1.387
	Glass's delta	.8452460	1.197	.734	1.652

Note. Cohen's *d* uses the pooled standard deviation. Hedges's correction uses the pooled standard deviation, plus a correction factor. Glass's delta uses the sample standard deviation of the control group. CI = confidence interval.
[a]The denominator used in estimating the effect sizes.

In SPSS, the confidence intervals for Cohen's *d* are calculated using Equation 9.6 for the standard error and the noncentral *t* distribution, which produces values slightly different from those calculated earlier using R code. Again, the differences between the alternate equations are small (third decimal point) in this example. Larger differences between the alternate calculations would be expected if the samples size was small (e.g., less than 20).

EXERCISES

The following exercise continues the hypothetical study conducted by Professor Leary of predictors of relapse for individuals attending substance abuse programming. Table 9.3 presents a selection of four additional variables that were

TABLE 9.3. A Selection of Variables Considered as Predictors of Relapse Among 100 Individuals Treated at a Residential Drug Treatment Center (Hypothetical Data)

	Relapsed			No relapse					
Variables	*n*	*M*	*SD*	*n*	*M*	*SD*	$M_o - M_{no}$	SD_{within}	*d*
Neuroticism (*Z* scores)	56	.011	1.2	40	−.032	1.1	?	?	?
IQ	50	99.8	14.1	37	102.3	16.3	?	?	?
Negative social influences (0–8)	55	4.4	1.5	40	1.7	0.9	?	?	?
Positive social influences (0–8)	57	2.9	1.4	38	4.0	1.6	?	?	?

coded as potential predictors. Neuroticism was assessed by a 40-item self-report questionnaire, with the total scores standardized to a mean of zero and standard deviation of one. A brief intelligence test was also administered at intake, with the result expressed in typical IQ format (expected mean of 100; standard deviation of 15). The final two variables were counts of the total number of Negative and Positive social influences among the clients' family, coworkers, and friends. Negative influences were those that used substances, encouraged the client to use substances, or had a history of criminal convictions. Positive influences were those that provided helpful psychological support, were prosocial, or created barriers to high-risk situations in which relapse was likely. Count variables are unlikely to be normally distributed (they typically follow a Poisson distribution); nevertheless, Cohen's *d* is still a reasonable heuristic for examining the size of the group differences.

Question 9.1

This exercise is intended to develop your skills at eyeballing effect sizes from tables of means and standard deviations. Consequently, try to answer the questions without using a calculator.

(i) Which of the four variables in Table 9.3 has the strongest relationship with relapse?
(ii) Which two variables have little or no relationship with relapse?

Question 9.2

Now complete the missing cells of Table 9.3.

Question 9.3

How well did your initial ranking of the importance of the variables correspond to the ranking provided by the *d* values?

ANSWERS TO EXERCISES

Question 9.1

(i) Think about how you answered this question. The approach introduced in this chapter is to compare the size of the differences between groups to the size of their standard deviations. The difference between groups for Negative social influences was more than 2, with a standard deviation between 0.9 and 1.5. Consequently, a large *d* is expected (> 1). None of the other differences are bigger than their standard deviations.

(ii) For both Neuroticism and IQ, the group differences were a fraction of their standard deviations.

Question 9.2

The *d* value for Negative social influences was 2.10, which is the largest for this set of variables (see Table 9.4). It is also unusually large. Most predictor variables in psychology are small to moderate (.20–.50). Rarely do prediction tools demonstrate *d* values >1. The *d* value for Neuroticism (0.037) was close to zero, and the *d* value for IQ was small (−0.17). For Positive social influences, the *d* value was moderate to large (−.74).

Question 9.3

The predictor variables in rank order of importance would start with Negative social influences (2.10), then Positive social influences (−0.74), IQ (−0.17), and finally, Neuroticism (0.037). Did you rank them in the same order before calculating *d* values?

TABLE 9.4. A Selection of Variables Considered as Predictors of Relapse Among 100 Individuals Treated at a Residential Drug Treatment Center (Hypothetical Data)

	Relapse			No relapse					
Variables	*n*	Mean	*SD*	*n*	Mean	*SD*	$M_o - M_{no}$	SD_{within}	*d*
Neuroticism (*Z* scores)	56	.011	1.2	40	−.032	1.1	0.043	1.160	0.037
IQ	50	99.8	14.1	37	102.3	16.3	−2.5	15.07	−0.17
Negative social influences (0–8)	55	4.4	1.5	40	1.7	0.9	2.7	1.28	2.10
Positive social influences (0–8)	57	2.9	1.4	38	4.0	1.6	−1.1	1.48	−0.74

10

Cox Regression

Cox regression is a type of survival analysis that estimates how much predictor variables are associated with the outcome (relative risk) when not all individuals are followed for the complete follow-up period.

Cox regression survival analysis measures the extent to which predictor variables are associated with the outcome (i.e., discrimination). For dichotomous (yes–no) predictors, it compares the likelihood of the outcome when the predictor is present to the likelihood when it is absent. For a risk tool with ordered levels or scores, it describes how much the likelihoods increase as the scores increase. Follow-up time is coded as a continuous variable and, like all survival analyses, not all cases need to be followed for the complete follow-up period. The relative risk statistic calculated by Cox regression is called a *hazard ratio*. A *hazard* is the likelihood of having the outcome in the next instant if the case has not already experienced the outcome. Hazard ratios are the ratios of the hazard rates for adjacent levels of the predictor variable. When the base rates are low for the outcome of interest (less than 25%), hazard ratios can be interpreted as rate ratios. Cox regression is an excellent method of describing relative risk, that is, how much riskier are cases with high scores compared with cases with lower scores. It is poorly suited, however, to estimating overall likelihoods or for identifying periods of increased or decreased risk during the follow-up period.

https://doi.org/10.1037/0000275-010
Prediction Statistics for Psychological Assessment, by R. K. Hanson

WHY USE COX REGRESSION SURVIVAL ANALYSIS?

As a developer of prediction tools, I am very interested in how well these tools work in new samples and settings. This turned out to be more complicated than I initially anticipated. In graduate school, I was taught that a finding was replicated when it was statistically significant in a new sample. Evaluators, however, are not interested in whether the measure predicts better than chance; evaluators want to know the size of the relationship and if the predictive accuracy is similar across samples and settings. This requires learning new statistics, many of which are included in this book. Most psychological tests are norm-referenced, meaning that their results can be interpreted as relative positions (rank order) of individuals on the latent construct measured by the test (Crawford & Garthwaite, 2009). For example, a questionnaire designed to measure anxiety (the latent construct) may indicate that the individual has an unusually high level of anxiety compared with adults in the general population. Although scores on prediction tools can be interpreted in terms of percentile ranks (see Chapter 16), that is not the basic information that they are designed to assess. Risk prediction tools are more fundamentally concerned with the likelihood of the outcome.

The interpretation of actuarial risk tools is simplified when there is one, and only one, likelihood associated with each score. In our early work with the Static-99 sexual recidivism risk prediction tool (Hanson & Thornton, 1999, 2000), this is what we found. The sexual recidivism rates per Static-99 score were remarkably consistent across three diverse samples from Canada and the United Kingdom. I remember my enthusiasm when I reported this finding to research colleagues and government decision makers. It turns out we were wrong. As we collected more Static-99 validation studies, it soon became obvious that the expected recidivism rates per score were meaningfully different across studies (Helmus, 2009; Helmus, Hanson, et al., 2012). The reasons for this variation were not fully known, and it remains an important topic of research for applied users of this risk tool (Boccaccini et al., 2017; Elwood et al., 2017; Hanson, Thornton, et al., 2016). In contrast, relative risk was remarkably consistent. A 1-point increase in Static-99 (or the revised version, Static-99R) was associated with a 30% to 40% increase in the likelihood of recidivism for most samples; furthermore, our initial studies found that the amount of variability in relative risk across studies was no more than would be expected by chance (Helmus, Hanson, et al., 2012).

Subsequent research did find that there was some variability across samples in the effectiveness of Static-99R at discriminating between risk levels (Hanson, Thornton, et al., 2016); however, the amount of variability in the overall base rates has a much greater influence on the expected recidivism rates than the relatively minor variability in relative risk. A similar pattern of stable relative risk and variable base rates has been observed in other areas of prediction, such as the risk of accidents (e.g., Ingre et al., 2006) and medical prognosis (e.g., Weinberger et al., 2010). This led us to the view that relative risk could perhaps be the most trustworthy information provided by risk prediction tools (Babchishin et al., 2012a; Hanson et al., 2013).

We now routinely include relative risk tables in the user guidance for the Static-99R, Static-2002R (Phenix et al., 2016) and STABLE-2007 risk tools (Brankley et al., 2017). For example, an individual who scored 4 on the Static-99R would be described as being approximately twice (1.94 times) as likely to sexually reoffended than individuals in the middle of the risk distribution (Static-99R median score of 2). Cox regression is used to calculate these relative risk estimates. Although the STATIC Development Group is almost continuously working on updates to the recidivism rates (e.g., Lee & Hanson, 2021), there has been no need to update the relative risk tables. The relative risk tables calculated on recent samples would be substantively similar to the tables produced on samples of individuals released 20 years ago.

A selection of statistics for describing relative risk have already been presented in the earlier parts of Part III, such as the odds ratios, the area under the curve (AUC), and Cohen's *d*. These statistics are most informative when the likelihood of the outcome is estimated from fixed follow-up studies (see Chapter 4). Cox regression survival analysis is well suited to studies where the follow-up time is not the same for all cases. Incomplete follow-up is the norm in real-world studies. A very common research design involves collecting outcome data at one point in time for individuals who became at risk at different times. In this design, the follow-up time for individuals would vary from the longest possible (i.e., the first individual to be at risk, e.g., the first patient discharged) to almost zero (i.e., the individual who became at risk just before the follow-up data were collected). Although it is possible to truncate ragged follow-up time to a fixed follow-up period, retaining all available data provides more reliable estimates (i.e., increased statistical power).

Cox regression is a flexible technique that does not require strong assumptions about the data. The survival curves can be any shape, and the shapes can be different for different subgroups in the same analysis. Although time is coded on an interval scale (e.g., days, months), it is only used to identify the order in which the outcomes occurred (i.e., time functions as an ordinal variable). Consequently, outcomes that occur unusually quickly or unusually late do not have a disproportionate influence on the results of Cox regression analyses.

Like odds ratios, Cox regression hazard ratios are not expected to be influenced by the base rate of the outcome or by restriction of range of the predictor variables. This facilitates comparisons across studies. Many effect sizes, such as AUCs, vary across studies even when the rate of the outcome per risk level is exactly as expected (i.e., perfect calibration). When hazard ratios are used as the effect size indicator, the consistency among such studies becomes obvious. On the other hand, when differences in hazard ratios across studies are observed, the differences in predictive accuracy are likely to be real in nature and not due to arbitrary features of the designs of the studies (e.g., length of follow-up, preselected high-risk sample).

LIMITATIONS

Cox regression is poor at estimating absolute risk. The quantity estimated by Cox regression is an instantaneous hazard, which is the likelihood of the outcome in the next, vanishingly small instant given that the individual has not yet had the outcome. Given that these time intervals are almost zero, so, too, is the likelihood of the outcome in that instant. To estimate absolute risk, the instantaneous hazards must be aggregated over time. Consequently, other forms of survival analysis are recommended for estimating base rates and overall likelihoods. These include discrete-time survival analysis, discussed in Chapter 5, and Kaplan–Meier survival analysis, discussed in Chapter 6. Given that the same data can be used for most forms of survival analysis, it is common to use either discrete-time or Kaplan–Meier survival analysis to estimate absolute risk, and then Cox regression survival analysis to estimate the effects of predictor variables.

Cox regression is poorly suited to finding periods of increased or decreased risk during the follow-up time. Although Cox regression does compute a baseline survival function, this is an intermediate step in the calculation of the hazard ratios and is not intended to be interpreted on its own. If the primary question is when the outcome is most likely or whether risk is above or below a threshold, use discrete-time survival analysis (Chapter 5).

Another limitation is that Cox regression assumes that relative risk is constant over time (i.e., the proportional hazard assumption). For individual difference measures in psychology, this is a reasonable assumption. Individuals with chronic risk factors for depression, for example, are those most likely to have major depressive episodes both now and later. The proportional hazard assumption is not tenable, however, when the predictor is expected to have a time-limited or intermittent influence on the outcome. For example, a treatment for depression may be expected to accelerate the speed of recovery, with full recovery expected in both the treatment and comparison groups. This would result in large differences between the groups in the middle of the follow-up period and little or no differences at the beginning and the end. There are certain statistical tests that can be used to check for violations in the proportional hazard assumption, the most common of which is plotting Schoenfeld residuals (Hanson et al., 2013; Singer & Willett, 2003, Section 15.4.3). A significant correlation between the Schoenfeld residuals and time indicate a violation of the proportional hazard assumption. All such approaches, however, are low-powered tests that are unlikely to detect violations unless the number of events is large (i.e., more than 100 cases with the outcome).

If the effects of the predictors are expected to change over time, it is good practice to examine the Schoenfeld residuals, even if low powered, as well as to examine the raw data. Change in the effects of the predictors over time is a violation of the proportional hazard assumption and should not be confused with changes in the values of the predictor variables over time, which is not a problem for Cox regression (using time-dependent covariates). To check the proportional hazard assumption, a useful way of visualizing the data is to divide cases into two or three levels of the predictor variable and then plot the survival curves using either discrete-time or Kaplan–Meier survival analysis. If the data support the proportional hazard assumption, the survival curves should be roughly parallel. When the survival curves cross, then the proportional hazard assumption is likely violated. Note, however, that survival curves are unstable when the sample size is small (less than 20 cases remaining at risk). Plotting Cox regression survival curves for different levels of the predictor variable is not recommended; it will always produce neatly parallel curves because the proportional hazards assumption is imposed on the data (it is not a finding).

Cox regression works best when no two outcomes happen at the same time. In practice, it is common for some cases to have the outcome in the same survival time. When this happens, a random process is used to break ties, placing one event before the other. When many events are clumped together, however, the randomizing process introduces unwanted error into the Cox regression estimates. If many events share the same survival time, use discrete-time hazard analysis instead of Cox regression. As a rough heuristic, when the proportion of ties is less than 10% the estimates are minimally distorted, whereas 30% or more ties would add considerable instability to the results. To reduce the proportion of ties, sometimes it is possible to use a finer unit of measurement for time (e.g., days rather than months).

Another limitation is that Cox regression coefficients can be difficult to interpret. They are unstandardized, meaning that they describe the amount of change in hazard rates based on a one-unit increase in the raw scores of the prediction tool. Although hazard ratios can be roughly interpreted as rate ratios when the base rates are low (less than 25%), the meaning of hazard ratios are not intuitive when the base rates are high. Consider a base rate of 70% and a hazard ratio of 2.0 for a dichotomous predictor. This seems to imply that the likelihood of the outcome would be 70% × 2 = 140%, which is clearly impossible. Although hazard ratios should be considered in conjunction with base rates, large hazard ratios may appear to say more about absolute likelihoods than they really do.

Furthermore, because the scaling of prediction tools lacks common conventions, it is impossible to tell whether a hazard ratio of 1.09 for one scale is better or worse than a hazard ratio of 1.45 for another scale. Fortunately, there is an effect size indicator for Cox regression similar to the AUC that provides an overall summary of how strongly the predictor is related to the outcome, namely, Harrell's C, or concordance (Harrell et al., 1982). Harrell's C can roughly be interpreted as the probability of two cases, the one with the highest score will have the outcome before the other. The magnitudes of concordance values are interpreted in the same way as AUCs—namely, .56 indicates a small relationship, .64 indicates a moderate relationship, and .71 indicates a large relationship (Rice & Harris, 2005).

Other general limitations of survival analysis are discussed in Chapter 5, such as changes in the composition of the at-risk group over time, competing risks, and frailty (i.e., selective attrition of the most vulnerable cases).

THE NUTS AND BOLTS

Data Requirements

The following data are required for Cox regression survival analysis:

1. a dichotomous outcome variable,
2. survival time, and
3. one or more predictor variables.

The following is a brief summary of the structure of survival data. For a longer description, see Chapter 6. Survival times are calculated from a start date, a follow-up end date, the outcome variable, and the date that the outcome occurred. Survival times start at the at-risk date and end when either (a) the outcome occurs or (b) follow-up ends. Cases without the outcome are referred to as *censored*, meaning that they are removed from the data set before the event occurs. For Cox regression survival analysis (and Kaplan–Meier), survival times are continuous (e.g., 1.22 years, 24.34 minutes). Ideally, the precision of measurement should be such that no events happen at the same time. When there is more than one event at the same time, ties are artificially broken using one of several available algorithms (IBM Corp., 2020; Singer & Willett, 2003, Section 14.2.2; Therneau, 2020). Cases that are censored before the first outcome do not contribute to the analysis.

The stability of Cox regression coefficients is primarily determined by the number of events. For a single predictor (categorical or continuous), reasonably stable estimates are provided when the overall sample size is greater than 100 and there are 20 events. Minimally, there should be 10 events per predictor variable. When there are fewer than 10 events, it is not unusual for the estimation programs to provide impossible (misspecified) values. Misspecified values can be identified because they are unusually large (e.g., a regression coefficient of 5.0, indicating a relative risk increase of 148 times for each unit increase in predictor variable) or the program will simply crash.

Calculating Cox Regression Survival Analyses

Cox regression is almost always calculated using specialized computer software, which is discussed later in this chapter. Readers interested in the specifics of the calculations are referred to Section 14.2.1 of Singer and Willett (2003). The general principles described here, however, should satisfy most readers.

In Cox regression survival analysis, the units of risk are instantaneous hazards, which express the likelihood of having the event during the next instant if the outcome has not already occurred. Because these numbers are vanishingly small, the instantaneous likelihood is transformed into a hazard rate by dividing it by the size of the interval (see Chapter 6, Equation 6.1; Aalen et al., 2008, Equation 1.2). The quantities estimated by Cox regression are hazard ratios—that is, the hazard rate for one level of the predictor variable divided by the hazard rate of the adjacent level of the predictor. Cox regression assumes that the increase in risk is the same between each value of the predictor variable. For example, consider a risk scale with scores from 1 to 10. If individuals with a score of 2 were 20% more likely to have the outcome than individuals with a score of 1, then individuals with a score of 8 would also be 20% more likely to have the outcome than individuals with a score of 7. The consistency in incremental risk means that relative risk for nonadjacent scores is calculated by repeating the size of the difference between scores by the 1-unit increase in risk. For example, the relative risk difference between a score of 3 and 4 would be 1.20, and the relative risk difference between a score of 3 and a score of 5 would be 1.20 × 1.20 = 1.44. The difference between a score of 3 and a score of 5 would be 1.20 × 1.20 × 1.20 = 1.728. Mathematically minded readers will notice that this is an exponential distribution ($y = B^n$, see the Appendix: Useful Algebra and Notation).

Hazard ratios are computed by comparing the features of each case at the time of the outcome to all other cases still at risk when the event occurred. Cox regression hazard ratios are the average of these comparisons. The number of comparisons is equal to the number of events. The precision of the Cox regression estimates is primarily determined by the number of events and secondarily by the overall size of the risk set (those still at risk). Consequently, estimates based on large samples (greater than 100) but few events (fewer than 10) will lack precision.

Averaging hazard ratios assumes that the influence of the predictor variable is reasonably constant over time (i.e., the proportional hazard assumption). Cox regression also assumes it is constant for adjacent values of a risk prediction tool. When relative risk is constant, then the natural log transformation creates a linear relationship between risk scores and hazard ratios. The natural log transformation is the number that when used as power of *e* (2.71828 . . .) produces the original number. For example, the logarithm of 1.2 is 0.18232 and the logarithm of 0.8333 [1/(1.2)] is −0.18232. It is the *ln* function on many hand calculators, although it is sometimes called *log*. To transform from log hazard ratios back to hazard ratios, simply use the log hazard ratio as the exponent of *e*. For example, $e^{(0.18232)} = 1.2000$. On hand calculators, this is often referred to as e^x, or *exp(x)*.

The preceding steps may seem like hocus pocus, and do not worry if it doesn't make sense right away. It is, however, a common feature of nature that logarithmic transformations make percentage increases appear linear, which applies to population growth, corporate profits, and the life expectancy of members of different species (West, 2017). It also applies to the risk prediction tools commonly used in corrections and forensic mental health (Hanson, Babchishin, et al., 2013; Howard et al., 2009; Wilson & Gutierrez, 2014). Consequently, it is worth developing some proficiency at transforming numbers into logarithms and back again.

With one predictor (e.g., a risk prediction tool), Cox regression produces one regression coefficient, often symbolized by *B*. There is no coefficient for the intercept; in Cox regression, the baseline survival function is only considered as an intermediate step in the calculations. Positive *B* values indicate that high scores are associated with increased risk, whereas negative *B* values indicate that high scores are associated with decreased risk. A regression coefficient of zero indicates no relationship between the predictor and the outcome. Although *B* values could, in principle, range from very small to very large, they typically fall in the range of −2 to +2. Very large regression coefficients (e.g., less than −4 or greater than +4) typically indicate that the model is misspecified (i.e., the computer program ran, but the output is nonsense). Misspecification is most likely when the number of events is less than 10.

Cox regression coefficients are log hazard ratios. They are often transformed into hazard ratios for the purposes of interpretation. When the base rate is low (less than 25%), hazard ratios have similar meaning to odds ratios and rate ratios. For example, a hazard ratio of 1.20 ($B = .1823$) would indicate that for each one unit increase in the score on the prediction tool, the likelihood of the outcome increased by 20%. When considering the relationship of age (in years) to criminal recidivism, a hazard rate of 0.96 ($B = -.0408$) would indicate that an individual who was 1 year older was 4% less likely to reoffend.

Worked Example

This example uses a random selection of 767 cases from the Static-99R norms (Hanson, Thornton, et al., 2016), of which 83 were identified as sexual recidivists. Static-99R is a sexual recidivism risk tool containing 10 items related to demographics (e.g., age) and criminal history (e.g., number of prior sexual offenses, any nonsexual violent offenses). In this example, the dates have already been organized into survival times. To conduct Cox regression survival analysis, three variables are necessary: (a) survival time (in this example, the variable *Time.Sex* coded in years), (b) whether the survival period ended with a recidivism event (*Recid.Sex* coded as *1* = *yes* and *0* = *no*), and (c) the predictor variable (*Stat99Rtot*, Static-99R total scores coded from −3 to 12). For the distinction between survival time and follow-up time, see Chapter 6. The data set contains one row per case, with case number included for organizational purposes.

```
ROW   CASE   Recid.Sex    Time.Sex     Stat99Rtot
1        8       0        3.00591327       -2
2       13       0        5.15768725       -1
3       20       0        3.49047306       -1
4       27       1        2.94568550        1
5       34       0        2.87998248       -3
6       46       0        2.91830924       -3
7       48       0        3.76423565        0
.
.
.
762   9202       0       12.34223135        2
763   9212       0       12.12594114        1
764   9224       0       13.33880903       -1
765   9248       0       13.07049966       -3
766   9252       0       11.32375086        3
767   9261       0       12.89527721        3
```

The **coxph** routine in R Statistics (Therneau, 2020) produces the following output:

```
coxph(formula = Surv(Time.Sex, Recid.Sex) ~ Stat99Rtot)
n= 767, number of events= 83
                coef    exp(coef) se(coef)   z       Pr(>|z|)
Stat99Rtot 0.30334   1.35437   0.04046 7.497 6.54e-14 ***a
---
Signif. codes: 0 '***' 0.001 '**' 0.01 '*' 0.05 '.'
0.1 ' ' 1
                exp(coef)  exp(-coef)  lower .95  upper .95
Stat99Rtot        1.354       0.7384       1.251      1.466
Concordance= 0.743 (se = 0.028 )
Rsquare= 0.07 (max possible= 0.743 )
Likelihood ratio test= 55.51  on 1 df,  p=9.293e-14
Wald test            = 56.2  on 1 df,  p=6.539e-14
Score (logrank) test = 58.97  on 1 df,  p=1.599e-14
```

This output contains a lot of numbers, which can be confusing. The most important numbers are in bold. In this artificial data set, the Cox regression coefficient for the relationship between Static-99R scores was $B = 0.30334$, with a standard error of 0.04046. These are logged hazard ratios. To transform into hazard ratios, use the values as exponents for *e*, that is, 2.71828^B, or $2.71828^{0.30334} = 1.354$. These values are expressed in the next line. The hazard ratio was 1.354 with 95% confidence interval of 1.251 to 1.466. In other words, a 1-point increase in Static-99R scores was associated with a 35% increase in the hazard rate of sexual recidivism. The confidence interval for the estimate does not include 1; consequently, the association is more than would be expected by chance.

The overall relationship between the full range of Static-99R scores and sexual recidivism can be summarized by the concordance statistic (Harrell's C), which in this example was $C = .743$. This indicates that there was a 74.3% chance that of two cases, the one with the higher Static-99R score would reoffend before the other. The standard error of the concordance ($SE_C = 0.028$) can be used to create a 95% confidence interval, using the usual formula: $C \pm 1.96\ (SE_C) = .743 \pm 0.05488$, or .688 to .798. In this example, there was a large relationship between Static-99R scores and sexual recidivism ($C = .743$).

Standard Errors and Confidence Intervals

There are several options for calculating the standard errors of Cox regression coefficients (SE_B), and there is no consensus concerning which approach is best (Pencina & D'Agostino, 2004; Singer & Willett, 2003, Section 14.2.2; Therneau, 2020). The differences in the options mostly concern different approaches to ordering events that happened at the same time (breaking ties). Consequently, do not be surprised if you find slightly different numbers with different software, or even with different editions of the same software. The standard errors are for the log hazard ratios, such that the 95% confidence intervals are calculated as follows: $B \pm 1.96(SE_B)$. To transform into the metric of hazard ratios, take the exponent of each of the values.

Comparing Regression Coefficients

Returning to the concern raised at the beginning of this chapter, evaluators are often interested in the extent to which risk tools generalize to other samples. For example, researchers may want to know whether a risk tool developed in Canada has the same relationship with the outcome in Singapore. One approach to making these comparisons is to use the usual formula for the standard error of the difference (SE_{diff}):

$$SE_{diff} = \sqrt{SE_1^2 + SE_2^2}. \tag{10.1}$$

In this equation, SE_1 and SE_2 are the standard errors of the Cox regression coefficients to be compared. Use the standard error of the difference to create a 95% confidence interval for the observed difference, which can then inform decisions concerning whether the differences across settings is more than would be expected by chance. For example, if the B value in the Canadian sample was 0.390 ($SE_1 = 0.086$) and 0.456 ($SE_2 = 0.156$) in Singapore, the difference between settings would be $0.456 - 0.390 = 0.066$. Using the these numbers, the standard error of the difference would be $((0.086)^2 + (0.156)^2)^{1/2} = 0.1781$. This would result in a 95% confidence interval for the difference of $Difference \pm 1.96(SE_{Difference})$, which in our example would be $0.066 \pm 1.96\ (0.1781)$; 95% confidence interval of $-.283$ to .415. Given that the confidence interval for the difference includes zero, the amount of variability in the Cox regression coefficients across these settings was no more than would be expected by chance.

The degree of overlap of confidence intervals for each study can also be used to compare Cox regression coefficients from different studies (Cumming & Finch, 2005), as can meta-analysis (see Chapter 14). Sometimes the research question is not generalizability but whether one scale predicts better than another. For example, test developers may want to know if changing the scoring criteria leads to meaningful improvement in predictive accuracy. The raw, unstandardized regression coefficients are not well suited for this purpose because they are dependent on the scaling of the measures (which can change with revisions). Instead, researchers need to compare global measures of predictive accuracy, such as Harrell's C. Kang and colleagues (2015) have presented a method for comparing the Harrell's C values for different scales used on the same sample; however, it has yet to be widely used. A more common approach for comparing the accuracy of predictors in the same data set is to use global fit indices, such as the Akaike information criteria (Raftery, 1995) and the Bayesian information criteria (Burnham & Anderson, 2004). The specifics of these approaches, however, are beyond the scope of the current book.

Other Uses

When Cox regression is used to describe the discrimination properties of a risk tool, the risk tool is typically the only predictor variable examined. It is common, however, for researchers to use Cox regression with multiple predictor variables to examine the incremental effects of different constructs and measures (e.g., Brouillette-Alarie et al., 2016; Brown et al., 2000). Such analyses have similar strengths and weaknesses as standard multiple regression. The major weakness is that the common explanatory power of correlated predictors can be hidden. If two correlated variables both have strong univariate relationships with the outcome, the multivariate analyses may make it appear that neither are related to the outcome. Another reason not to get too excited about the incremental contribution of variables is that, with large enough sample sizes, almost all univariate predictors will also be incremental predictors (Babchishin et al., 2012b).

Researchers can also use Cox regression to examine interactions, that is, multivariate analyses in which the effect of one variable varies depending on the value of another variable. Although interactions are often theorized, they are difficult to find and interpret in practice. The primary problem is that the interpretation of interactions requires assumptions about the measurement model of the variables in the analysis (Busemeyer & Jones, 1983; Kenny & Judd, 1984). The measurement model is the mathematical relationship between the latent construct (e.g., psychopathy) and the indicators (e.g., scores on the Psychopathy Checklist–Revised; see Michell, 1990). Although linear models are often assumed, exponential relationships between the construct and the indicators are equally plausible. For most psychological measures, their measurement models are unknown. Consequently, it is hard to tell whether an observed interaction (or lack thereof) speaks to the relationship between the latent variables or simply their indicators.

Another important research use of Cox regression is examining time-dependent covariates. Previously, we discussed variables whose relationship with the outcome may change over time (violating the proportional hazard assumption). In contrast, time-dependent covariates are predictor variables whose values change over time (Altman & De Stavola, 1994; Singer & Willett, 2003). For example, a researcher may be interested in the relationship between stress and self-harm. The time-invariant approach would assess stress levels at the beginning of the study, and link initial stress levels to the first incident of self-harm during the follow-up period. The time-dependent approach would keep reassessing stress levels throughout the follow-up period (perhaps with a smart phone app). The incidents of self-harm could be linked to the stress level in the most recent assessment or to some form of average stress level during the past few months (see Babchishin & Hanson, 2020, and Lloyd et al., 2020, for examples of using Cox regression to examine time-dependent prediction of criminal recidivism).

GOING FURTHER

Readers who have made it this far should have a sufficient understanding of Cox regression survival analysis to be educated consumers of studies using this statistical approach. The following sections are designed to deepen this understanding through further reading and exercises. These sections can be worked with in any order, and it is not necessary to do all (or any) of them.

Recommended Readings

Allison, P. D. (1984). *Event history analysis: Regression for longitudinal event data*. Sage Publications.

A short introduction to various forms of event history (survival) analysis, including a clear introduction to Cox regression (proportional hazards) survival analysis.

Singer, J. D., & Willett, J. B. (2003). *Applied longitudinal data analysis: Modeling change and event occurrence.* Oxford University Press.

Chapter 14 provides an in-depth coverage of Cox regression. Readable and authoritative.

Computer Code

Both R Statistics (Therneau, 2020) and IBM/SPSS (IBM Corp., 2020) have Cox regression survival analysis programs. Three variables are required: (a) survival time, (b) whether the event occurred by the end of follow-up, and (c) a predictor variable. The predictor can be continuous (ordinal) or dichotomous (present–absent). The following elaborates on the analyses described in the worked example above concerning the Static-99R risk tool as a predictor of sexual recidivism. The data set contains 767 cases, 83 of which were known to have reoffended sexually during the follow-up period. The original dates were transformed into survival time using the steps described in the earlier chapter on Kaplan–Meier survival analysis. Data are organized the same for Cox regression and Kaplan–Meier, with the exception that Cox regression requires a predictor variable (for Kaplan–Meier, predictor variables are optional).

R Code

Cox regression survival analysis is included in the *survival* package in R Statistics (Therneau, 2020). If you have not used it before, download it using the following command:

```
install.packages ('survival')
```

The next line identifies the data file to use, which, in this case, is an EXCEL.csv file (Chap10_Cox_example.csv; https://www.apa.org/pubs/books/prediction-statistics-for-psychological-assessment). You will need to specify where it is stored on your computer if you decide to download it. The next line tells R that you want to work with this data set.

```
Cox.data <-read.csv("c:\\run.files\\Book\\Chap10_Cox_
example.csv")
attach (Cox.data)
names (Cox.data)
[1] "CASE"  "Recid.Sex"  "Time.Sex"  "Stat99Rtot"
```

Time.Sex is survival time in years. *Recid.Sex* indicates whether the individual was identified as a sexual recidivist (1) or not (0). *Stat99Rtot* is the predictor variable (possible range of −3 to 12). *CASE* is a unique case identifier. Sometimes when reading EXCEL.csv files, R will distort the label for the first variable read. For example, instead of "CASE", the label may be "ï..CASE". One option for avoiding this problem is to explicitly define the labels in advance:

```
labels <- c("CASE", "Recid.Sex", "Time.Sex",
"Stat99Rtot")
Cox.data <- read.csv("c:\\run.files\\Book\\Chap10_Cox_
example.csv", col.names = labels)
```

Another option is to change the variable label using the **fix ( )** command, as in **fix (Cox.data)**. This will lead you to a separate window in which you can direct edit the variable labels.

The next line indicates that you will be using the survival package.

```
require ('survival')
```

Cox regression is calculated using the **coxph** command. The basic syntax is as follows:

```
model1 <- coxph(Surv(Time.Sex, Recid.Sex) ~ Stat99Rtot)
```

In this syntax "model1" is your variable name; again, you can use almost any name. The next few characters, <-coxph(Surv(, are R commands (watch the capitalization). *Time.Sex* is the time variable, and *Recid.Sex* is the outcome variables defined in the data set. The little squiggly thing (the diacritical mark tilde), ~, is an R command identifying *Stat99Rtot* as the predictor variable. Once you have specified the model correctly and run it, nothing will happen. You need to ask R for output using the *summary* command. This will produce the same output as described in the earlier worked example.

```
summary (model1)
Call:
coxph(formula = Surv(Time.Sex, Recid.Sex) ~ Stat99Rtot)
n= 767, number of events= 83
               coef    exp(coef) se(coef)   z       Pr(>|z|)
Stat99Rtot 0.30334  1.35437  0.04046 7.497 6.54e-14 ***a
---
Signif. codes: 0 '***' 0.001 '**' 0.01 '*' 0.05 '.'
0.1 ' ' 1
              exp(coef)  exp(-coef)  lower .95  upper .95
Stat99Rtot     1.354       0.7384       1.251      1.466
Concordance= 0.743 (se = 0.028 )
Likelihood ratio test= 55.51  on 1 df,  p=9e-14
Wald test             = 56.2  on 1 df,  p=7e-14
Score (logrank) test = 58.97  on 1 df,  p=2e-14
```

In this data set, the Cox regression coefficient is 0.30334, with a standard error of 0.04046. The 95% confidence interval for the hazard ratio was 1.251 to 1.466. The Harrell's C is 0.743 ($SE = 0.028$).

If Cox regression is used with more than one predictor variable, the basic syntax is as follows:

```
Model2<-coxph(Surv(Time.Sex, Recid.Sex) ~ Stat99Rtot +
Age)
```

In this syntax, both Static-99R and age are used as predictors, and the regression coefficients would indicate the incremental effect of each variable. If the data were collected from distinct samples and you want to allow for the baseline survival curves to vary across samples, then specify a categorical variable as strata, as in the following example:

```
Model3<-coxph(Surv(Time.Sex, Recid.Sex)~ Stat99Rtot +
strata (location))
```

IBM/SPSS Code

IBM/SPSS Version 27 uses the same algorithms as ***coxph*** in R Statistics for calculating Cox regression coefficients and their standard errors. SPSS does not have a routine for calculating concordance (Harrell's C). The SPSS data set contains the following variables on 767 cases: (a) *Time.Sex* is survival time in years, (b) *Recid.Sex* indicates whether the individual was identified as a sexual recidivist (1) or not (0), (c) *Stat99Rtot* is the predictor variable (possible range of −3 to 12), and (d) *CASE* is a unique case identifier. Unlike R, variable names in SPSS are not case sensitive. A copy of the SPSS data set is available for download (Chap10_Cox_example.sav; from https://www.apa.org/pubs/books/prediction-statistics-for-psychological-assessment).

The **Cox Regression** command is found by following **Analyze**, **Survival**, then **Cox Regression**. At the **Cox Regression** screen, specify which value of the dichotomous outcome variable indicates that the event occurred (in our case, the value 1). The predictor variable, Stat99Rtot, goes in the box labelled "Block 1 of 1". Under **Options**, check "CI for exp (B), 95%". The **Cox Regression** command has the option for aggregating survival curves across groups (*Strata*). This option is not needed when estimating the regression coefficients from a single sample. An example of SPSS syntax is provided below:

```
COXREG Time.Sex
/STATUS=Recid.Sex(1)
/METHOD=ENTER Stat99Rtot
/PRINT=CI(95).
```

A selection of the most important output is presented below:

Variables in the Equation

							95.0% CI for Exp(B)	
	B	*SE*	Wald	*df*	Sig.	Exp(B)	Lower	Upper
Static-99R total score	.303	.040	56.202	1	.000	1.354	1.251	1.466

Note. CI = confidence interval.

All the numbers are the same as those produced by the **coxph** program in R Statistics. The Wald statistics is a significance test (chi square), indicating whether the relationship between the predictor variable and the outcome was more than would be expected by chance (it is).

EXERCISES

Question 10.1

You just started a staff position in a secure forensic hospital, where one of your tasks is to assess new admissions for the likelihood of violence against staff and other residents. Given that no formal process was previously used, you scour the research literature for a risk tool that could help you. Of the various risk tools available, you select the Risk and Management Assessment (RaMA) because it is easy to implement and has the highest AUC value of the measures you examined. The RaMA uses a combination of 15 self-report and file review items to place individuals into one of five risk levels: 1—*well below average*, 2—*below average*, 3—*average*, 4—*above average*, and 5—*well above average*.

You use the RaMA in your first assessment, Mr. Gupta, and assign him to the below-average risk category. Feeling pleased with yourself, you present your assessment of Mr. Gupta at the weekly case conference. Your colleagues, who are unfamiliar with the RaMA, ask how much lower is Mr. Gupta's risk than that of other residents. A recent administrative review found that about 10% of residents had at least one significant incident of threats or physical force during their stay (which typically lasted about 6 weeks). Given that you do not know the answer, you praise your colleagues for their insightful questions and promise to get back with the answer shortly.

Returning to your PDF collection of research studies on the RaMA, it is hard to identify reliable incident rates for the RaMA risk levels. The rates vary considerably across studies due to differences in the settings, the length of follow-up, and the criteria used to define a violent incident. You do notice, however, that five of the studies used Cox regression to estimate the relationship between the RaMA and subsequent violent incidents. Using the meta-analytic techniques you recently learned from Chapter 14, you calculate an average Cox regression B value of .70 with a standard error of 0.043.

(i) The hazard rate for individuals in Level 2, *below average risk*, is how much lower than for individuals in Level 3, *average risk*?

(ii) What is the 95% confidence interval for this relative risk reduction?

(iii) The hospital implements the RaMA and several years later evaluates its ability to predict violent incidents. On the basis of 150 cases (20 incidents), the study finds a Cox regression coefficient of $B = .53$ with a standard error of 0.145. Using the formula for the standard error of the difference (Equation 10.1), does the predictive accuracy of the RaMA in this setting differ from that in other settings (i.e., the meta-analytic average) more than would be expected by chance?

Question 10.2

Because Cox regression is almost always calculated using statistical programs, it is useful to run the programs described in the computer code section of this chapter. The data sets used in the Static-99R example above can be found at https://www.apa.org/pubs/books/prediction-statistics-for-psychological-assessment. The Chap10_Cox_example.csv file is for R Statistics; Chap10_Cox_example.sav is an IBM/SPSS file. Using R Statistics, IBM/SPSS, or any software of your choice, calculate the following statistics for the Static-99R as a predictor of sexual recidivism: B (the raw Cox regression coefficient), exp(B), and the 95% confidence interval for the hazard ratio.

ANSWERS TO EXERCISES

Question 10.1

(i) The hazard rate for Level 2 is about half the rate for Level 3. The Cox regression *B* indicates the change in hazard rates (in logged units) for each unit change in the risk scale. The scale has five levels, each coded as being one unit apart. Level 2 is therefore 1 unit below Level 3. A 1-unit decrease would be −1 * B, or −.70 in logged hazard units. To obtain the hazard ratio, take the exponent: exp(−.70) = 0.497. A hazard ratio of 0.497 indicates that individuals in risk Level 2 on the RaMA are about half as likely to be involved in a violent incident than average (Level 3).

(ii) The 95% confidence interval is calculated as $B \pm 1.96\ (SE_B)$, that is, .70 ± 1.96 (0.043), or 0.6157 to .78428. Consequently, the relative risk for Level 2 compared with Level 3 could range from −0.78428 to −0.6157 in logged hazard units. In hazard units, the 95% confidence interval for the relative risk reduction would be 0.456 to 0.540.

(iii) The difference is 0.70 − 0.53 = 0.17. The standard error of the difference is $((SE_1)^2 + (SE_2)^2)^{1/2}$, $((0.043)^2 + (0.145)^2)^{1/2} = 0.1512$. The 95% confidence interval for the difference would be $Difference \pm 1.96\ (SE_{Difference})$, 0.17 ± 1.96 (0.1512), or −.126 to .466. Given that the confidence interval includes zero, the amount of variability is no more than would be expected by chance. The hospital continues to use the RaMA.

Question 10.2

B = .303, exp(*B*) = 1.354, with 95% confidence interval of 1.251 to 1.466. You can check your answer by referring to the computer code section above. The most common problems for R Statistics involve correctly identifying the data set to use. You will need to know where the Chap10_Cox_example.csv file is stored on your computer. My recommendation is that you place it near the top of the hierarchy of directories to minimize the opportunity for typographical errors. In my example, data are stored in a directory called "run. files\Book" on the c:\ drive. Note that the double back slashes, \\ , are necessary and that R is case sensitive (Cox.data ≠ Cox.Data).

```
Cox.data <-read.csv("c:\\run.files\\Book\\Chap10_Cox_
example.csv")
```

In Windows 10, downloaded files are sent to a specific directory (Downloads). If you want to leave the file in Downloads, use the following syntax:

```
Cox.data <-read.csv("c:\\Users\\Karl\\Downloads\\
Chap10_Cox_example.csv")
```

You would of course need to change "Karl" to your user name in your system.

11

Logistic Regression

Logistic regression describes how predictor variables are associated with a dichotomous outcome variable and estimates the likelihood of the outcome for each value of the predictor variables.

Logistic regression estimates the likelihood of a dichotomous outcome for different values of predictor variables (Hosmer et al., 2013). In the context of risk tools, logistic regression indicates how differences in the likelihood of the outcome are related to different levels of the risk tool. It indicates both relative risk (how much riskier is this case from others?) and absolute risk (what are the expected rates of the outcome for cases with these characteristics?). Predictor variables can be dichotomous, categorical, or ordinal/linear. In logistic regression, the outcome is coded as *logits* (logged odds). Transforming dichotomous outcomes into logits releases useful statistical properties, such as symmetrical variances and values bounded by zero and one. Although the extent to which data fit a logistic function needs to be verified, the logistic distribution fits a wide range of naturally occurring processes (e.g., population growth). Logistic regression is the preferred method for prediction studies with a fixed follow-up period. Compared with life-table survival analysis on the same data, logistic regression estimates are more accurate because the estimates for each risk level are informed by the data for adjacent risk levels.

https://doi.org/10.1037/0000275-011
Prediction Statistics for Psychological Assessment, by R. K. Hanson

WHY USE LOGISTIC REGRESSION?

Before extolling its many virtues, readers are warned that logistic regression is more complicated than many of the other statistics discussed in this book. In most introductory statistics texts, logistic regression is well at the back, if it is included at all. This is unfortunate because logistic regression is a key tool for describing and evaluating prediction tools (Royston et al., 2009; Steyerberg, 2019). Readers may be comforted to know that many of the core concepts have already been presented (e.g., relative and absolute risk, fixed follow-up, odds ratios). The distinction between relative risk and absolute risk is an organizing theme of many of the chapters. The fixed follow-up research design was discussed in detail in Chapter 4. Odds ratios and logged odds ratios (i.e., logits) were introduced in Chapter 7. Although these concepts are reprised in this chapter, do not hesitate to skip back to other chapters as needed.

A key advantage of logistic regression is that, in one swoop, it addresses both relative risk (how does this case compare with others?) and absolute risk (how likely is this individual to have the outcome?). Logistic regression produces two coefficients. One of the coefficients, B_0, identifies the base rate of the outcome in the sample (B_0 is also called the *intercept*). The intercept can be used to evaluate calibration, that is, the extent to which the observed rates in the current sample match those estimated by the prediction tool. The other coefficient, B_1 (the relative risk or *slope* parameter) indicates the extent to which differences in the predictor variables are associated with differences in the likelihood of the outcome. Although logistic regression is grouped in Part III with measures of discrimination, it would also fit with the calibration measures in Part IV. Chapter 14 specifically extends the discussion of logistic regression as a tool for comparing observed rates across samples and settings.

Compared with many other prediction statistics, the relative risk coefficients (the B_1s) are less influenced by arbitrary features of the research design. A change in the base rate of the outcome is expected to influence the base rate coefficient (B_0, as it should) but not the relative risk coefficient (B_1). Furthermore, the relative risk coefficients are not expected to change based on the distribution of scores for the predictor variable. Although the area under the receiver operating characteristics curve (AUC from ROC curves) is minimally influenced by base rates of the outcome, AUC values are influenced by the range of risk scores (narrow range = small AUC values; Howard, 2017; Humphreys & Swets, 1991). Consequently, logistic regression relative risk coefficients are particularly useful for comparing results across studies.

One of my early professional preoccupations was the identification of empirical risk factors for sexual recidivism (Hanson & Bussière, 1996, 1998; Hanson & Morton-Bourgon, 2004, 2005). This required reviewing hundreds of recidivism studies for common patterns. The sample size in these studies varied from less than 10 to more than 10,000. Some had recidivism base rates of less than 2%, whereas others had recidivism rates close to 50%. The predictors included characteristics both common (e.g., not currently married) and rare (e.g., active psychosis). After exploring different effect size indicators, I became increasingly

FIGURE 11.1. A Comparison of Three Methods of Estimating Recidivism Rates Associated With Static-2002 Scores

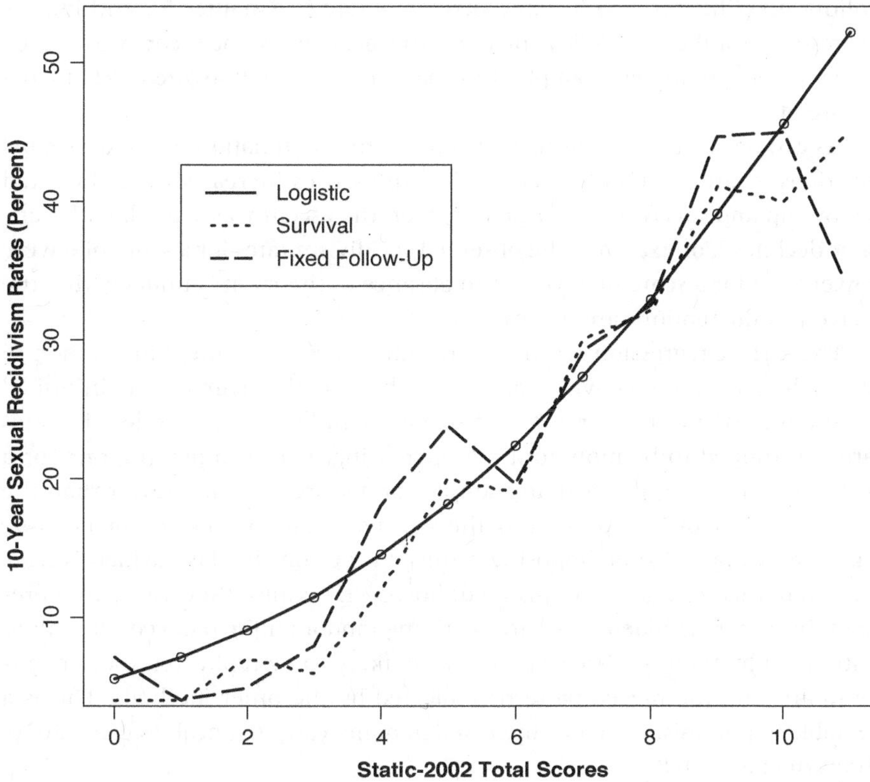

enamored with logits. Collections of findings that appeared divergent would often coalesce into a clear pattern when viewed through the lens of logistic regression. Nature speaks in logarithms (West, 2017).

Logistic regression is well suited to estimating likelihoods associated with specific scores or risk levels. Imagine a risk tool based on a simple count of the presence or absence of 20 risk factors, creating a scale with 21 levels (0, 1, 2, 3, up to 20 risk factors present). If the test developer wants to know the likelihood of the outcome for each risk level, one approach would be to divide the sample into the 21 groups (one for each risk level), then examine the rate of the outcome for each group. This is rarely optimal. The groups can become quite small even when the overall sample size is large. With small samples, observed rates will fluctuate based on sampling error, resulting in counterintuitive and unexpected patterns. Logistic regression reduces this noise.

Figure 11.1 presents an empirical example based on data from the Static-2002 sexual recidivism risk tool (N = 1,104 with 238 recidivists; Hanson et al., 2010).[1] The Static-2002 scores ranged from 0 to 11, with higher scores

[1]This figure is presented for illustrative purposes only. It is not intended for use in applied evaluations.

indicating greater likelihood of sexual recidivism (median score of 5). Three approaches were used to estimate the likelihood of sexual recidivism: fixed follow-up (Chapter 4), life-table survival analysis (Chapter 5), and logistic regression. For the fixed follow-up and survival analyses, each score was treated as a separate group, with sample sizes that ranged from 28 (score of 11) to 443 (score of 5).

As can be seen from Figure 11.1, for all three estimation methods, sexual recidivism rates generally increased as the scores increased. For the fixed follow-up and survival estimates, however, the ascent was ragged, with periodic declines. For example, the observed recidivism rates for a score of 6 were lower than for a score of 5. Given an absence of theory, it is unlikely that the perceived fluctuations are meaningful.

The logistic regression estimates, in contrast, are smoothed. In addition to using the observed recidivism rates for each score, the estimates are informed by the recidivism rates for adjacent scores. With the logistic model, the rates are constrained to be monotonically increasing. For example, the rate for a score of 6 must be higher than the rate for a score of 5, and lower than the rate for a score of 7. Representing the recidivism rates by a smoothed logistic curve may appear to be imposing artificial order on the data, which is true. The smoothed estimates are justified, however, because they aspire to represent the patterns hidden in nature. With the random noise reduced, the values estimated by the logistic curve are more likely to be replicated (better calibration) than the ragged patterns indicated by the other methods. This is a testable hypothesis, which is supported in many cases (Gonçalves et al., 2020; Hanson et al., 2018).

LIMITATIONS

The relationship between the predictor and the outcome is not always logistic. This is not a problem for dichotomous predictors because there is only one "distance" between the two values. For most measures in psychology, the shape of the relationship between scale scores (the indicators) and the underlying risk (the latent constructs) is unknown (Michell, 1990). With multiple risk categories or levels, logistic regression assumes that the separation between each level is the same (on a logarithmic scale). In other words, the relative risk increase for each point increase in the risk tool is the same for the full range of possible values. This is unlikely ever to be completely true; however, it is often reasonably approximated.

When the relationship has small deviations from the logistic curve, it is often possible to improve the fit by adjusting the risk scale. Typically, the adjustments involve adding more weight to the items with the strongest relationship to the outcome and less weight to weaker predictors. The fit can also be improved by allowing the curve to bend (adding a curve to the curve). In logit metric, logistic curves are straight lines. If the observations do not follow a straight line (in logit metric), it is relatively simple to bend the line to better fit the data

(Hosmer et al., 2013, Section 4.2.1). For the applied evaluator, however, this is not much comfort. If the logistic model is known to be a poor fit to the expected values for a measure, then other methods should be used to assign likelihoods to risk levels.

Logistic regression estimates are easiest to interpret when calculated from a fixed follow-up period. For example, consider a measure designed to evaluate the risk of substance abuse relapse. If researchers coded relapse within a fixed, 3-month follow-up period, then the likelihoods from logistic regression would indicate the likelihood of relapse within 3 months. Truncating follow-up times to make them all equal facilitates interpretation at the cost of statistical power. If there is wide variation in the at-risk time, then survival analysis provides more accurate estimates than logistic regression.

Like Cox regression, another limitation of logistic regression relative risk coefficients are that they are difficult to interpret. They are unstandardized, meaning that they describe the amount of change in the odds of the outcome for a 1-unit increase in the raw score of the prediction tool (say that five times fast!). Because the scaling of prediction tools lacks common conventions, a 1-unit increase could be a little or a lot. For example, if the total possible range is between zero and 2 (e.g., Psychopathy Checklist–Revised [PCL-R] item scores), a 1-unit increase would be substantial. If the possible range was between zero and 40 (e.g., PCL-R total scores), a 1-unit increase would be small. Consequently, it is impossible to directly compare the size of the regression coefficients for the items and the total scores of measures. Similarly, because different risk tools are scaled differently, an odds ratio of 1.25 for one scale could be better or worse than an odds ratio of 1.56 for another scale. To facilitate comparisons across measures, it is necessary to use an overall index of discrimination (e.g., calculating AUCs from the predicted values; Hosmer et al., 2013).

Finally, although odds ratios can be roughly interpreted as rate ratios when the base rates are low (less than 25%), the meaning of odds ratios is not intuitive when the base rates are high (see the discussion below).

THE NUTS AND BOLTS

Data Requirements

Logistic regression for prediction studies requires the following data:

1. a dichotomous outcome variable (preferably from fixed follow-up),
2. a predictor variable (dichotomous, ordinal, or linear), and
3. the predictor variable exists prior to the outcome.

Logistic regression will always have only one outcome variable; however, it is possible to have many predictor variables. The predictor variables can be dichotomous or categorical; however, the benefits of logistic regression are most apparent when the predictor variables have ordered levels. Ideally, each increment in the predictor variable would capture roughly the same amount of difference in relative risk. The sample size required will depend on the purpose of the logistic regression analysis. If the question is simply whether a single predictor variable has any relationship with the outcome, then 10 events in an overall sample of about 150 will have reasonable power to detect a moderate size relationship (Hosmer et al., 2013). Estimating likelihoods for specific scores of risk tools requires 100 cases with the event and 100 cases without the event (Vergouwe et al., 2005), and preferably many more. Researchers planning prediction studies can get some guidance concerning sample size requirements from Hsieh's (1989) tables. These tables, however, are only suggestive because they are based on null hypothesis statistical testing and are influenced by features of the data that are difficult to anticipate in advance.

The outcome variable should be based on a fixed follow-up time (e.g., 6 months, 10 years). This means that only cases that are followed for the complete follow-up time are included in the analysis. Individuals who are followed for less than the complete follow-up are excluded, regardless of whether they have the outcome. Individuals who have the outcome after the end of the fixed follow-up period are considered not to have had the outcome. Directions for computing fixed follow-up times by hand are presented in Chapter 4. Computer code for calculating follow-up times from raw dates (e.g., at-risk date, end of follow-up, lost to follow-up) are presented in Chapter 5.

Calculating Logistic Regression Coefficients

Logistic regression is almost always calculated using specialized computer software, which is discussed later in this chapter. Logistic regression is a form of regression that uses grouped data. Like regular linear regression, logistic regression generates an equation with a dependent variable, an intercept, and a slope coefficient: $\hat{y} = B_0 + B_1X$. In this equation, $\hat{y}$ is the predicted likelihood (as a logit), B_0 is the intercept, B_1 is the slope coefficient, and X is the predictor variable. Because the only possible outcomes are one (event) or zero (no event), the predicted values are averages of the zero's and one's for each value of the predictor variable. These average proportions are analyzed as logits (logged odds). Interpreting logistic regression coefficients requires understanding logits and how logits relate to more familiar concepts of likelihood and relative risk.

To motivate the calculations, consider the practical problem of predicting which musicians or music groups will be profitable. Starbound Corporation is a large talent management and production company. Its business model involves identifying promising acts and then investing in them through recording sessions, videos, branding, and other marketing services. Its minimum investment in an act is \$100,000, for which they need a return of \$150,000 over 5 years to stay in business. Although Starbound has had a number of spectacular successes, most of their acts do not make money for the company. Overall, only one out of five acts (20%) are considered financial successes by the preceding definition. The recruiters would like to increase that proportion.

Starbound hires a research group to develop an actuarial prediction tool for identifying financially successful music acts. Using archival data from Starbound and other interested production firms, they create the Starlight prediction tool. Starlight contains items related to musical ability, productivity (number of minutes of marketable music produced annually), motivation and drive, age (the younger the better), style sense (rated by an expert panel), and the affluence, accessibility, and absolute size of the demographics to which the music may appeal. Starlight weights these items using an empirically derived logistic regression equation, with the outcome being a predicted probability of financial success that potentially ranges from near zero to almost one.

Bier Cooler is the leader of Mĭn.E.Frĭj, a pop music band that was considered by Starbound and rejected based on a low Starlight score. Mr. Cooler thinks that they have made a bad decision (his band is musically talented and super cool). He asks Starbound to justify their decision. After considerable back and forth, Starbound provides Bier Cooler with the Starlight logistic regression equation and the score for Mĭn.E.Frĭj, which indicated only a 15% likelihood of being profitable. Mr. Cooler, whose coolness extends to being good with numbers, wants to sufficiently understand the Starlight algorithm to determine whether it is feasible to improve his score and, consequently, whether Mĭn.E.Frĭj has a realistic chance of making a living in the music business.

Probabilities and Odds

Understanding logistic regression equations requires understanding probabilities, odds, and logits. Starting with probabilities, Mr. Cooler was told that his act has a 15% likelihood of being profitable, which means that out of 100 acts like his, 15 of them will make money. In general, the *probability* of having the outcome (p) is the number with the outcome divided by the total number at risk (N): $p = n_{outcome}/N_{total}$. In this example, the probability of the outcome would be $p = .15$ (15/100). Although rarely distinguished in natural language, probabilities and odds have different statistical meanings. To calculate odds, the number with the outcome is divided by the number without the outcome (not the total at risk). Because the number with the outcome plus the number without the outcome equal the full sample, odds can be expressed as $p/(1 - p)$, which, in our example, would be the probability of being profitable divided by the probability of not being profitable.

Probabilities vary between 0 and 1, whereas odds vary between almost zero and almost infinity. When the probability of the outcome is .5, the odds of the outcome are 1 (.50/.50; in gamblers' language: "the odds are even"). When the probability is less than .5, the odds will vary between 0 and 1. When the probability is greater than .5, the odds will be greater than 1. For Mĭn.E.Frĭj, the odds of outcome was estimated as .176 (15/85, or .15/.85). When base rates are low (20% or less), the odds of the outcome are similar to the probability.

Comparing Risk Levels: Rate Ratios and Odds Ratios

With actuarial risk tools, risk levels are associated with likelihoods. These likelihoods can be expressed as probabilities or as odds. Both probabilities and odds can be used to compare likelihoods for different risk levels. When likelihoods are expressed as probabilities, the ratio of these likelihoods is the *rate ratio*, calculated as rate ratio $= p_1/p_2$. For example, consider a sample of 100 promising acts (40 out of 100 would be expected to succeed) and 100 average acts (of which 20 will succeed). The probability of being profitable is .40 for the promising acts (40/100) and .20 for the average acts (20/100). The rate ratio is 2.0 (.40/.20), which means that the promising acts are twice as likely to succeed than average (see Chapter 7).

Odds ratios are calculated in a similar manner, but using a ratio of the odds:

$$\text{Odds ratio} = \frac{n_{outcome(Group\ 1)} / n_{no.outcome(Group\ 1)}}{n_{outcome(Group\ 2)} / n_{no.outcome(Group\ 2)}} = \frac{Odds_{Group\ 1}}{Odds_{Group\ 2}} \tag{11.1}$$

Continuing our example, the odds of success for the promising acts is .6667 (.40/.60), and the odds of success for the average acts is .25 (.20/.80), which would result in an odds ratio of 2.67 (.6667/.250). Unfortunately, odds ratios are less intuitive to interpret than rate ratios. When the base rates are low, the odds can be interpreted as probabilities, and odds ratios approximate rate ratios. As the probability of the outcome increases, their interpretation is more complicated. For example, if the average success rate was 60% and the promising acts increased the likelihood by an odds ratio of 2, the success rate would not double (to more than 100%). Instead, an odds ratio of 2 indicates a doubling of the odds. For average acts, the odds is 1.5 (.60/.40). Doubling the odds would equal $2 \times 1.5 = 3.0$. An odds of 3 to 1 is equivalent to ¾ of the acts being successful and ¼ not being successful (.75/.25). In other words, an odds ratio of 2.0 corresponds to an increase in the likelihood from 60% to 75%. This was not obvious to Mr. Cooler before he did the calculations.

When odds ratios are used to describe associations in two by two tables (Chapter 7), it is often desirable to add 0.5 to each cell to stabilize the variance and permit the analysis of tables with empty cells (Fleiss et al., 2003). This adjustment is not needed for the calculation of logistic regression coefficients.

From Odds to Logits

As Mr. Cooler gets further into his studies, he realizes that one challenge with using odds and odds ratios in statistical analyses is that their variance is not symmetrical. For odds, recall that when the probability is less than .5, the odds can vary between 0 and 1, whereas the odds for probabilities over .5 can vary between 1 and infinity. Similarly, for odds ratios, if the group in the numerator has a lower rate than the group in the denominator, the odds ratio will be somewhere between 0 and 1. If the rate is higher for the group in the denominator, the odds ratio can vary between 1 and infinity.

To remedy this problem, odds and odds ratios are transformed to their natural logarithm (also referred to as the Napierian logarithm, or logarithm to the base *e*). The natural logarithm of a number (*x*) is the power to which *e* would have to be raised to equal *x*, where *e* is an irrational constant approximately equal to 2.71828. To learn more about this fascinating number, see the Appendix on Useful Algebra and Notation at the end of the book. When an odds has been transformed to its natural logarithm (ln), it is called a *logit*:

$$\text{logit} = \ln\frac{p}{1-p} \tag{11.2}$$

For example, in a sample of 100 acts of which 15 are expected to be profitable, the odds of financial success is .17647 (i.e., .15/.85 = .17647), and the logit is −1.7346. This is the number (−1.7346) that Mr. Cooler would have seen on his assessment by the Starlight prediction tool. To go from odds to logits, take the natural logarithm of the odds. On calculators, the natural logarithm function is indicated by symbols such as *ln*, *LN*, *lnx*, and log_e. Generically, ln (odds) = logit, and, in the current example, ln(.17647) = −1.7346. If the Starlight prediction tool was constructed to predict failures (not successes), then out of 100 acts like Mĭn.E.Frĭj, 85 would fail, and the odds of failure would be 5.66667 (i.e., .85/.15 = 5.66667), and the logit is 1.7346 (i.e., ln[5.66667] = 1.7346). Notice that switching the outcome from success to failure only changes the sign (direction) of the logit, not its absolute value.

To transform a logit into a probability, either of the following formulas can be used,

$$p = \frac{e^{LOGIT}}{1+e^{LOGIT}} \tag{11.3}$$

which is equivalent to Equation 11.4.

$$p = \frac{1}{1+e^{-LOGIT}} \tag{11.4}$$

For the logit of −1.7346, applying either formula gives a probability of .150, which is where we started in the example.

Equation 11.3: p = $(e^{[-1.7346]})/(1 + e^{[-1.7346]})$ = 0.17647/(1 + 0.17647)
= 0.17647/1.17647 = 0.150

Equation 11.4: p = $(1/(1 + e^{-[-1.7346]}))$ = (1/(1 + 5.666666)) = 1/6.66666
= 0.150.

I usually use Equation 11.4 because it requires only entering each number once.

Logistic Regression Coefficients

With one predictor variable (i.e., the score on a prediction tool), logistic regression estimates two regression coefficients (B_0 and B_1). These coefficients are often referred to as the slope (B_1) and intercept (B_0). B_0 is a logit (logged odds). Specifically, it is the logit of the likelihood of the outcome for a score of zero. Logits with negative values (e.g., −1.2) indicate probabilities less than 50%; positive logits indicate probabilities greater than 50%. It is often useful to rescale the predictor variable so that zero has a substantive meaning. For example, when the predictor is centered on its median value, B_0 indicates the likelihood for individuals in the middle of the risk distribution. To center a scale on the median value, simply subtract the median value from all raw scores. If a risk scale goes from zero to 11 with a median of 5, the median centered version of the scale would have scores that ranged from −5 to 6, with a median of 0. Adding or subtracting a constant will change the value of B_0, but it will not change B_1 or the likelihoods for the various risk levels.

It is worth developing some facility at transforming logits to proportions and back again. After studying the Starlight algorithm, Mr. Cooler finds he could increase the score for Mĭn.E.Frĭj by expanding their portfolio to include ballads for older audiences. This single change would increase his success rate from −1.7346 to −1.40. Simply looking at the logits, it is hard for Mr. Cooler to tell whether this change would be worthwhile. Consequently, he transforms the logit of −1.40 to a probability (proportion). Taking the exponent of −1.40 gives an odds of .2466. On calculators, the function that gives the exponent of a number is indicated by symbols such as *exp, exp(x),* e^x, and *(INV)lnx* (the inverse of the natural logarithm function). To go from odds to proportions, use p = odds/(1 + odds), or .2466/(1 + 0.2466) = .1978. Mr. Cooler decides that this change alone is unlikely to make his career, for his score still remains slightly below the average.

To go from proportions to odds, p/(1 − p) = .1978/(1 − .1978) = .2466. Take the natural log of the odds to get the logit: ln(.2466) = −1.40, and you are back to where you started. Mr. Cooler considers other changes in his act and the potential effects on his likelihood of success as indicated by his Starlight score. In the process, he spends considerable time transforming logits into probabilities and back again. You should, too.

Now do Exercise 11.1 (at the end of this chapter) before continuing with the rest of this chapter.

Have you done Exercise 11.1? If yes, great. You should be able to follow the next section. If not, well . . . I warned you.

The slope coefficient, B_1, indicates the average increase in the likelihoods associated with each 1-unit increase in the prediction tool. It is expressed as a logged odds ratio. The exponent of B_1 is an odds ratio. For example, if each risk level was associated with doubling the odds of success, B_1 would be 0.6931 indicating that the average increase would be 2.0 in odds units ($e^{(0.6931)}$ = 2.00). Notice that the slopes are logged odds ratios, not rate ratios; consequently, doubling the odds does not double the probability. Positive B_1 values indicate that the likelihoods increase with higher scores. Negative B_1 values indicate that the likelihoods decrease with higher scores. Using Cohen's (1988) conventions, odds ratios of 1.39, 2.28, and 3.74 indicate small, medium, and large effect sizes, respectively.[2] If the factor is associated with decreased likelihoods, 0.72, 0.44, and 0.27 would be small, medium, and large effects. These effect size ranges are for dichotomous predictors. For ordinal predictors, effects sizes can be expressed as the odds ratios associated with a 1 *SD* change in the predictor (e.g., Hsieh, 1989). For example, if the standard deviation of the risk scale was 3.0 and B_1 was 1.32, then a 1 *SD* change would correspond to an odds ratio of 2.30, or a moderate effect ($odds\ ratio^{SD} = 1.32^{3.0} = 2.30$).

Now complete Exercise 11.2.

Given the difficulty of interpreting logits, researchers are encouraged to report logistic regression coefficients in other, more intuitive metrics. The intercepts (B_0) can be reported as proportions, and the slopes (B_1) as odds ratios. For certain audiences, it may be worthwhile to further transform the odds ratios into rate ratios, using the base rates observed in the current study. For example, the logistic regression coefficient for productivity (annual minutes of marketable music) in the hypothetical Starlight prediction tool is $B_1 = 0.027$. On average, the acts reviewed by Starbound produced 40 minutes a year with a standard deviation of 20. If Mĭn.E.Frĭj was to increase its production from 40 to 60 minutes (a 1 *SD* increase), it would increase their logit of success by $20 \times 0.027 = 0.54$, and their odds of success by 1.716 ($e^{0.54} = 1.716$). This would increase their likelihood of success from 15% to 23% ([new odds]/[15/85] = 1.716; new odds = 0.3028; which equals a new success rate = 0.3028/[1 + 0.3028] = 0.232).

For the typical act, a 1 *SD* increase in productivity would increase the success rate from 20% (the base rate) to 30% ([new odds]/[20/80] = 1.716; new odds = 0.429, which equals a new success rate of .300 (0.429/[1 + .429] = 0.300). The new success rate compared with the original [average] success rate gives a rate ratio of 1.5 (.30/.20). In other words, the regression coefficient of 0.027 indicates that the typical act can increase their likelihood of financial success by 50% if they were to increase their annual production of marketable music by 20 minutes (1 *SD*). For most working musicians, a 50% increase in their chances of success for 20 more minutes of music would be more understandable than a regression coefficient of 0.027. This is how Bier Cooler explained it to his band members when he was encouraging them to get back to their warehouse studio after their rejection by Starbound. When presenting transformed versions of the coefficients, however, it is still good practice to report the raw regression coefficients and their standard errors in their original units (logits), particularly for atypical musicians like Bier Cooler who are motivated to fully understand the evidence. It is also good practice to report the base rate. Knowing that the base rate of success is only 20%, members of Mĭn.E.Frĭj will appreciate that they need to be more marketable than most acts—and lucky—to make it in the music business.

[2]Cohen's $d = Ln(odds.ratio)/(1.65)$; Sánchez-Meca et al. (2003).

Computing Likelihoods for Prediction Tool Scores

As previously stated, the basic form of the logistic regression equation is $\hat{y} = B_0 + B_1X$. The predicted value $\hat{y}$, is determined by B_0 and B_1 (which are constants) and the score on the prediction tool (X, a variable). For example, assume the B_0 for a risk scale is −2.800 and the B_1 is 0.320. This means that the predicted rate for a score of 0 would be −2.800 (in logit units, or 5.73%). Each 1-unit increase in risk score would increase the likelihood of the outcome by a logit of .320. The predicted rate (as a logit) for a risk score of 1 would be $\hat{y} = B_0 + B_1X = -2.800 + 0.320(1) = -2.48$. For a risk score of 5, the predicted rate (as a logit) would be $\hat{y} = -2.800 + 0.320(5) = -2.800 + 1.60 = -1.2$. Using Equation 11.4, $p = (1/(1 + e^{-[-1.2]})) = (1/(1 + 3.320)) = 1/4.320 = 0.231$, or 23.1%.

Checking the Credibility of the Logistic Model

The credibility of logistic regression estimates rests on the assumption that the relationship between the predictor and the outcome can be reasonably approximated with a logistic distribution. The simplest way to check is to plot the raw, observed proportions against the fitted logistic estimates, as in Figure 11.2 (see Worked Example later in the chapter). If it fits the logistic distribution, the line connecting observed values should wander back and forth across the line drawn by the logistic estimates. Some deviation from the logistic line is expected because of sampling error; however, there should not be areas of substantial divergence.

A more formal test is provided by the Hosmer–Lemeshow goodness-of-fit test (Hosmer et al., 2013, Section 5.2.2). This is a variation of the chi-square goodness-of-fit test described in Chapter 12. In the Hosmer–Lemeshow test, the full range of predictor scores are divided into eight to 10 equally sized groups. For example, if the total sample size was 250, each group would have approximately 25 cases. The number of events and nonevents in each of these groups is then compared with the numbers expected by the fitted logistic regression model. The resulting chi-square value is tested for significance against a distribution with $k-2$ degrees of freedom, where k is the number of groups. The degrees of freedom are $k-2$ (not $k-1$) because 1 degree of freedom is lost by creating the groups from the observed data. If the data fit the logistic function, the chi-square value will be small and not more than would be expected by chance.

Like most significance tests, the power of the Hosmer–Lemeshow test depends on the sample size. If overall the sample is small ($N < 100$; < 20 events), only the most flagrant deviations from the logistic curve would be detected. If the sample size is large ($N > 1{,}000$; >100 events), the Hosmer-Lemeshow test may detect small deviations of little practice concern (Altman et al., 2009). Consequently, it is useful to supplement the Hosmer–Lemeshow with other indicators, such as E/O index discussed in Chapter 13.

A technical discussion of how to detect and address deviations from the logistic distribution is provided in Hosmer et al. (2013, Section 4.2.1). The basic point, however, is that if any a priori distribution is used to estimate likelihoods, the model should reasonably represent the data. The default model in logistic regression is a linear relationship between the predictor and the *logit* of the outcome; however, the relationship between the predictor and the logit of the outcome need not be a straight line (i.e., there could be curves in the logistic curve). An example of improving the fit of a logistic regression prediction equation by allowing curves is provided in Wilson and Gutierrez (2014).

Worked Example

This example uses a random subset of 555 cases from the study previously presented in Figure 11.1 (Hanson et al., 2010). The cases were adult males released to the community following a charge or conviction for a sexual offense. The outcome variable was sexual recidivism (charge or conviction) during a fixed 10-year follow-up period. Of the 555 cases, 125 were known to have reoffended sexually during that period (22.5% sexual recidivism rate). The number of events was greater than 100, which allows for reasonably stable logistic regression coefficients. The predictor variable was the Static-2002 sexual recidivism risk tool (Phenix et al., 2009), with scores from zero to 13 (median value of 5; only nine cases had scores of 11 or higher). These data are used for illustrative purposes only and are not intended to inform the research or applied use of this risk tool.

Using IBM/SPSS, the logistic regression coefficients were as follows: B_0 = −2.822 (SE = 0.284) and B_1 = 0.279 (0.0429). The B_0 indicates that the expected recidivism rate for individuals with a score of zero was $1/(1 + e^{-(B0)}) = 1/(1 + e^{-(-2.822)}) = 5.6\%$, and that the odds of recidivism increased by 32% for each 1-point increase in Static-2002 scores ($e^{0.279} = 1.3218$).

The next step is determining the extent to which a logistic distribution represented the relationship between Static-2002 scores and sexual recidivism. Figure 11.2 is a graph of the logistic estimates and the estimates from fixed follow-up.

The distribution appears to reasonably fit the logistic shape, with the exception of scores 11 and 13. Given that there were few observations for scores 11 and 13 (5 and 1, respectively), the logistic assumption remains plausible.

The second test of the logistic fit was the Hosmer–Lemeshow test. The results of the IBM/SPSS analysis are presented in Table 11.1. The algorithm divided the 555 cases into nine groups, with sample sizes ranging from 34 to 68. The Hosmer–Lemeshow tests propose groups that are a compromise between equal sample size and full coverage of the predicted likelihoods. The groups are rarely exactly equal when the number of distinct scores or levels is less than 20. In our example, there were only 14 possible groups; consequently, most of the Hosmer–Lemeshow groups contained only cases with a specific score, and the remaining groups combined two or more Static-2002 risk levels. Visual inspection suggests reasonable concordance between the observed and expected values. The Hosmer–Lemeshow chi-square value was not significant (chi-square = 6.647, df = 7, p = .467), which provides further support for the

FIGURE 11.2. Logistic and Fixed Follow-Up Estimates of 10-Year Sexual Recidivism Rates Based on Static-2002 Scores (N = 555)

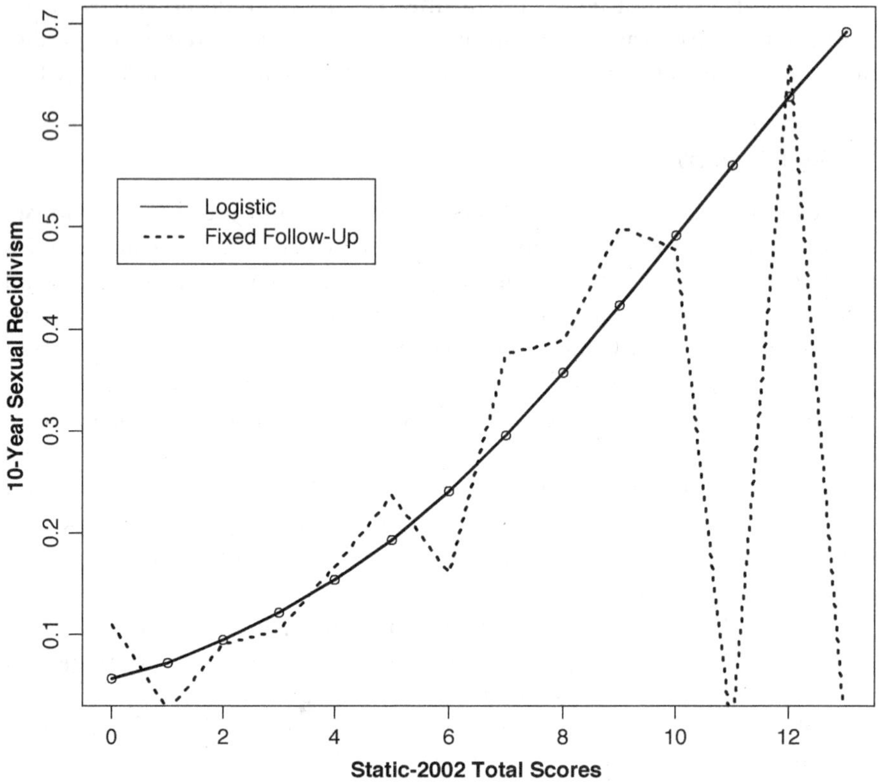

TABLE 11.1. Hosmer-Lemeshow Test for Worked Example of Static-2002 Validation Study (From IBM/SPSS)

	Contingency Table for Hosmer-Lemeshow Test				
	Sexual recidivism at fixed 10-year no		Sexual recidivism at fixed 10-year yes		
	Observed	Expected	Observed	Expected	Total
Step 1	46	44.651	2	3.349	48
2	50	49.821	5	5.179	55
3	51	50.114	6	6.886	57
4	55	55.855	11	10.145	66
5	58	61.285	18	14.715	76
6	68	61.485	13	19.515	81
7	35	39.449	21	16.551	56
8	33	34.735	21	19.265	54
9	34	32.604	28	29.396	62

logistic model. Consequently, it is reasonable to go the next step and use the equation to generate predicted values.

Standard Errors and Confidence Intervals

All logistic regression programs will produce B_0 and B_1 coefficients along with their standard errors: SE_{B0} and SE_{B1}. The standard errors are in the units of logits. They can be used in the usual way to create confidence intervals for the coefficients: 95% confidence interval is $B \pm 1.96\ (SE_B)$. After the calculations are completed (in logits), it is often useful to transform them into a more familiar metric for the purposes of communication. For example, B_0 can be expressed as a proportion, and B_1 as an odds ratio.

For example, if B_0 is −2.800 with a standard error of 0.800, the 95% confidence interval in logit units would be −2.800 ± 1.96 (0.800), −2.800 ± (1.568), or −4.368 to −1.232. In percentages, this would be 5.7% with a confidence interval of 1.25% to 22.6%. One advantage of doing the calculations in logits is that the range of the confidence intervals will never be lower than zero or higher than one. If B_1 is 0.320 with a standard error of 0.120, the 95% confidence interval would be 0.320 ± 1.96 (0.120), 0.320 ± 0.2352, or 0.0848 to 0.5552 (as logged odds ratios). This would correspond to an odds ratio of 1.377 with a 95% confidence interval of 1.088 to 1.742. The lower end of confidence interval does not include zero, indicating that the variable has a significant relationship with the outcome. The upper end of the confidence interval is less than 2, indicating that a 1-unit change in the predictor is associated with a small increase in the likelihood of the outcome.

The standard errors of the predicted likelihoods, $SE_{\hat{y}}$, are based on the standard errors of the coefficients (SE_{B0} and SE_{B1}) and the score on the risk tool. Each score on the risk tool is associated with a different degree of error. The scores with the lowest error are the well-populated levels in the middle of the risk distribution. Extreme scores are associated with the highest degree of prediction error (Equation 1.18 from Hosmer et al., 2013).

$$SE_{\hat{y}} = \sqrt{(SE_{B0})^2 + 2 \cdot x \cdot r \cdot SE_{B0} \cdot SE_{B1} + x^2 (SE_{B1})^2} \tag{11.5}$$

Equation 11.5 contains one additional parameter, r, which is the correlation of estimates. This is a scaling parameter that ensures that groups maintain the same predicted values when a constant is added or subtracted to the raw scores of the prediction tool.

Most logistic regression programs will automatically calculate 95% confidence intervals for the predicted values, minimizing the need for Equation 11.5. This equation is needed, however, when conducting meta-analyses of logistic regression coefficients, which are covered in Chapter 14. Readers should note that the confidence intervals for the predicted values are more strongly influenced by the overall sample size than by the measure's ability to discriminate recidivists from nonrecidivists. Confidence intervals for predicted values can be narrow (desirable) when the predictor has only a minimal relationship with the outcome (not desirable).

Unlike linear regression with a continuous outcome variable, the sampling errors of the predicted values in logistic regression are fully determined by the sampling variability of the parameters (B_0 and B_1). The basic model for ordinary least squares regression is $\hat{y} = B_0 + B_1X + e$, where e represents the deviations from the predicted values. Logistic regression does not have a residual error term, indicating the extent to which the observed outcome for an individual case deviates from the predicted outcome (Hosmer et al., 2013, p. 7). In contrast, the basic model for logistic regression is simply $\hat{y} = B_0 + B_1X$. The additional error term disappears because the dichotomous outcome follows a binomial distribution (see Chapter 4).

Confidence Intervals for Predicted Values in the Worked Example

The 95% confidence intervals can be calculated in R Statistics (see below) or in Excel based on Equation 11.5 (from above). In this data set, SE_{B0} was 0.284, SE_{B1} was 0.042916, and r was −.927. The scores (x) ranged from 0 to 13. Adding or subtracting a constant to the scores will change B_0, SE_{B0}, and r. However, B_1, SE_{B1}, the predicted values, and their 95% confidence intervals remain unchanged. When expressed as proportions, the confidence intervals are widest for predicted values close to 50% and narrower for values close to 0 or 1. Confidence intervals are also relatively narrow for values close to the middle of the risk distribution. In logit units, the confidence intervals are narrowest in the middle of the distribution and wider at both ends (Table 11.2).

The confidence intervals provide a range of plausible values for interpretation. Imagine that a jurisdiction had a policy of civilly committing individuals whose risk for sexual recidivism over 10 years is 30% or more. The individual in question, Mr. Wiley, was given a score of 8 on the Static-2002. On the basis of the data in our example, a score of 8 would presumptively meet the threshold given that the recidivism rate associated with this score is 35.7%. Furthermore, the prosecution argues, even individuals with scores of 7 would also meet this criterion: The upper end of the confidence interval for a score of 7 is 34.4%. The defense attorney, who happens to be unusually well trained in statistics, responds that Mr. Wiley should go free. Civil commitment is a serious consequence that should only be used with high levels of certainty (more than balance of probability). Consequently, high confidence that Mr. Wiley's likelihood is greater than 30% would require that the low end of the confidence interval should be above the threshold (a score of 9). The jury stopped listening at the first mention of statistics. They decide to commit Mr. Wiley because his index offense was abhorrent.

Comparing Regression Coefficients

Given the importance of logistic regression for evaluating prediction tools, a separate chapter is devoted to comparing logistic regression coefficients

TABLE 11.2. Predicted Values With 95% Confidence Intervals for Worked Example of Static-2002 Predicting Sexual Recidivism (N = 555)

Static-2002 scores (original metric)	Observed sexual recidivism rate (%)	n/N	Logistic regression estimates		
			Predicted probability ($\hat{y}$, %)	95% confidence interval	
				Lower	Upper
0	11.1	1/9	5.6	3.3	9.4
1	2.6	1/39	7.3	4.6	11.3
2	9.1	5/55	9.4	6.5	13.5
3	10.5	6/57	12.1	8.9	16.1
4	16.7	11/66	15.4	12.1	19.3
5	23.7	18/76	19.4	16.0	23.2
6	16.0	13/81	24.1	20.5	28.1
7	37.5	21/56	29.6	25.2	34.4
8	38.9	21/54	35.7	29.9	41.9
9	50.0	15/30	42.3	34.8	50.2
10	47.8	11/23	49.2	39.7	58.8
11	0.0	0/5	56.2	44.7	67.0
12	66.7	2/3	62.9	49.8	74.3
13	0.0	0/1	69.1	54.8	80.5
Total	22.5	125/555			

across studies. The general framework for these comparisons is fixed-effect meta-analysis (Chapter 14). The analyses described in this chapter and in Chapter 14 are often the preferred methods for conducting replication studies of actuarial prediction tools in new settings and for detecting prediction bias across racial and ethnic groups (for examples, see Hanson, Lunetta, et al., 2014; Lee et al., 2020).

Logistic regression coefficients for different risk measures are difficult to compare because they are unstandardized. The average change in the odds ratios described by the slope coefficient (B_1) is based on the changes in the raw units of the risk tool. Consequently, a scale that has scores from 0 to 10 would have different B_1 than an identical scale that had scores that ranged from 0 to 100 (e.g., multiplying each score by 10). There are a number of commonly reported R^2 (percentage of variance explained) measures for logistic regression (Mittlböck & Schemper, 1996); however, they are difficult to interpret because they are heavily influenced by base rates. One versatile approach to reporting overall discrimination is the AUC for the ROC curve (see Chapter 8). With only one predictor variable, the raw scores of the predictor variable can be used to create an AUC. If the risk prediction tool is a weighted combination of variables (a logistic regression equation with more than one slope coefficient, $\hat{y} = B_0 + B_1X_1 + B_2X_2 \ldots + B_nX_n$), then the overall accuracy (discrimination) can be described using the predicted values from the logistic regression analysis ($\hat{y}$) as the predictor variable in the AUC analysis (Hosmer et al., 2013, Section 5.2.4).

GOING FURTHER

If you have gone this far through the chapter, your understanding will be more than sufficient to read research articles and use risk scales based on logistic regression. The following sections are designed to deepen this understanding through further reading and exercises. These sections can be worked with in any order, and it is not necessary to do all (or any) of them.

Recommended Readings

Field, A. (2017). *Discovering statistics using IBM SPSS statistics* (5th ed.). Sage Publications.

Andy Field is a leading statistics educator in psychology. Clear and lighthearted. The full title of a previous edition was *Discovering Statistics Using SPSS (and Sex and Drugs and Rock n' Roll)*. A good introduction to logistic regression for students who choose psychology hoping to avoid statistics.

Hosmer, D. W., Lemeshow, S., & Sturdivant, R. X. (2013). *Applied logistic regression* (3rd ed.). Wiley.

A comprehensive, authoritative text. Moderately advanced. Full of wise, practical advice.

Computer Code

Both R Statistics (R Core Team, 2020) and IBM/SPSS (IBM Corp., 2020) have logistic regression programs. As usual, R is more complicated to run but does everything. IBM/SPSS does almost everything except compute confidence intervals for predicted values. Both programs generate identical values for the logistic regression coefficients, their standard errors, and predicted values. The computer code examples use data from the worked example above (555 cases, Static-2002 as predictor of fixed 10-year sexual recidivism rates, average recidivism rate of 22.5%).

R Code

Logistic regression is included in the base R program (R Core Team, 2020). Logistic regression is a variation of the general linear model (**glm**). If you have the R prompt, you should be able to run logistic regressions.

The first line below specifies the labels, then the next line reads an EXCEL.csv file (Chap11_LR_example.csv; available at https://www.apa.org/pubs/books/prediction-statistics-for-psychological-assessment) into an R data frame. You will need to specify where the Excel file is stored on your computer. The subsequent line (*attach*) tells R that you want to work with this data set.

```
labels <- c("CASE", "sexRCD10yr", "Static2002")
LR.data <- read.csv("c:\\run.files\\Book\\Chap11_LR_
example.csv", col.names = labels)
attach (LR.data)
names (LR.data)
[1] "CASE" "sexRCD10yr" "Static2002"
```

The *sexRCD10yr* variable indicates whether the individual was identified as a sexual recidivist (1) or not (0). *Static2002* is the predictor variable (possible range of 0 to 13). *CASE* is a unique case identifier. Remember variable names are case sensitive CASE ≠ Case. The following syntax conducts the logistic regression analysis:

```
LR.model<-glm(sexRCD10yr ~ Static2002, family=binomial)
```

LR.model is a variable name that you assign, which can be almost anything. The next few characters, **<- glm (** , are R commands for the general linear model. The next variable, *sexRCD10yr,* is the dichotomous outcome variable. The little squiggly thing (tilde), ~, tells R that *Static2002* is the predictor variable. Given that there are many possible linear models, you need to specify that the link function is binomial. This is another way of saying that you want to conduct a logistic regression, that is, a regression analysis with a linear relationship between the predictor and the logit of the outcome.

Once you have specified the model correctly and run it, nothing will happen. You need to ask R for output using the *summary* command.

```
summary (LR.model)
```

A selection of the output is reproduced here:

```
Call:
glm(formula = sexRCD10yr ~ Static2002, family = binomial)
[. . . .]
Coefficients:
              Estimate  Std. Error  z value    Pr(>|z|)
(Intercept)  -2.82200   0.28365    -9.949   < 2e-16 ***
Static2002    0.27906   0.04292     6.503   7.9e-11 ***
```

The most important elements of this output are the regression coefficients and their standard errors. The intercept coefficient (B_0) is –2.82200 with a standard error of 0.28365. The slope coefficient (B_1) for Static2002 is 0.27906 with a standard error of 0.04292.

To examine the data's fit to the logistic curve, you will need to compute the observed and predicted proportions. Use the *fitted.values* command for the predicted proportions.

```
p.recidivism <- fitted.values (LR.model)
```

P.recidivisim is a variable name you choose; <- fitted.values (LR.model), tells R that you want the predicted values from the logistic model created in the previous commands. To verify that it did what you want, ask for the mean and the length:

```
mean (p.recidivism)
[1] 0.2252252
length (p.recidivism)
[1] 555
```

The mean of the fitted values should be the same as the overall recidivism rate for the sample. The length of 555 indicates that there is a predicted value for each case. To graph the curve, first average the predicted recidivism rates by Static-2002 scores:

```
expected <- tapply (p.recidivism, Static2002, mean)
length (expected)
[1] 14
```

Now there are 14 expected values, one for each Static-2002 score. To get the observed rates, average the observed recidivism rates by Static-2002 score:

```
observed <- tapply (sexRCD10yr, Static2002, mean)
length (observed)
[1] 14
```

Before plotting, the values of the predictor variable need to be created.

```
scores <- c(0:13)
```

The following commands create a basic figure with the observed and expected rates (run both lines at the same time).

```
plot (scores, expected)
lines (scores, observed)
```

The following commands create Figure 11.2.

```
plot (scores, expected, ylab="10-year sexual recidivism",
xlab="Static-2002 total scores", cex.lab = 1.3)
lines (scores, expected, lwd = 2)
lines (scores, observed, lty = 3, lwd = 2)
legend(.12, .55, legend=c("Logistic", "Fixed Follow-
  up"),lty=c(1,3), cex=1.1)
```

The Hosmer–Lemeshow test is included in the package **generalhoslem** (Matthew, 2019). If you have not used it before, you will need to get it using the following command:

```
install.packages ("generalhoslem")
```

Once you have downloaded it, tell R that you want to use it now:

```
library ("generalhoslem")
```

The basic syntax is as follows:

```
HL.test <- logitgof(sexRCD10yr,p.recidivism, g = 10)
```

HL.test is a name of your choice, **<- logitgof(** , is an R command. The next two variables are the observed outcomes (in our example $N = 555$ 0s and 1s) and the predicted values ($N = 555$ probabilities). You need to specify the number of groups, with the default being 10. If you choose too many groups, it will let you know with a message like "Not possible to compute 10 rows. There might be too few observations." Don't worry. The Hosmer–Lemeshow test still works reasonably well with fewer than 10 groups. Furthermore, the program will automatically decrease the number of groups. If, however, your data are really limited and the groups are reduced to six or fewer, then the Hosmer–Lemeshow test may be uninformative. To see the results, type the name of the object you created using *logitgof*.

```
HL.test
     Hosmer and Lemeshow test (binary model)
data: sexRCD10yr, p.recidivism
X-squared = 8.6763, df = 7, p-value = 0.2767
```

The degrees of freedom indicate that the program created nine groups, not 10 ($g - 2 = 7$). The chi-square value is not significant, supporting the credibility of the logistic model for this data set. If you want to see the table of values, type the following:

```
cbind (HL.test$observed, HL.test$expected)
```

And it will generate the following table:

	y0	y1	yhat0	yhat1
[0.0561,0.0942]	96	7	94.47269	8.527309
(0.0942,0.121]	51	6	50.11397	6.886028
(0.121,0.154]	55	11	55.85468	10.145319
(0.154,0.194]	58	18	61.28510	14.714899
(0.194,0.241]	68	13	61.48503	19.514974
(0.241,0.296]	35	21	39.44882	16.551177
(0.296,0.357]	33	21	34.73530	19.264696
(0.357,0.423]	15	15	17.30962	12.690383
(0.423,0.691]	19	13	15.29478	16.705215

The following syntax generates the 95% confidence intervals for the predicted values and reports them as proportions.

```
inverse_logit = function(x){exp(x)/(1+exp(x))}
```

The confidence intervals are computed in logits. The preceding syntax creates a function for transforming logits into proportions, which follows:

```
LR.values <- predict(LR.model, type='link',
se.fit=TRUE)
se_high <- inverse_logit(LR.values$fit +
(LR.values$se.fit*1.96))
se_low <- inverse_logit(LR.values$fit - (LR.values$se.
fit*1.96))
upper <- tapply (se_high, Static2002, mean)
lower <- tapply (se_low, Static2002, mean)
```

```
table.ci <- cbind (0:13, lower, expected, upper)
table.ci
          lower        expected      upper
0     0  0.03299134  0.05614688  0.09397514
1     1  0.04644363  0.07290257  0.11265436
2     2  0.06483843  0.09415975  0.13482905
3     3  0.08944349  0.12080750  0.16122224
4     4  0.12126821  0.15371696  0.19294187
5     5  0.16034003  0.19361709  0.23189314
6     6  0.20483248  0.24092560  0.28113009
7     7  0.25169937  0.29555673  0.34354758
8     8  0.29926919  0.35675363  0.41868245
9     9  0.34760980  0.42301278  0.50218168
10   10  0.39696917  0.49216236  0.58792729
11   11  0.44716421  0.56161315  0.66986138
12   12  0.49764926  0.62873089  0.74325490
13   13  0.54767812  0.69122249  0.80539921
```

IBM/SPSS Code

IBM/SPSS Version 27 produces the same logistic regression coefficients and predicted values as R. SPSS does not have a routine for calculating confidence intervals of the predicted values. The IBM/SPSS file (Chap11_LR_example.sav, available at https://www.apa.org/pubs/books/prediction-statistics-for-psychological-assessment) contains the same data used in the worked example earlier in the chapter (555 cases, Static-2002 as predictor of fixed 10-year sexual recidivism rates, average recidivism rate of 22.5%). It contains three variables: (a) *sexRCD10yr,* which indicates whether the individual was identified as a sexual recidivist (1) or not (0); (b) *Static2002,* the predictor variable (possible range of 0–13)' and (c) *CASE.* a unique case identifier. Unlike R, variable names in SPSS are not case sensitive.

The logistic regression routine is found by following **Analyze**, **Regression**, then **Binary Logistic**. At the **Logistic Regression** screen, specify the dichotomous outcome variable (in our case, it is *sexRCD10yr*). The predictor variable, *Static2002,* goes in the box labelled "Block 1 of 1". Under **Options**, check "Hosmer–Lemeshow goodness-of-fit test." Under **Save**, check "Probabilities". An example of SPSS syntax is as follows:

```
LOGISTIC REGRESSION VARIABLES sexRCD10yr
/METHOD=ENTER Static2002
/SAVE=PRED
/PRINT=GOODFIT CORR
/CRITERIA=PIN(0.05) POUT(0.10) ITERATE(20) CUT(0.5).
```

The Hosmer–Lemeshow test is presented before the regression coefficients (reproduced as Table 11.1 earlier in the chapter). The cases are divided into nine groups; however, the groups are different from the groups created by R. Consequently, the chi-square values are not identical, although neither are statistically significant.

In IBM/SPSS, the constant is the intercept (B_0) and the variable name (Static-2002 total score) is used to identify the slope coefficient (B_1). These are the same values previously calculated. The Exp (B) of the Static-2002 total score is an odds ratio indicating that each increase in Static-2002 score was associated with a 32% increase in the odds of recidivism. The Exp (B) of the constant (B_0) is an odds. Use Exp(B)/(1 + Exp(B) to transform it into a proportion: (.059)/(1 + .059) = .056. This is the expected recidivism rate for Static-2002 scores of zero.

Variables in the Equation

		B	*SE*	Wald	*df*	Sig.	Exp(B)
Step 1[a]	Static-2002 total score	.279	.043	42.283	1	.000	1.322
	Constant	−2.822	.284	98.975	1	.000	.059

[a]Variable(s) entered on step 1: Static-2002 total score.

The predicted values will automatically be added to the active data set, with the variable name of *PRE_1*. Use the **Means** command for a table of the observed and predicted values (follow **Analyze**, then **Compare Means**, then **Means**).

```
MEANS TABLES=sexRCD10yr PRE_1 BY Static2002
/CELLS=MEAN.
```

Report

	Mean	
Static-2002 total score	**Sexual recidivism at fixed 10-year FU?**	**Predicted probability**
0	.11	.0561469
1	.03	.0729026
2	.09	.0941598
3	.11	.1208075
4	.17	.1537170
5	.24	.1936171
6	.16	.2409256
7	.38	.2955567
8	.39	.3567536
9	.50	.4230128
10	.48	.4921624
11	.00	.5616131
12	.67	.6287309
13	.00	.6912225
Total	.23	.2252252

The observed and predicted values are the same as those computed by R Statistics and displayed in Figure 11.2. Graphing functions are available in IBM/SPSS; however, the specifics of the SPSS graphing programs are beyond the scope of the current book.

EXERCISES

Question 11.1

Each of the columns in the following table presents three ways of representing a likelihood (logits, odds, and proportions). Complete the missing entries.

	A	B	C	D	E
Logit (B_0)	?	−1.735	?	0.0	1.386
Odds	0.05263	0.17647	?	?	?
p	?	0.1500	0.3500	?	?

Question 11.2

Each of the columns in the following table contains logistic regression slope coefficients (B_1, logged odd ratios) and odds ratios.

(i) Complete the missing entries.

	Variable			
	A	B	C	D
B_1 (logged odds ratio)	0.600	−.600	?	1.240
Odds ratio	?	0.5488	0.961	?

(ii) For which of the variables are high scores associated with increased risk?

(iii) For which of the variables are low scores associated with increased risk?

Question 11.3

Because logistic regression is almost always calculated using statistical programs, it is useful to run the programs described in the computer code section above. The data sets used in the Static-2002 example above can be found at https://www.apa.org/pubs/books/prediction-statistics-for-psychological-assessment. The Chap11_LR_example.csv file is for R Statistics; Chap11_LR_example.sav is an IBM/SPSS file. Using R Statistics, IBM/SPSS, or any software of your choice,

(i) Calculate the following statistics for Static-2002 as a predictor of sexual recidivism: B_0, SE_{B0}, B_1, SE_{B1}, and a table of the predicted values for each Static-2002 score.

(ii) Two evaluators scored Mr. Risky on the Static-2002. The prosecution evaluator obtained a score of 6. The defense evaluator obtained a score of 5. If they based their risk assessment only on these scores, the prosecution evaluator would estimate Mr. Risky's odds of recidivism as being how much higher than that estimated by the defense?

ANSWERS TO EXERCISES

Question 11.1

	A	B	C	D	E
Logit (B_0)	**−2.944**	−1.735	**−0.6190**	0.0	1.3863
Odds	0.05263	0.17647	**0.5385**	**1.0**	**4.000**
p	**0.0500**	0.1500	0.3500	**0.5000**	**0.8000**

Column A. To transform from odds to logit, take the natural log of the odds: ln(0.05263) = −2.944. Use p = odds/(1 + odds) to get the probability from an odds: .05263/(1.05263) = 0.0500 (with rounding).

Column C. Use odds = p/(1 − p) to get the odds from a probability: .35/(1 − .35) = 0.5385.

Use ln(p/(1 − p)) to transform from proportions to logits: ln(.35/(1 − .35)) = −0.6190.

Column D. To transform from logits to odds, take the exponent, $e^{logit} = e^{(1.3863)} =$ 4.000.

To transform from logits to probabilities, use either Equation 11.3 or Equation 11.4: $p = e^{logit}/(1 + e^{logit}) = 4/(1 + 4) = .8000$, or $p = 1/(1 + e^{-logit}) = 1(1 + e^{(-1.3863)}) = 1/(1 + 0.2500) = .800$.

Question 11.2

(i) The completed entries are in **bold.**

	Variable			
	A	B	C	D
B_1 (logged odds ratio)	0.600	−.600	**−.040**	1.240
Odds ratio	**1.822**	0.5488	0.961	**3.456**

The steps to calculating the entries are as follows: Variable A: Use $e^{odds.ratio} = B_1$, $e^{(0.600)} = 1.822$;

Variable C: Use ln(odds.ratio) = B_1, ln(0.961) = −0.03978 (rounds to −0.040); Variable D: Use $e^{odds.ratio} = B_1$, $e^{(1.240)} = 3.456$.

(ii) Increased scores for Variable A and Variable D are associated with increased risk.

(iii) Low scores for Variable B and Variable C are associated with increased risk.

Positive slope coefficients indicate that high scores are associated with increased likelihood of the outcome (increased risk). Negative slope coefficients indicate that low scores are associated with increased likelihood of the outcome. For example, the odds of the outcome for a case with a score of two on Variable B would be approximately half (0.5488) the odds of the outcome for a case with a score of zero.

Question 11.3

(i) $B_0 = -2.822$, $SE_{B0} = 0.284$, $B_1 = 0.279$, $SE_{B1} = 0.04292$

Static-2002 total score	Predicted probability
0	.0561469
1	.0729026
2	.0941598
3	.1208075
4	.1537170
5	.1936171
6	.2409256
7	.2955567
8	.3567536
9	.4230128
10	.4921624
11	.5616131
12	.6287309
13	.6912225
Total	.2252252

(ii) The *B1* coeff is 0.279. Exp(*B1*) give the odds ratio: Exp(0.279) = 1.32. Consequently, the odds of recidivism for a score of 6 would be 32% higher than for a score of 5. In raw proportions, this would be a rate of 24.1% versus 19.4%.

IV

CALIBRATION

INTRODUCTION: CALIBRATION

Calibration is one of two fundamental properties by which prediction tools should be evaluated. *Calibration* refers to the match between the predicted rates of the outcome and the rates observed in new samples. In other words, to what extent are the rates indicated by the risk tool stable features of nature? For example, if a risk tool estimates a recidivism rate of 10%, then for a well-calibrated prediction tool, the observed recidivism rates in new samples would be close to 10%. The other fundamental property of prediction tools is *discrimination*, also called relative risk (discussed in Part III), which is the extent to which individuals with the outcome are different from individuals without the outcome. Whereas good discrimination is a desirable property of all risk tools, calibration is a feature only of risk tools that have rates associated with scores or risk levels. Risk tools that provide only relative risk labels (e.g., low, moderate, or high) cannot be judged by how many individuals in the high-risk group have the outcome.

For certain decisions, the rate or likelihood of the outcome is more important than relative risk. Legal statutes, for example, may specify a threshold that triggers the application or removal of restrictive measures. For example, in some U.S. states, individuals can be confined indefinitely if they are considered more likely than not to commit another sexually motivated offense (Levenson, 2004). The courts hearing such cases are not deciding whether the individual is more likely than other individuals to commit a sexual offense; the question concerns this individual's likelihood of reoffending. A related example is that individuals on sexual offender registries in some states may be released from the duty to register if they are not a cognizable risk for sexual recidivism. Again, the question is not whether the individual is lower risk than other individuals on the registry; the question is whether their likelihood is very low in absolute terms.

Calibration cannot be evaluated from a single observation, except in the rare case where the predicted likelihood is zero or one. Calibration statistics are calculated from a collection of observations. When a weather forecaster states that there is a 40% chance of rain on Tuesday, whether it in fact does rain on Tuesday provides little information concerning the forecaster's accuracy. Instead, the accuracy of the estimated likelihood is evaluated based on a collection of days "like Tuesday." If the weather forecast is perfectly calibrated, then it would rain on exactly 40 out of 100 days that have the same meteorological conditions as the Tuesday in question. If a forensic evaluator states that Mr. Harris is a member of a risk group with a 40% chance of violent offending within 2 years, the accuracy of this risk estimate can only be empirically verified by reference to group data for individuals like Mr. Harris. Determining what it means to be "like Mr. Harris" requires the disciplined insight of researchers and the sound professional judgment of evaluators.

Part IV begins with the chi-square goodness-of-fit test (Chapter 12). It is a well-known statistic and the only calibration statistic that I was taught in graduate school. The limitation of chi-square is that it only provides a significance test, meaning that it is poorly suited to estimating the magnitude of the deviations from perfect calibration. Chi-square is included because it is perhaps the most common calibration statistic in the published literature. The next section provides a versatile effect size indicator for evaluating calibration (the E/O index; Chapter 13), which is often the preferred statistic for comparing an observed value to norms asserted by test developers. Chapter 14 examines the degree of consistency of findings observed in different samples and settings. The framework for these comparisons is meta-analysis. Part IV concludes with a brief overview of calibration plots for visualizing the degree of similarity between the expected and observed values (Chapter 15).

12

Chi-Square Goodness-of-Fit

The chi-square goodness-of-fit test is a measure of calibration that compares the expected number of outcomes with the observed number of outcomes in a replication study.

The chi-square goodness-of-fit test is a versatile statistic for assessing calibration between expected and observed values. In research articles, chi-square tests are often reported using the small Greek letter, chi, squared: χ^2. The chi-square statistic has many uses, of which the chi-square calibration goodness-of-fit test is only one. The χ^2 goodness-of-fit statistic is a statistical significance test, meaning that it estimates the likelihood that the observed results could be due to chance alone. Good fit is indicated by small, nonsignificant chi square values. Poor fit is indicated by large chi-square values. Good fit means that the observed values are close to the expected values; poor fit indicates that the distribution of outcomes is inconsistent with expectations (poor calibration). For prediction tools, a large chi-square value may indicate that the overall rates of the outcome were too high or too low. It could also indicate that the predictor was only weakly related to the outcome or, conversely, that the relationship between the predictor and the outcome was unusually strong. It could also indicate various combinations of the preceding patterns. Consequently, the interpretation of significant χ^2 values requires examining how the observed rates differed from the expected results.

https://doi.org/10.1037/0000275-012
Prediction Statistics for Psychological Assessment, by R. K. Hanson

WHY USE THE CHI-SQUARE GOODNESS-OF-FIT TEST?

Calibration tests, such as the chi-square goodness-of-fit test, are useful when absolute rates are more important than relative rates. The criminal justice and forensic mental health systems often restrict individual liberty based on defined thresholds of risk for violence. The question in such decisions is not whether Mr. Jones is riskier than other individuals; the clinical question is whether Mr. Jones is sufficiently dangerous to himself or others to justify involuntary commitment (provided, of course, that he meets other statutory criteria for civil commitment).

Calibration tests compare the observed rates in a replication study to the rates estimated by a prediction tool. Consequently, calibration tests only apply to prediction tools that assign likelihoods to cases. For many prediction tools, likelihoods are expected to increase steadily as the scores increase. For other prediction tools, the relationship between the risk levels and the outcome is not linear, or not even monotonically increasing. One advantage of the chi-square goodness-of-fit test is that it can easily evaluate prediction tools that do not have orderly increases in likelihoods for increasing risk scores. Any predefined pattern can be tested. The χ^2 test is particularly helpful when the risk classifications function as categories rather than as relative risk placements. Examples of categories commonly used in research are gender (e.g., male, female, nonbinary), race, and geographic region.

Categorical risk predictors allow for distinct groups to be higher risk, lower risk, or the same risk as other groups. An example of prediction using categories would be anticipating the onset of psychosis based on genetic or racial characteristics. For example, clinical practice guidelines might indicate that the likelihood of schizophrenia is higher among African Americans (with a history of slavery and discrimination) than for either (a) Caucasian Americans or (b) Indigenous Africans in Africa (e.g., individuals with similar genetic heritage as African Americans but without the history of slavery and dislocation). Perhaps a research study found prevalence rates of psychosis of 3.2%, 1.2%, and 1.1% for African Americans, Caucasian Americans, and Indigenous Africans in Africa (e.g., respectively). If a replication study found rates of 4.2%, 0.9%, and 1.4% for these groups, the chi-square goodness-of-fit could be used to test whether the variation in the rates between studies was more than would be expected by chance.

Some risk prediction procedures do not provide total scores; instead, the output of the algorithm are likelihoods (Duwe & Freske, 2012; Howard & Dixon, 2012). Some prediction tools are explicitly constructed to sort cases into categories with predefined levels of risk. An example of this type of prediction tool is the decision tree (e.g., Monahan, 2021; Monahan et al., 2006). Decision trees involve a series of binary decisions about risk-relevant characteristics, with the results of previous questions guiding subsequent questions. For measures that provide likelihoods as their primary output, it is appropriate to evaluate these risk tools using the chi-square goodness-of-fit test.

LIMITATIONS

The major limitation of the chi-square goodness-of-fit test is that it is only a significance test. Consequently, standard errors and confidence intervals do not apply, nor is there an obvious way of comparing the degree of fit across studies. The test provides information about whether the observed results are different from the expected results but provides no information about the size or nature of the deviations. The observations could be too high, too low, or some combination of the two. The deviations could be large and practically important, or too small to worry about. With very large sample sizes, even tiny deviations from perfect calibration will be statistically significant.

In general, a statistically significant chi-square value is bad news for a risk tool because it indicates poor calibration. Large chi-square values, however, can be found when a risk prediction tool works better than expected. For example, consider a risk tool with three risk levels associated with expected likelihoods of 20%, 40%, and 50%. If a replication study found rates of 10%, 35%, and 70% for these levels, the chi-square value may be statistically significant; nevertheless, most evaluators would still consider the study supportive of the risk tool because of the increased discrimination in the replication study (i.e., the relative risk differences between the top third and the bottom third increased from an odds ratio of 4.0 to an odds ratio of 21.0).

The E/O index discussed in the next chapter (Chapter 13) should be considered as an alternative to the chi-square test because the E/O index provides an estimate of the size and direction of the deviations from expectations. When there is the expectation of an orderly, consistent relationship between risk scores and the likelihood of the outcome, then meta-analysis of logistic regression coefficients is recommended (Chapter 14), as are calibration plots (Chapter 15).

Another limitation of the chi-square test is that it is an approximation. It was developed to solve probability problems that were too laborious to solve by brute calculation. With the advent of cheap computing power, it is now possible to calculate the exact probabilities directly for most goodness-of-fit problems. The chi-square approximation is nonetheless still used because it works well; there are rarely meaningful differences between the chi-square estimates and the exact probabilities when the sample size is not small. There is some debate about what is small. Most guidelines recommend against using the chi-square test when the number of expected events in the smallest cell is less than 10 or less than 5. If in doubt about whether the sample size is big enough, calculate the exact probability, which is available in most standard statistical software.

THE NUTS AND BOLTS

Data Requirements

The following data are required to calculate the chi-square goodness-of-fit test in prediction studies:

1. a dichotomous outcome variable,
2. the number with the outcome is not small,
3. a predictor variable with two or more levels, and
4. expected rates linked to levels of the predictor variable.

The simplest predictor would have two levels (e.g., predictor is present, predictor is absent); however, the χ^2 test can also be used with any number of ordered levels or (unordered) categories. Because the χ^2 test is an approximation for large samples, the expected number of events should not be small. Hayes (1981) recommended that the expected number of events should be at least 10 for fourfold tables and at least five for tables with more cells.

Calculating the Chi-Square Goodness-of-Fit Test

The elements of the χ^2 test are the number of observed events (O, an integer) and the number of expected events (E) in each possible cell. When both the predictor and the outcome are dichotomous, these are the cells of the fourfold table (Chapter 7). If the predictor has three levels (e.g., low, moderate, high), there would be six cells: 3 levels × 2 outcomes = 6. In general, the number of cells is equal to the number of levels or categories (L) of the predictor times the number of possible outcomes, which in our case in two (outcome present, outcome not present): total cells = $L \times 2$.

The chi-square goodness-of-fit statistic is calculated as follows (Gail & Pfeiffer, 2005; Hayes, 1981, Section 15.4):

$$\chi^2 = \sum_{i=1}^{C} \frac{(O_{\cdot i} - E_{\cdot i})^2}{E_{\cdot i}} \tag{12.1}$$

The Greek letter, capital sigma, Σ, indicates summation (i.e., calculate for each cell, then add them all together). The subscript $.i$ indicates that the observed (O) and expected (E) frequencies are computed for each cell, that is, all cells with events and all cells without events. In this equation, C is the number of cells. For example, four numbers would be added together to obtain the chi-square value for a fourfold table. Because the number with the outcome in each level fully determines the number without the outcome ($O_{0i(\text{no.outcome})} = n_i - O_{1i(\text{outcome})}$), Equation 12.1 can be rewritten as follows (Hosmer et al., 2013, Equation 5.8):

$$\chi^2 = \sum_{i=1}^{L} \frac{(O_{1i} - E_{1i})^2}{E_{1i}(1 - p_i)} \tag{12.2}$$

In this formula, p_i is the likelihood of the outcome for level i asserted by the norms of the risk prediction tool (expected rate of the outcome). L is the number of levels. The subscript $1i$ indicates that the observed and expected frequencies are only for the number of events. In a fourfold table, for example, there would be only two risk levels (predictor present, predictor absent); consequently, if the chi-square is calculated for a fourfold table using Equation 12.2 only two numbers would be added together (one number for each risk level).

The resultant chi-square value is associated with a significance level by referring to theoretical chi-square distributions. The shape of a chi-square distribution is determined by the number of degrees of freedom (*df*). In replication studies for a prediction tool, the degrees of freedom are equal to one less than the number of levels or categories in the risk prediction tool (Steyerberg, 2009, Section 15.3.8): $L - 1 = df$. The number of degrees of freedom are the same regardless of whether the chi-square value is calculated using Equation 12.1 or Equation 12.2 (both equations result in the same chi-square value). It may seem that Equation 12.1 should have more degrees of freedom because there are more cells to add together; however, because the number with the outcome fully determines the number without the outcome, the extra cells do not actually provide more degrees of freedom.

The chi-square values can be compared to certain critical values; for example, the critical value $p < .05$ for a one degree of freedom chi-square value is 3.84. If the calculated χ^2 value was 4.52, it is larger than 3.84; consequently, it is reasonable to conclude that the observed pattern would be unlikely to arise by chance alone, that is, the observed and expected distributions are different. Instead of simply checking whether a χ^2 value is bigger or smaller than a critical value (e.g., 3.84), a more precise estimate of the probability associated with the observed χ^2 value can be obtained through many statistical software programs. For example, the probability of $\chi^2 = 4.52$ with one degree of freedom is 0.0335 (computed using the **pchisq** command in R).

The chi-square goodness-of-fit test can also be used to identify findings that are too good to be true. A famous example concerns the experiments reported by Abbé Mendel, the father of Mendelian genetics. The match between the monk's predictions concerning the shape and color of his beloved pea plants matched his expectations all too well. The χ^2 value was 0.470 ($df = 3$), $p = .0745$ (Ferguson, 1976, §13.4), indicating that there was less than a 10% chance (p = .0745) that he would have obtained such results by chance alone. This inspired a century of debate on whether Mendel should be considered a father of scientific fraud (Radick, 2015). The current consensus is probably not. His data were unusually good, but that, too, can happen by chance. There is no other evidence that would raise suspicions about Mendel's scientific integrity.

Worked Example

The example is an evaluation of a simplified risk prediction scheme advanced by a certain Dr. Elisabeth von Ebing-Krafft (no relationship to Richard von

Krafft-Ebing, the Viennese author of *Psychopathia sexualis*). In this hypothetical example, Dr. Ebing-Krafft is the leader of the assessment unit for a hospital for sexual psychopaths. Her job is to determine whether the individuals referred for assessment should be committed as sexually dangerous persons, potentially for life. The criteria for commitment are that the individual (a) has committed a sexually violent offense, (b) suffers from a mental disorder, and (c) is more likely than not to commit a sexual or violent offense if not detained for treatment. Although there is no time limit on when the new offense could occur, decision makers usually commit individuals whose risk level corresponds to a violent recidivism rate of at least 35% after 5 years. Individuals whose recidivism risk is less than 35% are usually sent to serve determinant sentences in regular prisons.

Dr. Ebing-Krafft has been working at the hospital since its inception. Early in her tenure, she developed the prediction scheme now routinely used to assess sexual dangerousness. The assessment has two questions: (a) Does the individual have intense, enduring sexual interests in illegal sexual behaviors (e.g., pedophilia, sadism)? and (b) Does the individual suffer from psychopathy, a personality disorder characterized by lack of remorse, indifference to the rights of others, superficial charm, and persistent rule violation? Each construct is considered a discrete taxon, not a dimension (i.e., she is not interested in the level of sexual deviancy or psychopathy, only whether it is present or not). The decision rules for her prediction scheme are presented in Figure 12.1.

On the basis of the assessment results, individuals can be placed into one of four categories. Individuals who have neither deviant sexual interests nor psychopathy are considered low risk (Group D). They are sent elsewhere.

FIGURE 12.1. Dr. Ebing-Krafft's Decision Tree For Sexual Dangerousity

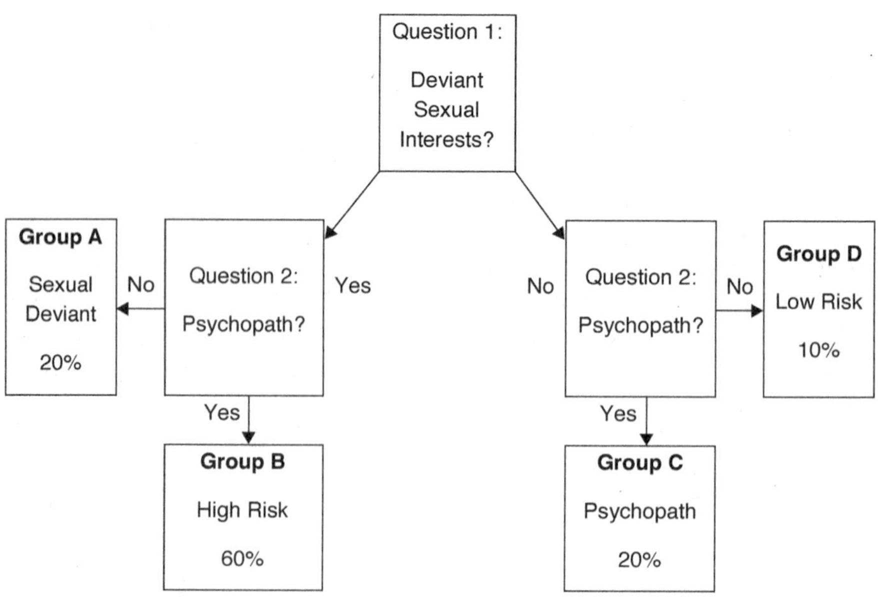

Individuals who only have deviant sexual interests but not psychopathy (Group A) and individuals who have psychopathy but not deviant sexual interests (Group C) are considered problematic but below the risk threshold. The only group of individuals recommended for commitment are those that have both deviant sexual interests and psychopathy (Group B). Each group is associated with an expected 5-year recidivism rate: 10% for Group D (low risk), 20% for Group A (sexual deviance present, psychopathy absent) and Group C (sexual deviance absent, psychopathy present), and 60% for Group B (sexual deviance and psychopathy present).

The procedures that Dr. Ebing-Krafft used to construct her prediction scheme have general acceptance in her professional community, thereby meeting the Frye test for the admission of scientific evidence (a standard used in many U.S. courts to determine whether judges and juries should hear the opinions of an individual who proports to be an "expert"). Mr. Baxstrom, one of the individuals committed under Dr. Ebing-Krafft's scheme, objects. He complains that general acceptance of the procedures is not sufficient: Risk prediction tools should only be used when their error rates are known (an element of the Daubert criteria, the other U.S. standard for admissibility of scientific evidence), and they have been rigorously evaluated. On these grounds, he files a court action against Dr. Ebing-Krafft, the hospital, the Department of Mental Health, and various individuals who work in the hospital, including you, the intern who conducted his initial assessment.

Faced with this lawsuit, the hospital contracts with a local academic, Dr. S. C. Lee, to evaluate Dr. Ebing-Krafft's prediction scheme. The results of Dr. Lee's study are summarized in Table 12.1. The sample size of each group may or may not be an empirical finding. Researchers may oversample certain risk categories to ensure that each category is adequately presented. The expected number of recidivists in each group is the sample size for the group multiplied by recidivism rates expected for that group. For example, the expected number of recidivists in Group B is $29 \times 0.60 = 17.4$. The observed values will be whole numbers (a count of individuals); however, the expected values are often not whole numbers. Do not round the expected values to whole numbers for the purposes of calculating the chi-square values.

The overall recidivism rate in the validation sample (20.1%) is very similar to the expected rate (21.2%). Inspection of the recidivism rates for each group suggest that in the validation sample, the rates for Group C and Group D were higher than expected, and the rates for Group A and Group B were lower than expected. Statistical tests are required, however, to determine whether the observed variation from the expected values is more than would be expected by chance.

To compute the chi-square statistic using Equation 12.1, the findings of the validity study were reorganized as in Table 12.2. The total number of observations will always equal the total number expected because each case will be placed into one of the eight possible cells.

The chi-square goodness-of-fit is the sum of the squared deviations for each cell (divided by the number expected), which sum to 8.308.

TABLE 12.1. Validation Study Results of Dr. Ebing-Krafft's Risk Scheme for Sexual Psychopathy

1	2	3	4	5	6	7	8
		Observed			Expected		
Group	Sample size	No. of recidivists	No. of nonrecidivists	Recidivism rate	No. of recidivists	No. of nonrecidivists	Recidivism rate
A	50	7	43	.140	10	40	.200
B	29	12	17	.414	17.4	11.6	.600
C	40	12	28	.300	8	32	.200
D	90	11	79	.122	9	81	.100
Total	209	42	167	.201	44.4	164.6	.212

TABLE 12.2. Calculation of Goodness-of-Fit Chi-Square for Validation Study for Dr. Ebing-Krafft's Risk Scheme Using Equation 12.1

Group	Status	No. observed (*O*)	No. expected (*E*)	$(O - E)^2/E$
A	Recidivist	7	10	0.900
	Nonrecidivist	43	40	0.225
B	Recidivist	12	17.4	1.676
	Nonrecidivist	17	11.6	2.514
C	Recidivist	12	8	2.000
	Nonrecidivist	28	32	0.500
D	Recidivist	11	9	0.444
	Nonrecidivist	79	81	0.049
Totals		209	209	$8.308 = \chi^2$

When using Equation 12.2, the data would be organized as in Table 12.3. Again, the chi-square value is 8.308, which is as expected because Equation 12.1 and Equation 12.2 are different ways of calculating the same chi-square value. It is easier to see the logic of Equation 12.1; however, Equation 12.2 is usually easier to calculate (half the number of rows).

The degrees of freedom for the chi-square value (calculated using either formula) equal one less than the number of levels, in our case, $L - 1 = 4 - 1 = 3$, which results in $p = 0.040$. This p value is lower than the $p < .05$ convention, meaning that the observed recidivism rates were not as expected.

Mr. Baxstrom feels vindicated. The hospital administration concedes that the recidivism rates do not precisely follow Dr. Ebing-Krafft's predictions. Nevertheless, the lawyer for the state points out that the observed violent recidivism rate for individuals in Group D was 41.4%, which is still higher than the presumptive threshold for commitment (> 35%). Mr. Baxstrom stays put, for now.

GOING FURTHER

The following sections are intended for individuals who wish to deepen their understanding, typically because they plan to use the chi-square goodness-of-fit in research, or appear as an expert witness on either side of Mr. Baxstrom's appeal.

TABLE 12.3. Calculation of Goodness-of-Fit Chi-Square for Validation Study for Dr. Ebing-Krafft's Risk Scheme Using Equation 12.2

Group	No. at this level	*p*	No. of events expected (*E*)	No. of events observed (*O*)	$(O - E)^2/(E(1 - p))$
A	50	0.200	10	7	1.125
B	29	0.600	17.4	12	4.190
C	40	0.200	8	12	2.500
D	90	0.100	9	11	0.494
Totals	209	0.212	44.4	42	$8.308 = \chi^2$

Recommended Reading

Hosmer, Jr., D. W., Lemeshow, S., & Sturdivant, R. X. (2013). *Applied logistic regression* (3rd ed.). Wiley.

This text describes how to calculate the Pearson chi-square goodness-of-fit statistic for prediction tools (Section 5.2.2; Equations 5.7 and 5.8), which is the same as the Hosmer–Lemeshow statistic. The difference is that Hosmer–Lemeshow test assumes that the levels are aggregated after the fact from continuous predictions, decreasing the degrees of freedom for the chi-square value from $L - 1$ to $L - 2$. When a prediction tool has a small set of discrete levels specified in advance, then the appropriate degrees of freedom are $L - 1$ (Steyerberg, 2009).

A version of the Pearson chi-square goodness-of-fit test is found in almost all intermediate-level statistics textbooks in psychology, so dust off the statistics textbook on your shelf. The examples in psychology statistics textbooks typically focus on evaluating the shape of a frequency distribution and not on the calibration of a prediction scheme with a dichotomous outcome. When applied to prediction schemes, it is important to remember that the frequencies evaluated are for each cell of the prediction table, with separate cell counts of cases with and without the outcome.

Computer Code

Both R and IBM/SPSS have programs for calculating the chi-square goodness-of-fit test. Both routines, however, require some extra steps. One initial step is computing the expected values, that is, the sample size multiplied by the expected rate for each level of the predictor. This can be done using a hand calculator or spreadsheets. As well, neither program associates the chi-square value with the correct degrees of freedom; consequently, it is necessary to separately calculate the appropriate degrees of freedom and the significance level of the chi-square values generated by these programs.

R Code

The R code that follows assumes that the data are already organized into a frequency table similar to Table 12.2 earlier in the chapter, that is, the observed and expected frequencies have already been tabulated. The R command for the chi-square goodness-of-fit test is **chisq.test**. It will assume, however, that each observation is fully independent, which is not the case for predictors of dichotomous outcomes. Consequently, after R calculates the chi-square value (which is correct), disregard the degrees of freedom and the significance level (which are incorrect). Instead, refer the chi-square value to a table of significance levels, or use the R command **pchisq** to find the associated significance level for the correct degrees of freedom. For a risk tool with L levels, the degrees of freedom will be $L - 1$.

The example uses the data from the evaluation study of Dr. Ebing-Krafft's risk scheme presented in Table 12.2. The first two lines of the syntax that follow are the data used in the calculation. These are the number of observed and expected cases in each cell. The entries must be in the correct order. In this example, the first entry for O and E is the number of recidivists in Group A, and the second entry for O and E is the number of nonrecidivists in Group A. The pattern continues up to the eighth and final entry, which are the observed and expected number of nonrecidivists in Group D. The **chisq.test** command defines expectations in terms of probabilities (out of 1.0); consequently, the next command line transforms the expected frequencies as numbers into expected frequencies as percentages.

```
O <- c(7,43,12,17,12,28,11,79) #the observed frequencies
E <- c(10,40,17.4,11.6,8,32,9,81) #the expected frequencies
EP <- E/sum(E) #the expected frequencies as proportions
chisq.test (O, p = EP)
```

This produces the following results:

```
  Chi-squared test for given probabilities
data: O
X-squared = 8.3085, df = 7, p-value = 0.3062
#chi-square value is correct, disregard df and p-value
#use pchisq (chi-square value, correct df) to obtain
cumulative chi-square probability
#use 1 - pchisq (chi-square value, correct df) for the
upper tail p-value
1 - pchisq (8.3085, 3)
[1] 0.04004818
```

IBM/SPSS

The IBM/SPSS example assumes that the expected frequencies have already been calculated. The observed frequencies are tabulated by the **CHISQUARE** option in the **NPAR TESTS** command. The **NPAR TESTS** command is found in Version 27 by following the drop-down menus from **ANALYZE**, then **Nonparametric Tests**, **Legacy Dialogues**, and finally **Chi-Square**.

This example uses the same data from Table 12.2 earlier in the chapter, organized as a data set with 209 rows (cases). This data set (Chap12_Chi2_example.sav) is available at https://www.apa.org/pubs/books/prediction-statistics-for-psychological-assessment. The data are entered as two variables: *Risk.Group* (Group A, Group B, Group C, or Group D), and *Recidivism* (1 = *yes*, 0 = *no*). To compute the chi-square goodness-of-fit there must be a single variable that identifies the groups. Consequently, the four-level *Risk.Group* variable and the two-level *Recidivism* variable are combined to create a variable with eight levels (Group A/recidivists, Group A/nonrecidivists, Group B/recidivists, . . . Group D/nonrecidivists). The combined variable is called *Group.Outcome*.

As with R, the expected frequencies are specified as proportions. In our example, the expected frequencies were n = (10, 40, 17.4, 11.6, 8, 32, 9, 81). Dividing each entry by the total sample size (209) results in expected proportions of p = (0.04784689, 0.19138756, 0.08325359, 0.05550239, 0.03827751, 0.15311005, 0.04306220, 0.38755981). All eight decimal points are not necessary (four would do); however, it is good practice to retain lots of decimal points during intermediate calculations. The probabilities will be entered into the **NPAR TESTS** command. These need to be entered manually because they are not derived from the data; instead, they are specified in advance by the prediction tool.

```
NPAR TESTS
/CHISQUARE=Group.Outcome
/EXPECTED=0.04784689, 0.19138756, 0.08325359,
0.05550239, 0.03827751, 0.15311005, 0.04306220,
0.38755981
/MISSING ANALYSIS.
```

Which produces the following output:

Test Statistics

	Group.Outcome
Chi-Square	8.308
df	7
Asymp. Sig.	.306

Again, the chi-square value is correct but the degrees of freedom and p value are not. The chi-square value can be compared with a table of significance levels or computed using the following command:

```
compute variable.name = 1 - cdf.chisq (value, degrees
of freedom)
compute probability = 1 - cdf.chisq (8.308, 3).
execute.
```

This creates a new variable in the main data set called *probability*. In our case, the chi-square value of 8.308 with 3 degrees of freedom has a p value of .0401.

EXERCISES

Based on the results of Dr. Lee's study, Dr. Ebing-Krafft decides to revise her risk scheme (see Figure 12.2). For Group A and Group B, she adjusts her predictions downward to be closer to the observed recidivism rates in Dr. Lee's initial validation study (Group A moves from 20% to 15%; Group B from 60% to 40%). The expected rate Group D (low risk) remains unchanged at 10%. She decides, however, to divide Group C (Psychopath) into two. When reviewing the recidivism results, she noticed that individuals with psychopathy who reoffended were predominantly young (18–25 years old) at time of assessment. Consequently, in the revised scheme, individuals with psychopathy who

FIGURE 12.2. Dr. Ebing-Krafft's Revised Decision Tree for Sexual Dangerousity

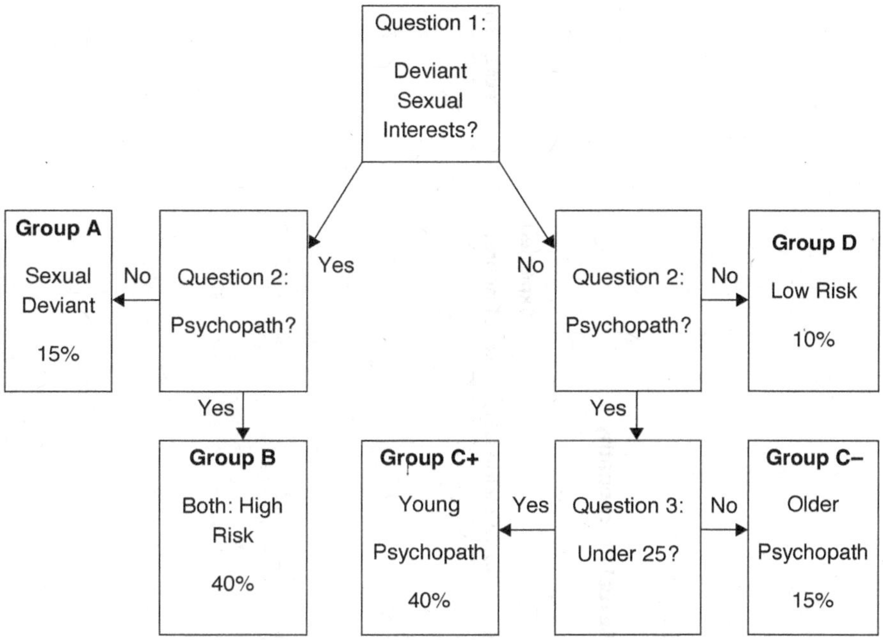

are under age 25 are placed in Group C+ (40% expected recidivism rate), whereas those over the age of 25 are placed in Group C– (15% likelihood of recidivism).

Her risk scheme now has five categories, two of which are expected to be above the commitment threshold (Group B and Group C+). Given the hospital's recent experience with litigation, they again hire Dr. Lee to conduct a validation study on a new sample. The results are presented in Table 12.4.

Question 12.1

Complete columns 5, 6, 7, and 8 of Table 12.4.

Question 12.2

Use the chi-square goodness-of-fit test to decide whether the observed recidivism rates are significantly different ($p < .05$) from the expected rate. The calculations can be done with a hand calculator or any statistical software of your choice.

Question 12.3

What does the statistical analysis in Question 12.2 say about the validity of Dr. Ebing-Krafft's revised prediction scheme?

TABLE 12.4. Validation Study Results of Dr. Ebing-Krafft's Revised Risk Scheme for Sexual Psychopathy

1	2	3	4	5	6	7	8
		Observed			Expected		
Group	Sample size	No. of recidivists	No. of nonrecidivists	Recidivism rate	No. of recidivists	No. of nonrecidivists	Recidivism rate
A	38	8	30	?	?	?	?
B	33	16	17	?	?	?	?
C–	25	3	22	?	?	?	?
C+	30	20	10	?	?	?	?
D	81	5	76	?	?	?	?
Total	207	52	155	?	?	?	?

ANSWERS TO EXERCISES

Question 12.1

Column 5, the recidivism rate, is calculated by dividing the number of recidivists (Column 3) by the sample size of that risk group (Column 2). For example, the first entry in Column 5 is 8/38 = .211, or 21.1%. Column 6, the expected number of recidivists is calculated by multiplying the expected recidivism rate (Column 8) by the observed sample size (Column 2). For example, the first entry in Column 6 is .150 × 38 = 5.7. The expected number of nonrecidivists (Column 7) is the sample size of the risk group minus the number of recidivists (e.g., 38 – 5.7 = 32.3). The expected recidivism rates for each risk group (Column 8) are asserted by Dr. Ebing-Krafft's prediction scheme presented in Figure 12.2. See Table 12.5.

Question 12.2

The chi-square value can be calculated by hand (or spreadsheet) using either Equation 12.1 or 12.2. Equation 12.2 is demonstrated in the answer because it is the simplest version for hand calculations. The first step is identifying the data to be used in the calculation, as in Table 12.6.

The essential data are (a) the expected recidivism rate (p) expressed as a value between zero and 1 (Column 3); (b) the expected number of events (E; Column 4), which is Column 2 multiplied by Column 3; and (c) the observed number of events (O; Column 5). Equation 12.2 is then used to compute the row values of Column 6. The sum of these row values is 12.465. The degrees of freedom are one less than the number of levels in the prediction scheme: 5 – 1 = 4. The p value associated with chi-square = 12.465 ($df = 4$) is $p = .014$.

Question 12.3

The goodness-of-fit test indicates that the distribution of scores was not as expected. It does not indicate how they were different. Visual inspection of Table 12.5 indicates that the recidivism rates for the two high risk groups were higher than expected, with a particularly high rate in the new Group C+ (expected 40%, observed 66.7%). For the purpose of separating out risk groups above and below the 35% threshold, there was complete concordance with expectations. Although the pattern of observed results was different from expectations, Dr. Lee's validity study supported the utility of Dr. Ebing-Krafft's revised prediction scheme for the purpose that it was intended.

TABLE 12.5. Validation Study Results of Dr. Ebing-Krafft's Revised Risk Scheme for Sexual Psychopathy

1	2	3	4	5	6	7	8
		Observed			Expected		
Group	Sample size	No. of recidivists	No. of nonrecidivists	Recidivism rate	No. of recidivists	No. of nonrecidivists	Recidivism rate
A	38	8	30	21.1	5.7	32.3	15.0
B	33	16	17	48.5	13.2	19.8	40.0
C–	25	3	22	12.0	3.75	21.25	15.0
C+	30	20	10	66.7	12	18	40.0
D	81	5	76	6.2	8.1	72.9	10.0
Total	207	52	155	25.1	42.75	164.25	20.7

TABLE 12.6. Calculating Chi-Square Goodness-of-Fit Using Equation 12.2

1	2	3	4	5	6
Group	No. at this level	Expected recidivism rate (p)	No. of events expected (E)	No. of events observed (O)	$(O - E)^2/(E(1 - p))$
A	38	.150	5.7	8	1.092
B	33	.400	13.2	16	0.990
C–	25	.150	3.75	3	0.176
C+	30	.400	12	20	8.889
D	81	.100	8.1	5	1.318
Total	207	.207	42.75	52	$12.465 = \chi^2$

13

The E/O Index

The *E/O* index is a measure of calibration that assesses the similarity between the rates of the outcome predicted by a risk tool and the observed rates in replication studies.

The E/O index, or E/O ratio, evaluates the performance (calibration) of a risk tool in a replication study. The E/O index is the ratio of the expected number of individuals who have the outcome (E) and the observed number of individuals who have the outcome (O). An E/O index of 1.0 indicates perfect calibration. Values greater than 1 indicate that the measure overestimates the likelihood of the outcome. Values less than one indicate that the measure underestimates the likelihood of the outcome. The use of the E/O index requires that the risk tool has numeric likelihoods associated with scores or levels on the risk tool. The E/O index can be used to evaluate specific scores, a range of scores, or total scores. Although there currently are no agreed-on standards for describing the magnitude of E/O deviations from perfect calibration, E/O values of greater than 2.0 or less than 0.5 are usually meaningful for applied decision-making. In general, the same E/O deviation is less problematic when the predicted value is based on a small proportion than when it is based on a large proportion.

This chapter includes excerpts from "Assessing the Calibration of Actuarial Risk Scales: A Primer on the E/O Index," by R. K. Hanson, 2017, *Criminal Justice and Behavior, 44*(1), pp. 26–39 (https://doi.org/10.1177/0093854816683956). Copyright 2017 by Her Majesty the Queen in Right of Canada, as represented by the Minister of Public Safety and Emergency Preparedness. Modified with permission.

https://doi.org/10.1037/0000275-013
Prediction Statistics for Psychological Assessment, by R. K. Hanson

WHY USE THE E/O INDEX?

The E/O index is a simple, intuitive measure of calibration. It originated in the medical field for assessing the calibration of statistical models designed to assess the likelihood of a dichotomous outcome (e.g., does the number of observed breast cancer cases match the number predicted by a screening tool? Gail & Pfeiffer, 2005; Rockhill et al., 2003). The E/O index provides both a statistical significance test and an effect size measure.

For evaluating the calibration of a prediction tool, the expected number would be calculated from the tool's norms, typically the outcome rates specified in the manual and endorsed by the scale developers. It is also possible to define expected recidivists from previous validation studies of the scale; this would be useful for scales without official estimates or if a researcher wants to compare calibration to a particular group examined in another study (e.g., from another jurisdiction or setting). A general assumption of the statistic is that the current data are being compared with a population value. In other words, the E/O index is analogous to a single-sample *t* test, where the current data are compared with a known value (this is why only the current data are incorporated in the confidence interval calculation, as discussed later in the chapter).

To illustrate the use of the E/O index, consider that your psychological services company has been asked to bid on a contract for employee assistance counseling. To put in a competitive bid, you need to know how many hours of service to expect. The company has not had an employee assistance program before, so there are no records of how many of their 500 employees will make use of the service. Your company, however, has provided employee assistance programs to other companies for many years. From this history, you have developed a prediction tool to estimate the uptake of employee assistance services. The prediction algorithm includes demographic information (age, gender), employment stability (rate of turnover in each sector), and the profitability of the company as a whole (negative cash flow increases employee stress). Although it is possible to use this algorithm to identify individuals more or less likely to use the service, the primary function of this risk tool is for budgeting. You obtain the necessary information about the company and its employees and use it in your budget calculation.

You are awarded the contract. During the first year of operation, 15 employees made use of your services; your algorithm had expected 20. For this year, the E/O index would be 1.33, indicating that uptake of the services was somewhat less than expected. The 95% confidence intervals for this estimate, however, indicate that it is within the range expected by chance (.88 to 1.66). You continue to use your prediction tools to plan for subsequent years.

LIMITATIONS

Although good calibration is an important feature of valid prediction schemes, it is but one of two essential features (the other being discrimination). For example, a scale may predict criminal recidivism rates for low-, moderate-, and high-risk groups as 15%, 18%, and 20%, respectively. Validation studies may repeatedly replicate these expected recidivism rates. However, the differences between the groups would be too small to make practical differences. The extent to which small differences have meaningful impacts will, of course, vary by context (consider the enormous impact of a 5% change in the national unemployment rate). Nevertheless, good discrimination is a requirement of useful prediction tools. In the extreme, betting the base rate without using any risk tool at all may result is virtually perfect calibration (E/O = 1.0), but no discrimination (area under the curve [AUC] = .50; Cohen's $d = 0.00$).

One limitation of the E/O index is that its sampling variance is determined by the number of observed events (*O*). When the event is rare, the absolute number of observed events can be quite small. For example, if the observed rate is 5% and the sample size is 120 cases, there would only be six observed events. If the expected value is also six, then a difference of plus or minus two cases can change the E/O values from .667 to 1.25. When the observed rate is zero, the E/O index cannot be calculated.

The E/O index is most appropriate given rates asserted by the prediction tool's developers. Different effect size statistics are recommended when comparing the outcome rates of two groups, neither of which takes priority. In such cases, other relative risk indices are recommended, such as rate ratios, odds ratios, or hazard ratios (see Chapter 7, this volume; Fleiss & Berlin, 2009; Hanson et al., 2013). Like the E/O index, these risk ratios are ratios of two risks (variously defined); however, instead of one being considered a population value, both risks are considered to be estimates measured with error (see Fleiss & Berlin, 2009).

Another valuable option for estimating calibration is to compare the stability of regression equations (see Chapter 14; Reynolds, 1982). The simplest regression equation includes two parameters: the intercept (predicted outcome for score of zero) and slope (how much change in outcome is associated with a unit change in scores). Given a dichotomous outcome (completion of high school, return to work after injury, criminal recidivism), logistic regression is often the most appropriate regression model. Examples of assessing calibration of risk tools using logistic regression can be found in Chapter 14 (see also Hanson, Lunetta, et al., 2014; Wilson & Gutierrez, 2014). Like E/O indices, calibration plots are another easy and intuitive way to visualize correspondence between observed and expected data points (see Chapter 15, this volume; see also Altman et al., 2009; Lehmann et al., 2013).

THE NUTS AND BOLTS

Data Requirements

The following data are required to calculate the E/O index in a prediction study:

1. a dichotomous outcome variable,
2. a predictor variable with two or more levels, and
3. expected rates linked to levels of the predictor variable.

The E/O index can only be used with risk tools for which there are probabilities associated with scores or levels. These probabilities are used to calculate the expected number with the outcome. The ideal calculation of the observed would be based on an unbiased and complete fixed-follow-up period (although alternatives are discussed later in the chapter). When calculating a fixed 5-year follow-up, for example, this requires using all cases with a *minimum* of 5 years of follow-up data, regardless of outcome status or time to the outcome. For example, should some individuals have the outcome after 2 years, but their maximum follow-up was 4 years (the difference between the at-risk date and their follow-up end date was 4 years), they would not contribute to analyses based on fixed 5-year follow-up (see Chapter 4). Such cases, however, would be included when the observed number is estimated from survival analysis using ragged (variable) follow-up.

Calculating the E/O Index

With fixed follow-up (and no attrition), the E/O index can be easily calculated by dividing the expected number with the outcome (*E*) by the observed number with the outcome (*O*; Method M_0 from Viallon et al., 2009). The number of observed events is straightforward when the replication study uses the same fixed follow-up as the norms. The number of expected outcomes requires more effort. With most risk prediction tools, it involves identifying the probabilities associated with each score or level (e.g., Level 1 has an expected probability of .12) and then multiplying these probabilities by the number of individuals at each level (e.g., 20 individuals at Level 1, each with a probability of 0.12, 20 × .12 = 2.4, indicating that there are 2.4 individuals expected to have the outcome among those classified as Level 1). Sum across all levels, keeping the decimals (the expectations will rarely be integers).

This calculation method is appropriate and unbiased with complete and fixed follow-up information (i.e., when all cases have the same length of follow-up). Viallon and colleagues (2009) provided and evaluated adjustments for calculating the E/O index and its confidence interval when the follow-up period varies. When the research uses survival data (where the follow-up ends after varying intervals), the observed number of recidivists can be estimated through Kaplan–Meier survival analyses (see Chapter 6). Directions for obtaining the Kaplan–Meier estimate is provided in Chapter 6 and reprised later in this chapter.

Worked Example

This example uses hypothetical data to evaluate the calibration of the Static-99R sexual recidivism risk tool (https://www.static99.org; Helmus, Thornton, et al., 2012). It examines calibration for the overall sample, as well as within each risk level, which can highlight particular areas of concern. Examining calibration at each score would provide even greater detail, but few studies have sufficient sample size for this type of analysis (for an exception, see Helmus, 2015), so examining risk levels is a more practical application. The example also reports discrimination accuracy, given that the two should be reported together.

To bring this hypothetical examination to life, imagine that a new island has been discovered in the Pacific Ocean, called Akuarl Atoll. Although the rest of the world was oblivious to this island paradise, Akuarl Atoll had studied the rest of the world in great detail. Furthermore, they have been using Static-99R for all individuals convicted in their jurisdiction of a sexual offense (OK, not a complete paradise). They collected 5-year follow-up data for 1,100 individuals and wanted to assess the scale's utility with their population, given recent media concerns in the atoll that there are important cultural differences with the Akuarl Atoll population compared with the rest of the world. They sent you their data to analyze.

Table 13.1 summarizes the raw data from Akuarl Atoll, presenting each Static-99R score, the risk category for that score, the number of individuals with that score, the number who sexually reoffended during follow-up, and the recidivism rate (as a percentage). From Table 13.1, the overall sexual recidivism rate for this sample was 7.5% after 5 years. As would be expected, the distribution of risk scores was largely clustered around the average risk category, with sample sizes getting smaller for the highest risk scores. None of the 1,100 individuals in this study scored higher than 10 on Static-99R. Discrimination accuracy in this sample was moderate (AUC = .68, 95% confidence interval of .62 to .74), which is comparable to other international studies (AUC = .69; Helmus, Thornton, et al., 2012).

TABLE 13.1. Hypothetical Observed Data From Study Validating Static-99R

Static-99R score	Risk category	*n*	Sexual recidivists, *n*	Recidivism rate, %
−3	I—Very low risk	45	0	0.0
−2	I—Very low risk	50	1	2.0
−1	II—Below average	97	2	2.1
0	II—Below average	129	5	3.9
1	III—Average risk	169	10	5.9
2	III—Average risk	181	13	7.2
3	III—Average risk	138	12	8.7
4	IVa—Above average	86	10	11.6
5	IVa—Above average	77	9	11.7
6	IVb—Well above average	72	7	9.7
7	IVb—Well above average	36	6	16.7
8	IVb—Well above average	16	5	31.3
9	IVb—Well above average	3	1	33.3
10	IVb—Well above average	1	1	100.0
11	IVb—Well above average	0	0	—
12	IVb—Well above average	0	0	—
Total		1,100	82	7.5

To calculate the E/O index, the information required is the number of observed recidivists (available in Table 13.1) and the number of expected recidivists. The expected number of recidivists was based on the 5-year predicted recidivism probabilities for Static-99R in routine/complete (i.e., fairly unselected) samples (see the Static-99R Evaluators Workbook; Phenix et al., 2016, p. 8). Table 13.2 reproduces each Static-99R score and category and provides the observed sample size and the number of recidivists (from the hypothetical data in Table 13.1) and the expected recidivism percentages from the Static-99R norms (page 8 of the 2016 Evaluator Workbook; for ease of tracking, this information is listed as both a percentage and a probability). In the last column, the expected number of recidivists for the Akuarl Atoll study is calculated by multiplying the proportion (from the normative data) and the sample size with that score (from the current study).

When calculating the E/O index, report the expected number of recidivists with decimal points (in this case, one decimal). Although it is impossible to observe fractions of a recidivist, the use of decimals allows for greater precision than would be provided if values were rounded to whole numbers. If the expected rates are really small, use 2 (or more) decimal points. Second, although the goal is to examine calibration for each risk level, the expected number of recidivists are calculated for each score because that is how the normative data is presented. After identifying the expected number of recidivists for each score, this information is then aggregated for each category. For example, there are two scores in risk Level I, namely, –3 and –2. The expected number of recidivists for the 45 individuals with a score of –3 is 0.4 (45 × .009 = 0.4). The expected number

TABLE 13.2. Observed and Expected Recidivists in the Akuarl Atoll Replication Study

Static-99R score	Risk category	Observed *n*	Observed Recidivists, *n*	Expected %	Expected Proportion	Expected *n*
–3	I	45	0	0.9	.009	0.4
–2	I	50	1	1.3	.013	0.6
–1	II	97	2	1.9	.019	1.8
0	II	129	5	2.8	.028	3.6
1	III	169	10	3.9	.039	6.6
2	III	181	13	5.6	.056	10.1
3	III	138	12	7.9	.079	10.9
4	IVa	86	10	11.0	.110	9.5
5	IVa	77	9	15.2	.152	11.7
6	IVb	72	7	20.5	.205	14.8
7	IVb	36	6	27.2	.272	9.8
8	IVb	16	5	35.1	.351	5.6
9	IVb	3	1	43.8	.438	1.3
10	IVb	1	1	53.0	.530	0.5
11	IVb	0	0	—	—	—
12	IVb	0	0	—	—	—
Total		1,100	82			87.2

of recidivists for the 50 individuals with a score of −2 is 0.6 (50 × .013 = 0.6). Consequently, the expected number of recidivists in Level I is 1.0 (0.4 + 0.6 = 1.0). From Table 13.2, we see that the current study of 1,100 individuals had 82 sexual recidivists. On the basis of the distribution of Static-99R scores and the predicted probability of recidivism per score from the scale's Evaluator Workbook, Static-99R would have predicted 87.2 sexual recidivists for this sample. This is not hugely different from the observed number. We can also examine correspondence at each score. For example, 129 individuals in this study scored a 0 on Static-99R, and of those, five sexually reoffended. On the basis of the normative data for the scale, 3.6 offenders would have been predicted to reoffend. Looking in the higher risk ranges, 36 offenders scored a 7 on Static-99R, and six of them sexually reoffended, whereas the scale would have predicted about 10 recidivists (specifically, 9.8).

Now it is time to calculate the correspondence between observed and expected recidivism rates. This step is presented in Table 13.3. First, the data in Table 13.2 are aggregated for each risk category. The number of observed recidivists for each category was obtained by summing the number of observed recidivists in each score within that category (from Table 13.2). The expected number of recidivists was also summed. The E/O index was obtained by dividing the expected number by the observed number.

Standard Errors and Confidence Intervals

Following Rockhill et al. (2003), the 95% confidence interval for the E/O index can be calculated using the Poisson variance for the logarithm of the observed number of cases (*O*):

$$\text{Upper limit of 95\% CI of } \frac{E}{O} \text{ Index} = \left(\frac{E}{O}\right)e^{\left(1.96\sqrt{\frac{1}{O}}\right)} \quad (13.1)$$

$$\text{Lower limit of 95\% CI of } \frac{E}{O} \text{ Index} = \left(\frac{E}{O}\right)e^{\left(-1.96\sqrt{\frac{1}{O}}\right)} \quad (13.2)$$

The preceding formula looks daunting, but it is manageable with careful attention to the order of operations. Given that an E/O index of 1 means the

TABLE 13.3. E/O Index and 95% Confidence Intervals (CIs)

Risk category	*n*	Observed recidivists (O)	Expected recidivists (E)	E/O index	95% CI
I—Very low risk	95	1	1.0	1.00	[0.14, 7.10]
II—Below average	226	7	5.4	0.77	[0.37, 1.62]
III—Average risk	488	35	27.6	0.79	[0.57, 1.10]
IVa—Above average	163	19	21.2	1.12	[0.71, 1.75]
IVb—Well above average	128	20	32.0	1.60	[1.03, 2.48]
Total	1,100	82	87.2	1.06	[0.86, 1.32]

expected number with the outcome matches the observed number, a 95% confidence interval that includes 1 means there is no statistically significant difference between observed and expected rates ($p > .05$). In contrast, a 95% confidence interval that does not include 1 indicates that the expected and observed rates differ to an extent greater than would be expected by chance ($p < .05$).

In terms of statistical power, the confidence interval formula only includes the sample size for the observed number with the outcome, not the expected number (or the number without the outcome). This means the power is derived from the validation study and is unaffected by the precision/quality of the norms that are used to obtain the expected number. The index and its statistical power are based solely on the number with the outcome. In other words, a study of 1,000 individuals with 50 positive cases (a 5% rate) would have the same statistical power as a study of 100 individuals with 50 positive cases (a 50% rate).

When the study involves unequal follow-up, Kaplan–Meier survival analysis should be used to calculate the observed number with the outcome. When Kaplan–Meier is used, the variability of the E/O index should also consider the error associated with the Kaplan–Meier estimate (Viallon et al., 2009, Equation 14):

$$\textit{Upper limit of } 95\% \textit{ CI of } \frac{E}{O} \textit{ Index} = \left(\frac{E}{O}\right)e^{\left(1.96\left[\frac{SE}{O}\right]\right)} \tag{13.3}$$

$$\textit{Lower limit of } 95\% \textit{ CI of } \frac{E}{O} \textit{ Index} = \left(\frac{E}{O}\right)e^{\left(-1.96\left[\frac{SE}{O}\right]\right)} \tag{13.4}$$

In Equations 13.3 and 13.4, *SE* is the Greenwood approximation of the standard error (see Chapter 6, this volume; Singer & Willett, 2003, Equation 10.8), which is routinely reported in Kaplan–Meier survival software. Note *O* and *SE* are expressed in the units of cases (not proportions); for example, given 767 initially at risk, .083 failing by year 5, and a *SE* of 0.01047, the value of *O* would be $767 \times .083 = 63.66$, and the value of *SE* would be $767 \times .010147 = 8.03$.

Interpreting the Confidence Intervals in the Worked Example

In Table 13.3, the 95% confidence intervals for the E/O values were computed following the Equation 13.1 and 13.2 (fixed follow-up). In the Akuarl Atoll study there were 82 recidivists, whereas the recidivism norms for Static-99R would have predicted 87.2 recidivists. The E/O index for the total number of recidivists was 1.06, which is very close to the ideal ratio of 1. Although the Static-99R recidivism norms overpredicted recidivism in this validation study, the difference was small. Specifically, the scale predicted 6% more recidivists compared with what was observed, and the difference between expected and observed recidivists was nonsignificant, as evidenced by a 95% confidence interval that overlapped with 1 (0.86, 1.32). Consequently, from this analysis, it appears as though Static-99R was well calibrated for Akuarl Atoll.

It is often helpful, however, to examine subgroups of cases, as there may be differences. For example, the scale may overpredict or underpredict for certain risk levels or groups (e.g., based on age, victim type, offense type). In this example, the E/O index was calculated for the risk levels. Calibration was perfect for the lowest risk level (E/O index = 1.0; the scale predicted one recidivist, and there was only one). Note that the 95% confidence interval for the lowest risk level was exceptionally wide (from 0.14 to 7.10) because the E/O index was calculated based on only a single recidivist. Had one additional individual in this level reoffended, the E/O index would have halved from 1 to 0.5, indicating how unstable this estimate is with only one recidivist.

The scale was also well calibrated for offenders in Level IVa, where 19 offenders reoffended, and the scale would have predicted 21.2 recidivists. Specifically, the E/O index was 1.12, which means the scale predicted about 12% more recidivists than what was observed, which was a slight overestimation and not statistically significant (the 95% confidence interval includes 1). Static-99R underpredicted recidivism for risk Levels II and III, but, again, the differences were not significant. Specifically, Static-99R predicted about three quarters of the observed number of recidivists in Level II (E/O Index = 0.77) and four fifths of those in Level III (E/O = .79). There was a significant difference, however, between observed and expected recidivism rates in the highest risk level (IVb; E/O = 1.60, 95% confidence interval of 1.03 to 2.48). For this risk level, the scale predicted 60% more recidivists than what was actually observed. From this hypothetical study, there was acceptable overall calibration for Static-99R in Akuarl Atoll, but that the scale tended to underestimate recidivism for low and moderate risk cases (this difference was not statistically significant) and overestimate recidivism for highest risk cases.

This pattern of calibration results may or may not be problematic depending on the purpose of the assessment. If the scale is used to estimate the recidivism rates of the highest risk cases, then decision makers should interpret the results cautiously because Static-99R significantly overestimated the recidivism rates of this category in Akuarl Atoll. On the other hand, if the scale is used to classify individuals in the middle of the risk distribution (or lower), decision-makers can have reasonable confidence that the recidivism rates in this jurisdiction are similar to norms asserted by the risk tool's developers.

GOING FURTHER

Readers who have made it this far should have sufficient understanding of the E/O index to be educated consumers of research studies using this statistic. The following sections are intended for those who want further mastery, typically because they are considering using the E/O index in their own research projects. These sections can be worked with in any order, and it is not necessary to do all (or any) of them.

Recommended Readings

Hanson, R. K. (2017). Assessing the calibration of actuarial risk scales: A primer on the E/O index. *Criminal Justice and Behavior, 44*(1), 26–39. https://doi.org/10.1177/0093854816683956

This article covers much of the same material as the current chapter, including the same worked example (Akuarl Atoll/Static-99R). It also includes, however, some additional background material.

Viallon, V., Ragusa, S., Clavel-Chapelon, F., & Bénichou, J. (2009). How to evaluate the calibration of a disease risk prediction tool. *Statistics in Medicine, 28*(6), 901–916. https://doi.org/10.1002/sim.3517

A technical article, providing useful guidance concerning calculating the E/O ratio when fixed follow-up periods are impractical or impossible (e.g., researchers are interested in death by cancer, but some patients are dying from other causes).

Computer Code

Neither R nor IBM/SPSS has dedicated programs for calculating the E/O index. It can nonetheless be calculated in either program using syntax. It is also relatively easy to calculate using a generic spreadsheet, such as Excel. The syntax that follows assumes the expected (E) and observed (O) values have already been calculated.

R Code

The following R syntax computes the E/O index with 95% confidence interval for studies with fixed follow-up and no attribution. In this example, the expected number has already been calculated (23), and the observed is the raw number of observed events in the study (20). R syntax is in Courier New 10 font; output is preceded by [1].

```
E <- 23
O <- 20
EO <- (E/O)
EO
[1] 1.15
upper95 <- EO*exp((1.96)*(sqrt(1/O)))
upper95
[1] 1.782526
lower95 <- EO*exp((-1.96)*(sqrt(1/O)))
lower95
[1] 0.7419248
```

The first two lines identify the basic data, the third line creates the E/O index (as an object—you will not see anything), and the fourth line requests the value of the object labeled "EO," which, in this case is 1.15 (the risk tool slightly overestimates risk). The subsequent lines calculate the upper and lower limits of the 95% confidence intervals using Equations 13.1 and 13.2 provided earlier in the chapter.

With ragged follow-up, the *O* is estimated from the Kaplan–Meier survival curve. The *E* is calculated in the usual way (i.e., the expected rate if all cases had been followed for the full follow-up period). The first two lines identify the data set containing the survival data, in this case, it is an Excel csv file called "c:\run.files\Book\Chap13_EO_KM_example.csv". R syntax is case sensitive and the **read.csv** command requires double backslashes. If readers are interested in running this analysis for themselves, a copy of the data set is available at https://www.apa.org/pubs/books/prediction-statistics-for-psychological-assessment.

```
data <- read.csv(file="c:\\run.files\\Book\\Chap13_EO_
KM_example.csv")
attach (data)
require ('survival')
Loading required package: survival
KMmodel <- survfit(Surv(time, outcome) ~ 1,
type="kaplan-meier")
```

In this syntax, the labels for the variables *KMmodel, time,* and *outcome* are set by you, the researcher. Because Kaplan–Meier is the default, you can simply use the following:

```
KMmodel <- survfit(Surv(time, outcome) ~ 1)
```

The syntax requires a predictor variable, which in this example is "1". The value "1" is noninformative. It simply tells R to fit the survival model without predictors.

```
summary (KMmodel)
```

The **summary** command reproduces all the points of the Kaplan–Meier survival curve. There is a new point for each new instance of the outcome.

```
Call: survfit(formula = Surv(time, outcome) ~ 1, type =
"kaplan-meier")
                                               lower   upper
 time    n.risk  n.event  survival  std.err  95% CI   95% CI
0.0250    767       1       0.999   0.00130   0.996   1.000
0.0301    766       1       0.997   0.00184   0.994   1.000
0.0575    765       1       0.996   0.00225   0.992   1.000
0.0825    763       1       0.995   0.00260   0.990   1.000
0.1232    762       1       0.993   0.00291   0.988   0.999
0.1670    760       1       0.992   0.00318   0.986   0.998
0.1779    759       1       0.991   0.00344   0.984   0.998
0.2108    757       1       0.990   0.00367   0.982   0.997
.
.
.
4.2500    537       1       0.922   0.01006   0.902   0.942
4.2926    531       1       0.920   0.01019   0.900   0.940
4.4815    513       1       0.918   0.01032   0.898   0.939
```

```
4.8237    489    1    0.917    0.01047   0.896    0.937
5.2015    454    1    0.915    0.01064   0.894    0.936
5.2672    452    1    0.913    0.01081   0.892    0.934
5.4807    446    1    0.910    0.01098   0.889    0.932
5.6833    435    1    0.908    0.01115   0.887    0.930
```

In this example, 767 individuals were initially at risk, and time is reported in years. To obtain the number of observed events at 5 years, use the cumulative survival rate for the last event before 5 years—the row is underlined in the preceding example. At this time, the survival rate is 0.917 and the rate of the outcome is .083 (1 – 0.917). The standard error is 0.01047. To obtain *O* and *SE*, multiply these values by the number initially at risk (767). Assume that the expected number given by the norms is 53.4 (calculated separately). The E/O index is calculated as usual; however, studies with ragged follow-up should use Equations 13.3 and 13.4 to estimate the 95% confidence intervals.

```
E <- 53.4
O <- (767)*(.083)
O
[1] 63.661
EO <- E/O
EO
[1] 0.8388181
SE <- 767*(.01047)
SE
[1] 8.03049
upper95 <- EO*exp((1.96)*(SE/O))
upper95
[1] 1.074099
lower95 <- EO*exp((-1.96)*(SE/O))
lower95
[1] 0.6550755
```

In this data set, the E/O index is 0.84, indicating some underestimation (the observed rates are higher than expected); however, the confidence interval includes 1 (.66 to 1.07), so the observed rates are not necessarily more than would be expected by chance.

IBM/SPSS

The first step is to create an SPSS data file (.sav) with two variables: *E* and *O*. Repeating the same example, then enter values of 23 for *E* and 20 for *O*. This is a very simple SPSS file with only two variables, with one value each (see Chap13_EO_example.sav available at https://www.apa.org/pubs/books/prediction-statistics-for-psychological-assessment). The E/O index and 95% confidence intervals are then calculated using the following syntax:

```
compute EO = E/O.
compute LL = EO*(exp(-1.96*(sqrt(1/O)))).
compute UL = EO*(exp(1.96*(sqrt(1/O)))).
Execute.
```

The preceding syntax can be copied from the SPSS syntax file called "Prediction Statistics SPSS syntax.sps" available at https://www.apa.org/pubs/books/prediction-statistics-for-psychological-assessment. This will recreate three new variables—EO, LL, and UL—with values of 1.15, 0.74, and 1.78, respectively.

EXERCISES

Question 13.1

A hospital-based clinic for treating depression is interested in whether their treatment is more effective than average. Previous studies have found that recovery rates vary predictably based on well-known features, such as gender, prior history of depression, and comorbid personality disorders. These features are used in a decision-tree algorithm that places individuals into one of four groups. In Group A, half are expected to recover within 4 months, whereas only a third of Group B, one out of 10 in Group C, and one out of 20 in Group D are expected to recover in this time period (4 months). The outcome statistics for the four groups apply to individuals receiving treatment as usual in the same region as the hospital clinic.

The clinic received a small grant to prospectively record the recovery rates of its patients for 1 year. Patients were contacted 4 months after the initial interview and asked (a) whether their symptoms were interfering with routine activities and (b) their level of subjective well-being. Individuals whose symptoms were not interfering with daily life and whose subjective well-being was within normal limits were considered recovered. Individuals were excluded from the study if the time between their initial assessment and the end of data collection was less than 4 months (regardless of whether they had recovered or not). The results are tabulated in Table 13.4.

(i) Use the E/O index to determine whether the rate of recovery for this year was higher than expected for their region. Calculate 95% confidence intervals.

(ii) For which group (A, B, C, or D) was the E/O index the most favorable for the clinic? Calculate 95% confidence intervals for this group.

TABLE 13.4. Number of Patients Who Recovered Within 4 Months Fixed Follow-Up According to Risk Groups

Group	Total no. of cases	No. recovered
A	24	15
B	64	28
C	22	5
D	27	4
Total	137	52

Question 13.2

The clinic was encouraged by their results, particularly for Group D, who usually only have a 5% chance of recovering within 4 months when they receive treatment as usual (i.e., at other clinics). Given the low number of cases in Group D in the prospective study, however, the hospital decides to collect more cases retrospectively. They hire research assistants to code the outcome for 100 Group D cases from existing records. The survival time for these patients began at the date of their intake interview, and, for those who recovered, ended at the date they were deemed recovered according to the case notes. For patients who had not recovered, the survival end date was one of the following: the date data collection ended for cases still in treatment, the date they dropped out of treatment, or the date they were lost to follow-up for other reasons. The survival time for these 100 patients ranged from 1 day to just under 6 months (mean = 2.9, SD = 1.8, range of .01 to 5.8 months).

Because of the ragged (variable) follow-up period, Kaplan–Meier survival analysis was used to calculate the number of observed cases in remission at four months. The results are presented below (from R Statistics with a mock data set; Chap13_EO_KM_Question2.csv available at https://www.apa.org/pubs/books/prediction-statistics-for-psychological-assessment). During the study period, 17 of the 100 cases were judged to have recovered. The earliest remission was at .33 months. There were six cases that were followed for less than .33 months and consequently were not included in the calculation of any of the survival rates. This resulted in an effective sample of 94 at-risk cases (100 – 6 = 94).

```
KMsurv <-survfit (Surv (Months, Remission) ~ 1)
summary (KMsurv)
Call: survfit(formula = Surv(Months, Remission) ~ 1)
                                       std.    lower    upper
time  n.risk  n.event  survival        err    95% CI   95% CI
0.33     94        1      0.989     0.0106    0.969    1.000
0.65     87        1      0.978     0.0154    0.948    1.000
0.93     81        1      0.966     0.0194    0.929    1.000
1.39     75        1      0.953     0.0230    0.909    0.999
1.80     70        1      0.939     0.0264    0.889    0.993
1.99     66        1      0.925     0.0296    0.869    0.985
2.67     57        1      0.909     0.0332    0.846    0.976
2.98     51        1      0.891     0.0370    0.821    0.967
3.04     50        1      0.873     0.0404    0.798    0.956
3.91     36        1      0.849     0.0460    0.764    0.944
4.34     31        1      0.822     0.0520    0.726    0.930
4.41     29        1      0.793     0.0574    0.688    0.914
4.61     25        1      0.762     0.0633    0.647    0.896
4.62     24        1      0.730     0.0681    0.608    0.876
4.85     14        1      0.678     0.0808    0.537    0.856
4.87     13        1      0.626     0.0898    0.472    0.829
4.94     11        1      0.569     0.0980    0.406    0.797
```

(i) What is the survival rate at 4 months? The remission rate?

(ii) What is the raw number of patients in remission at 4 months? What is the survival estimate of the number of patients in remission at 4 months?

(iii) If the at-risk sample was increased to 200 (instead of 94), and the survival rates stayed the same, how many patients would be estimated to be in remission at 4 months?

(iv) Using the E/O index, was the recovery rate of Group D patients at 4 months significantly higher than expected?

ANSWERS TO EXERCISES

Question 13.1

The first step to answering this question is to construct a table like that shown in Table 13.5.

(i) The E/O index for the overall sample was 38.86/52 = .709, indicating that the number in recovery was greater than expected. In other words, the algorithm used to classify patients underestimated the recovery rate at this clinic. Given that the confidence interval (calculated using Equations 13.1 and 13.2 in Excel) did not include 1, the increased rate of recovery at the clinic was more than expected by chance.

(ii) The E/O index most favorable to the clinic was for Group D (1.35/4 = 0.338). Given that the confidence intervals did not include 1, the recovery rate for this group was significantly higher than expected by chance.

Question 13.2

(i) To find the survival rate at 4 months, look at the survival rate for the last case in remission before 4 years (underlined below as .849). This is the proportion of Group D individuals who have not recovered at 4 months. The remission rate would be 1 – .849 = .151

time	n.risk	n.event	survival	std. err	lower 95% CI	upper 95% CI
0.33	94	1	0.989	0.0106	0.969	1.000
0.65	87	1	0.978	0.0154	0.948	1.000
0.93	81	1	0.966	0.0194	0.929	1.000
1.39	75	1	0.953	0.0230	0.909	0.999
1.80	70	1	0.939	0.0264	0.889	0.993
1.99	66	1	0.925	0.0296	0.869	0.985
2.67	57	1	0.909	0.0332	0.846	0.976
2.98	51	1	0.891	0.0370	0.821	0.967
3.04	50	1	0.873	0.0404	0.798	0.956
3.91	36	1	0.849	0.0460	0.764	0.944
4.34	31	1	0.822	0.0520	0.726	0.930
4.41	29	1	0.793	0.0574	0.688	0.914
4.61	25	1	0.762	0.0633	0.647	0.896
4.62	24	1	0.730	0.0681	0.608	0.876
4.85	14	1	0.678	0.0808	0.537	0.856
4.87	13	1	0.626	0.0898	0.472	0.829
4.94	11	1	0.569	0.0980	0.406	0.797

(ii) The raw number of patients in remission is 10. The survival estimate is (1 – survival rate) ∗ (initial sample size) = (1 – 0.849) ∗ (94) = 14.19. This is the observed value (*O*) in the E/O index. Note that when Kaplan–Meier survival analysis is used to calculate *O*, it is rarely an integer.

TABLE 13.5. Observed and Expected Number of Patients Recovered Within 4 Months

Group	Sample size	Observed Number	Observed Proportion	Expected Proportion	Expected Number	E/O	Lower CI	Upper CI
A	24	15	0.625	0.500	12.00	0.800	0.482	1.327
B	64	28	0.438	0.333	21.31	0.761	0.526	1.102
C	22	5	0.227	0.100	2.20	0.440	0.183	1.057
D	27	4	0.148	0.050	1.35	0.338	0.127	0.899
Total	137	52	0.380		38.86	0.709	0.540	0.930

Note. CI = confidence interval.

(iii) If the total sample size was 200 instead of 94 and the survival curve was the same, the observed number of recidivists would be (1 − 0.849) * (200) = 30.2.

(iv) According to the E/O index, the recovery rate of Group D patients was significantly higher than expected. With a sample size of 94, the expected number was 0.05 × 94 = 4.7, and the observed number was 14.19, resulting an E/O index of 4.7/14.19 = .3312. The confidence intervals were 0.182 to 0.602, calculated using Equations 13.3 and 13.4. These equations consider the standard error for the survival rate, which for 4-month survival was 0.0460, or 4.324 individuals given an initial sample size of 94 (0.046 * 94 = 4.324).

$$Upper\ limit\ of\ 95\%\ CI\ of\ \frac{E}{O}\ Index = 0.602 = \left(\frac{4.7}{14.19}\right)e^{\left(1.96\left[\frac{4.324}{14.19}\right]\right)}$$

$$Lower\ limit\ of\ 95\%\ CI\ of\ \frac{E}{O}\ Index = 0.182 = \left(\frac{4.7}{14.19}\right)e^{\left(-1.96\left[\frac{4.324}{14.19}\right]\right)}$$

Note that the confidence intervals calculated using Equations 13.3 and 13.4 will be larger than those calculated using Equations 13.1 and 13.2, although the difference is usually small.

14

Meta-Analysis

Meta-analysis is a quantitative method of summarizing results across studies and for identifying whether the variability across samples is more than would be expected by chance.

Science advances through orderly replication. The findings of a single study are useful in identifying potential risk factors; however, we have increased confidence in risk factors or prediction tools when the same results are found in diverse samples and settings. The statistical methods for combining and comparing studies are called meta-analysis (Borenstein et al., 2021). In meta-analysis, the findings from each individual study are transformed into a common metric (effect size) and then averaged. There are different ways of averaging effect sizes, which can be broadly classed as fixed-effect and random-effects methods. Fixed-effect meta-analysis produces a *Q* statistic, which indicates the extent to which the observed variability across studies is more than would be expected by chance. When replication studies consistently find the same results (i.e., good calibration), the Q statistic is small and not statistically significant.

WHY USE META-ANALYSIS?

We underestimate the influence of chance on observed research findings. When an effect is statistically significant ($p < .05$), we are tempted to believe that the effect is a genuine feature of nature. Furthermore, we expect that similar effects will be found in most studies. This is rarely the case. Although tests of statistical significance provide some protection against believing random

https://doi.org/10.1037/0000275-014
Prediction Statistics for Psychological Assessment, by R. K. Hanson

results to be real, the best protection is replication. Whenever we use research evidence to inform our risk assessments, we must consider generalization. For research findings to apply to individual cases, we need some confidence that patterns previously observed will apply to new instances.

The major information contained in risk prediction tools concerns relative risk and the absolute likelihood of the outcome of interest. How risky is this case compared with others? And what proportion of individuals similar to the case at hand will go on to have the outcome? A number of statistics have been presented that help answer these questions. Until now, however, the examples in this book have been based on statistics estimated from single studies. This chapter considers multiple findings on the same topic. In particular, the focus is on fixed-effect meta-analysis for proportions and for logistic regression parameters (intercept [B_0] and slope [B_1]). The exercises at the end of the chapter include a meta-analysis of area under the curve (AUC) values. Proportions are privileged because of their fundamental importance for estimating base rates. Logistic regression is the preferred framework for simultaneously comparing the discrimination and calibration of prediction tools across settings and samples.

Quantitative summaries of previous research findings are not new, dating back at least to Karl Pearson and Ronald Fisher in the early 1900s (Olkin, 1995). It was Glass's study of psychotherapy outcome (Glass, 1976; Smith & Glass, 1977), however, that introduced the term *meta-analysis* and inspired a generation of reviewers interested in quantitative alternatives to the traditional, narrative literature review (Hunt, 1997). After the expected criticisms and scrutiny, meta-analysis has long been the accepted method for answering questions concerning the magnitude and direction of empirical relationships (Cooper, 2003).

Meta-analysis is particularly well-suited to examining the calibration of actuarial risk prediction tools. Single studies can estimate the extent to which a risk tool discriminates between cases with the outcome and cases without the outcome. Multiple samples are required, however, to examine the extent to which the expected rates of the outcome are observed in new samples (i.e., calibration). Meta-analysis is also recommended for establishing norms. Because meta-analytic averages are based on large, diverse samples, meta-analytic averages should be more generalizable than norms based on any single sample.

Limitations

A common, early criticism of meta-analysis was "garbage in, garbage out" (Eysenck, 1978). In other words, the credibility of meta-analytic averages crucially depends on the credibility of the original studies. A related criticism was that reviewers often do not agree about which studies to include (Moher et al., 1995). Depending on the inclusion criteria, meta-analyses could come to opposite conclusions (Jüni et al., 1999). Choosing the studies to include in a meta-analytic review is a creative research activity, which will never be fully systematized (any more than any other *pattern of discovery*; Hanson, 1958).. The studies worthy of aggregation change as theory and research advances. Early meta-analyses may simply identify whether there is likely to be any relationship at all between the variables. As the pool of available studies increases, meta-analyses can focus on increasingly precise estimates. Current best practice in meta-analysis encourages systematic reporting of the hypotheses, search strategies, and selection criteria (e.g., Moher et al., 2015).

Another limitation is that averages can hide meaningful variability. Although there are methods for detecting whether the variability across studies is more than would be expected by chance (the *Q* statistic), they are only so good. With nonsignificant *Q* values, it is still possible (actually, likely) that there are real differences in the studies included in the meta-analysis. Another reason to be cautious about meta-analysis is that sometimes the results from one good study can be more conclusive than the meta-analytic average. For example, a large correctional system may want to establish its own norms, independent of whatever norms are asserted by the test developers. My experience, however, is that it is not uncommon for jurisdictions to want local norms because the decision-makers overestimate the extent to which their settings are unique. This leads decision-makers to be less critical of research in their own jurisdiction than they would be if the same study was done elsewhere. Unless the jurisdiction is exceptionally large and well-integrated, it is difficult to accumulate a sufficient sample size. Norms based on small samples (e.g., less than 100 events) rarely replicate in subsequent samples, even samples from the same jurisdiction. In many cases, the jurisdiction seeking local norms would have obtained more reliable estimates if they had merged their local data into existing meta-analytic averages.

A major advantage of meta-analysis is that it overcomes the weak statistical power of most single studies. Periodically researchers have the opportunity to conduct very large, well-controlled studies, with sample sizes comparable to the aggregated sample size of all previous studies on the topic. If the assumptions of meta-analysis are correct, then the findings of the very large single studies should align closely with the meta-analytic averages (Chalmers & Lau, 1993). This is not always the case (Sivakumar & Peyton, 2016). Sometimes the available studies contain subtle biases that can only be detected by a large, rigorously controlled study. Although I remain a strong advocate for meta-analysis, no research design is infallible. Evaluators should consider both meta-analyses and the best individual studies when making decisions about the validity of a risk factor or risk prediction tool.

THE NUTS AND BOLTS

Data Requirements

The basic information required to conduct a meta-analysis are the following:

1. Two or more effect sizes, *E*s, and
2. their standard errors, SE_E.

Effect size is a general term for statistics that describe the properties of samples (e.g., proportions) and the magnitude of relationships between variables (e.g., odds ratios). Meta-analysts' choice of effect sizes depends on the data available.

The previous chapters of this book presented a number of effect size indicators for prediction tools, and most are appropriate for meta-analysis. Researchers should remember that many effect size statistics are interchangeable, being simple transformations of each other. For example, correlations can be expressed as Cohen's *d*, as can AUCs and odds ratios (see the appendix of Hanson & Morton-Bourgon, 2004). Each transformation, however, introduces a certain amount of error because the statistical models of the different statistics are not identical. If the goal is estimating a common effect size, then best practice involves calculating the same effect size indicator (the same statistic) for all samples directly from the raw data. Of course, calculating a common effect size presupposes that there is a common effect to calculate. This is most likely when there is substantial similarity in the studies being considered.

Calculating Meta-Analyses

The two major approaches to aggregating findings in meta-analysis are fixed-effect and random-effects (Borenstein et al., 2010, 2021). What differentiates the fixed-effect and random-effects meta-analytic models is how they deal with variability between samples. A fixed-effect method assumes that all variability between samples is attributable to sampling error and that the participants come from the same population. The random-effects model incorporates variability across samples into the error term, allowing for the samples to represent different populations. When there is little variability across samples ($Q <$ degrees of freedom), random-effects and fixed-effect meta-analysis produce identical results (Borenstein et al., 2021). Random-effects models are often preferred because they are designed to reduce the possibility of Type 1 error (Borenstein et al., 2021; Schulze, 2007). As variability increases, however, the random-effects method gives more weight to the smaller samples, which can introduce another source of instability into the results. One practical problem with random-effects models is that the estimate of the between-study variability is usually derived from the same samples that are being meta-analyzed. When the number of studies is small ($k < 30$; Schulze, 2007), the estimate of between-study variability is imprecise, which adds additional noise to the random-effects estimates. This noise can increase or decrease the size of the meta-analytic average. For questions concerning generalizability of prediction tools, the fixed-effect model is often appropriate. The most useful prediction tools are intended to work more or less the same across samples. Consequently, the focus on this chapter is fixed-effect meta-analysis.

The Fixed-Effect Model

In the fixed-effect model (Hedges & Olkin, 1985), the averaged effect size, $\bar{E}$, is calculated by weighing the effect sizes from each study (E_i) by the inverse of its variance.

$$\bar{E} = \left(\sum_{i=1}^{k} w_i E_i \right) \Big/ \left(\sum_{i=1}^{k} w_i \right) \tag{14.1}$$

In Equation 14.1, k is the number of studies, $w_i = 1/v_i$, and v_i is the variance of the individual findings (E_i). In other words, Equation 14.1 says to create a weighted sum of the effect sizes and divide it by the sum of the weights. The variance of the weighted mean is the inverse of the sum of the weights.

$$Var(\bar{E}) = 1 \Big/ \left(\sum_{i=1}^{k} w_i \right) \tag{14.2}$$

The denominator of Equation 14.2 is the same as the denominator of Equation 14.1—namely, the sum of the weights for the individual effect sizes.

The 95% confidence interval for the meta-analytic average can be computed as follows:

$$95\%C.I. = \bar{E} \pm 1.96\sqrt{Var(\bar{E})} \tag{14.3}$$

One advantage of using fixed-effect models is that it provides a convenient test of whether the amount of variability across studies is more than would be expected by chance—namely, Cochran's Q statistic:

$$Q = \sum_{i=1}^{k} w_i (E_i - \bar{E})^2 \tag{14.4}$$

The Q statistic is distributed as a χ^2 with $k - 1$ degrees of freedom (k is the number of studies). It is a weighted sum of squares of the effect sizes.

Although the Q statistic is helpful, it is only a significance test. It does not provide information concerning the amount of variability. To describe the amount of variability, Higgins and colleagues (2003) introduced the I^2 statistic. I^2 is the proportion of the overall variability (i.e., Q) beyond what would be expected from random sampling error (Borenstein et al., 2021).

$$I^2 = \frac{(Q - \text{df})}{Q} \times 100 \tag{14.5}$$

In Equation 14.5, Q is the sum of squared deviations (of each effect size from the mean effect size; Equation 14.4) and the degrees of freedom (df) is 1 less than the number of studies/samples (k). In this equation, the degrees of freedom are subtracted from the Q because, with random numbers, the expected value of Q is equal to its degrees of freedom. For example, if six studies are examined, the degrees of freedom for Q would be $6 - 1 = 5$, that is, the expected value of Q would be approximately 5. I^2 is usually reported as a percentage, with 25%, 50%, and 75% representing low, moderate, and high variability, respectively (Higgins et al., 2003). When Q is less than the degrees of freedom, most researchers report I^2 as zero.

Identifying Outliers

The predictive accuracy of a risk tool found in one study is unlikely to be exactly the same as the predictive accuracy found in other studies. Sometimes, however, there is a study (or two) that is way off. When this happens, consider whether the extreme findings represent experimenter error, or unique features of the sample or study design, or other features that would be unrepresentative of the research on this topic. If a finding is very different from other findings on the same topic, then it may or may not make sense to include it in a meta-analytic average. Rejection of a study based on its results risk introducing bias; keeping outliers can introduce other types of bias. Consequently, it is worth having a decision rule for deciding whether a study is an outlier. The rule we developed was as follows (first published in Hanson & Bussière, 1998): (a) the variability (Q) needs to be more than expected by chance ($p < .05$); (b) the effect size of the sample is an extreme value (highest or lowest); and (c) removing the one sample reduces the variability across study (Q) by more than 50%. Typically, it is good practice to report results with and without outliers. The exception is that when there are three or fewer studies in an analysis, it makes little sense to reject one and average the other two. Instead, either report an average of all three (indicating significant variability) or abandon the meta-analytic average and discuss each study separately.

WORKED EXAMPLES

Worked Example 1 (Proportions)

The first worked example concerns the estimation of an average proportion based on the results of different studies. This type of meta-analysis is particularly relevant when the research question concerns the overall base rate of an outcome, or estimation of likelihoods associated with categorical predictors. For a published example of a meta-analysis of base rates using the methods described in this chapter, see Seto et al. (2011).

This fictious example continues the hypothetical scenario introduced in Chapter 12 (chi-square). Dr. Elisabeth von Ebing-Krafft, the assessment leader at a secure forensic hospital, proposed criteria for identifying individuals who meet the legal definition of sexual psychopathy. Individuals who meet the legal definition could be detained until they are deemed safe, potentially until the end of their natural life. The legal criteria require certain types of mental disorders and being likely to commit a violent offense if not civilly committed. Decision-makers had been interpreting "likely" to be above the threshold of an observed recidivism rate of 35% after 5 years. Dr. von Ebing-Krafft's assessment grid includes several steps; however, for the purpose of this exercise, we will only consider one of the final groups: individuals who are high on sexual deviancy and high on psychopathy. This group is expected to have an observed violent recidivism rate of more than 40% after 5 years.

On the basis of the promising results of the fictitious pilot studies (reviewed in Chapter 12), other centers are considering adopting Dr. von Ebing-Krafft's assessment procedure. Given the highly litigious nature of the assessment context, the administrators want a local evaluation before implementation.

A consortium of academics and public health administrators obtain a research grant for a multisite study. Six settings are selected on the basis that they do not have this type of civil commitment provision or have only implemented it recently. Consequently, individuals who would have met the criteria would not have been detained, allowing for their recidivism rate to be calculated. Pilot studies at each of the six sites found that it was possible to retrospectively code von Ebing-Krafft's criteria for sexual psychopathy with adequate reliability.

The outcome criterion was a new instance of violence as evidenced by arrest, hospital admission, or institutional misconduct in a secure setting. The follow-up records were not centralized (individuals could be rehospitalized almost anywhere); consequently, the cost of obtaining recidivism information was high. To keep costs manageable, recidivism information was only obtained for individuals identified as sexual psychopaths, not for the other (control) cases. The primary research question was whether this potentially high-risk group had observed violent recidivism rates above the legal threshold for civil commitment (a question of calibration). The question of relative risk (were these cases higher risk than other cases?) was deferred pending additional grant funding.

The results of the calibration study are presented in Table 14.1.

The overall rate of violent recidivism of 40.6% (138/340) was very close to the expected rate of 40%. In four of the six settings, the observed rates were above the commitment threshold of 35%. In two settings, however, the observed rates were below 35%. In Fridgewater Secure Treatment Center, only 10 of 35 cases reoffended (28.57%), and in Caligula State Hospital, five of 15 cases (33.33%) reoffended. The administrators at Fridgewater and Caligula are not sure how to interpret the results. On the one hand, some random variation from a common (population) mean is expected. If the assessment actually identifies a group with a true likelihood of 40%, then the observed likelihoods in any particular sample will not be exactly 40%, particularly when the sample size is not large. On the other hand, there could be real variation in the recidivism rates because of site differences in release conditions, treatment opportunities, and police practices.

The patients at Fridgewater are excited by the results because they support what they have been saying all along: We are not a particularly dangerous group. Without civil commitment, the average likelihood (28.6%) is below the legal threshold of 35% after 5 years. The president of Fridgewater hospital

TABLE 14.1. Violent Recidivism Rates for Individuals Assessed as High Risk at Six Settings

Setting	No. of high-risk cases	No. known to recidivate with violence	Violent recidivism rates (%)
Penetongue	80	32	40.00
Fridgewater	35	10	28.57
Fort Worth It	72	30	41.67
Mouse Lake	110	50	45.45
Candy Ridge	28	11	39.29
Caligula	15	5	33.33
Total	340	138	40.59

is under strong pressure to keep the system; consequently, he hires a second set of researchers to review the results. Although the observed rate is less than 35%, he argues this does not mean that it is representative of the population being studied. If the researchers repeated the study, they would find a different rate. Conducting a new study will take time; until the results are available, they decide to estimate the expected rate in the common population (if there is one) based on a meta-analysis of all six settings.

Variance Stabilization Transformation

Before conducting the meta-analysis, a detour is needed. The basic meta-analysis formula assumes that means are not correlated with their variances. This is not true for dichotomous outcome variables. Consequently, it is good practice to adjust the raw proportions with a variance stabilization transformation (Cohen, 1988; Eisenhart, 1947; Fleiss et al., 2003). Variance stabilization transformations are not really needed in the current example. When the observed proportions are between .25 and .75, the correlation between the observed proportion and its variability is negligible. The correlations become increasingly important, however, when the rates are very small (<.10) or very large (>.90). Nevertheless, a variance stabilization transformation will be used for illustrative purposes.

In our example, the raw proportion, p, is the proportion of recidivists (i.e., the number of recidivists divided by n, the sample size in each study). The standard formula for the variance of p is $(p(1 - p))/n$, which is the Wald method discussed in Chapter 4 (Fleiss et al., 2003, § 2.4). This variance is largest when the rate of the outcome is 50% and decreases as the proportions approach zero or one. For meta-analysis, the typical effect of using the Wald variance for proportions is to give the most weight to studies with the lowest rates, biasing the estimates to be artificially low.

The most common variance stabilization transformation for proportions is the arcsine transformation, which we will denote by $\breve{A}$, defined as $\breve{A} = 2\ arcsin\ \sqrt{p}$. The reason for using this transformation is that the variance of the arcsine transformation is only influenced by the sample size. Specifically, the variance for all the transformed proportions can be expressed as the inverse of the sample size ($1/n$). In other words, the variance of $\breve{A}$ depends only on the sample size and not the size of the proportion. This is as it should be.

The variance stabilization transformation $\breve{A} = 2\ arcsin\ \sqrt{p}$ requires several steps. First, take the square root of the observed proportion. If the proportion was .40, the square root of the proportion would be 0.632455 (0.632455 × 0.632455 = .40). Next use the arcsine transformation, often called arcsine (x) or $\sin^{-1}(x)$, which is the inverse of the sine transformation. Sine is a unit for describing angles. Arcsine x is the angle (in radians) whose sine is x. For example, arcsine 0.63245 is 0.6847. Consequently, $\breve{A}$ for a proportion of .40 would be $2 * \text{arcsine}(.40)^{1/2} = 2 * \text{arcsine}\ (0.632455) = 2 * 0.6847 = 1.3694$.

Do not worry too much about why we are aggregating probabilities using angles. They are not actually angles, just numbers. A further complication is that for this transformation, the units are radians. Whereas you are probably most comfortable describing a pirouette as rotating 360 degrees, the same rotation can be described as 2π radians. Although meta-analyses of proportions are conducted in radians, the results are most easily communicated in their original units of proportions. You do not need a deep understanding of this transformation to conduct the meta-analyses. In most cases, it is sufficient to learn which buttons to push on your calculator or how to run the R syntax presented later in the chapter.

Table 14.2 sets out the steps in calculating the meta-analytic average. Column 2 presents the sample size per group, which is used to calculate the variance of the estimate (Column 3). In meta-analysis, the individual studies are weighted by the inverse of their variance. For the transformed proportion, the inverse of the variance is simply the sample size, which brings us back to where we started. For example, Setting A had a sample of n = 80 cases, which results in a variance of (1/80) = 0.0125. The inverse of the variance is 1/.0125 = 80. Transforming sample sizes into a variance and back again may seem pointless, which it is in this case; however, I have retained these steps to demonstrate the logic of meta-analytic averages.

The proportion with the outcome is copied from Table 14.1. For example, for Penetongue, the transformed proportion is $\breve{A} = 2arcsin\sqrt{p} = 2\ arcsin\sqrt{.40} = 2 *$ arcsin(0.632455) = 2 * 0.6847185 = 1.3694. Column 7 presents the weighted effect sizes: w_iE_i, which is Column 4 times Column 6. If you are feeling numerate, try calculating some of the values in Column 6. Remember to set the units for the arcsine transformation to radians (not degrees).

The meta-analytic average can now be calculated using Equation 14.1. In Table 14.2, the sum of Column 7 is the numerator of Equation 14.1 and the sum of Column 4 is the denominator: 469.235/340 = 1.3801. This is the meta-analytic average in radians, which translates to 40.5% as a proportion. To transform $\breve{A}$ to a proportion, you can use the R computer code presented later in this chapter, or follow these steps:

1. divide by 2 (e.g., 1.3801/2 = 0.69005),
2. take the sine (e.g., sine[0.69005] = 0), and
3. square it (e.g., $[0.636575744]^2 = 0.40522$).

TABLE 14.2. Steps to Calculating Meta-Analytic Average of Violent Recidivism Rates for Individuals Assessed as High Risk at Six Settings

1	2	3	4	5	6	7
Setting	n	Variance (1/n)	Weights (w_i) inverse of variance	p	$\breve{A}$ 2 *arcsin* $\sqrt{p}$	$\breve{A}$ weighted by inverse of variance $\breve{A} *$ (n)
Penetongue	80	0.01250	80	.4000	1.369438	109.55507
Fridgewater	35	0.02857	35	.2857	1.127854	39.47488
Fort Worth-It	72	0.01389	72	.4167	1.403416	101.04594
Mouse Lake	110	0.00909	110	.4545	1.479670	162.76373
Candy Ridge	28	0.03571	28	.3929	1.354719	37.93213
Caligula	15	0.06667	15	.3333	1.230889	18.46333
Total	340		340			469.23508

Cohen (1988) provided a simplified table for converting proportions to Ă, which could be useful for checking your conversions.

The variance of the meta-analytic average (in radians) is given by Equation 14.2: variance = 1/(Σweights), which is 1/(total of Column 4) = 1/340 = 0.0029411. Take the square root to get the standard error: $(.0029411)^{1/2} = 0.05223$. The 95% confidence interval is given as 1.3801 ± 1.96 (0.05223) = 1.2738 to 1.48650. When the radians are transformed back into proportions, the lower end of the confidence interval is 35.4% and the upper end is 45.8%.

The president of Fridgewater is pleased to see that the lower bound of the confidence interval is just above 35%, which is the commitment threshold. He argues that even though the observed proportion for 35 Fridgewater patients was 28.6%, the expected violent recidivism rate for the class of sexual psychopaths is between 35% and 46%. Addams Gomez, the lawyer for the patients, argues "not so fast." Although the average is in the commitment range, it is possible that there is meaningful variation in recidivism rates between the six settings, which has yet to be tested. Mr. Gomez asks Lunch, his statistically gifted manservant, to run the analysis.

Lunch uses Cochran's *Q* (Equation 14.4) to test whether the variability is more than would be expected by chance: $Q = \sum_{i=1}^{k} w_i \left(E_i - \overline{E}\right)^2$. The steps for this calculation are presented in Table 14.3. These analyses use the transformed proportions, Ă, shown in Column 4 of the table. The weighted, squared deviations from the mean (Ă. = 1.3801) are presented in Column 6. The sum of the squared deviation is Cochran's *Q*, which in this example was 3.72. It is distributed as a chi-square with degrees of freedom equal to one less than the number of the group ($df = k - 1 = 5$). The one-tailed critical value for $p < .05$ given 5 degrees of freedom is 11.07, which is much larger than the observed value. The probability associated with chi-square of 3.72, $df = 5$ is $p = 0.59$. The value of *Q* (3.72) is less than the number of degrees of freedom (5). Consequently, the between-study variability, I^2, was estimated at zero.

The small *Q* value indicates that the range of proportions across sites is pretty much what would be expected if the sites were random samples from the same population. In other words, there is no evidence that variability was

TABLE 14.3. Steps to Calculating Cochran's *Q*

1	2	3	4	5	6
Setting	**N (w_i)**	***p***	**Ă 2 *arcsin* $\sqrt{p}$**	**$(Ă_i - Ă.)^2$**	**$w_i(Ă_i - Ă.)^2$**
Penetongue	80	.4000	1.369438	0.00011367	0.00909357
Fridgewater	35	.2857	1.127854	0.06362822	2.22698757
Fort Worth-It	72	.4167	1.403416	0.00054363	0.03914131
Mouse Lake	110	.4545	1.479670	0.00991424	1.09056606
Candy Ridge	28	.3928	1.354719	0.00064420	0.01803772
Caligula	15	.3333	1.230889	0.02226401	0.33396015
Total	340				*Q* = 3.718

more than expected by chance or that the clients at Fridgewater were less risky than other settings. The president of Fridgewater has grounds to believe that the value of 40% is a reasonable estimate of the expected recidivism rates at all settings, including Fridgewater. Mr. Gomez disagrees. He argues that the observed differences between settings are real and that his clients will be vindicated when researchers are able to repeat the study with a larger sample size and more recent cases.

Worked Example 2 (Logistic Regression Coefficients)

The second example addresses the validity of a risk prediction tool. Specifically, it describes a meta-analysis of logistic regression coefficients derived from different samples. For prediction tools with ordered levels, logistic regression generates two regression coefficients: the slope coefficient (B_1) and the intercept (B_0). Both coefficients are informative. Slope coefficients (B_1s) describe discrimination, that is, the extent to which individuals with the outcome have higher scores than individuals without the outcome. The intercept coefficients (B_0s) can be used to measure calibration, that is, the extent to which the rate of the outcome is consistent across groups. Meta-analysis of logistic regression coefficients is a core method for evaluating the extent to which risk tools work as intended across samples and settings (e.g., see Helmus, Hanson, et al., 2012). It is also extremely useful for examining the racial and ethnic bias (e.g., see Hanson, Lunetta, et al., 2014; Lee et al., 2020). The following example concerns the possibility of bias of a hypothetical matchmaking algorithm for couples of the same gender.

If you are a busy professional, Bowlby's Secure Attachment Match Makers will find your soulmate. Although Bowlby's service will accept just about anybody who pays their fees, it markets extensively to individuals seeking marriage or marriage-like relationships within the LGBTQ2+ community. Matches are linked by a computer algorithm that considers physical, psychological, and lifestyle characteristics (e.g., desire to have family). Each potential couple is assigned a score from 0 = *poor match* to 15 = *ideal match*. The company recommends partners with a score of 6 or higher. Clients, however, are not bound by the scores of the algorithm and are free to request introductions based on any criteria available in Bowlby's database. Bowlby's has an affiliated company that provides marriage services, and an affiliated law firm that specializes in separation and divorce in LGBTQ2+ communities.

In their advertising materials, Bowlby's states that 80% of its introductions result in a romantic relationship lasting at least 12 months. Furthermore, the company advertises that couples who use their marriage service are less likely to get separated or divorce than the national average, which is 10% after 5 years. Annie Anxieuse used the service and was not happy. She was introduced to an intelligent, fun, beautiful woman named Lola Libre. All was going well for the first 10 months, at which point Annie caught Lola flirting (by text) with another woman. It turns out that Lola was having doubts about Annie and asked Bowlby's for a new referral. Annie is furious and starts legal

TABLE 14.4. The Proportion of Mixed-Gender and Same-Gender Couples Together at 12 Months and Their Average Scores on Bowlby's Hypothetical Matchmaking Algorithm

Type of couple	Sample size	Together at 12 months?		Proportion together (%)	Bowlby's algorithm score		
		Yes	No		Average	*SD*	Range
Mixed-gender	700	579	121	82.7	7.5	3.9	0–15
Same-gender men	350	299	51	85.4	7.5	3.7	0–15
Same-gender women	350	238	112	68.0	6.2	3.7	0–15

action against the company. Among the grounds for action, Annie claims that Bowlby's algorithm was based on mixed-gender couples and should not be applied to same-gender unions.

One way that Bowlby's responds to Ms. Anxieuse's complaint is to conduct a validity study of their matching algorithm. Bowlby's has been in business for many years and keeps records on whether their clients are still in a relationship after 12 months. They hire a research consultant, Dr. J. Hunsley, who pulls records for 700 mixed-gender couples, 350 same-gender couples of men, and 350 same-gender couples of women. The same-gender couples are oversampled to reduce sampling error for these groups. Dr. Hunsley uses logistic regression to describe the relationship between the predictive algorithm and whether the couples are still together at 12 months. The descriptive data are presented in Table 14.4, and the logistic regression analyses are presented in Table 14.5.

From Table 14.4, there are fewer same-gender women couples still together at 12 months (68.0%) compared with mixed-gender couples (82.7%) or same-gender men couples (85.4%). It looks like Bowlby's is not doing as well with women in same-gender couples compared with the other groups. The average score for the same-gender women couples is also lower than for the other groups; consequently, it is possible that the lower success rate could be attributed to

TABLE 14.5. Logistic Regression Coefficients Describing the Relationship of Bowlby's Hypothetical Algorithm to the Likelihood of Still Being in Relationship at 12 Months for Mixed-Gender and Same-Gender Couples

Couple type	%	Intercept B_0	Intercept *SE*	Slope B_1	Slope *SE*	AUC	95% CI
Mixed-gender							
Raw scores	54.1	0.16487	0.19802	0.21562	0.02991	.715	[.668, .762]
Centered on 6	81.1	1.45862	0.10533				
Same-gender men							
Raw scores	53.4	0.13647	0.30083	0.26036	0.04844	.735	[.651, .819]
Centered on 6	84.5	1.69860	0.16419				
Same-gender women							
Raw scores	33.2	−0.69700	0.23231	0.26082	0.03874	.738	[.683, .794]
Centered on 6	70.4	0.86795	0.12978				

Note. AUC = area under the curve; CI = confidence interval.

a relative high proportion of women in same-gender couples disregarding Bowlby's algorithm and choosing partners based on their own idiosyncratic criteria. Further analyses are required to identify the extent to which Bowlby's algorithm works equally well for each group.

The results of Dr. Hunsley's logistic regression analyses are presented in Table 14.5. For each group, three coefficients are presented: two intercepts (B_0 for a score of 0 and for a score of 6) and one slope coefficient (B_1). The slope coefficients (B_1s) measure discrimination; they are, however, difficult to interpret because they are unstandardized. Consequently, the discrimination of the algorithm is also expressed as AUC values, which can be interpreted as the probability that a couple who stays together has a higher score than a couple who broke up before 12 months (see Chapter 8). In Table 14.5, all three B_1 coefficients are similar, with the coefficients for the same-gender couples being slightly higher than for the mixed-gender couples. The AUC values indicate that for all groups, there were large differences in scores between the couples that were still together at 12 months and those that were not. Overall, in terms of discrimination, there does not appear to be bias against same-gender couples.

The intercepts (B_0s) address calibration, or the extent to which the expected values are similar for the different groups. The B_0's for the raw scores estimate the rate of successful matches for couples who start with an algorithm score of zero. For the mixed-gender couples and same-gender men couples, this is around 50%. In other words, approximately half of these matches would be expected to still be together after 12 months. For women in same-gender couples, however, this rate was closer to one third (33.2%). Because Bowlby's service recommend matches with scores of six and higher, it is useful to examine the intercept when the algorithm has been rescaled so that the characteristics that would normally result in a score of six, now result in a score of zero. Adding or subtracting a constant to a predictor variable does not change the AUC value or the slope coefficient in logistic regression. Consistent with the claims of Bowlby's Match Making Service, more than 80% of the mixed-gender couples and the men in same-gender couples who had a score of six were still together after 12 months. For the women in same-gender couples, however, only 70% were still together. This finding is consistent with Ms. Anxieuse's claim that Bowlby's algorithm does not work as well for women in same-gender couples as for mixed-gender couples. Bowlby's does not immediately accept Ms. Anxieuse's criticism, however, because some variation across groups would be expected based on chance alone. To test whether the variation in regression coefficients was more than would be expected by chance, Bowlby's ask Dr. Hunsley to conduct a meta-analysis. The results are presented in Table 14.6.

Column 2 and Column 3 of Table 14.6 are the logistic regression coefficients and their standard errors, which are copied from Table 14.5. Column 4 are the weights, which are the inverse of the variances. Column 5 are the weighted coefficients, which are used to calculate the meta-analytic average ($\bar{E}$, Equation 14.1). In this example, the meta-analytic average is not of primary interest; instead, it is used to calculate between group variability (Q in Column 6, based on

TABLE 14.6. Meta-Analysis of the Logistic Regression Coefficients for Bowlby's Matchmaking Algorithm

1	2	3	4	5	6
Coefficient	Effect size (E_i)	*SE*	Weight (W_i) $=1/SE^2$	$W_i * E_i$	$W_i(E_i - \bar{E})^2$
$B_0(0)$					
Mixed-gender	0.16487	0.19802	25.502449	4.20459	2.22884
Same-gender men	0.13647	0.30083	11.049884	1.50798	0.789093
Same-gender women	−0.69700	0.23231	18.529521	−12.91508	5.941078
			$\Sigma = 55.081854$	$\Sigma = -7.202510$	
				$\bar{E} = -0.13076$	$Q = 8.959011$
					$p = .011$, $I^2 = 77.7$
$B_0(6)$					
Mixed-gender	1.45862	0.10533	90.135492	131.47343	1.772465129
Same-gender men	1.69860	0.16419	37.094250	63.00829	5.362331574
Same-gender women	0.86795	0.12978	59.372380	51.53226	12.04642996
			$\Sigma = 186.602122$	$\Sigma = 246.013981$	
				$\bar{E} = 1.31839$	$Q = 19.181227$
					$p < .0001$, $I^2 = 89.6$
B_1					
Mixed-gender	0.21562	0.02991	1,117.807898	241.02174	0.553384773
Same-gender men	0.26036	0.04844	426.178691	110.95988	0.215561224
Same-gender women	0.26082	0.03874	666.316806	173.78875	0.350950727
			$\Sigma = 2{,}210.30339$	$\Sigma = 525.770372$	
				$\bar{E} = 0.23787$	$Q = 1.119897$
					$p = 0.57$, $I^2 = 0$

Equation 14.4, and I^2, Equation 14.5). To demonstrate the arithmetic, the first entry in Column 6 is $W_i(E_i - \bar{E})^2$, 25.502449*(0.16487 – (–0.13076))^2 = 2.22884.

Regardless of whether the intercept was centered on zero or on 6, the amount of between group variability was large ($I^2 > 75\%$) and statistically significant. In contrast, the amount of variability in the slope coefficient (B_1) was no more than would be expected by chance (Q value was not significant and small; $Q <$ degrees of freedom, $I^2 = 0$). This means that for all three groups, Bowlby's algorithm was equally effective at sorting couples into those who are most likely to remain together after 12 months (unbiased discrimination). Regardless of gender, couples with higher scores are those most likely to stay together, and for every 1-unit increase in score, the odds of staying together increase by about the same for all three groups ($\bar{E} = 0.23$). In contrast, the variability in the intercepts indicates that the same scores do not imply the same likelihoods of staying together. In particular, women in same-gender couples had a lower likelihood of being together than either the mixed-gender couples or men in same-gender couples. A visual representation of the fitted logistic regression curves is presented in Figure 14.1.

The opposing sides in the legal contest emphasize different aspects of Dr. Hunsley's findings. Bowlby's argues that its algorithm works as intended

FIGURE 14.1. Logistic Fitted Curves for the Relationship Between Bowlby's Hypothetical Algorithm and Couples Still Being Together at 12 Months

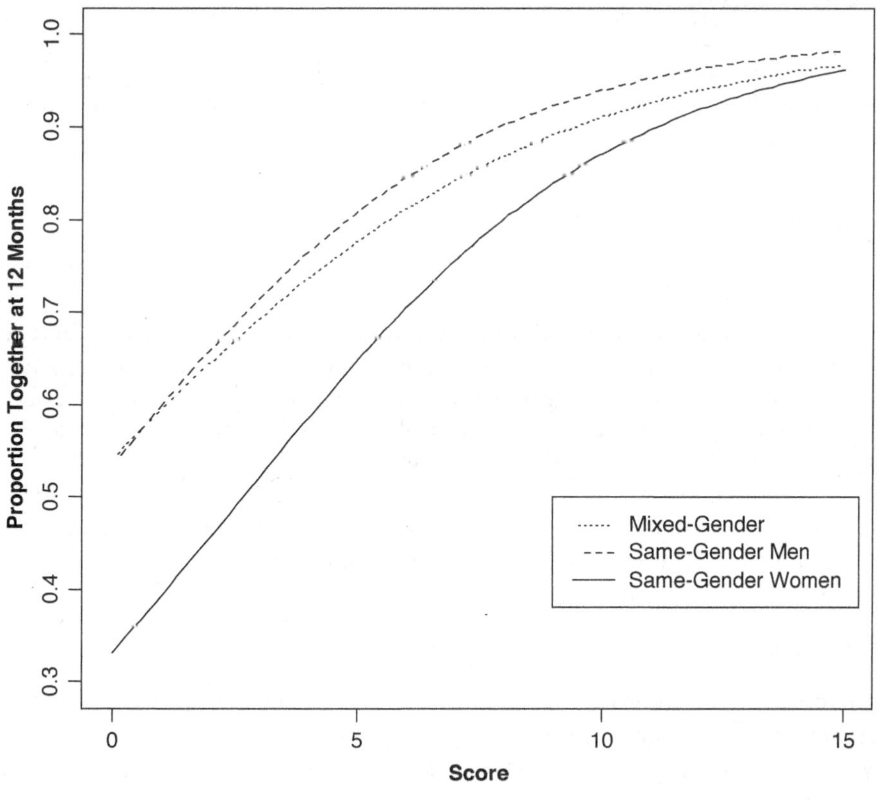

to identify couples likely to stay together, regardless of whether they are same-gender or mixed-gender. The lower stability of women in same-gender relationships compared with same-gender men or mixed-gender couples is a separate phenomenon beyond the scope of Bowlby's match making service (Kolk & Andersson, 2020). On the other side, the lawyers for Ms. Anxieuse charge Bowlby's with false advertising: the analysis clearly shows that less than 80% of women introduced to other women stay together for 12 months, even if they have the requisite minimum score of 6 on the matching algorithm.

Notice that the meta-analysis of the logistic regression intercept coefficients identified a weakness in the prediction tool that would have been difficult to identify with other statistics. Discrimination statistics, such as Cohen's *d* or the AUC, would conclude that the algorithm works equally well for all groups. The problem, however, is with calibration. It would be possible to examine calibration by comparing the raw rates for the three groups after combining ranges of scores; however, this would be underpowered, and the decisions concerning how to clump the data could appear ad hoc. In contrast, logistic regression provides a simple, efficient approach to calibration that does not require potentially arbitrary decisions concerning how to organize scores into levels. Consequently, the meta-analysis of logistic regression coefficients is one of the preferred approaches to examining the validity of prediction tools across settings, samples, and groups.

GOING FURTHER

The following sections are intended for individuals who wish to deepen their understanding, typically because they plan to use meta-analysis in research or teach it to others.

Recommended Readings

Borenstein, M., Hedges, L. V., Higgins, J. P. T., & Rothstein, H. R. (2021). *Introduction to meta-analysis* (2nd ed.). Wiley.

A very readable and authoritative introduction. Of the various different styles of meta-analyses, this is the dominant approach (and my preference).

Borenstein, M., Hedges, L. V., Higgins, J. P. T., & Rothstein, H. R. (2010). A basic introduction to fixed-effect and random-effects models for meta-analysis. *Research Synthesis Methods, 1*(2), 97–111. https://doi.org/10.1002/jrsm.12

A shorter, journal version by the same authors that covers the basic statistical approach to meta-analysis, with helpful worked examples. Meta-analysis aficionados will also enjoy browsing the whole journal.

Computer Code

There are several options for computing fixed-effect meta-analysis. Given that the computational demands are relatively low, it is often convenient to conduct these analyses using a generic spreadsheet (such as Excel) following the steps described in the worked examples described in this chapter. There are also a number of good, purpose-built meta-analysis software programs. Among the commercial programs, Comprehensive Meta-Analysis (https://www.meta-analysis.com/) deserves special mention because it is easy to use and closely aligns with Borenstein et al.'s (2021) excellent introductory text. R Statistics has several meta-analysis packages, one of which (**metafor**, Viechtbauer, 2010) figures in my example that follows. I choose to demonstrate **metafor** because it the most versatile of the R meta-analysis programs, and the most popular. IBM/SPSS does not have a meta-analysis program. It is possible to conduct these analyses using SPSS syntax files, examples of which can be found by searching the web.

R Code

If you have not used it before, you will first need to obtain the **metaphor** package.

```
install.packages ('metafor')
```

It will ask you to choose a CRAN site. Choose one geographically close to you.

Once you have obtained the package, tell R that you want to use it.

```
library ('metafor')
```

This example reanalyzes the data from the first worked example described earlier. The data can be in a preexisting datafile, or the datafile can be created using the following commands:

```
setting <- c("Penetongue", "Fridgewater", "Fort
Worth-It", "Mouse Lake",
      "Candy Ridge", "Caligula")
ni <- c(80, 35,72, 110, 28, 15)
xi <- c(32, 10, 30, 50, 11, 5)
```

The variable names (setting, ni, xi, Ai, vi) are your choice (and case sensitive). The following line transforms the raw proportion (xi/ni) into $A = 2\ arcsin\ \sqrt{p}$, and the next line creates the variances (vi) from the sample sizes (ni).

```
Ai <- 2*asin(sqrt(xi/ni))
vi <-(1/ni)
```

The next two lines create a datafile that can be read by **metafor**.

```
E1.data <- data.frame (setting, ni, Ai, vi)
E1.data <- escalc (measure = "GEN", yi=Ai, vi=vi,
data=E1.data)
```

In the above line, *escalc* is a **metafor** command that identifies the type of data to be analyzed. In this example, *measure* = "GEN" tells the programs that the data are generic effect sizes (*yi* = *Ai*) and their variances (*vi* = *vi*), which has already been calculated and are in the data file "E1.data"; *yi* and *vi* are **metafor** commands whereas *Ai* and *vi* are your variable names (which happened to be the same for vi). Now you are ready to run the meta-analysis:

```
Example1 <- rma(yi,vi, data=E1.data, method = "FE")
```

The *method* = *"FE"* command specifies fixed-effect meta-analysis (the default is random-effects). To see the results, type

```
Example1
```

This produces the following output:

```
Fixed-Effects Model (k = 6)
I^2 (total heterogeneity / total variability): 0.00%
H^2 (total variability / sampling variability): 0.74
Test for Heterogeneity:
Q(df = 5) = 3.7185, p-val = 0.5906
Model Results:
estimate   se     zval     pval    ci.lb   ci.ub
1.3801  0.0542  25.4484  <.0001  1.2738  1.4864   ***
---
Signif. codes: 0 '***' 0.001 '**' 0.01 '*' 0.05 '.'
0.1 ' ' 1
```

These are the same numbers that were previously calculated in the worked example. H^2 (H^2) is a measure of variability, similar to I^2 (I^2). H^2 is approximately equal to $Q/(\mathrm{k} - 1)$, with an expected value of 1. H^2 values less than one indicate that the variability was less than expected and H^2 values greater than one indicate that the variability was more than expected. In this example, H^2 is less than one (0.74) indicating that the amount of variability was low.

The following is syntax that converts variance stabilized/arcsine transformed *p* values ($\breve{A}$) back into proportions.

```
p <- (sin(Ai/2))^2
```

It can be used to report the meta-analytic average (1.3801 radians) in a more understandable metric (a proportion of 0.405, or 40.5%).

```
sin(1.3801/2)^2
[1] 0.4052287
```

The lower and upper limits of the 95% confidence interval (1.2728 to 1.4864) can be similarly converted to proportions (35.3% to 45.8%):

```
(sin(1.2738/2))^2
[1] 0.3536753
(sin(1.4864/2))^2
[1] 0.4578519
```

Forest plots are often used to display the results of meta-analyses (see Borenstein et al., 2021; Figure 14.2). The simplest syntax for creating a forest

FIGURE 14.2. A Forest Plot (From R) of the Multisite Study of Sexual Psychopathy (Worked Example 1)

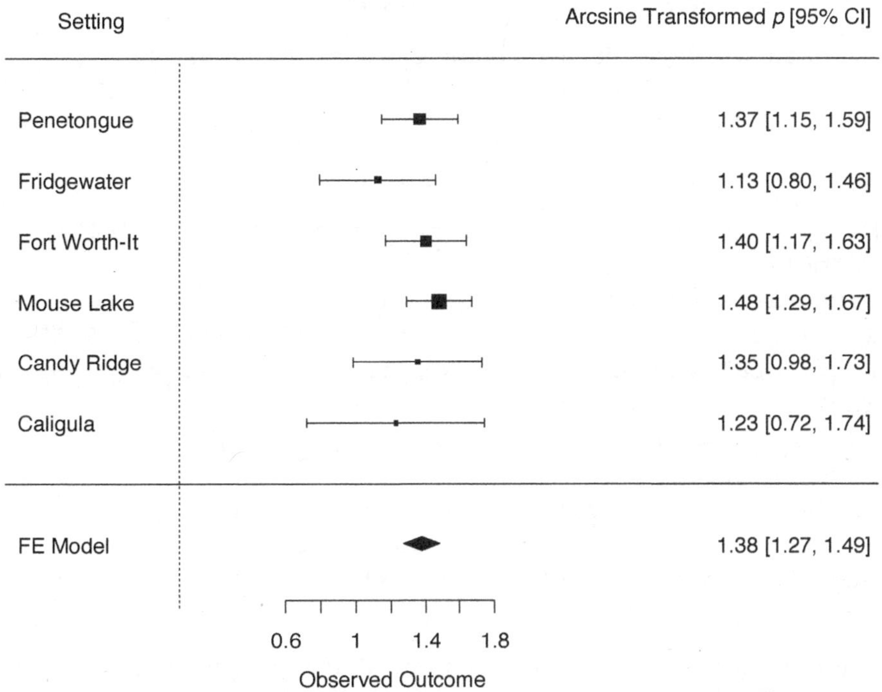

Note. CI = confidence interval; FE = fixed-effect.

plot in R is *forest(meta object)*, e.g., *forest (Example1)*. A somewhat prettier display can be created by tweaking the options, as in the following syntax:

```
forest (Example1, slab=paste(E1.data$setting), xlim =
c(-1, 4))
text(-.5, 8, "Setting", pos=1)
text(4, 7.7, "Arcsine Transformed p [95% CI]", pos =2)
```

The following R code conducts a fixed-effect meta-analysis of the logistic regression coefficients from Example 2. Specifically, it examines the between-group variability of the intercept centered on a score of 6 (B0[6]).

```
couple_type <- c("Mixed-Gender", "Same-Gender Men",
"Same-Gender Women")
B06 <- c(1.45862, 1.69860, 0.86795)
SEB06 <- c(0.10533, 0.16419, 0.12978)
VarB06 <- SEB06*SEB06
```

The first three lines identify the raw data (from Table 14.6), and then the standard errors are squared to create a vector of variances (*VarB06*) in the fourth line. Next, the data are organized into a format that can be read by **metafor**, with *yi* and *vi* being commands that tell the program which variables are the effect sizes and their variances, respectively.

```
E2.data <- data.frame (couple_type, B06, VarB06)
E2.data <- escalc (measure = "GEN", yi = B06, vi =
VarB06, data=E2.data)
```

The meta-analysis is then run on this data set (E2.data).

```
Example2 <- rma(yi,vi, data=E2.data, method = "FE")
Example2
Fixed-Effects Model (k = 3)
I^2 (total heterogeneity / total variability): 89.57%
H^2 (total variability / sampling variability): 9.59
Test for Heterogeneity:
Q(df = 2) = 19.1812, p-val < .0001
Model Results:
estimate    se      zval     pval     ci.lb    ci.ub
1.3184   0.0732   18.0095  <.0001   1.1749   1.4619   ***
Signif. Codes: 0 '***' 0.001 '**' 0.01 '*' 0.05 '.'
0.1 ' ' 1
```

The relevant values (Q, I^2, and mean) are all the same as those previously calculated in Example 2.

When there are a sufficient number of studies and reasons to expect that the effect sizes could vary based on another factors (e.g., ethnicity, gender), then researchers can examine whether these moderator variables account for a significant amount of the residual variance using the following syntax:

```
rma (yi ~ moderator1, vi, data = meta.data)
```

The default analysis uses random-effects. For fixed-effect moderator analysis, researchers can use the following:

```
rma (yi ~ moderator1, vi, data = meta.data, method = "FE")
```

EXERCISES

Given that Bowlby's Match Making Service states that its algorithm predicts stable marriages, it again hires Dr. Hunsley, this time to conduct a divorce study. Neither the marriage rate nor the divorce rate for Bowlby's matches are known, and it would be expensive to gather this information. Instead, Dr. Hunsley decides to compare couples seeking divorce services to a comparison group of couples who have remained married for at least 5 years. The divorce samples are drawn from Bowlby's affiliated legal service. The still married sample is selected from couples who used Bowlby's marriage services at least 5 years ago. Approximately equal numbers of divorced and married couples

TABLE 14.7. Comparison of Divorced and Married Couples on Bowlby's Hypothetical Matchmaking Algorithm

	Divorced couples			Married couples				
	N	*M*	*SD*	*N*	*M*	*SD*	AUC	*SE*
Mixed-gender	51	6.68	3.45	50	9.16	3.62	.678	0.0532
Same-gender men	48	6.95	3.49	47	9.03	3.20	.681	0.0555
Same-gender women	47	5.91	3.64	49	8.06	3.52	.654	0.0562

AUC = area under the curve.

are selected for each group (mixed-gender, same-gender men, same-gender women). Consequently, the proportion with the outcome is part of the research design, not a finding (calibration cannot be tested with this design). It is, nevertheless, possible to compare the discrimination of Bowlby's algorithm across groups. The basic findings are presented in Table 14.7

Answering the questions requires conducting a meta-analysis of the AUC values. You can conduct the analyses using a hand calculator or use any program you want.

Question 14.1

What is the meta-analytic average AUC value? What is the *SE* and 95% confidence interval for this value?

Question 14.2

How does the meta-analytic average AUC value compare to the simple average based on weighting each AUC by its sample size (e.g., the sample size for mixed-gender couples is 51 + 50 = 101)?

Question 14.3

Is the amount of variability in AUCs more than would be expected by chance?

Question 14.4

On the basis of these data, how would you respond to Ms. Anxieuse's complaint that Bowlby's algorithm works better for mixed-gender couples than for women in relationships with women?

ANSWERS TO EXERCISES

Question 14.1

Average AUC = .671, SE = 0.0317, 95% confidence interval = [.609, .734]. Note that the fixed-effect and random-effects estimates are the same because of the very low variability in this data set.

Question 14.2

The meta-analytic average and the simple weighted average are the same: AUC = .671. The simple weighted average and the meta-analytic average are usually close, so this is one way of checking that the meta-analytic average that you calculate is in the ballpark. In the current example, they are the same to three decimal points.

Question 14.3

The amount of variability is no more than would be expected by chance. The Q value is tiny ($Q = 0.1412$, $I^2 = 0$), corresponding to a p value of .932. The AUC values are almost too similar ($p = 1 - .932 = 0.068$). In other words, there is about a 1 in 15 chance that results this close would be found by chance alone. (The data were actually generated randomly specifying a common SD of 3.5 and a common group difference of 2.5 points for each group.)

Question 14.4

This analysis did not indicate any systematic group differences in the ability of Bowlby's algorithm to discriminate couples that will remain married and those who get divorced. However, this analysis had limited statistical power, and it is possible that group differences could be detected given larger sample sizes. The AUC value for the same-gender women couples was the lowest for the three groups. Calibration was not tested. In previous analyses, Bowlby's algorithm underestimated the likelihood of relationship breakdown for women in relationships with other women.

15

Calibration Plots

Calibration plots are graphs displaying the extent to which the observed likelihoods in a replication study are similar to the predicted likelihoods.

Calibration plots display the level of agreement between predicted values and observed values for prediction tools. There are several types of calibration plots, some well suited to categorical predictors and others well suited to linear or ordinal (ranked) predictors. All calibration plots require a set of observed proportions and a set of expected proportions that are specified in advance. Calibration plots display the extent to which the risk tool, on average, overpredicts or underpredicts (calibration-in-the-large; Steyerberg, 2019), as well as regions where the expected values are too high or too low. Calibration plots are excellent for identifying patterns in validation studies; however, they should be supplemented with statistical tests (e.g., E/O index, meta-analysis of logistic regression coefficients) to limit overinterpretation of chance findings.

WHY USE CALIBRATION PLOTS?

Many of us process visual displays more accurately and more quickly than we process printed text. As the saying goes, a picture is worth a thousand . . . numbers. The preference for visual processing of rates and proportions is not universal. Numbers work best for some. There are, however, enough people partial to visual displays that graphical representations are almost always a

https://doi.org/10.1037/0000275-015
Prediction Statistics for Psychological Assessment, by R. K. Hanson

worthwhile supplement to the other ways of presenting numeric information. Graphs and figures are particularly important when the numeric information is complex (Leonhardt & Robin Keller, 2018) and numeracy is low (Hilton & Helmus, 2020).

Different types of graphs lead viewers to pay attention to different information (Visschers et al., 2009). Although there are some general rules for making good graphs, it is also an art. One master of the art is Edward Tufte (1990, 2001, 2006). He has written a number of influential (and beautiful) books on how to present information in graphs and figures. One of his principles, which I support, is that visual displays of quantitative information should prioritize the data over decoration (avoid non-data-ink and chartjunk; Tufte, 2001). Viewers are most likely to get the intended message when that message is the most salient feature of the graph or chart.

In my own research, graphs are important in the beginning and at the end. In the early stages of data cleaning and analysis, graphs help me see what the data look like.[1] Simple scatterplots effectively display the relationship between two ordered variables. They are also great at identifying errant and impossible values during data cleaning. For dichotomous outcome variables, it is necessary to first clump the responses by scores or risk levels before plotting. It is almost impossible to see patterns in graphs when the only options are zero or one. Means of dichotomous variables (i.e., proportions) are much easier to graph than zeros and ones (see Example 2 of this chapter). Consequently, data cleaning with a dichotomous outcome variable usually benefits from exploring different ways of aggregating the data.

Once the data analysis is complete, researchers need to consider which information is best communicated by figures versus text or tables. In many cases, figures are the most effective way of communicating overall patterns in the data (e.g., the relationship between risk scale scores and criminal recidivism was well represented by a logistic curve). When group differences are large, a simple plot of raw values can be compelling. One of my graduate school professors, Ed Ware (1931–2020), called this the *interocular shock test*. Well-designed figures can also communicate the extent of sampling error by including confidence intervals (Cumming & Finch, 2005).

There are a number of variations on the calibration plot. One basic form plots the expected values along the x-axis (the horizontal line) against the observed values on the y-axis (the vertical line; Examples 1 and 2, this chapter). For dichotomous outcome variables, the observed values are averages for groups. The groups could be defined by risk scores or levels, or they can be equal-sized groups constructed from the observed data (e.g., deciles, which are 10 groups each comprising 10% of the total). When the calibration plot is based on deciles, it is a visual representation of the Hosmer–Lemeshow test (Hosmer et al., 2013). Whereas the expected values in the Hosmer–Lemeshow test are typically

[1]Note the deliberate use of visual language. A more tactile data analyst would get a feel for the data set.

generated from the observed data (to determine whether the data fit a logistic distribution), the expected values for calibration plots are specified in advance by the norms of the prediction tool. This type of calibration plot has a diagonal line indicating perfect calibration. Observations above the diagonal indicate that the risk tool underestimated the likelihood of the outcome, whereas observations below the diagonal indicate that the risk tool overestimated the likelihood of the outcome. Calibration plots also display information concerning discrimination. When the line that connects the observed values has a slope of 1.0 (i.e., it follows the diagonal), discrimination is the same in the replication study as it was for the norms (e.g., area under the curve [AUC] = .720 in both samples). When the slope of this line is flatter (less than one), the risk tool had poorer discrimination than expected (e.g., AUC < .720 in replication study). When the slope of the observed values is greater than one (steeper than expected), the risk tool demonstrated better discrimination in the replication study than expected (e.g., AUC > .720 in replication study).

Another type of calibration plot has separate lines for the observed and expected values. In this type of graph, the risk score or levels are plotted along the x-axis and the likelihoods are on the y-axis. There are two likelihoods plotted for each risk level: one for the expected values and another for the observed values (see Alba et al., 2017, Figure 2, and Examples 3 and 4, this chapter). I like calibration plots with risk scores on the x-axis because unlike calibration plots with expected values on the x-axis, it is easy to identify specific risk scale scores.

LIMITATIONS

Whereas figures are good at displaying overall patterns, tables are more effective at communicating precise numeric values (e.g., the average 2-year recidivism rate for individuals with the median score was 34.5%). Another limitation is that the graphs can appear to reveal patterns that are not really there, particularly when the sample sizes are small. Creating good graphs and figures requires judgment, and graphic design decisions can emphasize the wrong things or exaggerate chance features of the data. Conversely, it is difficult to detect small effects (Cohen's $d < .20$) from visual displays. When the relationship with the outcome is small (as many relationships are), real patterns may remain hidden in plots of the raw data. Skill is required to create meaningful graphs of small effects.

It is also worth remembering that not everybody likes visual representations of quantitative information. In graduate school, one of my statistic courses taught factor analysis based on visualizations of p-dimensional space. I thought the course was great and still think of factor analysis in geometric terms. For a significant minority of the class, however, the graphs added nothing. They were much more comfortable with words and equations. Consequently, it is best to consider graphs and figures as a supplement to other ways of communicating quantitative information.

THE NUTS AND BOLTS

Data Requirements

The following data are required to calculate a calibration plot:

1. expected values for the likelihood of the outcome provided by a risk prediction tool;
2. the observed rate of the outcome in a replication study; and
3. the expected must be specified in advance, prior to collecting the observed rates.

The expected values may be norms specified for actuarial risk tools, values observed in a previous study (or meta-analysis), or the values for an accepted reference group. For example, calibration plots can be used to compare the observed values for various ethic subgroups to the overall rates previously calculated for complete (mixed ethnicity) samples. The observed rates are easiest to interpret when calculated using a fixed follow-up period. Some calibration plots include an indicator of the variability associated with the observed and expected rates. These can be the standard error of the mean for proportions, or standard errors of fitted values (e.g., 95% confidence intervals for the predicted values from logistic regression).

Constructing Calibration Plots

The following sections present four types of calibration plots, two with the expectations on the x-axis, and two with risk scores on the x-axis. These calibration plots were featured because they are both informative and relatively simple to construct. Examples 1 and 3 can be plotted by hand on standard graph paper. This is not meant to be an exhaustive tour of all the options. Other variations on calibration plots can found in Steyerberg (2009, 2019). As well, researchers and test developers may construct other types of graphs tailored to their needs.

Example 1: Plotting observed values against expected values for discrete categories (expected values on x-axis)

The first example is based on the hypothetical validation study of Dr. Ebing-Krafft's risk scheme for sexual psychopathy. This scheme has four risk groups: neither sexually deviant nor psychopathic (low risk; Group A), sexually deviant but not psychopathic (Group B), psychopathic but not sexual deviant (Group C), and both sexually deviant and psychopathic (high risk; Group D). The observed and expected rates are summarized in Table 15.1. There is an observed and an expected value for each of the four risk groups.

The values in Table 15.1 are plotted in Figure 15.1. Although Figure 15.1 was constructed using R code (as described later in the chapter), this type of calibration plot can be easily constructed using a pencil and standard graph paper. In this figure, the expected likelihoods are on the x-axis (horizontal) and the observed values on the y-axis (vertical). The diagonal line going from (0, 0) to (1, 1) indicates perfect calibration. The recidivism rates for Group D and for

TABLE 15.1. Observed and Expected Recidivism Rates for the Hypothetical Validation Study of Dr. Ebing-Krafft's Risk Scheme for Sexual Psychopathy (From Table 12.1)

	Recidivism rates	
Group	Observed	Expected
A	.140	.20
B	.414	.60
C	.300	.20
D	.122	.10

FIGURE 15.1. Calibration Plot of the Hypothetical Validation Study of Dr. Ebing-Krafft's Risk Scheme for Sexual Psychopathy

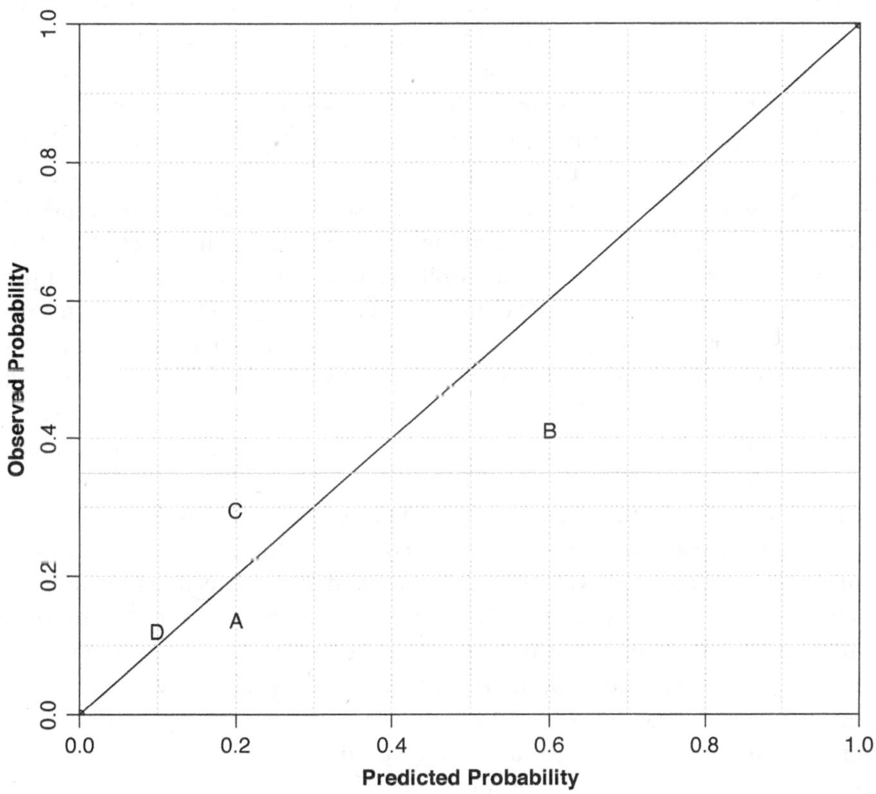

Note. Data can be found in Table 15.1. The letters indicate the four risk groups in the prediction scheme. The light gray horizontal line indicates the decision threshold in this example (35%).

Group A were pretty much as expected (both points were close to the diagonal). The observed rate for Group C was higher than expected, and the observed rate for Group D was lower than expected. Although Table 15.1 and Figure 15.1 contain identical information, many readers will find that they identify these patterns more quickly in the figure than in the table.

Whether this amount of imperfect calibration will have practical significance depends on the assessment question and the decision threshold. In this hypothetical example, the threshold for civil commitment as a sexual psychopath was 35%. The recidivism rate for Group C was higher than expected (30% instead of 20%); however, it was still below the decision threshold. Similarly, Dr. Ebing-Krafft's scheme overestimated the risk for Group B, but the observed rate was still above the decision threshold (41% instead of 60%).

Example 2: Plotting observed values against expected values for a risk scale with ordered scores or levels (expected values on the x-axis)

The second example reprises the hypothetical replication study of Static-99R in Akuarl Atoll, which was previously described in Chapter 13 (E/O index). Static-99R is an actuarial risk tool for estimating the likelihood of sexual recidivism (Hanson & Thornton, 2000; Helmus, Thornton, et al., 2012). It has 10 items, which generate scores from a possible minimum of −3 to a possible maximum of 12. The scores are then organized into five risk levels: Level I = *very low risk* (−3, −2), Level II = *below average risk* (−1, 0), Level III = *average risk* (1, 2, 3), Level IVa = *above average risk* (4, 5) and Level IVb = *well above average risk* (scores of 6 and higher). The median value is 2. Each score is associated with expected recidivism rates derived from fitted logistic estimates (Hanson et al., 2016; Phenix et al., 2016). In the Akuarl Atoll example, the observed values in the validation study are compared with the 5-year sexual recidivism rate norms for routine/complete samples (Phenix et al., 2016). The data used for the calibration plot were presented previously in Table 13.2 (Chapter 13). A quick look at this table indicates that the sample size per score ranged from one case (score of 10) to 181 (the median score of 2). The expected recidivism rates ranged from less than 1% to 53.0%.

Like the first example, the second example plots the expected values on the x-axis and the observed values on the y-axis. It also includes 95% confidence intervals for the predicted values, and a smoothed line connecting the observed values. To construct the calibration plot for a continuous predictor, the observed values need to be collapsed into groups, preferably groups of equal size. Following the conventions for the Hosmer–Lemeshow test, it is common practice to divide the sample into 10 equal sized groups (deciles). There are a variety of statistical programs that could be used to divide samples into deciles; however, in this example the groups will be constructed manually. With an overall sample size of 1,100, each group should have just over 100 cases (1,000 ÷ 10 = 110). Some adjustments are necessary, however, given that several scores already have more than 110 cases, and it is impossible to subdivide individual scores into groups smaller than a single score (Static-99R scores are integers). Consequently, to maintain a minimum of approximately 100 cases per group, there will be fewer than 10 groups. For this calibration plot, the scores were combined as follows: Group 1 (−3 and −2, *very low risk*), Group 2 (−1), Group 3 (0),

Group 4 (1), Group 5 (2), Group 6 (3), Group 7 (4 and 5, *above average risk*) and Group 8 (6 through 10, the maximum score observed in the replication study, *well above average risk*). Notice that when aggregation of scores was needed, the risk groups were constructed to correspond to the Static-99R risk levels.

The data for the calibration plot are presented in Table 15.2. For the risk groups that included just one score (Groups 2, 3, 4, 5, and 6), the expected values are taken directly from the Static-99R norms (Phenix et al., 2016). For the risk groups that contained more than one score (Groups 1, 2, and 8), the expected values are the average of the expected values for members of that group. To add confidence intervals, the standard error of the proportions was calculated using the Wald method (square root of $p_i(1 - p_i)/n_i$, where p_i and n_i are the observed proportion and sample size for each of the eight risk groups; see Equation 4.3 in Chapter 4, this volume). Each side of the 95% confidence interval is equal to the standard error times 1.96 (e.g., for Group 5 [Static-99R score of 2], $0.1919 \times 1.96 = 0.03761$.)

Figure 15.2 is the calibration plot based on the data from Table 15.2. As in the previous calibration plot (Example 1, for discrete categories), the diagonal line indicates perfect calibration. Seven of the eight groups are close to the diagonal, indicating adequate fit between the expected and observed values. For the highest risk group, however, the observed rates are lower than the expected rates, and the confidence interval for the observed rates did not cross the diagonal, indicating poor calibration for this risk group. The slope of the line connecting the observed values provides some guidance concerning whether the discrimination was better or worse than expected. The slope is slightly steeper than the diagonal between the low scores and middle scores, indicating better than expected discrimination at this range of scores. The slope is flatter than the diagonal between the middle scores and the high scores, indicating worse than expected discrimination for the higher scores. Overall, the slope is roughly parallel to the diagonal (slope close to one), indicating the overall discrimination is close to the expected value. Making this same comparison using statistics, the global AUC value for the Akuarl Atoll data was .68, compared with an expected value of .69.

TABLE 15.2. Observed and Expected Recidivism Rates for the Hypothetical Akuarl Atoll Static-99R Replication Study

1	2	3	4	5	6	7
Group	**Size of group**	**Static-99R (*M*)**	**Observed recidivism rate**	**Expected recidivism rate**	***SE* of observed**	**1.96 × *SE* (for 95% confidence intervals)**
1	95	−2.47	0.0153	0.111	0.01047	0.02052
2	97	−1.00	0.0206	0.019	0.01443	0.02828
3	129	0.00	0.0388	0.028	0.01699	0.03331
4	169	1.00	0.0592	0.039	0.01815	0.03557
5	181	2.00	0.0718	0.056	0.01919	0.03761
6	138	3.00	0.0870	0.079	0.02399	0.04701
7	163	4.47	0.1166	0.130	0.02513	0.04926
8	128	6.63	0.1562	0.250	0.03209	0.06290

FIGURE 15.2. Calibration Plot With Expected Values on x-Axis for Akuarl Atoll Example (Table 15.2)

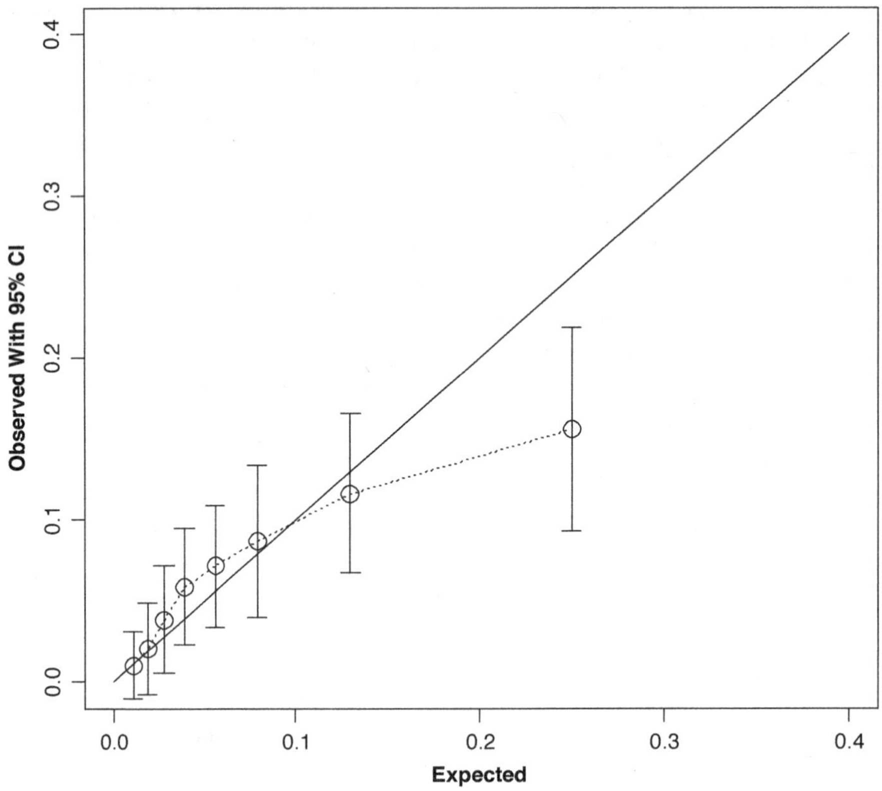

Note. CI = confidence interval.

Although calibration plots with expected values on the x-axis are informative and widely used (e.g., Altman et al., 2009), it is not my preferred style of calibration plot for prediction tools in psychology. Its major weakness is that it is hard to connect the risk groups on the graph to specific risk scale scores. The groups on the graph are defined by the frequency distribution of the observed sample, which may change from study to study. This is not a problem when the outputs of the actuarial risk tool are probabilities (e.g., MnSOST-3, Duwe & Freske, 2012). Often, however, risk scale scores have other meanings, such that risk level placement can support inferences concerning current functioning and treatment needs (Hanson, Babchishin, et al., 2017; Hanson, Bourgon, et al., 2017). Evaluators who are interested in specific risk scale scores will benefit from calibration plots that display the risk scale scores directly on the x-axis, such as the next two examples.

Example 3: Observed and expected values plotted by risk scale scores (risk scores on the x-axis)

Example 3 uses the same data as Example 2 (Static-99R validation study in Akuarl Atoll), slightly reorganized. Instead of plotting the observed rates against the expected rates, both the observed and expected rates are plotted for each risk scale score (for another example of this type of graph, see Alba et al., 2017, Figure 2). In Example 3, there are separate points (observations) for each Static-99R score. When there are many scores with few observations (few being less than 20), it is preferable to clump the scores to increase the sample size for each observation. When scores are clumped together, the risk groups will resemble those used in Example 2 of this chapter. In Example 3, however, scores are not grouped together to demonstrate the strengths and weaknesses of this approach. The expected values in Example 3 are plotted as a solid line. Given that the expected values were based on logistic regression, the line for the expected values is a logistic curve.

Table 15.3 holds the data that are plotted in Figure 15.3. The figure includes confidence intervals calculated as plus or minus the standard error of the observed proportions (68% confidence intervals; Cumming & Finch, 2005). As before, the standard errors were calculated using the Wald method (Equation 4.3, this volume). One limitation of the Wald method is that the standard error is zero when the observed values are zero (Static-99R score of −3) or one (Static-99R score of 10). The standard errors for the other values are nevertheless helpful in presenting the variability associated with the observed values. Once the standard errors are calculated, it is relatively simple to construct this type of calibration plot using a pencil and graph paper.

As with the previous calibration plot of this data (Figure 15.2), Figure 15.3 suggests that Static-99R was reasonably well calibrated for lower and average scores but overestimated recidivism rates for the *well above average* scores. In particular, the observed rates for a score of 6 were lower than expected and below the observed rates for the previous two scores (scores of 4 and 5)—that is, the expected monotonic increase in recidivism rates was not maintained. The

TABLE 15.3. Observed and Expected Recidivism Rates for the Hypothetical Akuari Atoll Static-99R Replication Study

1	2	3	4	5
Static-99R total scores	Sample size	Observed recidivism rate	Expected recidivism rate	*SE* of observed
−3	45	0.0000	0.009	0.00000
−2	50	0.0200	0.013	0.01980
−1	97	0.0206	0.019	0.01443
0	129	0.0388	0.028	0.01699
1	169	0.0592	0.039	0.01815
2	181	0.0718	0.056	0.01919
3	138	0.0870	0.079	0.02399
4	86	0.1163	0.110	0.03457
5	77	0.1169	0.152	0.03661
6	72	0.0972	0.205	0.03491
7	36	0.1667	0.272	0.06211
8	16	0.3125	0.351	0.11588
9	3	0.3333	0.428	0.27216
10	1	1.0000	0.530	0.00000

FIGURE 15.3. Calibration Plot With Risk Scale Scores on the x-Axis for the Hypothetical Akuarl Atoll Replication Study

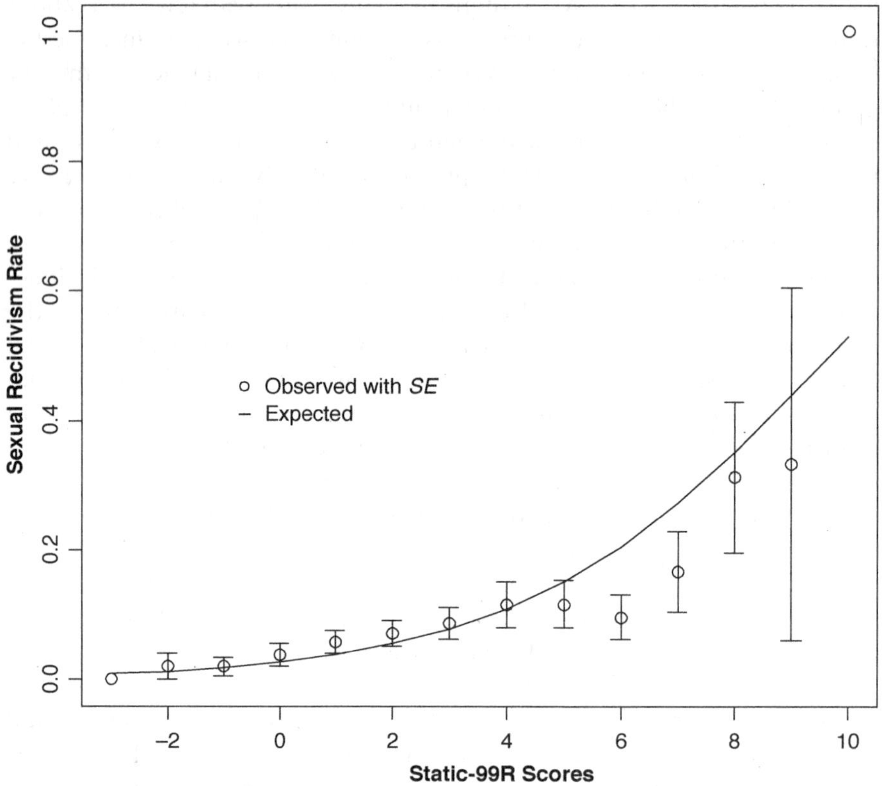

Note. The error bars indicate plus or minus one standard error for the observed proportions (68% confidence intervals). Data can be found in Table 15.3.

recidivism rate for a score of 10 was higher than expected (100%), but this was based on only one individual with this risk score.

Although Figures 15.2 and 15.3 tell essentially the same story, it is easier in Figure 15.3 to identify specific scores. The major disadvantage of plotting points for each risk scale score is that scores can be sparsely populated, hence unstable. In the current example, the overall sample size was large (1,100), which resulted in only a few scores having less than 20 cases (only the scores of 8, 9, and 10). With more typical sample sizes of 100 to 300, stable proportions can only be achieved with considerable aggregation. Even with the large sample in Example 3, it is difficult to evaluate the stability of the observed patterns. The decline for score 6 was unexpected, and could be due to chance features of this (hypothetical) data set. The logistic distribution of risk indicated by the norms may still hold true for the population (all individuals with a sexual offense conviction in Akuarl Atoll), but not for this particular sample (the 1,100 individuals in this study). Furthermore, given that the confidence interval for a score of 6 overlapped substantially with the confidence intervals for adjacent scores, it is impossible tell from this figure whether the observed values for score 6 are too low or the observed values for the adjacent, lower scores (4, 5) are too high.

Example 4: Plotting logistic regression curves for observed and expected by risk scale score (risk scores on x-axis)

This type of calibration plot is similar to Example 3 in that the observed and expected proportions are plotted against the risk scale scores on the x-axis. The distinctive feature of Example 4 is that both the observed and the expected are plotted as fitted (logistic) curves. Rather than plotting the observed proportion for each score, the proportions in the replication data are smoothed using logistic regression. Consequently, the graph has two sets of estimated values: (a) the smoothed, expected values based on the norms and (b) the smoothed distribution of proportions in the replication study. To appreciate the sample error associated with the observed proportions, there are two additional lines indicating their 95% confidence intervals (for another example, see Lee et al., 2020).

Table 15.4 presents the values that are plotted in Figure 15.4. The values in Table 15.4 were computed following the steps described in Chapter 11 ("Logistic Regression") using a data set with 1,100 cases (from Table 13.2). As a preliminary step, the Hosmer–Lemeshow test was computed as a check that the logistic distribution reasonably matched the observed data for Akuarl Atoll. It was not statistically significant ($\chi^2 = 3.21$, $df = 6$, $p = 0.782$), supporting the plausibility of the logistic model for the observed data.

The major comparison in Figure 15.4 is between the observed values indicated by the dotted line (with open circles) and the expected values indicated by the solid line. For Static-99R scores of 4 or less, these two lines are similar,

TABLE 15.4. Fitted (Smoothed) Observed and Expected Recidivism Rates for the Hypothetical Akuarl Atoll Static-99R Replication Study

1	2	3	4	5	6
Static-99R total scores	Sample size	Observed fitted recidivism rate	95% confidence intervals Lower	95% confidence intervals Upper	Expected recidivism rate
−3	45	0.01844	0.01010	0.03345	0.009
−2	50	0.02365	0.01405	0.03954	0.013
−1	97	0.03029	0.01948	0.04681	0.019
0	129	0.03871	0.02682	0.05558	0.028
1	169	0.04936	0.03655	0.06634	0.039
2	181	0.06274	0.04901	0.08000	0.056
3	138	0.07945	0.06404	0.09817	0.079
4	86	0.10013	0.08091	0.12330	0.110
5	77	0.12546	0.09897	0.15780	0.152
6	72	0.15609	0.11828	0.20320	0.205
7	36	0.19255	0.1392	0.26009	0.272
8	16	0.23516	0.16228	0.32795	0.351
9	3	0.28387	0.18764	0.40486	0.428
10	1	0.33822	0.21549	0.48741	0.530

FIGURE 15.4. Calibration Plot of Fitted Observed and Expected Recidivism Rates for the Hypothetical Akuarl Atoll Static-99R Replication Study

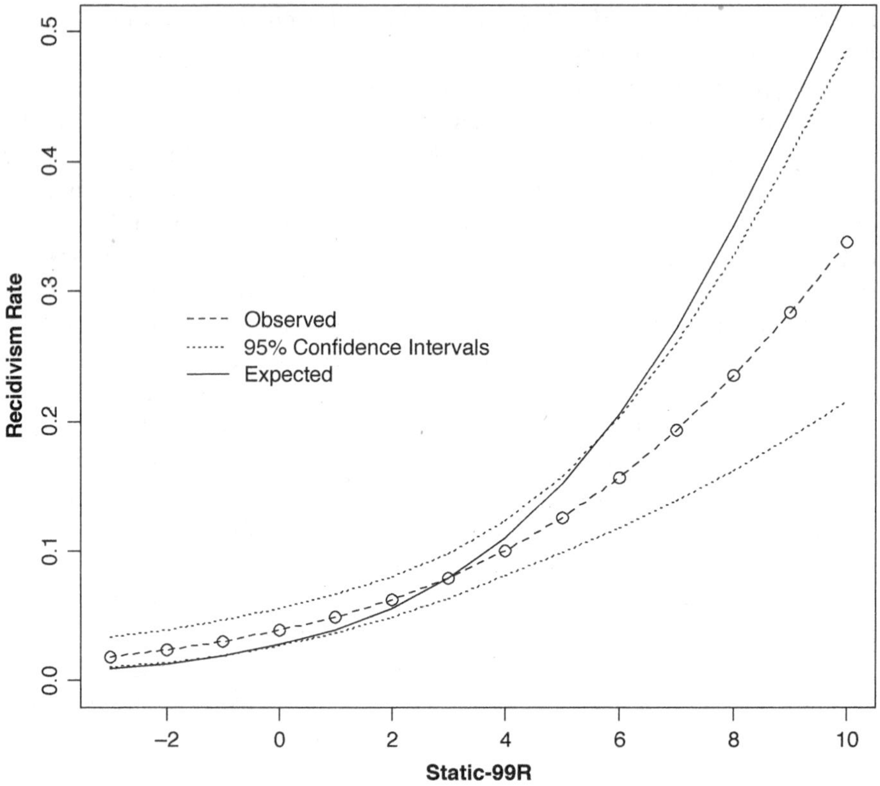

Note. Data can be found in Table 15.4.

deviating from each other by only a couple of percentage points. The lines start to diverge at a score of 5, with the fitted observed values being significantly lower than the expected values for scores of 6 or more. Statistical significance is indicated by the expected value being outside the 95% confidence interval for the fitted observed values.

Comparison of the Four Calibration Plots

This section presented four styles of calibration plots. Example 1 is most appropriate when the observations are necessarily grouped—that is, the risk prediction scheme generates discrete categories. One useful variation of Example 1 is to include confidence intervals or error bars for the observed proportions (keeners can do this on their own as an exercise). The second example is similar to the first example in that it plots observed values on the y-axis against expected values on the x-axis. In Example 2, however, the groups are constructed for the purpose of the calibration plot and do not necessarily align with the interpretive levels or categories of the risk tool. Example 2 is recommended for risk tools that have lots of different potential values, and there is little intrinsic interest in specific risk scale scores. The third example displays the observed and expected values for each value of the risk tool, with risk scale scores on the x-axis.

Example 3 is only possible when most of the risk scale scores are reasonably well populated (i.e., occupied by 20 or more cases). When the observed data are sparse, then the observed findings will need to be aggregated (as in Example 2) or smoothed (as in Example 4). Like Example 3, Example 4 also plots the risk scale scores along the x-axis against the observed and expected values on the y-axis. However, the observed values in Example 4 are smoothed, thereby minimizing opportunities to be distracted by chance features of the data.

All three calibration plots of the Akuarl Atoll replication study told the same story: the observed and expected values are similar for the low and average scores, but the Static-99R norms overestimated the observed recidivism rates for the highest risk group (*well above average*; scores of 6 or more). Of the three styles, my preference would be either Example 3 (observed for each score) or Example 4 (fitted observed values). I like being easily able to identify the specific scores, which were not displayed in Example 2. On the other hand, Example 4 is better than Example 3 at screening out noise. Viewers will make fewer inferences from Example 4 than Example 3, but the inferences they do make have a greater likelihood of being correct.

This chapter started with the premise that sometimes, for some people, graphs communicate quantitative information more effectively than tables. To check whether this is true for you, go back and take a quick look at Table 15.1, then Figure 15.1. Which one works best for you? Similarly, compare your immediate understanding of Table 15.2 with Figure 15.2, Table 15.3 with Figure 15.3, and Table 15.4 with Figure 15.4. My own experience of this exercise is that the figures are great at communicating the big picture. As I continue to ponder the graphs, however, I long for increased precision. For this, I turn to the tables. If I keep pondering the data, I soon yearn for statistical indicators of discrimination and calibration (e.g., AUC, E/O index, meta-analysis of logistic regression coefficients).

GOING FURTHER

Readers who have made it this far should be able to appreciate the information provided by various types of calibration plots. The following sections are designed to deepen this understanding through further reading, computer code, and exercises. These sections will be of interest primarily to researchers who are considering using calibration plots in their own studies.

Recommended Readings

Steyerberg, E. W. (2019). *Clinical prediction models: A practical approach to development, validation, and updating* (2nd ed.). Springer.

Both editions (Steyerberg, 2009, 2019) have great examples of calibration plots (see, in particular, Chapter 15). This is an advanced text, however, which is not easily accessible to the beginner. It is nevertheless worth serious study because Steyerberg has thought long and hard about prediction models and how to communicate their results to physicians and patients.

Altman, D. G., Vergouwe, Y., Royston, P., & Moons, K. G. M. (2009). Prognosis and prognostic research: Validating a prognostic model. *BMJ, 338,* b605. https://doi.org/10.1136/bmj.b605

This paper provides a basic introduction to calibration, accompanied by an excellent example of interpreting a calibration plot (the same type as Example 2 of this chapter).

Computer Code

Basic calibration plots do not require any specialized software. In agreement with Tufte (2001), I believe that much can be learned about data by plotting with a pencil and graph paper. There are, however, several excellent commercially available graphing programs, of which Excel deserves special mention because it is widely available and has a large set of flexible graphing algorithms. Good calibration plots can also be made with IBM/SPSS, although SPSS is more difficult to customize than Excel or R.

The following section presents the R code used to create the figures in this chapter. This section only touches on the graphic capacities of R. Readers seeking mastery of the R plotting functions should expect hours, if not days, of study and practice. R has a steep learning curve, but it can do just about anything you can think of. Fortunately, there are numerous helpful online resources.

R Code

The R code is for the four examples described earlier in the chapter. You may want to try them as an introduction to the graphic functions in R.

Example 1. The first figure does not require any special downloads. It can be run directly from the R prompt:

```
a <- c(0, 0, 1, 1)
A <- matrix (a, nrow = 2, ncol=2, byrow=TRUE)
plot (A, xlab = "Predicted Probability", ylab = "Observed
Probability", cex.lab = 1.3, xaxs = "i", yaxs = "i")
lines (A)
b <- c(0, .35, 1, .35)
B <- matrix (b, nrow = 2, ncol=2, byrow=TRUE)
lines (B, cex = 0.5, col = "gray85")
grid (10, 10)
text (.20, .14, "A")
text (.60, .414, "B")
text (.20, .30, "C")
text (.10, .122, "D")
```

The first two lines "a" and "A" create a matrix (i.e., rows and columns of numbers), which is used to set the size of the calibration plot. The **plot** function creates the actual plot. The simplest form is **plot (A)**, where A is the matrix previously defined. The rest of the syntax makes the plot prettier. For example, **cex.lab = 1.3** sets the font size of the labels, indicating that it is 30%

bigger than the default setting, **cex.lab** = **1**. The "b" and "B" syntax lines create a matrix for plotting the line indicating the decision threshold (at .35). I used the **grid** option to make this figure look more like it was plotted on graph paper. The following four lines—for example, text (.20, .14, "A")—place the risk groups "A,", "B", "C", and "D" on the graph. It is relatively easy to change the colors of the lines and text using the **col** = command, which accepts numbers and names (e.g., 1, 2, 29, "gray85", "blue") as options. For a list of color names type **colors ()**.

Example 2. The second graph was created using the **plotCI** routine from the **plotrix** package (Lemon, 2006). If this is the first time using this package, you need to download it. Use the following command in R:

```
install.packages ("plotrix")
```

It will ask you to select a CRAN site. Choose one geographically close to you. Once you have downloaded **plotrix**, tell R that you want to use it:

```
library ("plotrix")
```

For Figure 15.2, the datafile for the analysis is called Chap15_Fig2.table (available at https://www.apa.org/pubs/books/prediction-statistics-for-psychological-assessment). To load it into R, use the **read.table** command, thereby creating a working file called Fig2.data.

```
Fig2.data <- read.table (file = "c:\\run.files\\Book\\
Chap15_Fig2.table")
```

You will need to edit the preceding line to indicate where you have stored the data. In my case, it is in a subfolder called "Book" in the folder called "run. files" on my c:\ drive. To see what the data file looks like, type "Fig2.data" and hit return at the R prompt.

```
Fig2.data
   Static 99R   Observed     Expected     Group   n     SE.p         CI
1  -2.473684    0.01052632   0.01110526   1       95    0.01047077   0.02052270
2  -1.000000    0.02061856   0.01900000   2       97    0.01442843   0.02827973
3   0.000000    0.03875969   0.02800000   3       129   0.01699461   0.03330944
4   1.000000    0.05917160   0.03900000   4       169   0.01814966   0.03557333
5   2.000000    0.07182320   0.05600000   5       181   0.01919148   0.03761530
6   3.000000    0.08695652   0.07900000   6       138   0.02398597   0.04701250
7   4.472393    0.11656442   0.12984049   7       163   0.02513487   0.04926434
8   6.632812    0.15625000   0.25009375   8       128   0.03209312   0.06290251
```

The Observed values were computed from the data in Table 13.2; specifically, the values of the variable called "Observed" is the number of recidivists divided by the sample size for each risk group. For example, Group 1 included cases with scores of 1 or 2. Overall, there were 45 + 50 = 95 individuals in this risk group, only one of which was known to have reoffended during the follow-up period (see Table 13.2); consequently, the observed recidivism rate for Group 1 was 1/95 = 0.0105. The expected values were the average expected values from the Static-99R norms (5-year, routine and complete samples; Phenix et al., 2016). For example, in Group 1, there were 45 cases with an expected rate of 0.009 and 50 cases with an expected rate of 0.013, which averages to an expected rate of 0.0111; ([45 × .009] + [50 × .013])/95 = 1.055/95 = 0.0111. The standard errors of the observed values (SE.p) were calculated from the sample size and observed values, using the Wald method (see Chapter 4). The R commands for the Wald standard errors are as follows:

```
SE.p <- ((p.data$Observed * (1- p.data$Observed))/n)
**(1/2)
```

The statement "p.data$Observed" tells R to use the variable *Observed* in the data set *p.data,* which was the penultimate data set for this analysis (not shown). The standard errors were multiplied by 1.96 to create 95% confidence intervals.

The following syntax creates Figure 15.2:

```
plotCI (Fig2.data$Expected, Fig2.data$Observed,
Fig2. data$CI, xlim=c(0, .40), ylim = c(0, .40),
xlab="Expected", ylab = "Observed with 95% CI",
cex=1.8, cex.lab = 1.3)
b <- c(0, 0, .40, .40)
B <- matrix (b, nrow = 2, ncol=2, byrow=TRUE)
lines (B)
LWS <- loess (Fig2.data$Observed ~ Fig2.data$Expected)
lines (LWS, lty = 3)
```

The **plotCI** routine requires three variables: (a) the values of the x-axis (in this case, *Fig2.data$Expected*), (b) the values of the y-axis (in this case, *Fig2.data$Observed*); and (c) an indicator of the size of the confidence interval (e.g., standard errors [SE] or 1.96*[SE]), in this case, *Fig2.data$CI.* The rest of the **plotCI** syntax defines the labels and the size of the plot (i.e., making it prettier). The "b" and "B" syntax lines create a matrix for drawing the diagonal line of perfect calibration: **lines (B)**. The next two lines of syntax add a smoothed line (loess curve) connecting the observed values.

Example 3. The third figure was also plotted using the **plotCI** command in R. The data for Figure 15.3 has 14 rows, one for each populated Static-99R score. Observed values were calculated from Table 13.2 (number of recidivists divided by the sample size with each score). The Expected values were copied directly from the norms. The standard errors of the observed proportions (SE.p) were calculated using the Wald method.

The datafile for the analysis is called Chap15_Fig3.table (https://www.apa.org/pubs/books/prediction-statistics-for-psychological-assessment). To load it into R, use the **read.table** command, thereby creating a working file called Fig3.data.

```
Fig3.data <- read.table (file = "c:\\run.files\\Book\\
Chap15_Fig3.table")
```

Again, you will need to edit the above line to indicate where you stored the data.

```
Fig3.data
   Static99R   Observed   Expected   n       SE.p
1       -3    0.00000000   0.009     45 0.00000000
2       -2    0.02000000   0.013     50 0.01979899
3       -1    0.02061856   0.019     97 0.01442843
4        0    0.03875969   0.028    129 0.01699461
5        1    0.05917160   0.039    169 0.01814966
6        2    0.07182320   0.056    181 0.01919148
7        3    0.08695652   0.079    138 0.02398597
8        4    0.11627907   0.110     86 0.03456680
9        5    0.11688312   0.152     77 0.03661336
10       6    0.09722222   0.205     72 0.03491459
11       7    0.16666667   0.272     36 0.06211300
12       8    0.31250000   0.351     16 0.11587810
13       9    0.33333333   0.438      3 0.27216553
14      10    1.00000000   0.530      1 0.00000000
```

The R code for plotting Figure 15.3 is as follows:

```
library (plotrix) #telling R that you want to use this
set of programs
plotCI (Fig3.data$Static99R, Fig3.data$Observed,
Fig3. data$SE.p, ylim=(0:1), xlab="Static-99R Scores",
ylab = "Sexual Recidivism Rate", cex=1.3)
lines (Fig3.data$Static99R, Fig3.data$Expected)
label.names <- c("Observed with SE", "Expected")
label.symbols <- c(1, 95)
legend ( 1, .50, label.names, pch = label.symbols,
bty = "n")
```

As before, the **plotCI** command requires three variables: the x-axis (*Static99R*), the y-axis (*Observed*) and the size of the confidence intervals (*SE.p*). The range of observed values is restricted to between zero and one by **ylim** = **(0:1)**. The first two numbers in the **legend** command tell R where you want the legend to be placed on the graph (x and y coordinates). This is followed by syntax indicating the text (*label.names*) and the symbols (**pch** = *label.symbols*) used in the legend. The symbols are identified by numbers ("1" indicates an open circle; "95" indicates the dash from the top row of the keyboard). Codes for **pch** symbols can be found by the **help (pch)** command in R. They are also widely available on the internet (e.g., https://www.benjaminbell.co.uk/2018/02/quick-guide-to-pch-symbols-in-r.html).

Example 4. Figure 15.4 was constructed using the **plot** command in the base set of R routines. The most complicated step for this type of calibration plot is calculating the fitted values for the observed proportions. Steps for estimating fitted values (with confidence intervals) from logistic regression are provided in Chapter 11.

The datafile for the analysis is called Chap15_Fig4.table (https://www.apa.org/pubs/books/prediction-statistics-for-psychological-assessment). To load it into R, use the **read.table** command, thereby creating a working file called Fig4.data.

```
Fig4.data <- read.table (file = "c:\\run.files\\Book\\
Chap15_Fig4.table")
```

Remember that you need to specify where you stored Chap15_Fig4.table on your computer. Fig4.data have 14 rows, one for each populated Static-99R score. Instead of the raw observed proportions used in Figure 15.3, the observed proportions are smoothed using a logistic function (specifically, logit = −0.321214 + 0.25409 [Static-99R]).

```
Fig4.data
          lower      p.fitted     upper     p.norms
-3 -3 0.01009806 0.01844383 0.03345405  0.009
-2 -2 0.01405454 0.02365319 0.03954439  0.013
-1 -1 0.01947749 0.03028850 0.04681369  0.019
 0  0 0.02681833 0.03871139 0.05557743  0.028
 1  1 0.03655162 0.04935735 0.06634061  0.039
 2  2 0.04900579 0.06273997 0.07999946  0.056
 3  3 0.06403971 0.07944787 0.09817443  0.079
 4  4 0.08091227 0.10012981 0.12329941  0.110
 5  5 0.09897280 0.12546192 0.15779899  0.152
 6  6 0.11827960 0.15609118 0.20320462  0.205
 7  7 0.13925141 0.19255166 0.26008867  0.272
 8  8 0.16227930 0.23515557 0.32794716  0.351
 9  9 0.18763826 0.28387196 0.40486331  0.438
10 10 0.21549387 0.33821785 0.48741003  0.530
```

The R code for plotting Figure 15.4 is as follows:

```
ylim.values <- c(0, .50)
plot (-3:10, Fig4.data$p.fitted, xlab = "Static-99R",
ylab = "Recidivism Rate", ylim = ylim.values, cex=1.3,
cex.lab =1.2)
lines (-3:10, Fig4.data$p.fitted, lty=2)
lines (-3:10, Fig4.data$upper, lty = 3)
lines (-3:10, Fig4.data$lower, lty = 3)
lines (-3:10, Fig4.data$p.norms, lty = 1)
legend.names <- c("Observed ", "95% Confidence
Intervals ", "Expected ")
legend.lines <- c(2, 3, 1)
legend (-2, .30, legend.names, lty = legend.lines,
bty = "n")
```

The basic **plot** command is **plot (*x-axis values, y-axis values*)**. In this example, the Static-99R scores are across the x-axis, and are represented by the consecutive numbers from −3 to 10 (−3:10). The values on the y-axis are the fitted observed values (Fig4.data$p.fitted). Once the basic plot is constructed, additional lines are added that indicate the upper and lower confidence intervals, and the norms. The different line types are identified by **lty** ("1" is solid, "2" is dashed, and "3" is dotted).

EXERCISES

The exercises involve plotting calibration plots. Although it is possible to use software, they can also be done by hand with a pencil and graph paper. If you do not have graph paper, you can create it in MS Word by inserting a table with lots of columns and rows (e.g., 35 × 35).

Question 15.1

Plot a calibration graph in the style of Example 1 (observed vs. expected for discrete groups, with the expected values on the x-axis). This exercise continues the example of Dr. Ebing-Krafft's revised decision tree for sexual dangerousity from Chapter 12 (chi-square goodness-of-fit). On the basis of the results of the initial study, she revised her assessment scheme from four to five categories. The recidivism rates associated with these five categories were examined in Dr. Lee's next validation study (described in the exercises for Chapter 12; see Figure 12.2 and Table 12.5). The results of the validation study are summarized in Table 15.5.

(i) Using graph paper, construct a calibration plot for the data in Table 15.5. Follow the first example described earlier (expected along the x-axis and observed along the y-axis). Include the diagonal line for perfect calibration, and line indicating the decision threshold of 35%.

(ii) Which groups had expected rates above the decision threshold? Which groups had observed rates above the decision threshold?

(iii) For which categories did the prediction scheme overestimate the observed recidivism rates? Did the amount of overestimation look like it would have clinical significance?

TABLE 15.5. Validation Study of Dr. Ebing-Krafft's Revised Risk Scheme for Sexual Psychopathy

	Recidivism rates	
Group	Observed	Expected
A	.211	.15
B	.485	.40
C–	.120	.15
C+	.667	.40
D	.062	.10

(iv) The calibration (match between observed and expected values) was the poorest for which risk group? Did the degree of poor calibration look like it would have clinical significance?

Question 15.2

Plot a calibration graph in the style of Example 3 (risk scores on x-axis, observed and expected on y-axis). This question extends the hypothetical Bowlby's Secure Attachment Matchmaker's example introduced in Chapter 14 ("Meta-Analysis"). At issue is whether a prediction algorithm for romantic pair bonding works equally well for mixed-gender couples as for same-gender couples of women. The prediction scheme considers a large number of variables, which are combined into scores ranging from zero (unlikely to complete a coffee date) to 15 (ideal soul mate). There is one score per couple, such that 350 scores would involve 700 individuals. The company recommends matches with scores of 6 or higher. The outcome criterion in the validation study is whether the couple who were introduced by Bowlby's matchmaking service are still together at 12 months.

A female client, Annie Anxieuse, had a negative experience with the woman she met through Bowlby's service. Ms. Anxieuse is now suing the matchmaking service on the grounds that the algorithm does not work for same-gender women couples. For the purposes of this exercise, the expected values are those for mixed-gender couples, as estimated by logistic regression (Table 14.5, logit = 0.16487 + 0.21562 [Score]). The basic data to be plotted are presented in Table 15.6.

The total sample of 350 is divided into 10 equal groups of 35 each. These deciles were created from the distribution of observed scores. The expected

TABLE 15.6. Observed and Expected Success Rates for Same-Gender Women Couples by Bowlby's Scores (Deciles)

1	2	3	4	5	6
Risk group (deciles)	Group size	Average score	Expected success rate	Observed success rate	Half of 95% confidence interval *SE* * (1.96)
1	35	0.10	0.547	0.371	0.160
2	35	1.71	0.630	0.429	0.164
3	35	3.48	0.714	0.543	0.165
4	35	4.69	0.764	0.571	0.164
5	35	5.64	0.799	0.686	0.154
6	35	6.68	0.833	0.800	0.133
7	35	7.64	0.860	0.800	0.133
8	35	8.68	0.884	0.857	0.116
9	35	10.17	0.913	0.743	0.145
10	35	12.83	0.948	1.000	0.000
Total	350	6.16	0.789	0.680	

success rates are the logistic regression predictions for mixed-gender couples, which are averaged for each of the 10 risk groups. The observed success rate is the proportion of same-gender women couples that were still together at 12 months. The width of the confidence interval was calculated as 1.96 times the standard error of the observed proportions, with the standard errors estimated using the Wald method (Equation 4.3).

(i) Construct a calibration plot with risk groups along the x-axis, and the observed and expected proportions on the y-axis. Add the 95% confidence intervals to the observed success rates. Draw a line connecting the expected proportions. Hand-draw the figure on graph paper or use any programs of your choice.

(ii) Overall, does the prediction scheme overestimate or underestimate the likelihood of success of same sex women couples?

(iii) Is the calibration better for scores that are below average or that are above average (average score is 6.16)?

Question 15.3

(i) As a step toward learning to make your own graphs in R, recreate the four graphs in this chapter using the R code provided. For Examples 2, 3, and 4, you will need data sets that can be read by R. You can download them from https://www.apa.org/pubs/books/prediction-statistics-for-psychological-assessment. Alternately, you can re-create the data files from the tables. For example, the following syntax creates a vector with the observed values in Example 2 from the fourth column of Table 15.2:

```
Observed <- c(.0153, .0206, .0388, .0592, .0718,
.0870, .1166, .1562)
```

Once you have defined each of the necessary variables (e.g., Group, Observed, Expected, CI), they can be combined using the **data.frame** command.

```
Fig2.data <- data.frame (Group, Observed,
Expected, CI)
```

(ii) After you have recreated the figures in this chapter, try varying the look of the graphs using the **lty** = , **cex** = , **cex.lab** = , and **ylim** = commands. Try adding colors using **col** = "red", or **col** = 1, 2, 3, 4 . . . 657. For the names of the available colors, type **colors ()**. Have fun.

ANSWERS TO EXERCISES

Question 15.1

(i) The graph in Figure 15.5 was created using R code; however, your hand-drawn graph should be similar.

(ii) Group B and Group C+ had expected and observed values above the decision threshold of 35%. The expected value for both groups was 40%, and the observed values were higher.

(iii) Groups below the diagonal indicate overprediction—namely, Group C— and Group D. The amount of overprediction was small, however, as both groups were close to the diagonal. The same substantive conclusions would follow from the expected and observed rates.

(iv) Group C+ displayed the poorest calibration. The prediction scheme underestimated the observed rate (40% expected vs. 67% observed). The poor calibration would have little clinical significance, however, because both the expected and observed values were above the decision threshold of 35%.

FIGURE 15.5. Calibration Plot for Dr. Ebing-Krafft's Sexual Psychopathy Prediction Scheme

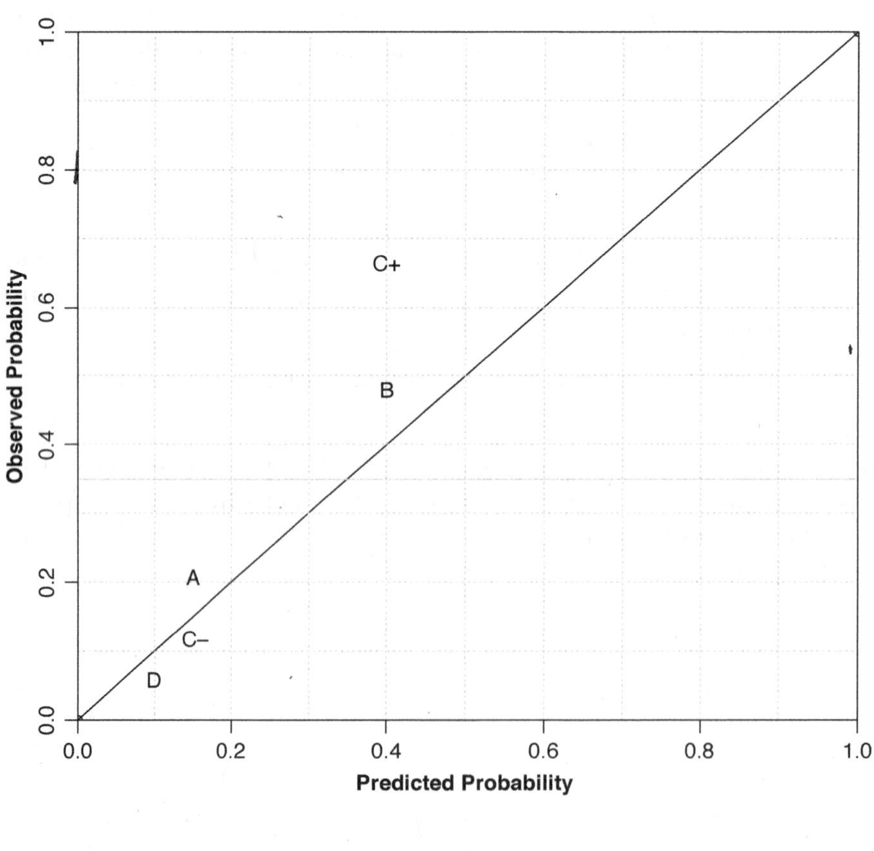

Question 15.2

(i) Your figure should resemble Figure 15.6. If you drew the figure by hand, expect some variation in the length of the confidence intervals. Notice that the line connecting the expected values is not logistic; even though the estimates were from logistic regression, after the data are grouped into deciles, the shape of the curve will no longer be logistic when there is an uneven distribution of scores.

(ii) Overall, the prediction scheme overestimated the likelihood of success of same-gender women couples. Most observed values are below the line connecting the expected values (i.e., the line of perfect calibration). For half of the risk groups, the 95% confidence intervals are below the line and do not include the expected values (Groups 1, 2, 3, 4, and 9). Group 10 is above the line, with a 100% success rate. However, it is the exception to the overall pattern.

(iii) The calibration is better for scores that are above average compared with scores that are below average. It is necessary to refer back to Table 15.6 to align the 10 risk groups to specific scores. The average score (6.16) would

FIGURE 15.6. Observed and Expected Success Rates in the Hypothetical Study of Bowlby's Prediction Algorithm for Same-Gender Women Couples

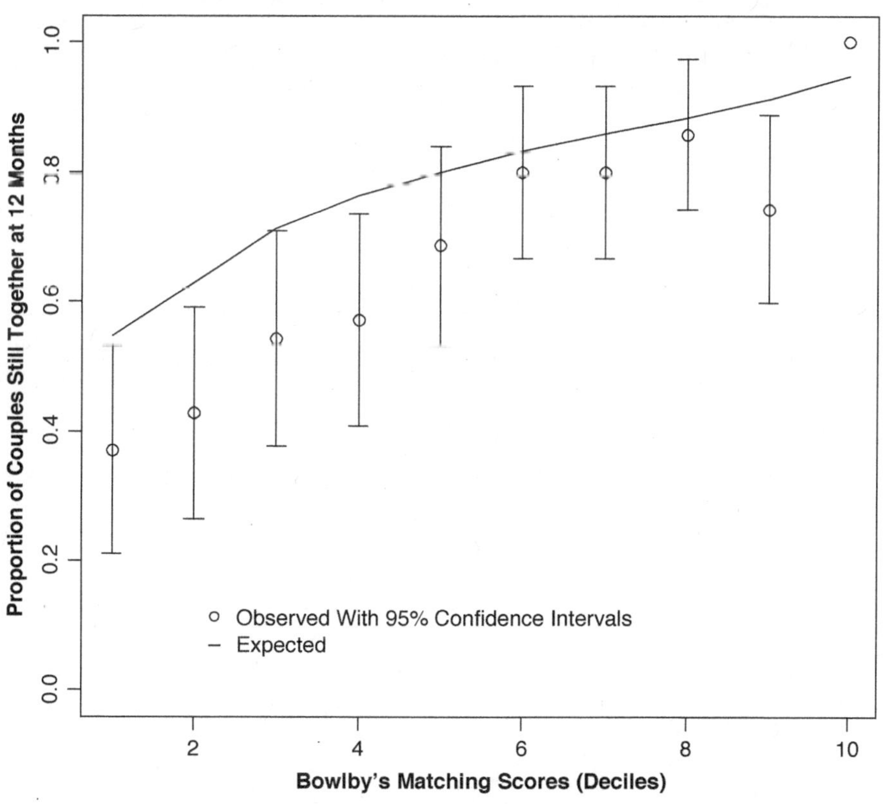

be either in Group 5 or Group 6. If Groups 6 through 10 are considered above average, then the observed values for these groups are reasonably close to expectations. In contrast, Groups 1 through 5 are consistently and substantially below the line of perfect calibration.

Question 15.3

(i) I hope you were able to recreate the graphs without too much trouble. The most common difficulty is setting up the data sets to be read by R. The only section of the syntax that you need to edit is the location of the data sets, which must match where you have stored them.

(ii) If you made your own variations, proudly show them to your colleagues, family, and classmates.

V

PERCENTILE RANKS

INTRODUCTION: PERCENTILE RANKS

Although percentile ranks are not a prediction statistic, they are included in this text because they are a useful metric for describing the results of risk assessments. For example, an evaluator could indicate that the individual's likelihood of on-the-job success was higher than 90% of applicants. As well, percentile ranks have the benefit of being easily understood and are by far the most common metric used to describe the results of psychological assessments. Although there is only one chapter in Part V, the discussion of percentile ranks is accorded its own section to clearly identify percentiles as a norm-referenced metric and distinguish them from the statistics used to describe base rates (Part II), discrimination (Part III), and calibration (Part IV) for criterion-referenced prediction tools.

16

Percentiles

Percentiles, or percentile ranks, indicate the extent to which a score is unusually high or unusually low.

In the context of risk assessment, percentile ranks indicate the proportion of cases who score the same, higher, or lower on a prediction tool. For example, percentiles may indicate that Mr. Jones is in the top 24% in terms of risk to reoffend or that Ms. Abebe's likelihood of repaying her loan is similar to that of most loan applicants (near the median). More generally, percentiles provide information concerning how common a particular pattern of results is in a reference population (Crawford & Garthwaite, 2009). Percentile ranks are ideal for describing characteristics for which there are established frequency norms and for which extreme values (high or low) are clinically significant. Percentiles are by far the most commonly used metrics for describing test results in applied psychology (e.g., T-scores, IQ, sten scores [standard ten scale], percentiles; see Ley, 1972). For risk prediction tools, they are an easily understood indicator of relative risk (is Mr. Jones riskier than Mr. Smith?) and may be sufficient for resource allocation decisions (e.g., provide treatment to the 20% most risky cases). Percentiles, however, do not indicate absolute

---

Sections of this chapter were adapted from "Developing Non-Arbitrary Metrics for Risk Communication: Percentile Ranks for the Static-99/R and Static-2002/R Sexual Offender Risk Scales," by R. K. Hanson, C. D. Lloyd, L. Helmus, and D. Thornton, 2012, *International Journal of Forensic Mental Health, 11*(1), pp. 9–23 (https://doi.org/10.1080/14999013.2012.667511). Copyright 2012 by Her Majesty the Queen in Right of Canada, as represented by the Minister of Public Safety and Emergency Preparedness. Modified with permission.

https://doi.org/10.1037/0000275-016
Prediction Statistics for Psychological Assessment, by R. K. Hanson

risk. Consequently, the use of percentile ranks in risk communication should be supported by base rate information. Percentiles also say nothing about the validity or predictive accuracy of the risk tool. Other statistics are required to know whether the risk tool is functioning as intended.

WHY USE PERCENTILE RANKS?

Percentile ranks are widely applicable and can be used with any method that ranks cases in terms of risk (e.g., unstructured professional judgment, structured professional judgment, empirical actuarial risk tools). Percentile ranks are a key metric for describing the results of norm-referenced tests. Norm-referenced tests are primarily interpreted on the basis of the unusualness of scores. For example, scores that are one standard deviation (or two standard deviations) away from the mean may be considered clinically significant.

Percentile ranks can also inform the interpretation of prediction tools. For example, percentile rank norms are provided in the Violence Risk Appraisal Guide (VRAG) and revised VRAG set of violence risk measures (Harris, Rice, et al., 2015), the Ontario Domestic Assault Risk Assessment intimate partner risk tool (Hilton, 2021), and the Static-99R, Static-2002R and STABLE-2007 sexual recidivism risk measures (Brankley et al., 2017; Hanson, Lloyd, et al., 2012; Phenix et al., 2016). All these measures are actuarial risk tools that include recidivism rate estimates. The use of percentiles, however, need not be restricted to actuarial risk tools. The 1999 version of the Spousal Assault Risk Assessment Guide (SARA; Kropp et al., 1999), a structured professional judgement (SPJ) measure, included percentile distributions for total scores and items. Users of the SARA were encouraged to consider these distributions when assigning their overall risk categorization based on professional judgment (Kropp & Gibas, 2010). Percentile ranks were not included, however, in the 2015 update of the SARA manual (Kropp & Hart, 2015). Developers of SPJ measures have rarely asserted normative data of any kind; Christopher Webster (2010), a key champion of SPJ assessment, has even actively opposed referring to normative data in risk reports. I believe that this is unfortunate. There is no inherent conflict between SPJ risk levels and the use of quantitative metrics to describe risk.

One benefit of percentile ranks is that they have a commonsense meaning that is easily understood by anybody with experience in ability and achievement rankings. At one point in my life, I regularly participated in cross-country running races. The courses would vary from relatively flat, smooth trails to steep climbs over rocky ridges. Although I noticed my times in these races, I paid more attention to my rankings, hoping to be in the top third. With large differences in the difficulty of the terrain, percentile ranks were more information than the raw times. Similarly, percentile ranks are the primary metric used for job, school, and grant applications. Many of us are all too familiar with being told that our submissions were great but was ranked below the applications that actually got the goods. The Olympic sprinter who finishes fourth gets no medal.

Percentiles are easily calculated with commonly available data. Consequently, they can be produced and updated without major investments of research resources. Unlike the prediction statistics described in this book, percentiles do not require a follow-up time. All that is required is a distribution of scores (i.e., how many cases were placed in each risk level). With little cost, researchers can quickly generate percentiles for unique settings and estimate the extent to which percentiles generalize across samples and settings.

For example, consider the True Test neuropsychological evaluation clinic, which specializes in return-to-work decisions. True Test has been using the ABC measure assessment developed in another state. The authors of the ABC measure have provided both percentile norms (for their setting) as well as absolute risk estimates linking ABC scores to the likelihood of returning to work within a year (in their state). True Test decides to collate their assessment data to compare the frequency distribution of their cases to those of the ABC normative sample. These percentile statistics can be calculated almost immediately after each new assessment. In contrast, evaluating the calibration of the ABC's estimated rates of returning to work in True Test's setting would require many years of prospective follow-up. Whereas the calculation of percentiles could be slipped into routine duties, the demands of the follow-up study are sufficient enough that it is unlikely to be done without dedicated resources.

Percentile ranks provide sufficient information for many applied decisions, particularly decisions concerning resource allocation. In the criminal justice system, for example, police can consider percentiles on risk tools to decide which individuals on large registries should be prioritized for follow-up and surveillance. Within the risk–need–responsivity model of offender rehabilitation (Andrews et al., 1990), percentile ranks can identify the higher risk cases who require more intervention than the lower risk cases. Similarly, child protection workers can consider percentile ranks when deciding which cases could most benefit from extra support and monitoring. None of the foregoing decisions require accurate estimates of absolute rates; instead, they can be based on relative riskiness of the cases, as indicated by percentile ranks.

A particularly important percentile is the *median*, defined as the value in the middle of the risk distribution (i.e., half the cases have lower scores and half the cases have higher scores). When considering the characteristics of groups, the median is a very informative measure of central tendency. When risk distributions are exponential or logistic (as they often are, see the Appendix: Useful Algebra and Notation), the median will not be the same as the mean, or average value.

LIMITATIONS

Although percentile ranks provide useful information for risk communication, they have limitations as a metric for quantifying risk. Percentile ranks are primarily an indicator for norm-referenced measures, that is, measures that compare individual scores to a reference group. Risk tools, in contrast, are prognostic tools that estimate the likelihood of future outcomes, not the unusualness of the score. Consequently, the basic information communicated by percentile ranks (i.e., relative risk placement) may be poorly linked to certain applied decisions (e.g., is Mr. Rogers too risky to release? Mr. Bean is the top-rated candidate, but is he good enough to do the job?). As well, it is easy for the casual reader to incorrectly infer that a high percentile rank (e.g., 95th percentile) indicates a high likelihood of the outcome. Likelihoods are determined by base rates and relative risk, not by percentile ranks. Similarly, the correspondence between percentile ranks and the underlying dimension measured by a risk tool is unlikely to be linear. Given a large number of cases with the same score, a one-unit change to an adjacent category could result in a substantial change in percentile rank, with only a minimal change in absolute or relative risk. Percentile ranks may or may not align with other indicators of relative or absolute risk. Decision-makers cannot tell.

A related limitation is that percentile ranks provide no information about the validity or predictive accuracy of the risk tool. Imagine a risk tool that ranked students' likelihood of completing college based on their height. The risk rankings would have high reliability, but a student in the 70th percentile would have essentially the same likelihood of completing college as a student ranked in the 10th percentile. The percentile ranks for this bogus risk tool may look informative, but they are not. In contrast, other metrics can provide information concerning relative risk along with information concerning the predictive accuracy of the risk tool. For example, if relative risk was reported as rate ratios or odds ratios (risk for each case compared with the base rate), then it would be immediately obvious that the height/education risk tool was uninformative (odds ratios for all cases would be close to 1.0).

THE NUTS AND BOLTS

Data Requirements

The data needed to calculate percentile ranks are the following:

1. a frequency distribution of scores or ordered risk levels, that is
2. based on a representative sample;
3. an outcome measure is *not* needed.

For risk scale scores that are ordered groups, or risk levels, the frequency distribution would indicate the proportion of the sample at each level. For continuous risk measures (i.e., those with many different values) the distribution is the list of cases ranked in order from least risky to most risky.

Because percentiles are interpreted as relative placement in a reference group, it is important to consider the reference group. These reference groups, or sampling frames, could be very broad (all women) or very narrow (first time applicants to Faint Hope University). Given that percentiles are commonly used in psychological assessment, there has been considerable discussion concerning the construction of samples for percentile norms (Joint Committee, 2014). Fundamentally, the reference groups should represent the class or category to which individual scores will be compared. For certain measures, the preferred samples would closely resemble the cases for which the risk tool will be used (a risk tool for probationers normed on probationers). For other measures, the normative sample is intended to represent the full range of population values, whereas the measure is primarily used for individuals suspected of deviating from the norm. An example of the latter sampling approach is intelligence testing. The normative samples of intelligence tests aspire to replicate the distribution of scores in the population (stratified by age), whereas these tests are disproportionately used with individuals suspected of cognitive or learning difficulties.

Calculating Percentile Ranks

The basic idea of percentile ranks is simple; however, their calculation is complicated by ties (i.e., more than one case with the same score). Given ties, several definitions of percentile ranks are plausible (Crawford et al., 2009; Joint Committee, 1999, p. 179). These definitions include the percentage with (a) lower scores, (b) higher scores, (c) equal or lower scores, and (d) equal or higher scores. It is also possible to calculate percentiles based on a midpoint average across the range defined by tied scores. For example, consider 100 scores distributed as follows: 30 cases were rated *low,* 50 were rated *moderate,* and 20 were rated *high.* Individuals with a moderate score could be described with the percentile rank of 30 (percentage with a lower score), 80 (percentage with the same or lower score), or 55 (midpoint average = 30 + 50/2). Similarly, it would be possible to describe the percentile rank of the moderate group as a range below (30–80) or as a range above (20–70).

Each of these definitions can be useful for specific decisions. If, for example, the decision requires selecting the 20% highest risk cases, then a definition based on "the same or riskier" would be closely aligned with the task at hand. If the decision is not specified and evaluators want to report a single value, some authorities have expressed a strong preference for reporting the midpoint average (Crawford et al., 2009; Ley, 1972). The 1999 Standards did not take a position concerning the preferred form of percentile ranks (Joint Committee, 1999, p. 179); however, the 2014 Standards, without elaboration, defined percentile ranks as the proportion below the score being ranked (Joint Committee, 2014, p. 221). Everyone agrees that the version of percentiles used should be described in enough depth that readers understand what they represent.

When percentiles are defined as the proportion below the score of interest, then

$$\text{Percentile}_{\text{below}} = \left(\frac{m}{N}\right)100 \tag{16.1}$$

where m is the number of members of the normative sample scoring below a given score and N is the overall size of the normative sample. When percentiles are defined as the proportion equal or below, then

$$\text{Percentile}_{\text{same+below}} = \left(\frac{m+k}{N}\right)100 \quad (16.2)$$

where k is the number of cases with the score of interest. When percentiles are defined as the midpoint average, then

$$\text{Percentile}_{\text{midpoint}} = \left(\frac{m+.5k}{N}\right)100 \quad (16.3)$$

Continuing our example of 100 cases scored on three-level risk tool (30% are *low*, 50% are *moderate*, and 20% are *high*), for the high-risk group, $m = 80$, $k = 20$, and $N = 100$. Consequently, the high-risk group could be described as the 80th percentile (80% of cases had lower scores, [80/100]100 = 80; Equation 16.1), the 100th percentile (nobody had a higher score; [(80 + 20)/100]100 = 100; Equation 16.2), or the 90th percentile (midpoint average, [(80 + .5[20])/100]100 = 90, Equation 16.3).

Calculating the Median

The median is the score that divides the population into two equal parts. If each case has a different value, the median is found by sorting the cases from lowest to highest, and then selecting the middle value. If there are an odd number of cases (each with a different score), there will be only one choice of the median. For example, in the set of nine numbers (1, 3, 4, 5, 6, 8, 10, 11, 12), the median is 6 (i.e., four values are lower and four values are higher). If there is an even number of cases, researchers must choose which of three values represents the median. With an even number of observations, there will be an observation just below the 50th percentile and another value just above the 50th percentile. The most common practice is to take the average of these two values. For example, if there are eight scores (1, 3, 4, 5, 6, 8, 10, 11), the median could be (5 + 6)/2 = 5.5. In some contexts, however, it is preferable to report the median as an observed (possible) value. Using this approach, the median could be either 5 or 6 (if the measure is reported in integers), provided that the choice was explained. If the working definition of percentile ranks was the proportion with lower scores, the median would be 6 (50% of cases are lower); if the working definition was the proportion with equal or lower scores, then the median would be 5 (50% of cases have the same score or lower).

With grouped frequency data (i.e., "ties"), there are two procedures commonly used to calculate the median value. The simplest approach is to identify the observed value capturing the range within which the median can be found (Anderson & Sclove, 1978; Grissom & Kim, 2005). For example, if 34% of the sample of 100 cases had a score of 3 or less and 56% of the sample had a score of 4 or less, the median value would be "4."

The second approach estimates an exact median by assuming that the observed, discrete values are markers for a latent continuous distribution. Specifically, a fraction of the interval containing the median value is added to the lower limit of that interval to bring the cumulative total to 50% (Ferguson, 1976, Equation 3.8; Hayes, 1981):

$$\text{median} = L + \frac{N/2 - m}{k} S \tag{16.4}$$

In this equation, L is the lower limit (on a continuous scale) of the interval containing the 50th percentile, and S is the size of that interval. As before, k is the number in the interval that contains the 50th percentile, m is the number with a lower score, and N is the total sample. Assuming that the scores are in increments of $S = 1$, the lower limit (L) of the interval for a score of 4 would be $L = 3.5$ (which is the upper limit for a score of 3). In the preceding example, $L = 3.5$, $N = 100$, $m = 34$, $k = 16$, and $S = 1$. Consequently, the exact median would be 4.23 (3.5 + [(100/2) − 34]/[16] × [1]). Readers will note that the median value estimated by the exact approach will rarely correspond to any observable value.

Worked Example

The worked example continues the fictional Akuarl Atoll Static-99R validation study introduced in Chapter 13 ("The E/O Index") and 15 ("Calibration Plots"). This example is a replication study of the Static-99R sexual recidivism risk tool involving 1,100 cases. Static-99R scores are integers (whole numbers) that can potentially range from −3 to 12. Consequently, the frequency distribution contains many ties, that is, cases with the same score. The distribution of Static-99R scores in the Akuarl Atoll study is provided in Table 13.1, and reproduced here in Table 16.1. The percentile information for each score is presented in four columns: the percentage below, the percentage with the same score, the percentage higher, and the midpoint average. This format contains a certain amount of repetition; however, it allows evaluators to easily select the form of percentage rank that most closely corresponds to the referral question.

To demonstrate the use of this table, consider the 77 cases with a Static-99R score of 5. Of the total 1,100 cases, 81.4% had lower scores, 7.0% had the same score, and 11.6% had higher scores. The percentile for a score of 5 expressed as a midpoint average would be 84.9%. If the top 20% riskiest cases were offered intensive treatment, it would be offered to individuals with a score of 5 and higher. If intensive treatment was offered to the top 10%, individuals with a score of 5 would not be included because 11.6% of cases had higher scores.

The only information required to calculate percentiles is the sample size per score (Column 2), which is divided by the total sample size ($N = 1,100$) to obtain the *same* percentages (Column 4). The percentages *below* are calculated

TABLE 16.1. Frequencies and Percentiles for Static-99R Scores in the Akuarl Atoll Example

Static-99R score	Sample size	Percentages Below	Same	Higher	Midpoint average
−3	45	0.0	4.1	95.9	2.0
−2	50	4.1	4.5	91.4	6.4
−1	97	8.6	8.8	82.5	13.0
0	129	17.5	11.7	70.8	23.3
1	169	29.2	15.4	55.5	36.9
2	181	44.5	16.5	39.0	52.8
3	138	61.0	12.5	26.5	67.3
4	86	73.5	7.8	18.6	77.5
5	77	81.4	7.0	11.6	84.9
6	72	88.4	6.5	5.1	91.6
7	36	94.9	3.3	1.8	96.5
8	16	98.2	1.5	0.4	98.9
9	3	99.6	0.3	0.1	99.8
10	1	99.9	0.1	0.0	100.0
11	0	100.0	0.0		
Total	1,100				

using the cumulative sum of the frequency distribution starting with the lowest score. The percentages *above* are calculated using the cumulative sum starting with the highest score. The midpoint average for a score is the percentage below the score of interest plus half of the cases with the score of interest (the *below* column plus half of the *same* column). For example, the midpoint average for a score of 5 is 84.9% because 81.4% had lower scores and 7.0% had the same score: 81.4 + (7.0/2) = 84.9.

When the predictor variable has lots of different values (e.g., 3.456, 4.478, 7.499, . . . 124.987), the frequency distribution may contain few, if any, ties. Without ties, a frequency distribution of 1,100 raw scores would be 1,100 rows long, making it impractical to calculate the percentile associated with each observed score. Instead, researchers find the scores associated with percentiles of interest. For example, scores can be grouped into 10 equal-sized groups (deciles), and risk communication would indicate to which group the case belongs. An example of this use of percentiles to collapse scores into ordered categories are the bins for the VRAG-R (Harris, Rice, et al., 2015, Tables C.1 and C.2). Similarly, if the top 20% of cases are offered intensive treatment, then the score associated with the 80th percentile rank would be identified as the decision threshold.

To identify the observed median in grouped data, find the observed value that includes the 50th percentile. In the Akuarl Atoll example, 44.5% of cases are below the score of 2, and 61.0% are below the score of 3; consequently, the middle case has a score of 2. Another way of finding the observed median is to identify the risk group that has a midpoint average percentile closest to 50%. Again, it is the score of 2 (midpoint average percentile of 52.8%).

The exact median is calculated using Equation 16.4 above (median = $L + ((N/2 - m)/k)S$). Calculating the exact median requires first identifying the observed median. The lower limit (L) is an (unobserved) value halfway between the observed median and the next lowest score. In this example the observed median is 2, and the next lowest score is (1); consequently, the lower limit (L) is 1.5, and $S = 1$ (the groups are one unit apart). The overall samples size is 1,100, so $N/2 = 550$. The number of cases with scores lower than 2 is 490 (45 + 50 + 97 +129 + 169 = 490, from Table 16.1), and $k = 181$ (the number of cases with a score of 2). From these numbers, the exact median is calculated as follows: $1.5 + ((550 - 490)/181) * 1 = 1.5 + 0.331 = 1.83$.

Standard Errors and Confidence Intervals

There has been relatively little interest in the standard errors of percentile ranks. Group comparisons and meta-analyses rarely use percentiles as the effect size indicator. Questions about the generalizability of frequency distributions are usually addressed using means, standard deviations, or the chi-square goodness-of-fit test (Chapter 12).

There are, however, a number of ways of estimating confidence intervals for percentiles, mostly of interest in neuropsychological assessment where small normative samples (less than 100) are common (Crawford & Garthwaite, 2009; Crawford et al., 2009). The basic approach to estimating confidence intervals for percentiles ranks is to treat them as binomial proportions, with variability influenced by the value of the proportion (largest variability near the median) and the sample size (larger samples result in smaller confidence intervals). Crawford et al. (2009) developed an approach to calculating 95% confidence intervals using a search procedure that finds the tails of the distribution of the binomial distribution that correspond to a probability of .025 (implemented in the *percentile_norms_int_est.exe* software). Unlike true binominal distributions (discussed in Chapter 4, "Proportions"), the precision of percentile ranks is reduced when multiple individuals share the same score. To account for ties, Crawford et al.'s method calculates the probability (.025) based on an average of all possible ranks within the tied category.

With grouped data and reasonably large samples (several hundred), there is relatively little difference between the confidence intervals calculated by Crawford et al.'s (2009) procedure and the lower and upper bounds of the proportions created by ties. The inherent imprecision created by many cases having the same score does not go away no matter how large the normative sample.

GOING FURTHER

Readers who have made it this far should have a sufficient understanding of percentiles to appreciate how they are calculated and used in risk communication. The following sections are designed to deepen this understanding through further reading and exercises. These sections can be worked with in any order, and it is not necessary to do all (or any) of them.

Recommended Readings

Crawford, J. R., Garthwaite, P. H., & Slick, D. J. (2009). On percentile norms in neuropsychology: Proposed reporting standards and methods for quantifying the uncertainty over the percentile ranks of test scores. *The Clinical Neuropsychologist, 23*(7), 1173–1195. https://doi.org/10.1080/13854040902795018

A useful discussion of the options for reporting percentiles. Moderately advanced. Although the paper focuses on norm-referenced test, the same concerns apply when percentiles are used to describe the results of prediction tools.

Hanson, R. K., Lloyd, C. D., Helmus, L., & Thornton, D. (2012). Developing non-arbitrary metrics for risk communication: Percentile ranks for the Static-99/R and Static-2002/R sexual offender risk scales. *International Journal of Forensic Mental Health, 11*(1), 9–23. https://doi.org/10.1080/14999013.2012.667511

An argument for the use of percentiles in risk communication in corrections and forensic mental health. There is some overlap with the current chapter.

Computer Code

Neither R (R Core Team, 2020) nor IBM/SPSS (IBM Corp., 2020) has dedicated programs for computing the different types of percentiles discussed in this chapter. Given a frequency table, it is often easiest to calculate the various percentiles using generic spreadsheets (e.g., Excel). A hybrid approach may also be convenient: use statistical software to reduce the full data set to a frequency table, and then calculate the desired percentiles either by hand calculator or by secondary syntax.

R Code

The R code that follows computes the four percentile columns of Table 16.1 (below, same, above, midpoint average) from the observed number with each risk score. Note that I have added a zero to either the bottom or to the top of the frequency distribution in certain calculations in order to align the output with the structure of Table 16.1. R commands are in Courier New 10 font, and output are the lines starting with [1].

```
n <- c(45, 50, 97, 129, 169, 181, 138, 86, 77, 72, 36,
16, 3, 1) #the data
N <- sum(n)
same <- (n/N)*100
same.pct <- round(same, 1) #rounding to one decimal
point
same.pct
```

```
[1] 4.1 4.5 8.8 11.7 15.4 16.5 12.5 7.8 7.0 6.5 3.3
1.5 0.3 0.1
n.1 <-c(0,45,50,97,129,169,181, 138, 86, 77, 72, 36,
16, 3, 1)#zero added
n.below <- cumsum (n.1) #cumulative sum of n.1
p.below <- round(((n.below/N)*100), 1) #calculating
and rounding in one step
p.below
[1] 0.0 4.1 8.6 17.5 29.2 44.5 61.0 73.5 81.4 88.4
94.9 98.2 99.6 99.9 100.0
n.below2 <- cumsum (n)
n.above <- (N - n.below2)
p.above <- round (((n.above/N)*100), 1)
p.above
[1] 95.9 91.4 82.5 70.8 55.5 39.0 26.5 18.6 11.6 5.1
1.8 0.4 0.1 0.0
n.2 <-c(45,50,97, 129, 169, 181, 138, 86, 77,72,36,
16, 3, 1, 0)#zero added
p.midpoint1 <- ((n.below + .5*n.2)/N)*100
p.midpoint <- round (p.midpoint1, 1)
p.midpoint
[1] 2.0 6.4 13.0 23.3 36.9 52.8 67.3 77.5 84.9 91.6
96.5 98.9 99.8 100.0 100.0
```

IBM/SPSS Code

The **Frequencies** command provides the proportion with each score, as well as cumulative proportions. These values can be used to calculate the *below, above,* and *midpoint average* columns in Table 16.1. The IBM/SPSS commands are based on a data set with one row per case (1,100 rows for Table 16.1; Chap13_Table2.sav, available at https://www.apa.org/pubs/books/prediction-statistics-for-psychological-assessment). The IBM/SPSS data set contains four variables: *case, Static99R, Observed,* and *Expected.* For this exercise, only one variable (the Static-99R scores) is required. In the menu click on **Analyze**, then **Descriptive Statistics**, then **Frequencies**. At the **Frequencies** screen, click and drag the variable of interest from the list on the left to the **Variable(s)** box (in our example, the variable of interest is *Static99R*). You will want the *frequency table,* which is checked as the default option. To obtain the median, click on **Statistics**, then **median**. The default median is the observed median. If you want the exact median, check the box labeled "Values are group midpoints." The SPSS syntax is as follows:

```
FREQUENCIES VARIABLES=Static99R
/STATISTICS=MEDIAN
/GROUPED=Static99R
/ORDER=ANALYSIS.
```

This produces the following output:

Statistics

	Static99R	
N	Valid	1100
	Missing	0
Median		1.83[a]

[a]Calculated from grouped data.

Static-99R

	Frequency	Percent	Valid percent	Cumulative percent
Valid −3	45	4.1	4.1	4.1
−2	50	4.5	4.5	8.6
−1	97	8.8	8.8	17.5
0	129	11.7	11.7	29.2
1	169	15.4	15.4	44.5
2	181	16.5	16.5	61.0
3	138	12.5	12.5	73.5
4	86	7.8	7.8	81.4
5	77	7.0	7.0	88.4
6	72	6.5	6.5	94.9
7	36	3.3	3.3	98.2
8	16	1.5	1.5	99.6
9	3	.3	.3	99.9
10	1	.1	.1	100.0
Total	1100	100.0	100.0	

To create Table 16.1 from the SPSS output, additional calculations are required. The sample size per score does not need to be calculated (it is labeled *Frequency*) nor do you need to calculate the percentage with the same score (it is labeled *Percent* or *Valid Percent,* given that there are no missing values in this data set). The percentage below is the same as the *cumulative percent,* except that a zero needs to be added for the score of −3 (there are no scores lower than −3), and all the remaining values shifted up one score. To obtain the percentage *higher,* subtract the *cumulative percent* from 100. For example, the percentage higher than a score of 4 is 100 − 81.4 = 18.6%. To obtain the midpoint averages, subtract half of the valid percent from the cumulative percent. For example, for the score of −1, the cumulative percent is 17.5, the valid percent is 8.8, so the midpoint average is 17.5 − (8.8/2) = 13.1%. Note that this value is slightly different from the value in Table 16.1 due to rounding. If greater precision is required, then use the raw numbers in Equation 16.3: $((m + .5k)/N) * 100 = (((45 + 50) + 97/2)/1100) * 100 = (143.5/1100) * 100 = 13.045$.

EXERCISES

The intake unit of a regional psychiatric facility has a five-level system for triaging admissions. The facility serves a large, mostly rural district with outpatient and inpatient services. Their five-level system is a brief, structured professional judgment measure intended to guide recommendations for the intensity of treatment services. It is also used by the hospital administration for the purposes of budgeting and performance measurement. Research has found that these ratings predict the length of time that individuals will be receiving services (discharge date), as well as whether they will return to the hospital within 12 months. The five levels are as follows: *Level 1*—the individual has a limited, acute crisis or concern that can be resolved at intake, no hospital follow-up needed (e.g., adverse drug reaction); *Level 2*—some ongoing concerns, would likely benefit from follow-up and outpatient treatment; *Level 3*—concerns that are sufficiently serious to justify inpatient admission, with the expectation of being discharged to outpatient services within one week; *Level 4*—concerns that are sufficiently serious or chronic to justify extended inpatient treatment; and *Level 5*—very serious concerns with behavioral problems that justify hospitalization and involuntary confinement, with the expectation that the individual will move to a higher security hospital when feasible.

As part of an accreditation cycle, the administration collates the admissions ratings for the past 12 months. Given that you are the only staff member who has a copy of *Prediction Statistics for Psychological Assessment*, your boss asks you to analyze the data. The frequency distribution is presented in Table 16.2. Your first step is to calculate percentiles.

Question 16.1

Complete the percentile columns in Table 16.2 (below, same, above, midpoint average).

Question 16.2

(i) What is the observed median?
(ii) What is the exact median?

Question 16.3

(i) In your completed Table 16.2, circle the number indicating the proportion of intake cases that should receive some inpatient treatment (i.e., Levels 3, 4, and 5).

(ii) Circle in two places the proportion of intake cases that were identified as needing no further service (i.e., Level 1).

TABLE 16.2. Frequency Distribution of Treatment Needs Ratings at a Hypothetical Psychiatric Hospital

Treatment need level	Sample size	Percentages			
		Below	Same	Higher	Midpoint average
1	284	?	?	?	?
2	189	?	?	?	?
3	169	?	?	?	?
4	80	?	?	?	?
5	18	?	?	?	?
Total	740				

ANSWERS TO EXERCISES

Question 16.1

See Table 16.3. To illustrate the calculations, consider the row for Treatment Need Level 2. The percentage below would be the number below (284 in Level 1) divided by the total sample size (284/740 = .38378, or 38.4%). The percentage with the same score would be 189/740 = .2554 or 25.5%. The percentage higher would be (169 + 80 + 18)/740 = .3608 or 36.1%. The midpoint average (calculated using Equation 16.3) would be (284 + [.5 * 189])/740 = .51149 or 51.1%.

Question 16.2

(i) The observed median is the value in the middle of the distribution. With 38.4% below Level 2, and 63.9% below Level 3, the 50th percentile is in Level 2. Note that the midpoint average percentile for Level 2 is 51.1%, which is the midpoint average percentile closest to 50%.

(ii) The exact median is calculated using Equation 16.4.

$$\text{median} = L + \frac{N/2 - m}{k} S$$

In this example, the boundary between the observed median and the next lowest level (L) is 1.5; $N/2$ = 740/2 = 370; the sum below (m) is 284; the sample size of the observed median (k) is 189, and the interval size (S) is 1. Consequently, the exact median is 1.5 + (370 − 284)/189 = 1.96.

Question 16.3

(i) Collectively, Levels 3, 4, and 5 account for 36.1% of intake cases (from Table 16.3, the percentage higher than 2). Alternately, it can be calculated as (169 + 80 + 18)/740 = .361 or 36.1%.

(ii) The proportion of Level 1 cases is 38.4%, which is the proportion who have the same score as Level 1 (38.4), and the proportion of cases who have scores below Level 2 (38.4).

TABLE 16.3. Frequency Distribution of Treatment Needs Ratings at a Hypothetical Psychiatric Hospital

Treatment need level	Sample size	Percentages			
		Below	Same	Higher	Midpoint average
1	284	0.0	38.4	61.6	19.2
2	189	38.4	25.5	36.1	51.1
3	169	63.9	22.8	13.2	75.3
4	80	86.8	10.8	2.4	92.2
5	18	97.6	2.4	0.0	98.8
Total	740				

VI

PRACTICE CONSIDERATIONS

INTRODUCTION: PRACTICE CONSIDERATIONS

Prediction tools are intended to improve decision making. By increasing the precision of our estimates, our decisions are less influenced by irrelevant factors, less biased, and more just. But the mere existence of a risk tool does not automatically improve decision making, any more than three eggs automatically make an omelette. Skill and judgment are required to select, administer, and draw inferences from prediction tools. Chapter 17 is intended to help evaluators weight the scientific credentials of prediction tools and decide whether the inferences implied by the risk tool are appropriately aligned with the referral question. As well, evaluators want prediction tools that are easy to understand, efficient, and do not exacerbate negative outcomes for already disadvantaged groups.

Chapter 18 discusses risk communication. Although evaluators and decision makers like natural language labels, such as *low, moderate,* and *high,* these labels lack common meanings. Careful consideration of the terms used to communicate the results of risk assessments would reduce misunderstandings. Although different terms will work best in different areas of practice, there are some common principles that could apply to many risk tools. Increased standardization is both possible and desirable.

The final chapter (Chapter 19) invites readers to consider an inherent limitation for any prediction task: People change, as do their circumstances. Although there is a certain stability to personality and behavior, many valued outcomes (e.g., falling in love, infectious disease) cannot be fully anticipated by any analysis of initial conditions. Consequently, evaluators are encouraged to regularly update their assessments and to be humble concerning their ability to predict the future.

17

Estimating the Quality of Prediction Tools

Previous chapters in this book considered the quality of prediction tools in terms of numeric indicators of predictive accuracy. Relative comparison of numbers is straightforward. A risk tool with an area under the curve (AUC) value of .73, for example, is slightly better than a risk tool with an AUC value of .72. Predictive accuracy, however, should not be the only criteria used to evaluate risk tools. Evaluators must consider other features when deciding which, if any, risk tool to use. Some of these features concern the types of inferences implied by risk scores. Other features consider the strength of the research supporting these inferences.

Risk tools serve many functions, perhaps the most important of which is promoting effective risk management. The use of a risk tool should result in better case-management decisions and support interventions that are both effective and efficient. Practitioners who use the tools should have fewer negative and more positive outcomes. Although there is value in risk tools that only estimate likelihoods, prediction tools are more valuable when they explain the nature, origins, and effects of the risk and protective factors. In other words, the most useful risk tools are supported by a theoretical model. Ideally, this model would inform etiology, intervention, and prognosis. Prediction tools supported by validated causal theories is a lofty goal, well beyond the minimum requirement for utility. A risk tool that provides reliable and valid estimates of the likelihood of the outcome is sufficient for many decisions. Nevertheless, appreciating what risk tools are measuring helps to protect against misinterpretation and misuse.

https://doi.org/10.1037/0000275-017
Prediction Statistics for Psychological Assessment, by R. K. Hanson

Consider the risk factor "diagnosis of schizophrenia," which appears in at least two violence risk assessment tools, the Violence Risk Appraisal Guide (VRAG; Harris et al., 1993) and the Classification of Violence Risk (COVR; Monahan, 2021). In both these measures, a diagnosis of schizophrenia is a protective factor, associated with a decreased likelihood of violence. This is not easily explained. In the general population, a schizophrenia diagnosis is positively associated with the risk of violence (Fazel et al., 2009). In contrast, the VRAG and COVR were developed to predict future violence in mental health samples. Although schizophrenia may be undesirable, the other individuals in the VRAG and COVR samples were worse (at least in terms of risk for violence). Although the direction of the schizophrenia item can be explained in terms of sample composition, this does not address practitioners' concerns about what can be done to manage the risk.

I do not doubt that individuals diagnosed with schizophrenia are lower risk than other individuals in certain data sets; however, I question the wisdom of including this item in a violence prediction tool. The concepts of risk and protective factors include empirical relationships to the outcome of interest, but these concepts also include judgments concerning the desired direction for change (i.e., fewer risk factors; more protective factors). Even when the developers of risk tools distance themselves from evaluative statements, the mere presence of an item in violence risk tool implicitly communicates values.

Risk factors that are comprehensible protect against irrelevant content. Risk tools should not be measuring the wrong things. In particular, evaluators want some assurance that the risk tools they use are not contaminated by cultural or racial biases against historically disadvantaged groups. Psychological and educational testing has long been concerned with fairness (Joint Committee, 2014, Chapter 3). Even though fairness has been an elusive goal, with multiple, incompatible definitions, it remains a core value of those conducting psychological assessments.

If used as part of treatment, risk tools should also make sense to the individuals being assessed. Risk tools can facilitate engagement in intervention by demonstrating the need for treatment (e.g., status quo = high likelihood of negative outcomes) and what needs to change. In the context of crime and violence, the targets for intervention have been referred to as *criminogenic needs* (Andrews et al., 1990), *dynamic risk factors* (Douglas & Skeem, 2005), and *psychologically meaningful risk factors* (Mann et al., 2010). Certain criminal recidivism risk tools have been explicitly designed to be completed as a collaboration between the person being assessed and person conducting the evaluation (e.g., Lasher et al., 2015). When used in this way, risk tools provide a common language for problem-solving. Therapists learn the problems of the individual assessed (intermediate targets); the individuals assessed learn what to do to maximize desired outcomes. For the purposes of treatment engagement, the client should look at the assessment results and agree that "Yes, this describes me," "Yes, these problems are worth changing," and "Yes, these strengths are worth building."

For most areas of practice, there is considerably more research on the predictive accuracy of the risk tools than there is research on their ability to promote desired outcomes. This is to be expected. Establishing the predictive accuracy is a necessary first step. Consequently, most of my comments that follow concern how to evaluate risk tools in terms of predictive accuracy. Some of my comments, however, address the potential (or lack thereof) of risk tools to advance effective interventions.

A summary of the concerns of this chapter is presented in Table 17.1. The table is not intended to be a formal quality control checklist (although it could probably function that way); instead, my hope is to remind evaluators what to consider when deciding to use, or not, a particular risk tool for a particular case. It should also be useful to researchers developing prediction tools for diverse contexts. Readers interested in other considerations for developing high-quality prediction tools are encouraged to read Baer (2019), who provided valuable practical advice (mostly for business decisions).

QUALITY OF THE RESEARCH FINDINGS

Good risk tools are supported by good research studies. The value of research studies depends on the nature and quality of previous research and on what is currently believed to be true by the community of experts. The scientific credibility of any assertion, method, or procedure is based on an evolving body of evidence. Scientific truth is not established by a single study, no matter how good. Instead, risk tools gain scientific credentials through a progressing program of research during which supportive evidence accumulates and potential alternate explanations become increasingly hard to justify (Lakatos's, 1970, advancing program of research). The activity of science involves arguing from evidence, with both the arguments and evidence under the scrutiny of peer review. Scientific findings are considered to be established when there is consensus in the community of knowledgeable experts. However, complete consensus is rare, and statements enter textbooks and practice standards based on the lesser threshold of recommendations by reputable groups of opinion leaders.

The next section reviews commonly accepted criteria for judging the quality of research. This is followed by a section on more specific criteria for evaluating prediction tools.

Large Sample Size

Sample size is a central indicator of study quality. Before becoming excited about a research finding, check the sample size. We underestimate the extent to which chance variation influences research and are prone to naively accept findings from small studies. How large does the sample size need to be? The bigger, the better. Jacob Cohen (of Cohen's *d* fame) spent much of his professional career reminding researchers that they need to collect large samples to

TABLE 17.1. Evaluating the Quality of Prediction Tools

Feature	Look for	Beware of
Quality of research findings	• Large sample sizes • Representative samples • Replication • Meta-analysis • Strong reputation of research team • Careful and appropriate statistical analyses • Quality control checks	• Improbable (or impossible) values • One-off findings • Research teams that do not learn
Open science practices	• Preregistration • Sharing of data and research materials	• Publication bias • p-hacking
Protection against overfitting	• Coherent theoretical model • Replication	• Counterintuitive variables • Tools developed on only one sample
Understandable	• Coherent theoretical model • Explicit method of risk tool construction • Simple method of assigning scores/levels to cases	• Undefined variables • Opaque algorithms
Fair/unbiased	• Historically disadvantaged groups (e.g., BIPOC) explicitly considered in model development • Similar inferences supported for different racial/ethnic groups	• Confounding of predictors and outcome • Bias in data collection • Indicators are proxies for ethnic group membership
Rater reliability	• Kappa/ICC >.75	• Kappa/ICC <.60
Comprehensive	• Items cover major domains known to be associated with the outcome • Variables based on strong theoretical model	• Small set of initial variables • Limited rationale for variables considered • Secondary analysis of existing administrative data
Fit for purpose	• Sampling frame matches the case at hand • Outcome variable(s) align with referral question	• Sampling frame undefined
Simple	• Ease of coding • Ease and availability of training	• Unusual variables • Complex/expensive training

Note. BIPOC = Blacks, Indigenous, and People of Color; ICC = intraclass correlation coefficient.

have adequate statistical power (i.e., the likelihood of detecting an effect that is actually there). Power increases with large sample size and few variables. In Cohen's research lab, his students would joke that their professor's ideal study would have 10,000 cases and no variables.

Cohen's (1988) power tables provide some guidance concerning the number of observations necessary to detect small, medium, and large effects. Assuming equal numbers of individuals with and without the outcome, 800 cases are required to have an 80% likelihood of detecting a small effect (400 in each group; $d = .20$), 130 to detect a medium effect (65 in each group; $d = .50$), and 50 to detect a large effect (25 in each group; $d = .80$; Cohen, 1988, Table 2.3.5, two-tailed alpha $p < .05$). For the prediction of crime and violence, most predictors have small relationships with recidivism (d values around .20; Andrews & Bonta, 2010, Table 2.7; Hanson & Morton-Bourgon, 2005). The median sample size in prediction studies is less than 200 (Hanson & Morton-Bourgon, 2005), which is well below the 800 recommended by Cohen (1988). Consequently, do not expect consistent results across individual studies. Low statistical power means that many studies will fail to detect effects that are actually there. Reliable identification of small predictors is possible, however, when the results of the individual studies are aggregated through meta-analysis (see Chapter 14, this volume).

One limitation of Cohen's (1988) power tables is that they are framed within null hypothesis statistical testing. That is, the sample size estimates assume that researchers are only interested in determining whether potential effects are greater than zero. This is rarely in doubt. In applied risk assessment, evaluators are not just interested in whether there is any relationship with the outcome, they want to know the size of the relationship. This requires larger samples than those indicated by Cohen's (1988) tables.

With low base rates, statistical power is primarily determined by the number of cases with the outcome. For example, a recidivism prediction study with 150 cases including 50 recidivists would have higher statistical power than a study with 300 cases but only 10 recidivists. If the only question is statistical significance (not the size of the relationship), then it is possible to detect moderate effects using logistic regression with 10 events out of total sample size of 150 ($p < .05$; Hosmer et al., 2013). Stable logistic regression estimates of moderate effects require about 100 individuals with the outcome and 100 without the outcome (Collins et al., 2016; Vergouwe et al., 2005).

Representative Sample

Evaluators using risk tools make inferences about a specific case from data collected on other people. Consequently, confidence in these inferences increases when the *other people* are similar to the case at hand. It is often difficult to judge the representativeness of samples because there are any number of ways that individuals differ from each other, some of which will be risk-relevant (discussed in Chapter 2, "The Nature of Probability"). In many cases, samples have been preselected on risk-relevant variables that are unknown to the researchers.

One oft-neglected selection process, for example, is that individuals who are currently receiving interventions are likely to be disproportionately in need of services (Cohen & Cohen, 1984; Rhodes et al., 2016; see Chapter 4, this volume). The ideal sample would be truly random (each member of the class has an equal likelihood of being selected), but this is extremely rare; instead, a more common approach to checking for sampling bias is replication. If a risk tool performs similarly across diverse groups (discrimination and calibration), then there should be less concern about matching the case-at-hand to specific research samples.

Formal tests of between-sample variability are provided by meta-analysis (see Chapter 14). Specifically, low variability is indicated by small, nonsignificant Q values and I^2 values of 25% or less. Real (significant) variability in predictive accuracy need not be a problem, however, when the full range of observed values implies the same inferences. For example, a risk tool may have moderate discrimination in most samples but large discrimination in a minority of samples. This pattern of findings would support the use of the risk tool to rank individuals in terms of risk. In contrast, if the risk tool showed moderate discrimination in most samples but no discrimination (AUC around .50) in some samples, then prudent evaluators would carefully consider the research studies before deciding to use (or not) the risk tool with the case at hand. Sometimes unusually poor or unusually good discrimination can be explained by features of the research design (e.g., restriction of range, extreme groups design). This would be unlikely to influence the choice of a risk tool for a specific individual. On the other hand, poor discrimination for a certain subgroup would be a concern if the case at hand was a member of that group (e.g., non-Europeans in Sweden; Långström, 2004).

Given that historically disadvantaged groups, such as Blacks, Indigenous people, and People of Color (BIPOC), are all too frequently overrepresented in the criminal justice and forensic mental health systems, these populations should be considered in the development of criminal recidivism risk tools. In particular, it may be worthwhile to oversample minority groups in research studies to have sufficient sample size for reliable statistical analysis. Similarly, when there are reasons to suspect differences between men and women, there should be enough cases of each gender to study each gender separately.

Open Science Practices

"L'art c'est moi; la science c'est nous" (Art is I; science is we). This quote by the French physiologist Claude Bernard (1813–1878) encapsulates the aspiration for science to be a collective, self-correcting enterprise. Although we all have our own ideas and beliefs, scientists search for ideas that are also true for others (whether the others believe them or not). The advancement of scientific research requires open debate, public criticism, and correction. In recent years, there has been concerns that certain research practices within psychology have stymied this process. In particular, there are numerous ways in which researchers working privately in their own laboratories can "game" the research process to generate findings that are not really there.

This concern about lack of transparency in research practices has motivated the development of open science practices, which have been adopted by many academic journals. These practices include preregistration of research studies (discussed in more detail later in the chapter), dissemination of null findings, and facilitating external researchers to review and replicate primary findings. For example, many journals now expect authors to include the forms, questionnaires, and computer code used in primary studies as supplemental online materials. As well, journal editors routinely ask whether the original data has (or will be) posted on a publicly accessible website. Although the impact of such measures is not yet known, open science practices send the right message. Claude Bernard would approve.

Publication Bias

Not all studies get published. Published studies, on average, have effects that are larger, and more novel, than the results of unpublished studies (Kühberger et al., 2014). Publication bias arises because we are particularly interested in new and surprising findings (i.e., they appear newsworthy). Publication bias, however, is a serious threat to cumulative knowledge (Ioannidis, 2005). When reviewing research studies, reviewers must consider the extent to which the evidence available is an unbiased selection of all the studies conducted.

It is difficult to tell whether any specific study has been preselected from other, less interesting, studies. A preselected study can look completely normal, and may well be. Bias is introduced not by the available studies but by those that are missing. This has been called the file drawer problem (Rosenthal, 1979): How many nonsignificant studies are collecting dust in some researchers' file drawers for each disseminated, significant result? Although publication bias is difficult to detect for any individual study, publication bias for a content area can be detected.

There are a number of technical approaches to detecting publication bias (see Borenstein et al., 2021, Section 35), of which I will discuss one, the funnel plot. *Funnel plots* display a collection of effect sizes against their expected variability. If the available studies are a representative sample of studies, then there should be a greater range of values for small studies than for large studies. As well, the funnel plot of unbiased samples should be symmetrical, with equal number of values above and below the overall average. Empty regions of the plot indicate reporting bias. In particular, small studies with small effects are those most likely to go missing. Large studies tend to be reported because (a) even small effects will be statistically significant with large enough samples and (b) researchers feel greater responsibility to report their results for large studies (which tend to have external funders and large research teams) than for small studies (which are often unfunded). In contrast, a researcher who finds a small, nonsignificant effect in a small sample is likely to either collect more data or shelve the project. Good luck trying to publish it.

Figure 17.1 presents a funnel plot based on data from a review I conducted with my then student, Seung Chan Lee (Lee & Hanson, 2015). The question at issue was whether violence risk assessment tools developed in Western settings worked as expected in China (Zhou et al., 2016). Figure 17.1 presents nine effects sizes (three from meta-analyses and six from individual studies) representing predictive accuracy of four risk tools in the West. The funnel plot shows clear evidence of publication bias. In this plot, the AUC values (a measure of discrimination) were plotted against the square root of the sample size (a measure of the expected variability). The effects from the largest studies (Study H and Study I) had AUC values around .70, which is typical for applied violence risk tools. The smallest studies, however, had unusually large effects. If the population value of the AUC is really around .70 (as suggested by the large studies), then the values observed in the small studies should be equally distributed above .70 (e.g., .71–.90) and below .70 (e.g., .50–.69). In contrast, all of the small studies had values above .70. The empty, triangular region indicates where studies with effect sizes below the mean would have been expected but were not found. We concluded that there was a publication bias effect for these Western studies. In contrast, the funnel plot for the Chinese studies in Zhou et al.'s (2016) review was symmetrical (not shown), indicating no publication bias.

FIGURE 17.1. Funnel Plot of the Predictive Accuracy (AUC Values) of Violence Risk Tools in Nine Western Samples

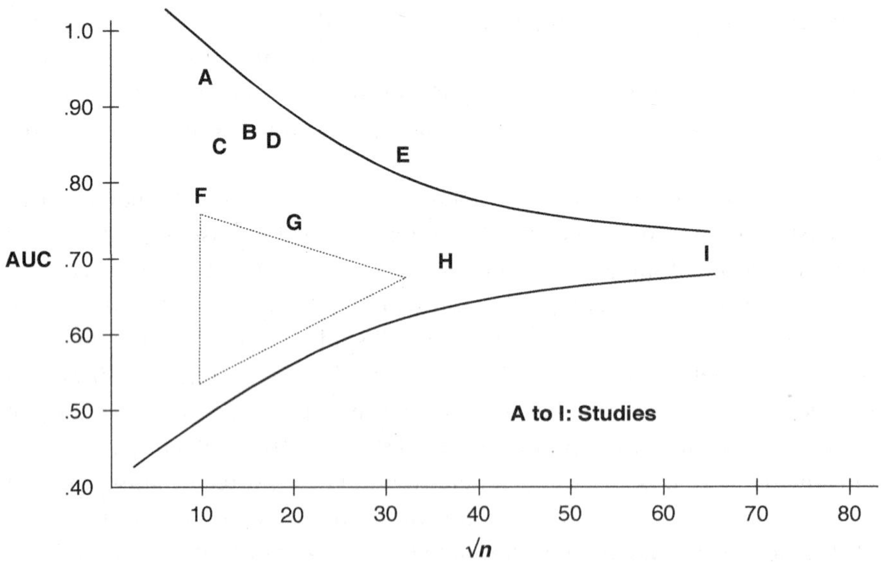

Note. The AUC values in each study are indicated by letters A to I. The empty, triangular region indicates where studies would be expected if this sample of studies were unbiased. AUC = area under the curve. Data from Lee and Hanson (2015).

Preregistration

One way of protecting readers against publication bias is preregistration (Lindsay et al., 2016). Preregistration involves documenting, in advance, the research methods, analyses, and associated hypotheses of a research study. These design features can then be posted at searchable websites, such as the Open Science Framework (https://osf.io). Preregistration also inhibits researchers from selectively reporting significant results from within a single study (called p-hacking; Head et al., 2015). The goal of preregistration is to increase the likelihood that the available research is filtered by relevance and methodological rigor, rather than by results. Readers who want to know whether a study has been preregistered should check its Method section. Some journals have adopted the laudable practice of awarding badges to preregistered studies.

Careful and Appropriate Statistical Analyses

There are many ways of reporting and presenting data. The most informative data analyses will address the questions of interest. For prediction tools, these questions typically concern base rates, discrimination (how different are those with the outcome from those without the outcome), and calibration (the extent to which the predicted likelihoods are replicated in new studies). My hope in writing this book is that evaluators will have increased ability to appreciate what is communicated by prediction statistics and to be well-informed consumers of research articles.

Once data are collected, more time is needed to clean the data than to compute the statistics of primary research interest. All data sets contain errors, and it is the responsibility of data analysts to minimize errors and their impact on the conclusions. Of the thousands of empirical articles I have coded for meta-analyses, most contain at least one obviously impossible value (e.g., the sample size does not correspond with degrees of freedom). Typically, these errors have minimal influence on the conclusions; however, certain studies or data sets contain so many errors that they are excluded from our reviews.

There are no firm rules concerning the number of errors or impossible values that would disqualify empirical data from the scientific conversation. Typically, I expect 2% to 3% of the entries in raw data sets to be incorrect, and in my own studies, I tolerate error rates up to 5%, provided the errors are not systematic. The data sets that I have excluded had detectable error rates around 10% (e.g., totals that do not add up; out-of-range values). Sometimes these discrepancies can be resolved by consultation with those responsible for the data set; often, however, the source of the errors is unknown. Just as proofreaders of written materials catch typos missed by the original author, it is good practice to have a second data analyst replicate the main analyses of research studies. Ideally, the data analysts should be blind to the hypotheses, although this is rare in practice. Minimally, the second analyst should be able to produce the key numbers after being provided with only the raw data set and the Method section. Our experience with double-running analyses is that everybody makes mistakes, but that most errors are minor (they do not change the substantive conclusions). We have found, however, that it is often necessary to revise Method sections to disambiguate the analytic choices (e.g., which of several potential approaches were used to estimate standard errors?).

Credible Research Team

Researchers and research teams vary in reliability and conscientiousness. They also vary in skill. In any specific research domain, there are numerous tricky decisions concerning study design and analysis that could influence the findings (some of which are discussed in this book). Teams with expertise and experience are likely to make better decisions than less skilled teams.

For various reasons, some teams are more trustworthy than others. Judging credibility based on reputation, however, runs counter to the culture of scientific inquiry (Shapin, 2010). The scientific revolution aimed to weaken the credibility of authorities and build knowledge from direct observations, that is, basic facts that could be verified by anybody. In practice, however, science is built on trust. For the edifice of science to stand, we must believe that researchers are making their best efforts to follow accepted standards and that they report what they did and what they found with accuracy and candor. This is not always the case. The numerous decisions required to conduct a research study present almost endless opportunities to influence the eventual findings. These range from regrettable distortions (e.g., adding a hypothesis after the results are known) to outright fraud (never collecting the data in the first place). Humans are prone to self-deception; researchers are no exception. Don't underestimate the temptation to bend the rules for personal and professional advantage.

At one point in my career, I was working on a project that aimed to establish scientific consensus on the criteria for evaluating sex crime recidivism intervention studies (Collaborative Outcome Data Committee, 2007a, 2007b). Part of the process involved asking opinion leaders about evaluation criteria. One of these experts suggested we have an item "I just don't believe them." He had had enough close experience with a certain research team that he no longer trusted anything coming from their lab. I argued back that this item was highly subjective and violates the values of science (and correctional rehabilitation—"OK, you may have caught them cheating once but that doesn't mean that everything they publish is wrong"). Although the item did not appear in the final list, our conversation sensitized me to how I actually judge research quality. For me, reputation matters. I judge studies published in top-rank journals by respected researchers as more credible than the findings of an unpublished master's student. I also place considerable weight on studies from researchers with a history of promoting one perspective who change their minds based on new evidence. My hope that these heuristics direct me quickly to the most reliable information. Although research evidence deserves to be evaluated on its own merits, not on who produced it, the credibility of the researchers cannot be ignored. Although we should make every effort to check our biases at the door, it would be foolish not to recognize that some researchers are more trustworthy than others.

QUALITY OF PREDICTION TOOLS

The above concerns (*sample size* to *credible research team*) are relevant to most quantitative research in psychology. There are, however, certain concerns of special importance for research on prediction tools. These will now be discussed.

Replication to Protect Against Overfitting

Overfitting of risk tools involves failing to distinguish chance features of a data set from features of nature. Due to the risk of overfitting, risk tools should be replicated in a fresh sample (not the one used to construct the measure) before being used in applied assessments. Overfitting is expected to be of particular concern for risk tools that are empirically derived from a large collection of candidate variables. Even when none of the candidate variables actually have any relationship with the outcome, some variables will appear to be related to the outcome based on chance alone. This is not a new concern, and diverse technical solutions have been proposed to limit overfitting of statistical models. These include corrections for shrinkage (e.g., Ferguson, 1976, §26.9), model fit indices (e.g., Burnham & Anderson, 2002), dividing the data into development and validation samples, and various forms of bootstrap resampling (Stine, 1989). None of these technical solutions provide strong protection against overfitting.

Each data set has its own unique features. Empirical analyses of any single data set cannot determine whether the patterns observed in that data set will be found in other data sets. This requires another data set. The problem with the technical solutions is that they all based their conclusions on information from the target data set. The technical solutions (e.g., bootstrapping) provide some protection against obvious overfitting, and help researchers identify the most stable features of a specific data set. These stable features may speak to the phenomenon of interest; however, they could speak only to that data set. The best way to tease apart these possibilities is to replicate the study in a new sample.

Consequently, before risk tools are used in applied assessments, it is necessary that the major inferences implied by the risk tool have been replicated in at least one sample that was not used to construct the measure. Preferably, the inferences are supported by multiple replication studies, conducted by diverse research teams. The only studies that do not require replication are those based on very large data sets. Data management practices during the past few decades have resulted in large administrative databases being available to researchers. Although still unusual, some risk tools have had the luxury of developmental samples in the tens of thousands (e.g., Howard & Dixon, 2012). If a risk tool was developed based on 20,000 cases and the other features of construction seem reasonable, I would trust these results for this setting, even without replication. If the risk tool is to be used in other settings, however, then replication is still necessary, regardless of the sample size on which the risk tool was based.

When I was developing risk tools, my preferred process was to start with candidate risk factors that had already been established as univariate predictors in meta-analysis. My team and I would then collect diverse data sets that contained these variables, which would allow us to examine their stability across samples and settings. In our analyses, we had the dual goals of (a) maximizing predictive accuracy and (b) increasing the likelihood that the resulting risk tool would be replicated in future studies. Often, the final version of the risk tool was not the most accurate; instead, it was a compromise between increased accuracy and low variability across samples. As a final check on generalizability, we typically would hold back one sample as a validation sample and refrain from analyzing it until decisions had been made about the new, or revised, risk tool we were creating. If the new risk tool worked as expected in the validation sample, we would (cautiously) recommend it for applied use.

It is not until the findings are replicated by an independent research group, however, that I really trust them. In 2000, we had just developed Static-99 (a risk tool for sexual recidivism among adult men with a history of sexual offending; Hanson & Thornton, 1999, 2000), and it was being used by various jurisdictions, including my own. I thought that we had done our due diligence as risk-tool developers; nonetheless, I felt a certain vulnerability knowing that decisions with major life consequences were being made based on a risk tool that David Thornton and I had put together in a hotel room the previous year. At a 2000 conference, a young Swede, Niklas Långström, introduced himself to me and insisted that I follow him. He led me to a poster by his then student, Gabrielle Sjöstedt, which described how they had tested Static-99 on a large, representative sample from Sweden. It worked pretty much as expected (subsequently published as Sjöstedt & Långström, 2001). That brief meeting greatly increased my confidence that the Static-99 risk tool was worthwhile. Although Niklas and I would go on to be friendly, professional colleagues, we had not met before then. That strangers from another continent had read our reports, scored 1,000+ new cases, conducted a credible study, and found substantially similar results was immensely reassuring.

Rater Reliability

Rater reliability is the extent to which independent evaluators obtain similar scores for the same cases. Rater reliability is usually indexed by numbers ranging from −1.0 to 1.0. A reliability coefficient of 1.0 indicates perfect agreement, and a coefficient of −1.0 indicates perfect disagreement. When ratings are random, the reliability coefficient is expected to be zero. Rater reliability is usually assessed in research studies by having two evaluators rate the same set of cases. It is possible, however, to have more than two evaluators, and not all evaluators need to rate the same cases. The design of the rater reliability study determines how reliability statistics should be calculated (Shrout & Fleiss, 1979).

For prediction tools that produce an ordered set of scores, the standard rater reliability statistic is the *intraclass correlation coefficient,* or ICC. ICCs are preferred over Pearson correlation coefficients (r), which are also used to measure reliability, because ICCs can account for differences in magnitude, not just relative ranking. For example, consider a risk tool that assigns individuals to five levels (1 is *no risk,* 3 is *moderate risk,* and 5 is *highest risk*). If Dr. T. K. Easy rates four cases 1, 2, 2, 3, and Dr. I. Worry rates the same cases 3, 4, 4, 5, the Pearson correlation between their ratings would be 1.0, indicating perfect agreement. In contrast, the ICC would only be 0.25, indicating poor agreement, which seems more appropriate given that the evaluators disagreed by two levels on each and every case. In this example, the ICC of 0.25 was calculated using two-way random effects/absolute agreement (Case 2, Model ICC [2,1] from Shrout & Fleiss, 1979). When there are only two raters for each case in the reliability study, the two-way random effects model is almost always the most appropriate.

With ICCs, there is the option of specifying the number of raters who are expected to rate the measure in applied practice. Reporting single rater or multiple rater ICC values is based on how the measure is used in practice, not the number of raters included in the reliability study. The greater the number of raters for each case, the higher the expected ICC value (following the Spearman-Brown formula; Ley, 1972, Equation 11:15). Most prediction tools are intended to be used by a single evaluator; consequently, the ICC value for a single rater is the one that should be reported in most circumstances. Certain measures, however, are designed to be scored simultaneously by two or more raters, with the final score being the average across the raters (e.g., ratings of inpatient adjustment completed by a treatment team). For such measures, the ICC value for multiple raters is appropriate.

For prediction tools that places cases into discrete categories, Cohen's kappa (κ; Cohen, 1960) is the standard index of rater reliability. Kappa is a measure of agreement for categorical variables that considers the amount of agreement expected by chance. For example, consider a decision about whether each of 100 individuals is a sexual psychopath. If a rater reliability study was conducted at a nonforensic outpatient clinic, few individuals would be expected to be sexual psychopaths. Dr. Easy may identify one individual as a sexual psychopath, whereas Dr. Worry identifies three entirely different individuals as sexual psychopaths; in this scenario, they would still agree that most cases, 96 out of 100 cases, were not sexual psychopaths. Expressed as 96% agreement, this may seem like the good doctors agreed. The kappa value tells a different story. With very low or very high base rates, there is a large amount of agreement expected simply by chance. When this chance agreement is removed, kappa in this example is close to zero ($\kappa = -0.015$), indicating that there was no agreement between the evaluators on which cases were sexual psychopaths.

Kappa has been criticized for attributing too much of the observed agreement to chance (Whitehurst, 1984). According to kappa, the amount of chance agreement is calculated from the proportions (base rates) provided by each evaluator. Assigning these base rates, however, is a professional judgment; if the raters agree on the base rates, this is a type of real agreement. For example, members of a hiring committee may agree than none of the candidates are fully qualified but disagree about which one is the best of a bad lot. Consequently, it is often useful to supplement kappa with other statistics, including the marginal totals (the base rates assigned by each evaluator) and overall percent agreement. If a category was never used by one rater, kappa cannot be calculated, and percent agreement may be the best option for reporting rater reliability.

A related concern is that both ICC and kappa are influenced by the variability in the cases rated. When there are large differences in the cases in a reliability study, ICCs and kappas will be larger than when the cases closely resemble each other. Ideally, the variability in scores in the research cases would be similar to the variability in the setting where it will be used (Joint Committee, 2014, p. 39).

So how good is good enough rater reliability? There are no absolute standards, as thresholds vary based on base rates and the intended use of the measures. Nevertheless, there are a number of useful guidelines (Byrt, 1996), of which those of Cicchetti (1994) and Fleiss et al. (2003) are widely referenced. For ICCs and for kappas, Cicchetti suggested that values less than .40 are *poor*, .40 to .60 are *fair*, .60 to .75 are *good*, and values greater than .75 are *excellent*. Another perspective for judging rater reliability is to consider the types of information coded. The simplest variables, such as age or whether the current sentence involved community supervision, should be coded with accuracy of greater than .80; it is not unusual to have ICC/kappa values greater than .90 for these types of variables. Coding items that require more professional judgment, such as poor cognitive problem-solving (from STABLE-2007; Fernandez & Helmus, 2017) or shallow affect (from the Psychopathy Checklist—Revised; Hare, 2003), typically have rater reliability (ICC values) in the .50 to .60 range. Rater reliability for total scores will be meaningfully higher than the rater reliability of the individual items. Consequently, Cicchetti's guidelines can be considered too lenient when applied to total scores from risk tools (particularly when the risk tool is based on easily coded items) and too stringent when applied to professional ratings of moderately complex, psychologically meaningful constructs. For example, the research team evaluating the reliability of *DSM-5* diagnoses considered that kappa values "above 0.8 would be almost miraculous; to see kappa between 0.6 and 0.8 would be cause for celebration. A realistic goal is kappa between 0.4 and 0.6, while kappa between 0.2 and 0.4 would be acceptable" (Kraemer et al., 2012).

For researchers planning their own rater reliability studies, I recommend that between 20 and 50 cases are coded by at least two raters. One popular heuristic is to double code 10% of the research sample. A minimum of 20 cases are required, however, for the statistics to be at all stable; as well, there is rarely any benefit to coding more than 50 cases, unless the cases are being coded by different sets of raters or under different conditions (e.g., different project sites). Although the cases in the reliability study should be coded independently, it is prudent for the coders to first collaborate on several practice cases and to periodically confer.

Software for calculating ICCs and kappa are available in both R Statistics and IBM/SPSS. The "psych" package in R Statistics (Revelle, 2020) has subroutines for ICCs (*ICC*) and kappa (*cohen.kappa*). In IBM/SPSS version 26, kappa is found by following **Analyze/Descriptive Statistics/Crosstabs/ Statistics**, and ICCs are found by following **Analyze/Scale/Reliability Analysis/Statistics.**

Understandable Risk Tools Are Better Than Black Box Predictors

Black box prediction schemes do not provide an explanation for the relationship between the risk tool and the outcome. No explanation is complete; nevertheless, it is desirable for evaluators to have some sense of why *this* individual should be considered *this* risky. In the context of treatment, these explanations provide direction for intervention and risk management. Even when a probability is the only information of interest, understandable risk tools provide some protection that the risk tool is predicting for the right reasons. Variables that predict for the right reasons are justified by credible, psychologically sound, causal theories. Variables that predict for the wrong reasons are those that capitalize on chance features of a specific data set, that reinforce discrimination against historically disadvantaged groups, or that are inadvertently proxies for the outcome (the outcome is predicting itself). Researchers, for example, may mistakenly use the outcome to predict itself when variables are coded from clinical files that were created because the outcome occurred. Black box predictors may predict for the right reasons, the wrong reasons, or some combination of both. Evaluators cannot tell.

Face validity provides some protection against predicting for the wrong reasons. Face validity involves the degree of association in natural language between the factor and the outcome. Face validity is particularly important when the risk assessment is used in intervention and planning processes directly with the individual being assessed. If the connection between the item and the outcome is not obvious, its inclusion in a prediction tool requires a strong evidence base. All risk and protection factors benefit from a coherent theoretical model articulating their causal influence on the outcome.

The prototypic black box measures are machine learning algorithms that are not intended to be understandable (Berk et al., 2009). Although the algorithm itself is understandable, its output may not be. These algorithms are referred to as machine learning because they make decisions based not only on the data but also on previous decisions. When successful, it is possible to train machine learning algorithms to identify relationships in complex data sets that would otherwise remain hidden. The problem, however, is that the relationships identified by the algorithm may never be known to the human users.

The Classification of Violence Risk (COVR; Monahan, 2021) is an example of an applied violence prediction scheme that prioritizes prediction over understanding. The COVR was developed using iterative classification tree (ICT) analyses (Steadman et al., 2000). The COVR's ICT algorithm divides cases into groups based on 40 possible factors, such as age at first hospitalization, diagnosis of antisocial personality disorder, substance misuse at admission, and father's arrest. The analyses are iterative in that each factor is used to divide the cases into groups, and the divisions stops when groups have observed failure rates that meet predefined thresholds for low risk and for high risk. For the COVR, the threshold for low risk is less than 9% after 20 weeks (half the violence base rate of 18%) and the threshold for high risk is greater than 37% (twice the base rate). The moderate-risk groups have recidivism rates between 9% and 37%.

A single classification tree is relatively easy to describe by a flow chart (e.g., see Figure 12.1 and Figure 12.2 in this volume). COVR total scores, however, are based on five different classifications trees, each starting with a different risk factor (Banks et al., 2004). Specifically, the COVR final score is a weighted count of the number of times that the case is classified as low risk, moderate risk, or high risk by each of the five classification trees (*low* = −1, *moderate* = 0, and *high* = +1). Consequently, the possible scores range from a low of −5 (all five trees indicated low risk) to maximum of 5 (all five trees indicated high risk).

The use of multiple classification trees increases predictive accuracy at the expense of transparency. Given the computational demands, COVR scores are generated by a computer program. The output is an expected rate (from 1% to 76%) and a list of the items (out of a possible 40) used to derive this estimate. Although evaluators could reconstruct the steps used to generate the violence rate estimate, it is neither easy to do nor easy to interpret. Consequently, evaluators using the COVR in applied assessments would be expected to know (and trust) its scientific basis without fully understanding how the COVR generates risk estimates for the case at hand.

The growing availability of large data sets combined with exponentially increasing computer power encourages the development of machine learning algorithms. A useful review of these algorithms in the context of criminal justice is provided by Brennan (2017). One popular machine learning approach is the random forest (Breiman, 2001). Random forest analyses proceed in two stages. The first stage generates a large number of ICTs (e.g., 500). The second stage applies decision rules for interpreting the results of these classification trees (e.g., individuals who are considered low risk in 251 of 500 trees are classified as low risk). Another intriguing approach to machine learning involves artificial neural networks (Schalkoff, 1997). These programs aim to replicate the structures and processes that biological brains use to process information. Artificial neural networks can learn from training examples and from past mistakes (classification errors). The major advantage of machine learning algorithms is that they are able to identify complex relationships in large data sets. The major disadvantage is that the inner workings are often opaque.

Just as human judgment is fallible, machines also make mistakes. The advancing program of science is based on publicly available observations, which are interpreted and reinterpreted in the light of new theory and fresh evidence. To quote Daniel Dennett (1995), science "is not just a matter of making mistakes, but of making mistakes in public" (p. 380). Given this perspective, the results of machine learning algorithms are not part of science. When the intricacies of the calculations are beyond the scope of our mental abilities, we want some machine learning equivalent of peer review. Ideally, there would be trustworthy procedures for verifying that black box prediction programs are working as intended, that is, they are robust across samples and settings, and not predicting for the wrong reasons. Until then, prudent evaluators will privilege risk tools they understand, even if it comes at the potential cost of lower predictive accuracy.

The extent to which machine learning algorithms outperform simpler approaches (e.g., counting the number of risk factors present) depends crucially on the patterns in the data. Machine learning shines when the data are actually complex. Examples of complexity include substantially nonlinear relationships or statistical interactions involving three or more predictor variables. The complexity of data will depend on the area of study and how the indicator variables are related to the constructs of interest. In the area of risk for crime and violence, the machine learning algorithms have not done meaningfully better than simpler approaches, such as logistic regression (see the review by Brennan, 2017). Consequently, choosing understandable recidivism risk tools does not currently require sacrificing predictive accuracy.

My own experience with criminal recidivism research is that there is little to gain from repackaging the same set of predictors (e.g., adding interactions, changing weights). In contrast, meaningful increases in accuracy are found when new types of information are added to risk tools. For example, adding interview data concerning psychologically meaningful risk factors (STABLE-2007; Fernandez et al., 2014; Hanson et al., 2015) to criminal history information (as measured by Static-99R; Helmus, Thornton, et al., 2012) meaningfully improves the prediction of sexual recidivism (Brankley et al., 2021). One of the promises of machine learning approaches is that they can extract information from messy sources that would otherwise be ignored, such as predicting inpatient violence from electronic health records (Menger et al., 2019). Once new relationships are identified, however, they need to be explained. Explanations require a different program of research from that used simply to identify empirical predictors.

The relative success of the basic additive model suggests that the predictors of criminal recidivism contain few complex interactions. Each risk factor slightly increases the risk of criminal recidivism, and individuals with more risk factors are higher risk than individuals with fewer risk factors. This is the *cumulative stochastic* model, meaning that there a number of risk and protective factors that each have a probabilistic (stochastic) relationship to the outcome. No single factor, or combination of factors, is necessary or sufficient. Although the cumulative stochastic model is an obvious simplification of nature, it is the default model against which other, less parsimonious models, must be compared.

Black box predictors are less valuable than risk tools that identify psychologically meaningful risk factors, which can become treatment targets. Identifying treatment targets requires a causal model justified by theory and evidence. These causal models not only promote effective intervention, they also contribute to the advancement of psychology as a science. Ideally, the results of the risk assessment should be comprehensible to both the evaluator and the individual assessed. Although it may be that the major determinants of human behavior are beyond our understanding (Yarkoni & Westfall, 2017), I doubt that this is the case. Instead, I believe that we can go a long way toward understanding each other by using evidence to discipline our insight and empathy.

Risk Tools Should Not Be Biased Against Already Disadvantaged Groups

There is no single definition of bias for risk tools; however, evaluators are most likely concerned about bias because of the potential for adverse consequences, particularly adverse consequences for already disadvantaged groups. Technically, bias in risk assessment occurs when the test results systematically mean different things for different groups. For example, a low score on a reading test could be an indicator of low intelligence for most children, but for children of recent immigrants, it could indicate that the test was not in the child's native language.

There are several possible sources of bias for prediction tools. When looking at cultural bias within the instrument itself, we can refer to both item bias and construct bias (Haag et al., 2016). *Item cultural bias* refers to different responses based on how individuals of different cultures would be expected to respond to the items (e.g., the term "unrelated victim" could mean something different to people from individualistic vs. collectivistic cultures). Raters can also introduce bias because of their expectations about certain types of people. *Construct cultural bias* occurs when the constructs measured by the scale do not apply equally to individuals with different cultural backgrounds. Given that we often do not know what risk tools are actually measuring, construct cultural bias is difficult to detect.

One popular definition of bias is that the decision process unfairly results in certain groups having fewer benefits or more harms (or both) than other groups. If Blacks and Whites are equally credit-worthy, for example, there should be no difference in their likelihood of obtaining low interest loans. Fairness can be defined at an individual level (i.e., same treatment for individuals with the same attributes) but it can also be defined at a cultural level. In both the United States (*Fisher v. University of Texas at Austin*, 2016) and

Canada (Friesen, 2019), affirmative action is used to correct historical injustices concerning access to education for certain marginalized racial groups.

In psychology, test bias is usually defined in terms of discrimination and calibration (Reynolds, 2000; Reynolds & Suzuki, 2013). In particular, prediction tools are considered unbiased when there are no systematic differences across subgroups in (a) the extent to which those with the outcome are different from those without the outcome (discrimination) and (b) the proportion with the outcome at each risk level (Reynolds, 2000). One of the most efficient methods for testing both discrimination and calibration is by examining the equivalence of logistic regression equations across subgroups. Differences between logistic regression equations can be tested using meta-analysis (see Chapter 14) or interaction terms. Examples of the meta-analysis approach to examining racial differences in the predictive accuracy of Static-99R (a sexual recidivism risk tool) can be found in Hanson, Lunetta, et al. (2014) and Lee and Hanson (2017).

Considerations of risk tool bias, however, are complicated when group membership is correlated with the outcome of interest (Chouldechova, 2017). If the risk tool is well calibrated, then group differences in the likelihood of the outcome will create systematic differences in risk scores across groups. To maintain equal risk scores across groups, the risk tool cannot remain well calibrated. If the groups actually differ on the propensity for the outcome, parity in risk scores can only be achieved by creating systematic differences in the rates of the outcome per risk score for each group.

Consider a numeracy test used to select candidates for employment at an international company. If Norwegians are less skilled with numbers than Japanese, then employment selection tests that assess numeracy would disadvantage Norwegians. Although Norwegians may be unhappy about not making the cut, the numeracy test could still be well calibrated if the rates of on-the-job success per score were the same for both ethnic groups. If there were political or social demands to hire equal numbers of both ethnic groups, then the company would hire some Norwegians who were less qualified than Japanese who were not hired. In this case, the Japanese who were not hired would be unhappy. If the test worked as intended, however, the Japanese who were hired should outshine the Norwegians at work because the average score for those hired would be higher for Japanese than for Norwegians. In this case, the numeracy test is unbiased, even if the hiring decisions may be.

One particularly problematic type of bias is when the test scores incorrectly indicate differences that are not really there. For example, assume that the Norwegians and Japanese applicants are actually equally good with numbers. A selection test would be biased if the questions were written to be intrinsically easier for Japanese than for Norwegians (e.g., all arithmetic questions involve Japanese yen). The Japanese candidates would be expected to do better than the Norwegians on the test, even though there are no ethnic group differences on the latent construct that the test was designed to measures. Given this type of bias, the high scores for the Japanese would not align with better on-the-job success because the selection test was contaminated with irrelevant content. Notice that the same pattern of scores (Japanese higher than Norwegians) can result from two quite different processes, one of which seems more patently unfair than the other.

When groups differ in the likelihood of the outcome, a further complication is that all indicators of group membership will also be empirical risk factors for the outcome. It is very difficult to disentangle direct and indirect effects in prediction studies. All factors that are correlated with each other will also be correlated with the outcome if any of the factors are causally related to the outcome. Theory and dedicated programs of research are required to identify how correlated variables are influencing the outcome, if at all. Consequently, when one ethnic group is actually more violent than another, then all characteristics that are more common in that ethnic group may appear to be empirical risk factors for violence. To protect against this type of bias, good risk tools should be supported by evidence indicating that they are predicting for the right reasons. For example, a risk tool for youth violence can be justified if it included items that psychology and criminology have identified as plausible risk factors for violence, such as lack of adult supervision, negative attitudes toward authority, and low engagement with education. A youth violence risk tool would be suspect if the indicators were cultural differences in clothing, language, and food even if these factors were reliable, empirical correlates of youth violence.

Empirical risk factors can also be biased by confounded outcome variables. The outcome in criminal recidivism studies, for example, is *detection* for a criminal offense, which is an imperfect indicator of criminal behavior. To the extent that different ethnic groups are more likely to be stopped and questioned by the police, membership in the targeted ethnic group will be an empirical risk factor for (officially recorded) crime, regardless of the actual incidence of criminal behavior. For example, there is evidence of racial bias in police stops in the United States (Pierson et al., 2020). Drivers with dark skin are more likely to be questioned but only during daylight hours. The association between skin tone and the likelihood of a police search disappears after dark.

When the cultural features are correlated with increase rates of crime, there is no purely empirical method for disentangling the features that are, or are not, associated with crime. Theory is required. Theory is a model of what people are like, and, importantly, what we should be like. By identifying *callous disregard for others* as a criminogenic need, evaluators are indicating that it is a change-worthy feature of individuals. Research may indicate that callousness is empirically related to increase risk for crime; however, when evaluators refer to callousness in a risk assessment, they are asserting that callous disregard for others is undesirable. There are any number of factors that are empirically related to crime that are not found on any of the commonly used recidivism risk tools. The reason that skin color or residency in the high north (arctic) are not risk factors on recidivism risk scales is that evaluators do not perceive that there is anything intrinsically wrong with these characteristics. The risk and protective factors included in the various risk scales express social values.

Cultural norms define what good people are supposed to do and rank the seriousness of social transgressions. These values are also built into the items selected for risk assessment tools. Content areas that are perceived as important are given more weight and attention. Content areas that are perceived as less important are given little weight, or no weight at all. These decisions are typically made by small groups of likeminded professionals. Few of the commonly used criminal recidivism risk tools, for example, have benefited from significant input for representatives of groups who have been targets of racism and who are overrepresented in the criminal justice system (e.g., Blacks in the United States; racialized Muslim ethnic groups in France; Indigenous Peoples in Canada, Australia, and New Zealand).

Given the commonalities in human nature, minority groups would be expected to concur that the items in the recidivism risk scales described widely accepted human values, such as lifestyle stability, nonviolent conflict resolution, work, and positive life goals. It is also likely, however, that there are certain values that are important for marginalized groups that are not well represented in the risk and protective factors currently addressed by existing criminal recidivism risk tools. For example, many Indigenous groups place a spiritual value on the land. This value is absent from criminal risk scales. Individuals who have caused massive environmental degradation are rarely subject to criminal code sanctions, if they receive any sanction at all.

Significant consultation with minority groups has the potential of improving risk tools. By listening to the perspective and concerns of the communities, risk tool developers are more likely to craft items that are broadly applicable and less likely to omit risk factors that have high importance for specific cultural groups. Meaningful consultation also supports sound implementation. In practice areas with high consequences (such as criminal justice and child welfare), it is common for marginalized groups to experience risk assessment as yet another form of systemic racism. Members of marginalized groups are more likely to see the merits of risk tools if the items address their values, lived experience, and aspirations. Once culturally specific items are articulated, however, research is still needed to determine whether the proposed risk factors function as intended. No cultural group is immune from bias, blindness, and self-deception.

In summary, culturally unbiased risk tools support the same inferences regardless of the culture of the person assessed. This may or may not imply that the average scores are similar across groups. Systematic differences in the scores of unbiased risk tools indicate real group differences in the constructs the measure was design to assess, not systematic error in the items. When the outcome of interest is more common in one group than another, however, special care is needed to disentangle psychologically meaningful risk factors from variables that could simply be correlates of group membership. Validation for a risk tool for a specific ethnic or cultural group requires more than empirical studies of risk tool with that subgroup. For risk tools used in high-stakes decisions, it also requires meaningful consultation to ensure that the risk tool aligns with the history, current circumstances, and values of that cultural group.

Good Risk Tools Are Comprehensive

The ideal risk assessment would consider all relevant risk and protective factors. This never happens. Risk tools have a finite (manageable) set of items; however, the number of potential influences on human behavior is very large, and changing. The best that evaluators can hope for are risk tools that address the most salient factors. Risk tools typically take years to develop and validate. They are not easily changed. It is relatively easy, in comparison, to conduct research studies that show improvements in predictive accuracy by considering variables not included in the original risk tool. With large enough sample sizes, incremental validity is almost guaranteed (Babchishin et al., 2012b). Consequently, evaluators will commonly be in the uncomfortable position of knowing that an external factor adds information beyond the information provided by a risk tool but not knowing how the external factor should be considered in the overall assessment.

There are several options for addressing this dilemma, none of which are completely satisfactory. Fully integrating the external factor into the risk tool is the most scientifically robust approach; however, it will create a new scale, which would then require its own validation studies. Too slow. Another option is to ignore them. When there are few external factors identified and their effects are small, special adjustments may not be needed; instead, weak external factors would simply be part of the overall error associated with the risk tool. At times, there may be reliable estimates of the magnitude of the incremental effect of the external variable (e.g., a meta-analysis of the incremental regression coefficients, e.g., Brankley et al., 2021). If the incremental effects of the external variable are known, it may be possible to calculate an adjusted score that mechanically combines the findings of the risk tool with the external variable.

But what if the external factors are not weak? Paul Meehl (1954), in *Clinical Versus Statistical Prediction*, introduced the concept of *broken legs* in actuarial prediction. Meehl's thought experiment concerned the question of whether Professor A will attend the movies on a particular Friday night. When the professor's previous behavior is subjected to time-series analysis, the actuarial prediction indicates a 90% probability that he will go to the neighborhood theater as usual this Friday. But what if the evaluator also knows that Professor A has recently broken his leg? "This single fact is sufficient to change the probability of .90 to a probability of approximately zero" (Meehl, 1954, p. 25). Broken legs in actuarial prediction are obviously consequential factors that are too rare to be included in the actuarial prediction scheme. Although the likelihood of a broken leg is small, there are a large number of rare and potentially consequential events (e.g., spouse leaves, global pandemic). Collectively, these rare events add up to a nontrivial likelihood that something out of the ordinary could interfere with an actuarial prediction.

The potential for broken legs has motivated research on professional overrides of actuarial risk tools. In the domain of crime and violence, the results have been clear. When evaluators are permitted to adjust actuarial predictions based on factors that are not specified in advance, the adjustments degrade predictive accuracy (Cohen et al., 2020; Duwe & Rocque, 2018; Gore, 2007; Hanson et al., 2015; Schmidt et al., 2016; Storey et al., 2012; Wormith et al., 2012; see also my earlier review, Hanson & Morton-Bourgon, 2009). When asked about the basis for their overrides, rarely do evaluators identify factors that correspond to Meehl's broken leg. Instead, they are likely to identify factors that are already included in the risk tool (e.g., a long criminal history), or factors that appear problematic (or helpful) but are not supported by recidivism research (e.g., denial, remorse).

In the Dynamic Supervision Project (DSP), we trained probation officers to monitor ongoing changes in recidivism risk levels using a brief rating scale, the ACUTE-2000 (149 officers submitted 7,050 ratings for 744 adult males supervised for a sexual offense; Babchishin & Hanson, 2020; Hanson et al., 2007). The ACUTE-2000 included seven items specified in advance (e.g., sexual preoccupations, substance misuse, victim access, lack of cooperation with supervision), as well as the option to add one other risk factor, which could be a unique concern for that individual's supervision (e.g., visits from ex-spouse). We thought that it was impossible to fully describe individuals' current psychological and community adjustment using just seven items; consequently, we wanted officers to identify significant, neglected factors using their professional judgment, just as they have been doing for all risk factors before the DSP training. The use of unique factors was popular, being used in 75% of the assessments. They were, however, unrelated to recidivism. Consequently, the unique factor item was dropped from the revised version of the measure (ACUTE-2007; Fernandez et al., 2015).

Despite the difficulties, I nevertheless encourage evaluators to consider external risk factors when using actuarial risk tools. No finite risk tool can measure all relevant factors. Furthermore, the scoring of the risk tool is not an assessment. Evaluators must consider (a) the extent to which the case at hand fits within the risk tool's sampling frame (see next section), (b) if there are obvious conditions that nullify the actuarial prediction (broken legs), and (c) how well the inferences implied by the risk scale score are supported by research evidence and the particulars of the specific case. Such judgments can be difficult; however, they are easier when the prediction tool has research evidence that there are few (if any) external factors, and their incremental effect is small. For an override to be justified, the external factors need to be obvious and consequential (broken leg). Avoid adjusting actuarial risk estimates based on variables similar to those already considered in the development of the actuarial tool.

A related concern is that evaluators need to make a judgement concerning the extent to which the risk tool speaks to the assessment question of interest. For example, the decision threshold may involve the lifetime rates of violent sexual recidivism whereas the prediction tool may only present 10-year rates for any sexual recidivism (i.e., sexual recidivism includes nonviolent sexual offenses, such as possession of child sexual exploitation images, that are outside the offenses specified in statute). In all cases, evaluators should be aware of potential gaps between the evidence supporting a risk tool and the assessment questions and then decide how best to link the evidence to the decision required for the case at hand.

Risk Tools Should Apply to the Population and Outcome of Interest

The field of psychological assessment has long been concerned with the representativeness of norms. Most psychological tests are norm referenced—that is, the primary meaning of the scores concerns relative placement on a latent dimension. For example, intelligence is a latent construct that is assessed by specialized tests. Intelligence tests results are typically presented as IQ scores with a mean of 100 and standard deviation of 15. Given this common metric, an IQ score of 115 is instantly recognizable as being one standard deviation above the mean. But what mean? The average performance on IQ tests vary across countries, sociodemographic factors, and time (e.g., the Flynn effect; Flynn, 2007). Consequently, the interpretation of psychological test results requires understanding the samples on which the numbers are based.

Prediction tools are criterion-reference measures—that is, their primary meaning concerns the likelihood of the outcome. Although scores on predictions tools can be used to infer placement on latent dimensions (see Chapter 16, "Percentiles"), that is not their primary purpose. Like norm-referenced measures, the interpretation of criterion reference measures also requires attention to their normative samples. The composition of the normative samples, or sampling frames, can influence both discrimination (how much the risk tool is related to the outcome) and calibration (the likelihood of the outcome) of prediction tools. For example, a diagnosis of schizophrenia is positively correlated with violence in the general population (Fazel et al., 2009) but negatively correlated with violent recidivism within forensic mental health populations (Harris, Rice, et al., 2015; Monahan, 2021). Consequently, if a violence risk tool contains a schizophrenia item, it would have a positive, negative, or zero weight depending on the composition of the risk tool's reference group. Risk factors that have opposite effects in different samples are, fortunately, rare. Poor calibration, however, is common. Given that risk tools never measure all relevant risk factors, samples that are preselected to be high risk are likely to have higher rates of the outcome, even after controlling for risk scale scores (Hanson, Thornton, et al., 2016).

Within psychology, norms for assessment measures are either based on representative samples of the general population (e.g., IQ tests, some personality measures), or samples from the settings in which the measure is likely to be used (e.g., criminal recidivism risk tools, Graduate Record Examinations; see Joint Committee, 2014). Although both sampling strategies have their merits, they address different questions and can generate very different norms.

One benefit of the defining the reference group in terms of the full population is that there is only one full population (e.g., adult women in the United States); furthermore, full populations are expected to change slowly on the latent constructs of interest (e.g., conscientiousness). In contrast, norms based on specific practice settings must consider the extent to which the individuals assessed at these settings have been preselected in different ways. It is not uncommon for certain practice settings to deliberately select cases that vary on the construct of interest (e.g., the average level of adaptive functioning is higher in outpatient psychotherapy practices than in secure, forensic hospitals).

Evaluators also need to consider the extent to which the outcome criteria align with the questions of interest. For example, if the referral question concerns the risk for intimate partner violence, how much consideration should be given to a risk tool that assesses general criminal recidivism? The extent to which risk tools inform the likelihood of different outcomes will vary across domains. In the criminal justice domain, there are common risk factors that are related to all types of crime (e.g., Andrews & Bonta's, 2010, central eight) as well as specific factors for specific offenses (e.g., arson, Edwards & Grace, 2014; sexual offending against children, Whitaker et al., 2008; intimate partner violence, Hilton, 2021). My colleague David Thornton has suggested that it is possible to create a recidivism risk tool for any specific outcome (e.g., fraud, prostitution) by using only three items: (a) the number of prior offenses for that specific type of crime, (b) the number of total prior offenses for anything, and (c) young age.

Variability in the outcome may not involve a difference in kind; instead, outcome criteria can be more or less inclusiveness. For example, in criminal recidivism studies, any subsequent arrest is a more inclusive outcome criterion than any new conviction. Variation in the inclusiveness of the outcome criteria will obviously influence calibration, but it may not influence discrimination. When the different outcome criteria track the same latent construct, analyses using appropriate discrimination statistics (e.g., AUC, Cohen's *d*) should be reasonably consistent across samples and settings, despite poor calibration (i.e., the rate of the outcome per risk level would not be consistent).

Mindful of the foregoing issues, evaluators considering using a prediction tool must decide if is fit-for-purpose. This will be a professional judgment, guided by the referral questions, the case at hand, and the available documentation for the risk tool (scoring guides, user manuals, research reports, etc.). Decisions concerning the degree of fit are made easier when the risk tool's documentation specifies the types of cases for which it is intended. This will likely involve a core group for which it is most suited, as well as secondary groups for which it may be used "with caution" or only for selected inferences (e.g., relative risk placements but not absolute risk). Similarly, it is useful for evaluators to know the latent constructs that risk tool is intended to predict, as well as a range of potential indicators of this construct. For recidivism risk tools, for example, the latent construct could be the propensity to commit crime and the indicators could be self-report, peer reports, cheating in controlled settings, and officially recorded charges or convictions. Decisions concerning fit are easiest when the inferences from the risk tool are supported by a well-developed and advancing program of research and when the inferences are robust across samples and settings.

Simple Is Good

Risk tools that are simple and inexpensive are more likely to be used, and to be used appropriately, than complex tools. Complexity can be introduced in many ways. The items can be more or less difficult to understand, the information needed to score the items may be harder or easier to obtain, and the requisite skill of the evaluators can vary from basic conscientiousness to advanced, specialized expertise. In terms of parsimony, the ideal risk tool would use clearly defined items that are easily scored from commonly available information. These items would then be combined into an overall evaluation using a straightforward, mechanical procedure. This ideal of parsimony, however, must face the complexity of the real world. All risk tools are simplifications of nature, and none address all potentially relevant risk factors. Consequently, the best that risk tools developers can strive for is to limit unnecessary complications.

My most popular risk tool is the Static-99 (Hanson & Thornton, 1999, 2000), now in its slightly revised form, Static-99R (Helmus, Thornton, et al., 2012). It is an actuarial risk tool designed to assess the likelihood of sexual recidivism among adult males with a history of sexual offending based on commonly available criminal history and demographic information. Although its predictive accuracy is no better than other measures (Hanson & Morton-Bourgon, 2009), it is by far the most commonly used sexual recidivism risk tool in the world (Bourgon et al., 2018; Kelley et al., 2020; Neal & Grisso, 2014). Its simplicity has contributed to its popularity. It has 10 items addressing objective characteristics such as the individual's age, the number of prior sexual offenses (based on official records), the characteristics of sexual offense victims (unrelated, males), and whether the individual has been convicted for a violent offense. Each item is given a weight (mostly zeros or ones), which are then summed into a total score.

Implementing such a seemingly simple risk tool, however, has turned out to be not that simple. The original Static-99 coding rules were only two and a half pages long (Hanson & Thornton, 1999). The most recent version is 104 pages (Phenix et al., 2017) plus a 49-page evaluators' workbook (Phenix et al., 2016). The training expanded from a couple of hours to a full day or more. Although we, the Static Development Team, have always aspired to limit complexity, the expansion of the coding rules was driven by a steady stream of questions from evaluators concerned with how to score specific cases: Does Static-99 apply to a transgendered individual who sexually offended as a male but now identifies as female? Are first cousins related? Should evaluators count victim characteristics when the victim is a farm animal? roadkill? Real-world complexity required us to add increased precision to the coding rules, based on our developing understanding of what the original items were intended to measure and why they should be related to the persistence of sexual crime. We perceived the updates and expansion of the coding rules as necessary; however, we are also very much aware that the added complexity makes Static-99R harder to use.

Another advantage of simplicity is that simple tools are more robust than complex tools to implementation challenges. Consider the following example. In the Dynamic Supervision Project, we trained more than 1,000 community supervision officers to score Static-99 and two new risk tools, one of which was STABLE-2000 (Hanson et al., 2007, 2015). STABLE-2000 was considerably more complex than Static-99, requiring a structured interview and inferences concerning the presence of risk-relevant psychological problems (e.g., hostility toward women, deviant sexual interests, lack of concern for others). Officers participating in the project were asked to complete a number of forms; however, data were frequently incomplete. A significant number of the trainees submitted no data at all, and half of the cases that were submitted had missing information. The lack of full cooperation and diligence from all volunteers is no surprise in field studies. What we did not expect, however, was the extent to which the data submitted by the fully cooperative officers demonstrated greater predictive accuracy than the data from incomplete cases. For STABLE-2000, the AUC value was a respectable .73 for the complete cases, whereas it was a dismal .56 (not significantly above chance) for the incomplete cases. Static-99R also demonstrated lower predictive accuracy among the incomplete cases (AUC = .68) than the complete cases (AUC = .80). Even among the incomplete cases, however, Static-99R scores still showed a moderate level of predictive accuracy, similar to the averages observed for other recidivism risk tools. Whereas STABLE-2000 was only related to recidivism when scored by the cooperative, conscientious officers, the simpler Static-99R worked at least adequately for all users.

CONCLUDING COMMENT

The quantity and quality of the scientific evidence necessary to inform applied decisions increase as the state of knowledge matures. The significance of a study depends on what is already known. In the early stages of knowledge development, minimal evidence may be helpful to evaluators because it provides some guidance, even if imperfect. As knowledge develops, higher levels of scientific rigor (e.g., larger samples sizes, better measurement) are required to revise or replace positions supported by previous research. The influence of scientific evidence on applied practice will also depend on the extent to which the new evidence is congruent or incongruent with our a priori expectations, biases, and assumptions. If something is commonly believed and, upon reflection, there are reasonable grounds to believe it to be true, then relatively little new scientific evidence is required before acting on those beliefs. In contrast, higher standards of scientific evidence are needed before considering propositions that appear, at first impression, to be implausible. This feature of human cognition facilitates decision-making while reinforcing our biases. Consequently, prudent readers strive to be aware of their own biases when judging the quality of research evidence, and make special efforts to seriously consider findings and narratives that are contrary to their deeply held beliefs. In 1876, Charles Darwin (1887) credited his scientific success, in part, to his long-standing habit of

> whenever a published fact, a new observation or thought came across me, which was opposed to my general results, to make a memorandum of it without fail and at once: for I had found by experience that such facts and thoughts were far more apt to escape from the memory than favourable ones. (p. 36)

May we follow his example.

18

Standardizing Risk Communication

The focus of this book has been on the numeric information contained in risk prediction tools, and the statistics used to describe their predictive accuracy. This chapter discusses options for communicating their results. Whereas there are established conventions for describing scores on norm-referenced tests, there are no such conventions for describing the results of criterion-referenced prediction tools. Both evaluators and decision makers favor named levels, such as *low, moderate,* and *high* (Grann & Pallvik, 2002; Heilbrun et al., 2000, 2004). The difficulty is that these terms do not have established meanings; consequently, there is considerable opportunity for risk communication to result in miscommunication. I and my colleagues having been working toward a common language for risk communication in corrections and forensic mental health (Hanson, Babchishin, et al., 2017; Hanson, Bourgon, et al., 2017; Kroner & Derrick, 2020). Although these standardized risk levels have attracted the attention of certain researchers and test developers (Davies et al., 2020; Kroner et al., 2020, Olver et al., 2018), this work is far from complete (Davies et al., 2020; Hogan, 2020). Furthermore, the risk levels useful for describing criminal recidivism risk cannot be expected to generalize to other psychological prediction tasks, such as estimating the likelihood of school success, the onset of psychosis, or recovery from depression. Nevertheless, our struggle with a common language for criminal recidivism risk has identified certain principles that may be helpful to psychologists considering how best to communicate the results of other types of prediction tools.

https://doi.org/10.1037/0000275-018
Prediction Statistics for Psychological Assessment, by R. K. Hanson

The interpretation of norm-referenced tests is largely based on the unusualness of the scores. Common scores are considered normal or unproblematic; extreme scores are worthy of special attention or concern. Although the definition of *unusual* varies, many norm-referenced tests label values that are one or two standard deviation away from the mean to be clinically significant (16th or 2nd percentile). The interpretation of extreme scores of norm-referenced personality tests, however, is not simply that the scores are uncommon or statistically rare. For measures of psychopathology, extreme scores carry an inference of dysfunction. With ability tests, unusually high scores indicate special abilities (e.g., gifted), whereas unusually low scores indicate deficits.

Although it is possible to use percentile ranks to communicate the results of prediction tools, relatively placement in a population is not what prediction tools are designed to assess (see Chapter 16). Instead, prediction tools are intended to assess relative risk (how much riskier is Mr. Jones compared with Mr. Singh?) and absolute likelihoods (what proportion of individuals like Mr. Singh are expected to how the outcome?). Risk communication also may indicate a recommended course of action.

One of my professional activities has been the development and maintenance of the Static-99 risk tool (Hanson & Thornton, 1999). It is an empirical actuarial measure, with sexual recidivism rates associated with specific scores. The original Static-99 had four risk levels: *low*, *moderate-low*, *moderate-high*, and *high*. The 1999 recidivism rate norms were estimated using life-table survival analysis on an aggregated data from three samples ($N = 1{,}086$). The Static-99 was quickly adopted and used for applied decisions concerning the likelihood that individuals with a sexual offending history would reoffend. In several jurisdictions, decision thresholds were explicitly defined in terms of Static-99 scores. For example, individuals who had scores of 4 or higher may be considered for postsentence civil commitment, whereas cases with a 3 or lower would not.

As research on the Static-99 continued, it became obvious that the original norms needed updating. The 1999 norms did not replicate in larger and more recent samples of routine or complete cases. With new samples and more precise statistical techniques, the observed recidivism rates were lower overall than the original estimates (Helmus, 2009) and were particularly lower for a score of 4 (Doren, 2004). We, the STATIC Development Team, also observed that recidivism rates were lower than expected for older individuals (e.g., age 50+; Hanson, 2006). On the basis of these findings, the Static-99 age weights were revised, creating Static-99R (Helmus, Thornton, et al., 2012). We then updated the recidivism rate estimates using 21 new samples ($N = 8{,}805$; Hanson, Thornton, et al., 2016).

As an empirically derived prediction tool, updating the Static-99/R recidivism rate estimates presented no conceptual challenges. The findings from bigger, newer, and more representative samples should be privileged over the findings from older, less representative samples. In contrast, it was not obvious what we should do with the risk levels. Given that the recidivism rates per score had changed, should we keep the same labels for the same scores but change the interpretive inferences? Could we change the score thresholds to preserve the interpretive inferences of the previous levels? Should we create entirely new risk levels, and, if so, on what basis? Should we abandon risk levels entirely, and direct evaluators to report only quantitative indicators, such as percentile ranks and estimated recidivism rates? Importantly, what should we recommend to jurisdictions that had already enshrined specific Static-99 scores in policy or legislation? As we pondered these questions, we realized that the original risk labels lacked scientific justification. As I was the one who had assigned the original labels, it was troubling that I did not know what they meant.

Following Wittgenstein (1976), the meanings of words are based on how they are used in language. Wittgenstein employed the example of a builder and an assistant. The builder can effectively communicate with the assistant by single words, such as *brick*, *slab*, or *pillar*. When the builder wants more materials, yelling "slab" tells the assistant to deliver a slab. Wittgenstein referred to the structure involving the words and the actions into which they are woven as a *language-game* (Wittgenstein, 1976, Section 8). In the same way, the meaning of the risk-level labels must be understood within the language-game that they are embedded.

One of my first jobs after graduation involved completing psychological assessments for presentence reports. Judges requested the reports because they wanted some guidance concerning the appropriate sentence for the individuals found guilty of certain types of offenses (typically, sexual crimes or violence against intimate partners). In most cases, the decision was between a short custodial sentence (less than 2 years), several years of community supervision, or both. Given the conventions of that setting, however, neither the psychologist nor the probation officer responsible for the presentence report were permitted to make direct recommendations to the judge. Recommendations were made, nonetheless. A psychologist's recommendation for a community sentence could be worded as "Mr. Sinclair is low risk to reoffend and, should he receive a community sentence, I would be available to see him." Conversely, judges would interpret "Ms. Sinclair has multiple needs that are unlikely to respond to outpatient counseling" as a recommendation for a custodial sentence.

Although I never conducted the research study, my impression was that there were few misunderstandings among the judges, psychologists, and probation officers at this setting. After being socialized into local practice, each professional understood the rules of the language-game. Similarly, a large number of specific professional communities use labels such as *low risk* and *high risk* to effectively communicate recommendations to decision makers. For example, the risk levels for many of the structured professional judgment violence risk measures (e.g., Sexual Violence Risk—20 [Boer et al., 1997], Spousal Assault Risk Assessment Guide—Version 3 [Kropp & Hart, 2015], Historical Clinical Risk Management—20, Version 3 [HCR-20^{V3}; Douglas et al., 2013]) are explicitly recommendations concerning the degree of supervision and intervention required and are likely interpreted as such in the local settings in which they are used.

Locally defined risk levels, however, present two types of challenges. The first is that local definitions are easily misunderstood by individuals who are not socialized into the same language-game. Hilton et al. (2008), for example, found that professionals inferred widely different recidivism rates from the same risk labels (see also Batastini et al., 2019; Krauss et al., 2018). This variation was even found for professional working in the same practice setting. The second problem is that locally defined risk levels inhibit the development of cumulative knowledge. For example, Andrews et al.'s (1990; Andrews & Bonta, 2010) risk/need/responsivity (RNR) model of correctional rehabilitation stipulates that those individuals who are most likely to reoffend should be provided with the most intervention. The *risk* principle seems reasonable and has some research support (Andrews & Bonta, 2010, Table 11.1.1). The practical question, however, is what level of intervention is needed for what level of risk? This is difficult to answer from the available research studies because the studies use diverse methods for assigning risk levels, with unknown concordance. A meta-analysis of research on the *risk* principle would need to first harmonize the findings using a standardized definition of risk.

Standardization does not happen by fiat. Communities adopt standards when they are better than the alternatives. One of the most ambitious programs of standardization was that which created the metric system shortly after the French Revolution (1789; Alder, 2002). In the previous system, the king and nobles had full authority to determine the size of weights and measures. A pound of bread was the size the local duke said it was. A laborer might be entitled to 10 pounds of bread, and 10 pounds would be given. However, the 10 pounds of bread could be more or less depending on the decrees of the duke. The postrevolutionary government considered these decrees to be arbitrary and abusive; in their place, they advanced weights and measures based on universal features of nature and represented these units in multiples of 10 with decimals. Although the metric system has become the universal standard of science and is now the official system in all countries (except the United States, Myanmar [Burma], and Liberia), not all metric units caught on. Few people ever used metric clocks (100 seconds to the minute, 100 minutes to the hour) nor metric calendars (10 days to the week). Even in officially metric countries, local units are still widely used (e.g., the English still measure their weight in stone; Canadian retailers sell building materials in feet and inches). Nevertheless, metric measures were widely adopted because they facilitated trade, increased the consistency of scientific observation, and permit advanced engineering. Imagine building a railway when each construction trade used different, subjective units of measurement. Now imagine applying Andrews et al.'s (1990) risk principle when each evaluator uses different, subjective units of risk.

To standardize language for risk communication, there must also be consensus on what it is that is being assessed. This requires a model of the features and processes that result in the outcome of interest. The first decision is whether risk classifications are better described as categories or a dimension. A categorical classification assumes that there are distinct groups in nature (taxon). The dimensional approach assumes that risk is a matter of degree; although risk tools may assign cases to levels or bins, the boundaries of the risk levels are for convenience, not because they carve nature at its joints. Given that most psychological variables are well represented as dimensions (Haslam et al., 2020), the default model should be that the information assessed by prediction tools is also dimensional. Theory and evidence are required to assert taxonic structure, which should be supported by the types of empirical analyses described by Haslam and Ruscio (Ruscio et al., 2006, 2018).

ABSOLUTE RATES

Of the various quantitative information implied by prediction tools, perhaps the most useful are absolute likelihoods (i.e., the proportion of cases with a specific risk profile expected to have the outcome within a specific time period). Many applied decisions can be framed as balancing the likelihood of the outcome with the costs and benefits of interventions (e.g., Rice & Harris, 1995). Although cost–benefit utility functions are rarely used in applied practice, it is not uncommon for decision thresholds to be linked to rates (e.g., involuntary civil commitment if the risk of harm to self or others is 20% or more during the next month). Consequently, there are some prediction tools that eschew labels entirely in favour of numeric likelihoods as the only output (Duwe & Freske, 2012; Howard & Dixon, 2012; Matheny et al., 2005).

Although the intentions of legislators are rarely transparent, I suspect that they focused on absolute recidivism rates when determining which Static-99 scores to enshrine in statute. If their decisions were based on absolute recidivism rates, then the Static-99 scores in statutes would need to be revised when the Static-99/R recidivism rate estimates are updated. For example, if the decision threshold for *high risk* was a Static-99R score of 4, this would correspond to an expected 5-year sexual recidivism rate of 26% in the original norms (Hanson & Thornton, 1999, 2000). In the 2016 update, a 26% recidivism rate corresponds to Static-99R scores of 6 or 7 (Phenix et al., 2016). Changing the decision threshold from 4 to 6 would conserve the same absolute risk level but reduce the number of individuals deemed high risk.

One problem with absolute recidivism rates is that, without further guidance, they can be difficult to interpret. One of my colleagues, Daryl Kroner, spent many years conducting risk assessments for parole board decisions. Concerned with the arbitrary nature of risk category labels, Dr. Kroner began to report violence risk estimates in purely numerical terms (e.g., a typical individual at this risk level, released in this jurisdiction, has a 26% likelihood of being convicted of a violent offense within 5 years). This practice was short-lived. Almost immediately, the parole board members came back with questions concerning whether 26% was *low, moderate,* or *high*.

In natural language, we commonly use words such as low, moderate, and high when describing the chances that a particular outcome will occur. There is no absolute correspondence, however, between these qualitative indicators and quantitative indicators. Nor should there be. A 10% chance of rain is low, whereas a 10% chance of your brakes failing is very high. Within our language-games (à la Wittgenstein), the names that describe risk levels are the justifications for actions, value judgments, and planning decisions. Low likelihoods may indicate high risk if the consequences are serious.

Another difficulty with absolute rates is that they are difficult to empirically estimate. The rates of the outcome will vary with follow-up time, outcome criteria, and cohort effects and by other factors that are not fully understood (Hanson, Thornton, et al., 2016; Helmus, Hanson, et al., 2012; Matheny et al., 2005).

RISK RATIOS

In contrast to absolute rates, relative risk is often remarkably consistent across samples and settings. Consequently, risk level labels could be aligned with relative risk indicators, such as rate ratios, odds ratios (see Chapter 7), or hazard ratios (Chapter 10). For example, the Risk Matrix-2000/Sex is an empirical actuarial risk tool for sexual recidivism with four risk categories: *low, moderate, high,* and *very high.* An increase in one Risk-Matrix level (e.g., from *low* to *moderate*) is associated with a doubling of the recidivism rate (e.g., from 4.4% to 10% after 5 years; Lehmann et al., 2016). Risk ratios are widely used in the communication of medical- and health-related risk (e.g., you can cut your risk of diabetes in half if you exercise regularly).

Unlike percentiles, there are no conventions within psychology for describing the magnitudes of risk ratios. One potential reference point would be Cohen's (1988) conventions for effects size, which, expressed as odds ratios would be 1.4, 2.3, and 3.7 for small, medium, and large differences, respectively (using Sánchez-Meca et al.'s [2003] conversion formula). It may be reasonable, for example, to consider risk ratios of less than 1.4 to be similar, risk ratios between 1.4 and 3.7 to indicate *elevated risk,* and risk ratios of 3.8 or more to indicate *highly elevated risk.* The most useful labels, however, will vary with the decision context and the base rate of the outcome. With small base rates, larger risk ratios would be required to justify action than if the base rates are high. For example, if the base rate was 1%, a fourfold increase in risk would still only indicate a 4% chance of the outcome (96% would not have the outcome even if the risk factor was present). In contrast, if the base rate was 40%, an increase to 60% (a rate ratio of 1.5) could be cause for concern. Consequently, it is often useful to supplement risk ratios with risk differences, that is, the difference between the proportions with and without the predictor (see Fleiss & Berlin, 2009).

An additional consideration is that risk ratios require a comparison group. If informed that a risk factor doubles the likelihood of the outcome, the first question should be "compared with what?" For risk prediction tools, there are several comparison groups that could be used. One type of comparison group would comprise cases that are considered normal or nonproblematic.

The risk in this group would be greater than zero but too small to justify special measures or interventions. For example, a risk tool that estimates the likelihood of first-episode psychosis could use the base rate of psychosis in the general population in statements such as the following: "Based on the prediction tool, Ms. Ellis's risk for having a psychotic episode during the next 10 years is 5 times higher than that of the general population of women her age." For low base rate outcomes, it would be important to also specify the base rate; otherwise, the persons reading the report are apt to overestimate the absolute likelihood (Akobeng, 2008).

Another comparison group would be individuals in the middle of the risk distribution. This approach can be helpful for risk tools designed for preselected samples, none of whom may be unproblematic. For example, the Static-99R and Static-2002R sexual recidivism risk tools include risk ratios for adult males with a history of sexual offending (Phenix et al., 2016). The risk ratios (calculated from Cox regression) compare the relative risk of sexual recidivism to that of individuals in the middle of the risk distribution (defined as the median). For example, individuals with a Static-2002R score of −1 could be described as having a risk for sexual recidivism that is approximately one quarter (0.28) the rate of individuals in the middle of the distribution (Static-2002R score of 3).

When there is a threshold defined by policy or practice, another option would be to use that threshold for risk ratio calculations. For example, a jurisdiction may have a law permitting civil commitment of individuals with major mental illness and a substantial likelihood of harm to self or other. On the basis of research and a series of legal decisions, substantial likelihood of harm to self may have been operationalized as a 20% chance of requiring medical treatment for self-inflected injuries within 30 days. If a risk tool indicated that the individual had a 10% likelihood of self-harm within 30 days, the individual's risk could be described as only one half of the risk level stipulated in statute. If the individual was assessed being more likely than not to self-harm (50% or more), then the individual's risk would be 2.5 times higher than the minimum (as a rate ratio: .50/.20 = 2.50), or 4 times higher ([.50/.50]/[.20/.80] = 4.0) when expressed as an odds ratio.

PERCENTILES

As discussed in Chapter 16, the most popular method of describing the results of psychological assessments are based on percentiles, or the relative position of the score in a reference population. Although most suited to norm-referenced measures, percentiles are, nonetheless, useful for interpreting and communicating the results of prediction tools. Returning to the question of whether a violent recidivism rate of 26% was *low*, *moderate*, or *high*, Dr. Kroner could have responded that 56% of the normative sample had scores of this level or lower (Violence Risk Appraisal Guide—Revised score of 3; see Harris, Rice, et al., 2015, Tables C.1 and C.2). In other words, this level of violence recidivism risk is common in forensic and correctional samples. Percentile ranks does not directly answer the question of whether a violent recidivism rate of 26% is low, moderate, or high. It does, however, provide the parole board members with additional information that they can use in their decision. The percentile for this case indicates that whatever is appropriate for the typical individual in the middle of the risk distribution would also be appropriate for the case at hand.

PSYCHOLOGICALLY MEANINGFUL RISK LEVELS

Another option is to define risk level that have construct validity—that is, risk level placement would imply a theoretically coherent set of associated features (Cronbach & Meehl, 1955). In practice, quantitative indicators such as rate ratios, absolute rates, and percentiles are often reliably associated with psychologically meaningful characteristics (Blais et al., in press; Hanson, Babchishin, et al., 2017). These features can include antecedents, current psychological and community functioning, and prognosis. By using psychologically meaningful risk levels, evaluators can communicate the types of problems the individual is expected to have and, potentially, what could be done about them.

One set of risk levels that aspire to construct validity are those we developed with the Justice Center of the U.S. Council of State Government with assistance from Public Safety Canada (Hanson, Bourgon, et al., 2017; Kroner & Derrick, 2020; Kroner et al., 2020). These risk levels were motivated by practical concerns with implementing the RNR model in U.S. corrections (Andrews et al., 1990). If a state wanted to follow the risk principle (provide increased supervision and services to high-risk cases), a decision threshold for *high risk* was needed. Determining what constituted high risk was complicated by the use of 47 jurisdiction specific recidivism risk tools across the United States, each with its own thresholds and risk-level labels (e.g., Illinois Risk Assessment Instrument; Illinois Risks, Assets and Needs Assessment Tool; Indiana Risk Assessment System; Iowa Board of Parole Risk Assessment; Desmarais & Singh, 2013, Appendix A). In one particular state, individuals could change risk level when they moved from parole to probation simply because the risk tool used by parole officers was different from that used by probation officers.

In the RNR model, criminal recidivism risk is considered an individual difference variable in the propensity to commit crime. Although it is conceptualized as a continuous dimension, different correctional responses are recommended for individuals at different points on this continuum. The Justice Center's classification system proposes five levels, which are aligned with the actions typically available to correctional systems. At the lowest level (Level I), no correctional response is needed because the individual's recidivism risk is already no different from that of the general population. At the highest level (Level V), individuals are virtually certain to reoffend unless they are closely supervised or detained in secure facilities. Each of the five levels is associated with an expected profile of criminogenic needs and strengths, recidivism rates without intervention, recommendations for the amount of supervision and correctional treatment, expected effect of treatment, and prognosis after appropriate correctional response (Hanson, Bourgon, et al., 2017; Appendix A, Table 1). For example, individuals in the middle of the risk distribution (Level III) have recidivism rates between 30% and 49% after 2 years, have multiple criminogenic needs, and are expected to benefit from change-focused community supervision and 100 to 200 hours of rehabilitative programing.

The Justice Center's Five-Level System presents a set of inferences based on evidence and a model of criminal conduct that is closely aligned with the RNR theory of correctional rehabilitation. Although the Five-Level System aspired to be evidence-based, not all of the associated features of the risk levels have strong empirical support. Consequently, the Five-Level System will undoubtedly be revised and updated as research progresses. It is unlikely to disappear. One of its most valuable features is that it is explicitly aligned with recommended correctional responses. Like the builder's assistant who hears "slab," correctional decision makers conversant in the Five Levels will instantly know what to do with an individual assessed as Level III, Level V, or any of the other levels.

Although risk prediction tools are intended to estimate the likelihood of the outcome, they also speak to individual differences in psychologically meaningful risk factors. Individuals with a high likelihood of criminal recidivism, for example, look different from individuals at low risk for recidivism. Consequently, the distinction between criterion-referenced prediction tools and norm-referenced measures is not absolute. A high score on a measure of antisocial personality traits implies high risk of criminal recidivism, just as a high score on a recidivism prediction tool implies unusually high levels of antisocial personality traits. Attention to construct validity can improve all types of psychological assessment, even though narrowly designed to estimate the likelihood of a specific outcome.

COMMUNICATING RISK ASSESSMENTS

The following section provides some recommendations and examples on how risk assessments can be communicated to both decision makers and those assessed. The following guidance is based on reviews of the academic literature on risk communication (mostly in the medical field) and consultations with evaluators and decision makers (mostly in corrections and forensic mental health). There are relatively few constants in the risk communication research, other than different people processes information differently. Some people like numbers, some words, some pictures. The cardinal rule for effective communication is "Know thy audience." It is prudent, however, not to expect high levels of numeracy.

Risk assessments usually address four topics: (a) the particulars of the case at hand, (b) the risk assessment procedure, (c) the outcome of the risk assessment (e.g., levels, rates, relative risk), and (d) recommendations for action. The degree to which each of these topics is elaborated depends on the setting. In many correctional settings, risk assessments follow a familiar pattern. The risk assessment procedures (e.g., the Level of Service/Case Management Inventory [LS/CMI] risk tool) is the same for all cases, as are the possible risk levels. So, too, are the options for action (e.g., low-, moderate-, or high-intensity community supervision). In such contexts, the reporting of the risk assessment can be short: "Mr. Yang's LS/CMI score placed him in the moderate risk level; consequently, he was assigned to moderate-intensity community supervision (as per Policy Directive AK-047)." The rest of the report would provide sufficient detail to reassure the reader that the risk tool was administered and interpreted correctly; however, there is no need to explain the risk tool, the risk levels, or the resulting policy recommendation. These would be already well known to all parties.

In other contexts, risk assessment reports function as teaching documents. This is particularly true for evaluations made by psychologists for courts and tribunals. When evaluators can choose their risk tools, these choices need to be explained and justified. For certain types of risk assessments (e.g., a threat assessment of a man who stalks celebrities), the primary concern may not be the likelihood of the outcome; instead, the primary concern is what can and should be done to manage the risk. Evaluation reports in this context are useful to the extent that they describe the options and resources available to the individuals who feel threatened.

In addition to whatever is written in risk assessment reports, psychologists can also directly teach the basic of risk assessment to the consumers of the reports. These trainings can be part of informal staff meetings, grand rounds, or other ongoing professional development activities. Briefing notes, research reports, and prerecorded videos can also be used but are less effective than interactive meetings. Communication works best when all parties can talk.

Communicating Base Rates and Likelihoods

The following are some general recommendations when evaluators want to communicate base rates and likelihoods for specific cases:

1. Report likelihoods as a number of people with the outcome from a larger sample of similar people. For example, out of 10 new members of the national track team, six are expected to still be on the team after 2 years.

2. Adjust the denominator according to the frequency of the outcome. For proportions between .10 and .90, a denominator of 10 often works (e.g., six out of 10 new members of the track team are likely to requalify). For rare events, consider using denominators of 100, 1,000, or 100,000 (e.g., the annual incidence of suicide in the United States is between 10 and 15 per 100,000).

3. Keep the same denominator for all comparisons. For example, for individuals like Mr. Bolt, 95 out of 100 are expected to still be on the track team after 2 years. This compares to a rate of 62 out of 100 for all new team members.

4. Report likelihoods for the outcome and for those not having the outcome. For example, out of 10 new members, six would be expected to still be on the team after 2 years; conversely, four out of 10 would not.

5. Use visual displays, such as bar graphs and icon arrays.

To continue this elite sport example, consider that coaches use the Athletic Persistence Prediction Tool (APPT) when recruiting members of the national track team. The prediction tool uses variables related to recent performance, biometrics (e.g., VO_2 max), and psychological stability and drive. Being a team member involves lots of work, low pay, and the faint hope of glory if they are still at the top of their game when the Olympics are held 2 years from now. APPT was developed for coaches to select athletes; however, APPT results are also shared with the athletes to inform the athlete's decision whether to join the team. In this context, the reports may be something like the following:

> The Athletic Persistence Prediction Tool (APPT) was developed to assess the likelihood of sustained elite performance among new members of the national track team. It has moderate predictive accuracy for estimating the likelihood that an individual will remain in elite athletics for a period of 2 years. On average, six out of 10 new members will remain on the team for at least 2 years. Compared with other athletes who qualify for the national track team, the APPT placed Mr. Swift in the low end of the average category. Mr. Swift scored high on psychological stability and drive, average on biometrics, and somewhat below average on recent performance. Out of 10 individuals with APPT scores similar to Mr. Swift, four would be expected to still be on the national team after 2 years; conversely, six out of 10 would not. The APPT does not measure all relevant factors, and Mr. Swift's likelihood of success may be higher or lower based on factors not measured by the APPT.

Relative Risk

The following are recommendations for reporting relative risk metrics, such as rate ratios or odds ratios:

1. Report relative risk as rate ratios or hazard ratios. When relative risk is calculated using odds ratios, convert the odds ratio to a rate ratio using a plausible base rate.

2. Always report base rates when reporting relative risk metrics.

3. Clearly identify the comparison group for the relative risk comparison (e.g., median of a preselected reference group, individuals without the risk factor or condition).

Relative risk metrics are often the most useful when reliable estimates of absolute likelihoods are not available. Nevertheless, it is important to provide some indication of absolute likelihoods (e.g., the expected success rate is between 20% and 40%). Unless grounded in base rates, risk ratios are interpreted as indicating higher likelihoods than they actually do.

Continuing with the hypothetical APPT example, consider that the research on the predictive accuracy of the tool used variable follow-up analyzed with Cox regression survival analysis (not a fixed 2-year follow-up). The primary output of this version of the risk tool were hazard ratios, which are centered on the median scores of new team members. Consequently, the hazard ratios can be interpreted as the relative likelihood of staying on the team compared with the average (median) individual on the team. In this context, the risk report may read something like this:

> The Athletic Persistence Prediction Tool (APPT) was developed to assess the likelihood of sustained elite performance among new members of the national track team. It has moderate predictive accuracy for estimating the likelihood that an individual will remain in elite athletics. On average, just over half will remain on the team for at 2 years or more. Compared with other athletes who qualify for the national track team, the APPT placed Mr. Swift in the low end of the average category. Mr. Swift scored high on psychological stability and drive, average on biometrics, and somewhat below average on recent performance. Overall, his likelihood of remaining on the team is estimated to be approximately two thirds of that of athletes in the middle of the distribution. The APPT does not measure all relevant factors, and Mr. Swift's likelihood of success may be higher or lower based on factors not measured by the APPT.

Percentile Ranks

The following recommendations should be considered when reporting percentile ranks:

1. Specify how the percentile rank was calculated (e.g., proportion below, proportion same or below, midpoint average).
2. Align the form of percentile rank to the referral question. For example, if there was no source of funding for the bottom 20% of an athletics team, the most useful percentiles would indicate the proportion with a lower ranking.
3. If no specific form of percentile is suggested by the referral question, report percentiles as midpoint averages.
4. Clearly specify the normative reference group on which the percentiles are based.

Continuing with the elite sports example, the national track team has a record of APPT scores on all team members for the past 10 years. They routinely collate these scores into updated frequency tables and calculate percentile ranks for the score of each new team members. For Mr. Swift, percentile ranks could be communicated as follows:

> The Athletic Persistence Prediction Tool was developed to assess the likelihood of sustained elite performance among new members of the national track team. Scores range from 1 to 100 with higher scores indicating increased likelihood of remaining in elite athletics. The average score is 74 among athletes who qualify for the national track team (based on a sample of 250 athletes assessed between 2010 and 2020). Most scores (approximately two of three scores) are in the

> range of 56 to 92. Mr. Swift's score was 61, placing him in the low end of the average category. Within a group of 100 new team members, 24 would have a lower score, eight would have the same score, and 68 would have a higher score. Mr. Swift's score is sufficiently high that funding is available should he join the team.

In this example, the standard deviation of scores was 18, which was expressed as two thirds of the scores being between 56 and 92. Consequently, an APPT score of 61 could also be expressed as a *Z*-score of $-.72$ ($[61 - 74]/18 = -.722$).

Communicating Nonquantitative Information

This book is about prediction statistics, and the preceding examples describe how quantitative information can be communicated in applied reports. For some reports, however, the most important information is not expressed in numbers. Instead, the report aspires to make the case comprehensible. Comprehensible, in this context, means providing a way of understanding the individual in question that informs what should happen next (remember Wittgenstein's language-games). This is an art. Somebody once told me that they became a psychologist because they did not have sufficient insight into people to be a novelist.

Psychological portraits (also called case formulations) are often necessary for scoring risk tools (is the individual hostile to women generally or just to his ex-spouse?). Case formulations are also highly valued by decision makers. The types of recommendations for action desired by decision makers, however, almost always go well beyond the evidence available. We may have strong evidence that Mr. Soprano is at high risk for criminal recidivism; in contrast, we may have only limited evidence concerning what types of intervention would be expected to reduce that risk. A further complication is that we may or may not know whether these interventions are even available.

CONCLUSION

The growing use of prediction tools in applied assessments motivates discussion concerning how best to communicate their results. Certain inferences that can be made from criterion-reference prediction tools are different from those made from norm-references tests; consequently, different language is required. Although it would be possible to report results in terms of quantitative indicators, such as risk ratios and absolute recidivism rates, there is a near universal preference for named levels, that is, categories with implications for action. How best to translate quantitative indicators into levels will depend on the context of the assessment and the base rate of the outcome of interest. Applied psychologists who are familiar with the statistics described in this book will be well positioned to shape these language-games of the future.

19

Going Even Further

When you are finished changing, you're finished.

—BENJAMIN FRANKLIN

All of the statistics in this book were based on assessments at Time 1 predicting outcomes at Time 2. This simple design works because there are stable individual differences in risk-relevant characteristics and there are some life trajectories that can be anticipated from initial conditions. Although this research paradigm is informative, it neglects an important and obvious fact: People change. An individual accurately assessed as high risk may defy expectations because the characteristics that initially elevated risk are no longer present. The whole project of applied psychology, psychotherapy, recovery, and healing is grounded in the expectation of deliberate, positive change on risk and protective factors. The past cannot be erased completely: Not everybody starts at the same place, and our choices, experiences, victories, and traumas have enduring consequences. Nevertheless, life is a process of adaptation that never ends until we do. Ongoing assessments of improvements and deterioration are standard practice for psychotherapists, educators, and case managers in corrections and child welfare.

The statistics for assessing change in risk-relevant characteristics, however, are considerably more complicated than those presented in this book. Compared with studies that assess each case only once, the available analytic options increase substantially for studies with multiple assessments. For example, how should data analysts address the correlations between multiple assessments of

https://doi.org/10.1037/0000275-019
Prediction Statistics for Psychological Assessment, by R. K. Hanson

the same individual? How should an individual's history and recent functioning be balanced in an overall assessment of risk? How do we know that any observed changes will endure?

Although the assessment of dynamic change is widely recognized as important, conventions for analyzing and reporting the findings of dynamic prediction studies are still developing. I will, nonetheless, provide some general recommendations for researchers interested in this topic. Warning: Ye who venture forth can expect divergent opinions, technically challenging articles, and the need to learn, or expand your fluency in, statistics and software programs. The journey, however, is worth the effort. Prediction models that include the capacity for change are an uncontroversial advance on models that only consider static, historical variables.

The three main steps required to identify a characteristic as a dynamic (changeable) risk factor are (a) establishing measurement invariance, (b) documenting individual-level change, and (c) demonstrating that updated assessments are more strongly related to the outcome than earlier assessments (dynamic reassessment).

MEASUREMENT INVARIANCE

Measurement invariance means that scores on an assessment measure support the same inferences over repeated administrations and for different groups (e.g., White Native Alaskans compared with Alaska Natives). For dynamic prediction studies, researchers are most concerned with invariance over time. An evaluator using a depression inventory with temporal measurement invariance could use the same cut-score to identify clinically significant symptoms, regardless of whether it was the first or the 15th time that the client had filled out the questionnaire. In contrast, temporal measurement invariance is unlikely in ability or knowledge tests because test-takers learn from previous administrations. Temporal measurement invariance is often considered a prerequisite for the analysis of individual-level change. Without some idea of the expected stability of scores (in the absence of true change), it is hard to determine the extent to which observed change is real (i.e., how much of the observed change should be attributed to change on the latent construct the measure was designed to assess).

The general approach to examining measurement invariance is longitudinal factor analysis (Asparouhov & Muthén, 2009; Chen, 2007; Liu et al., 2017). The measurement invariance analyses examine whether the patterns of scores are the same (invariant) across administrations. There are several features of the data that could be examined, the most important of which are the factor structure and item difficulty. *Factor structure* refers to how the items are related to the latent constructs assessed by the measure (i.e., which items load on which factor). *Item difficulty* refers to how individual differences on the latent construct influence the likelihood of item endorsements.

INDIVIDUAL-LEVEL CHANGE

After establishing that the scores are measuring more or less the same thing over time, the next step is examining the extent to which individuals change. In treatment outcome studies, change is often assessed by comparing posttest scores with pretest scores. Although pretest–posttest analyses can be informative, their interpretation is complicated by regression to the mean effects. Even when the treatment has no effect at all, high scores decline and low scores go up. This is a simple, predictable consequence of measurement error. Disentangling measurement error from true change is much easier when each case is assessed on three or more occasions. A single decline in a high score could be due to measurement error; two declines invite explanation.

The general framework for identifying individual change is *multilevel modeling,* also called *mixed models* or *hierarchical linear models* (Raudenbush & Bryk, 2002; Singer & Willett, 2003). Although these analyses can be conducted with a dichotomous predictor variable, they are most easily interpreted when the (changing) predictor variable is measured on an ordinal or linear scale. One useful feature of multilevel modeling is that assessments do not need to be equally spaced or all at the same times. On the contrary, unequal timing between the assessments will often produce more stable estimates than when all cases are assessed in a small number of discrete waves (provided that there are enough different assessment periods).

This analytic approach is called multilevel modeling because it separates the patterns of individual-level change (Level I) from variables that predict the shape of the individual-level patterns (Level II or higher). For example, physical stamina could be increasing, plateauing, or declining over time for a sample of marathon runners (Level I), and these patterns of individual-level change could be predicted by the characteristics of their diet and training regimes (Level 2). One useful feature of multilevel modeling is that it possible to test whether the variability in individual-level change is more than would be expected by chance. This provides some indication whether it is worth looking for variables that could account for individual differences in trajectories.

DYNAMIC REASSESSMENT

Whether or not measurement invariance has been established, it is still possible to examine whether reassessments improve prediction over earlier or baseline assessments. Measurement invariance is required to determined that individuals have changed. Without measurement invariance, the assessments could mean different things at different times. For example, reassessments could be more accurate than previous assessments because later assessments are based on more complete information or because evaluators have increased competence with their prediction tools. From a purely pragmatic perspective, however, it may not matter. If the most recent assessment is the most accurate, evaluators do not need to disentangle these possibilities to justify using the most recent assessment for decision-making purposes.

Like multilevel modeling, dynamic reassessment studies have increased reliability when there are three or more assessments per case (reduces regression to the mean effects). There is no requirement, however, that the assessments are done at the same time for all cases. Furthermore, the number of assessments can vary across cases. As with other prediction studies, it is assumed that the outcome variable is dichotomous.

My preferred analytic strategy for dynamic reassessment prediction studies is Cox regression with time-dependent covariates (Altman & De Stavola, 1994; Hanson et al., 2020; Singer & Willett, 2003). When the Cox regression model was introduced in Chapter 10, the predictor variables in that chapter were considered static—that is, whatever values of the predictor variables that were initially assigned to the case were assumed to remain unchanged through the follow-up period. In contrast, the time-varying Cox regression model allows the values of the predictor variables to change repeatedly during the follow-up period. For example, consider *degree of physical impairment* as a predictor of returning to work for injured employees. The amount of physical impairment at the time of injury should be a good predictor; however, it should be possible to improve predictive accuracy by considering subsequent assessments of physical impairment. Eventually, as workers recover, the severity of their initial injuries will have less importance than recent assessments of current functioning.

The preceding considerations were intended to help researchers identify whether risk and protective factors function as dynamic predictors. Once dynamic predictors have been identified by research, evaluators still need some method of determining whether the observed changes indicate meaningful change for any specific case (Jacobson et al., 1984). Despite the statistical complexities, the recent criminal recidivism reassessment studies have provided a simple message for practitioners: The most recent assessment is usually the most informative (Babchishin & Hanson, 2020; Davies et al., 2021; Hanson et al., 2020; Lloyd et al., 2020; Wanamaker & Brown, 2021).

CONCLUDING COMMENT

I wrote this book to increase psychologists' capacity to understand the statistics relevant to risk prediction and to appreciate the numeric information that could be used in risk communication. It is primarily addressed to evaluators using prediction tools in applied practice. My hope, however, was that it would also be of interest to evaluators in diverse fields who do not use predictions tools and even to those who object to their use. Constructive participation in debates about the strengths and weaknesses of prediction schemes requires some familiarity with the topics addressed in this book. Consequently, the teaching of prediction statistics is embedded within a broader discussion of the utility of prediction and prediction tools.

Like George Kelly (1963), I believe that we are continually predicting the future: These predictions shape who we are. Some of our predictions are so automatic that we experience them as perception (e.g., expecting the frame of the TV to remain the same but not the images on it). Other predictions are expressed as abstract principles, such as expecting long-term benefits from right conduct. The uncertainty we all experience when our expectations are not fulfilled, however, reminds us of the limitations of our predictive powers. The requirement to critically examine and justify our predictions also arises whenever we disagree with the strongly held expectations of others (e.g., prejudice).

During the past few centuries, we have developed methods for expanding our predictive powers through statistics. This is a major intellectual achievement. The potential of this achievement is still being worked out in diverse areas of human knowledge and concern. In correctional and forensic psychology, the value of prediction statistics is evident in the now-routine use of risk assessment tools for crime and violence. Although debate continues concerning how such risk tools should be constructed and used, there is consensus that prediction statistics can, and should, inform applied practice. Regardless of the approach used, risk assessments gain scientific credentials through evidence. The most important evidence is a replicated association between risk scale scores (or placements) and the likelihood of the outcome. After reading this book, evaluators and decision-makers should understand what that evidence could look like.

Finally, this book contains a lot of hypothetical studies and made-up data. These mock studies are deliberate simplifications of the actual studies conducted in applied settings and published in academic journals. The mock studies were primarily designed to illustrate specific points. My hope, however, is that evaluators interested in evidence-based prediction can use their understanding of these simplified, hypothetical studies to unlock the meaning of real studies relevant to their work. Similarly, professors may be able to accelerate their students' grasp of original research by pairing the analysis of academic articles with one or more of the relevant chapters in this book. A related hope is that students and other researchers will recognize how variations on the hypothetical studies in this book could advance knowledge in their fields of study and then conduct them for real.

APPENDIX

Useful Algebra and Notation

The following are some basic rules of algebra, functions, and conventions for notation, which could be helpful for readers who do not regularly work with formulae.

VARIABLE

A *variable* is a measure or indicator that can take a range of values (not a constant). Variables are often represented by letters. For example, the letter S could be used to represent a set of risk scale scores. It is common for variable names to have subscripts to further identify them. For example, S_o could indicate the risk scale scores for cases with the outcome (o). Sometimes the subscript indicates the number of cases. For example, S_i for $i = 1$ to $i = n$, would indicate risk scale score for n cases. In certain equations, variable names can have two subscripts. For example, S_{ij} could be used to indicate the number of cases ($i = 1, 2, 3, \ldots n$) within G groups ($j = 1, 2, 3 \ldots$ G). A subscript period ($_{.}$) indicates averaging. For example, $S_{.}$ indicates the average of the S values. The symbol $\bar{S}$ could also be used to indicate the average of the S values. $S_{.j}$ would be the average scores within each of G groups (G different values), and $S_{..}$ would indicate the overall average (a single value – the grand mean).

Variables are contrasted with constants, which can also be indicated by letters. For example, the constant e is always approximately 2.7182818 (discussed subsequently), whereas the variable S_o would take different values for different cases. The letters x and y are often used to indicate generic variables (as are the letters a and b).

INEQUALITIES

$x < y$ means that the value of x is less than the value of y. For example, if all psychologists work at multiple jobs, income from the private practice settings (x) will be less than total income (y).

$x \leq y$ means that the value of x is less than or equal to the value of y. If some psychologists work at multiple jobs, then income from private practice (x) will be less than or equal to total income (y).

$x > y$ means that x is greater than y.
$x \geq y$ means x is greater than or equal to y.
$x \neq y$ means that x does not equal y.
$x \approx y$ means that x is approximately equal to y, as in $4.323 \approx 4.3$.

MULTIPLICATION

The following expressions all indicate that 10 is multiplied by 4, and that the answer is 40.

$10 \times 4 = 40$
$10 * 4 = 40$
$10(4) = 40$
$(10)4 = 40$
$a = 10,\ a4 = 40,\ a(4) = 40$
$b = 4,\ 10b = 40,\ (10)(b) = 40$
$a = 10,\ b = 4,\ ab = 40$

The Greek capital pi, Π, is used to indicate that a set of numbers are multiplied together, as in

$$\prod_{i=1}^{5} x_i = (x_1)(x_2)(x_3)(x_4)(x_5)$$

Example, given a set of numbers 2, 3, 1, 1, and 4:

$$\prod_{i=1}^{5} x_i = (2)(3)(1)(1)(4) = 24$$

Tip: When two symbols are adjacent to each other, it usually means that they are multiplied together, for example, $ab = a \times b$, or $5\sqrt{4} = 5 \times 2 = 10$. In certain cases, adjacent symbols do not indicate multiplication. Instead, the adjacent symbols could be an identifier, for example, x_i indicates that there are a number of different x values; specifically, there are i different values of x. Here is another example: in Equation 5.3 the expression $SE(h_t)$ is a single number, the standard error of the hazard at time t. It does not mean SE multiplied by h_t.

DIVISION

The following expressions all indicate that 10 is divided by 5 and that the answer is 2.

$10 \div 5 = 2$
$10/5 = 2$

$$\frac{10}{5} = 2$$

$10 \times 5^{-1} = 2$

$10 \times 1/5 = 2$

$a = 10,\ b = 5,\ a/b = 2$

ORDER OF OPERATIONS

Multiply and divide before addition and subtraction.

$2 \times 3 + 2 \times 5 = 6 + 10 = 16$

Multiplication and division can be done in any order.

$2 \times 3 = 3 \times 2$

$2 \times 3/3 = 6/3 = 2 \times 1 = 2$

Whatever is in brackets is done first.

$2 \times (4 + 1) = 2 \times 5 = 10$

If there are multiple brackets, do the operations in the inner brackets first.

$2 \times ((2 + 1) \times (3 + 2)) = 2 \times (3 \times 5) = 2 \times 15 = 30$

Addition and subtraction can be done in any order.

$10 + 3 - 5 = (10 + 3) - 5 = (10 - 5) + 3 = (3 - 5) + 10 = 8$

Exponents are executed before anything else (except brackets).

$10 \times 3^2 = 10 \times (3 \times 3) = 90$

$(1 + 2)^2 = 3^2 = 3 \times 3 = 9$

One mnemonic for remembering the order of operations is BEDMAS (or PEDMAS), an acronym for brackets (or parentheses), exponents, division/multiplication, addition/subtraction.

SQUARES AND SQUARE ROOTS

A number multiplied by itself is said to be squared. Squaring is indicated by a superscript 2, as in $3^2 = 3 \times 3 = 9$. Square roots are the number that is squared, for example, the square root of 9 is 3. Square roots are typically written as $\sqrt{9} = 3$. Square roots do not have to be integers, for example, $\sqrt{7} = 2.645751311$. Square roots can also be indicated by ½ as a superscript, as is $9^{1/2} = 3$. Squaring a number is the same as raising the number to the power of 2. Taking the square root of a number is the same as raising the number to the power of ½.

When there are operations within a square root sign, complete the operations before taking the square root. For example, $\sqrt{3^2 + 4^2} = \sqrt{9 + 16} = \sqrt{25} = 5$. $\sqrt{a^2 + b^2} \neq \sqrt{a^2} + \sqrt{b^2}$.

Tip: Occasionally, the superscript 2 does not indicate an operation; instead, it is part of the name of a statistic, for example χ^2 (chi-square) and I^2 (I-square).

SUMMATION

The Greek capital epsilon, Σ, is used to indicate that numbers are added together.

$$\sum_{i=1}^{5} x_i = (x_1 + x_2 + x_3 + x_4 + x_5)$$

In other words, the five values of x are added together, as in

$$\sum_{i=1}^{5} x_i = (2+3+1+1+4) = 11$$

In certain tables, Σ is used as a shorthand to indicate that the values presented are the sum of a column.

NOTATION FOR EXPRESSING LIKELIHOODS

Likelihoods are often expressed with the letter p (for probability). These may have a subscript, indicating a set of p values, as is p_i. Conditional probabilities are written as p $(x \mid y)$, which is read as "the likelihood of x given that y is true." For example, p (living to age 94 | current age of 92) is the likelihood of living to age 94 if the individual makes it to 92. This is a bigger number than p (living to age 94), which would be interpreted as the probability of living to age 94 from the time of birth.

Likelihoods are typically expressed as values between zero (impossible) to 1.0 (certainly will happen). Alternately, they are expressed as percentages, for example, there is a 30% chance of rain tomorrow. This is equivalent to saying that the likelihood of rain tomorrow is 0.30.

SIGNIFICANT FIGURES

For decimal or whole numbers, their significant figures are those digits that convey precision of measurement. For example, 4.2 contains two significant figures, as does 0.42, 0.000042, and 42. The value 42,000 could indicate five significant figures if the zeros were real; if the expression was rounded to the nearest thousand, the number 42,000 would indicate only two significant figures. The concept of significant figures is part of scientific notation, such as 4.2×10^3 (forty-two thousand) or 4.2×1^{-1} (0.42).

It is generally good practice to report at least two significant figures in research articles (.0042, not .004). During calculations, it is useful to retain more significant figures that will be reported. For example, if you want to report numbers to two significant figures (e.g., 4.3), uses four or more significant figures in the intermediate calculations ($2.223 + 2.106 = 4.323 \approx 4.3$). My usual practice is to retain as many significant figures as my calculator allows until the final results, at which point I will round to units congruent with the units of measures. Remember that more decimal points may actually communicate less information: Readers are more likely to remember an average age of 22 years than 21.673 years.

LOGARITHMS AND EXPONENTS

Exponents are shorthand for indicating how many times a number is multiplied by itself. Exponents are written as superscripts. For example, 8×8 is the same as 8^2 (eight squared); $4 \times 4 \times 4$ is the same as 4^3 (four cubed). Exponents are also called "powers," for example, 2 to the power of 4 is the same as $2 \times 2 \times 2 \times 2$. Exponents do not have to be whole numbers: $3^{(2.34)} = 13.0757$ (three raised to the power of 2.34 equals 13.0757). Negative exponents indicate the multiplicative inverse or reciprocal: x^{-1} is the same as $1/x$, similarly $x^{-2} = 1/x^2$, and $4^{-2} = 1/16 = 0.0625$. By definition, $x^0 = 1$.

Logarithms are another way of talking about powers and exponents. Logarithms are the exponents that need to be applied to a base number to get the number of interest. For historical and practical reasons, the base numbers are either 10 or *e*. The number *e* is a constant that is approximately equal to 2.7182818 (more about *e* later). For example, given that $10 \times 10 = 10^2 = 100$, the base 10 logarithm for 100 is 2. Logarithms using base *e* are referred to as Napierian (after John Napier [1550–1617]) or natural logarithms. The natural logarithm for 100 is 4.60517 because $(2.7182818)^{(4.60517)} = 100$. Adding two logarithms is the same as multiplication. Subtracting one logarithm from another is the same as division. Before cheap calculators were available, this property of logarithms was the foundation of calculations in science and engineering, including the slide rule I used in my science classes in 1974 (by 1976 everybody was using pocket calculators).

To transform a number to its natural (base *e*) logarithm, use the *ln* function found on many hand calculators (and probably your smart phone), although it is sometimes called *log*. You may need to check which logarithm is which by calculating the logarithm of a number for which you already know the answer, for example, $\log_{(\text{base } 10)} 100 = 2$; $\log_{(\text{base } e)} 100 = 4.60517$. To transform from a natural logged number back to the original metric, take its exponent (again, base of *e*). For example, $\ln(.40) = -.91629$, and $e^{(-.91629)} = 0.40$. On hand calculators, this is often referred to as e^x, $exp(x)$, or the inverse of $\ln x$. All the logarithms in this book are natural logarithms using *e* as the base.

The number *e* may seem like a strange base for logarithms. It is, however, a feature of nature (like π), and the use of *e* simplifies many practical calculations. The number *e* is the basis of the exponential distribution, $y = e^x$, plotted in Figure 1. Another way of writing e^x is *exponent (x)* or *exp (x)*. For example, if x is 1, $y = e^1 = 2.7172818$. If x is 2, $y = e^2 = 7.38906$. Exponential distributions are found whenever the rate of change (i.e., the slope) in the y variable increases as the x values increase. This is common. A classic example is compound interest where the investor gets interest on interest previously paid. If a \$1,000 investment increase at a rate of 5% per year, the investor would be \$50 richer the first year, and \$52.50 richer the second year (5% of [1,000 + 50] = 52.50). As a historical aside, it was a problem of compound interest that led Jacob Bernoulli to first explicitly calculate *e* in 1683. In addition to compound interest, exponential functions describe many patterns in nature including the size and metabolic rate of animals, the number of patents in cities of different sizes, and the income of companies based on their number of employees (West, 2017).

For prediction tools, logistic functions are more important than exponential functions. The logistic function is a type of exponential function that includes a limit to growth. As the x values in exponential functions increase, the y values just keep getting bigger. In contrast, nature often imposes limits to growth. For example, the population of eagles may increase exponentially with the number of lemmings, but, at some point, the overall environment can no

FIGURE 1. The Exponential Distribution $y = e^x$

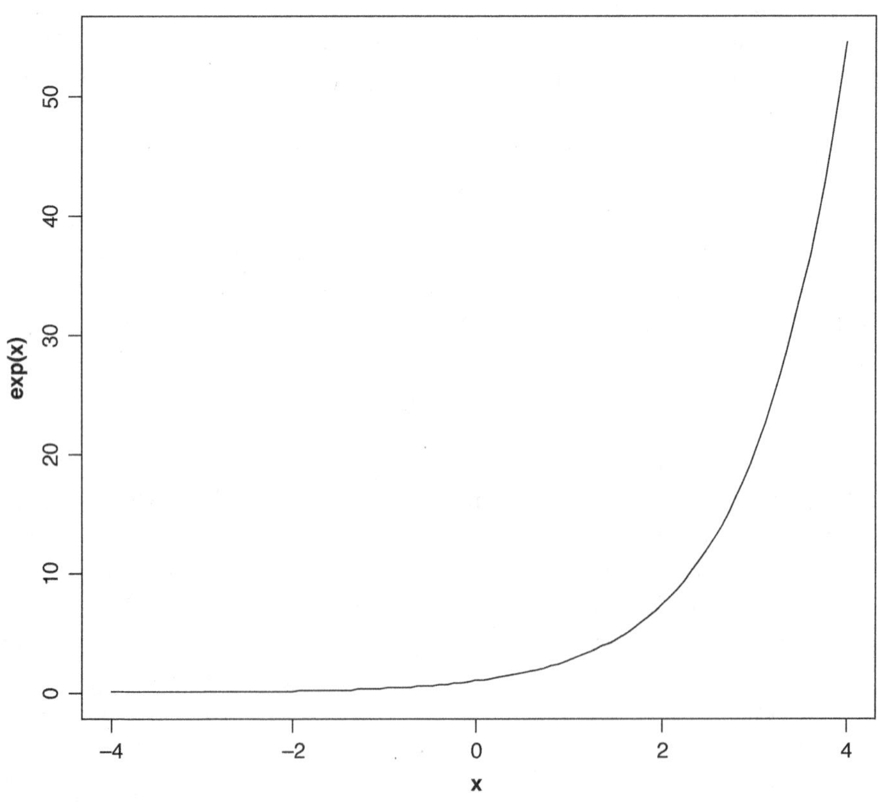

FIGURE 2. The Logistic Function: $y = e^x/(1 + e^x)$

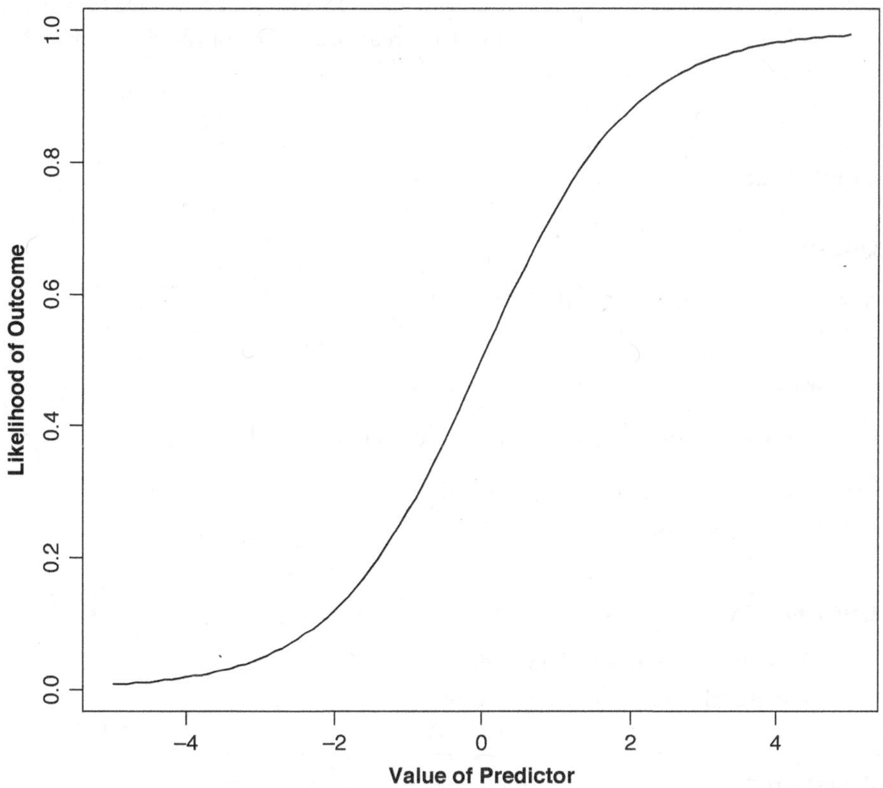

longer support more eagles. At that inflection point, the increase in the population of eagles slows down, stops, or reverses. Another example of a distribution with inherent limits is the likelihoods associated with actuarial prediction tools. The expected and observed proportions cannot be smaller than zero or larger than one. This often results in logistic distribution for the likelihoods estimated by prediction tools. The logistic distribution can be thought of as two exponential distributions: one that has an increasing slope between zero and .50, and a second that has a decreasing slope between .50 and 1.0. Figure 2 is a plot of the basic logistic function.

MISCELLANEOUS NOTATION

Δx is commonly used to indicate a change in x values, or the gap between two x values. It is read as "delta x".

$\Delta x \rightarrow y$ means the following: "as the gap between the x values approaches the value y." Commonly used in expressions such as $\Delta x \rightarrow$ zero (as the gap approaches zero) or $\Delta x \rightarrow \infty$ (as the gap approaches infinity). $\Delta x \rightarrow y$ is read as "as delta x approaches y".

y = **limit** $x \to$ **0 (expression)**, means the following: "as the x values approaches zero, the expression approaches the value y". Example: 10 = limit $x \to 0$ $(10 - x)$. This example would be read as "as x approaches zero, the expression $(10 - x)$ approaches 10."

EXERCISES

Question 1

$A = (3 + 6)(4 - 3)$. What is the answer (A)?

Question 2

Consider the following set of numbers: $x_i = (1, 2, 0, 4, 3, 6, 10, 1)$.

(i) What is the value of $\bar{X} = (\sum_{i=1}^{8} x_i)/n$?
(ii) What is the value of $Y = \prod_{i=1}^{8} x_i$?

Question 3

(i) The natural log of ½ is what value?
(ii) The natural log of 2 is what value?

Question 4

What is the value of P? $P = \exp(-.70)$

Question 5

What is the value of Z?

(i) Z = limit $x \to \infty$ $(x/[1 + x])$
(ii) Z = limit $x \to 0$ $(x/[1 + x])$

ANSWERS TO EXERCISES

Question 1

$A = 9$

Question 2

(i) $27/8 = 3.375$
(ii) 0 (anything multiplied by zero is zero)

Question 3

(i) −0.693147
(ii) 0.693147

Question 4

0.496585

Question 5

(i) 1
(ii) 0

Note that the expression $(x/[1 + x])$ is used to bound the logistic distribution between zero and one.

GLOSSARY

The glossary covers technical terms concerning probability, statistics, and prediction in psychology. Language is fluid. Words gain and lose associated meanings as they are used by different people in different contexts (Wittgenstein's, 1976, language-games). The glossary emphasizes the meanings that are most closely aligned with their meanings in this book. Do not think of them as complete, dictionary definitions. Instead, may they be a guide when passages in the book become ambiguous or just stop making sense.

Terms in the glossary are frequently defined using other terms in the glossary. Terms that are subject to their own entries are in *italics* the first time they are used in a definition.

absolute difference The size of the difference between two values, regardless of whether the difference is positive or negative. It is symbolized by $|x|$, as in $|3 - 5| = |-2| = 2$.

absolute risk Risk expressed as a *proportion* or a *likelihood*, for example, of 100 cases like Mr. Jones, 34 are expected to reoffend within 2 years. Contrasts with *relative risk*. Also called absolute likelihood.

actuarial prediction tool A risk tool that has an explicit method of combining items into scores or risk levels. The scores or risk levels are associated with *likelihoods* of the *outcome*.

algorithm A set of rules to be followed to arrive at a solution (e.g., risk estimate). Algorithms are an essential feature of *statistical* and *actuarial* risk tools.

alpha In *null hypothesis statistical testing*, the *likelihood* of incorrectly concluding an effect is there when it is not. Commonly set at $p < .05$ or $p < .01$. Also called *Type I error*.

arcsine transformation A *variance stabilization transformation* for *proportions.* Particularly useful in *meta-analyses* when the observed proportions are very low or very high.

area under the curve (AUC) A measure of the accuracy (*discrimination*) of prediction tools. Specifically, the value of the *AUC* is the *likelihood* that an individual with the outcome will have a higher score than an individual without the outcome. The curve in question is the *receiver operating characteristic (ROC) curve.*

artificial neural networks A *machine learning* approach to developing *statistical prediction* schemes modeled after the structures and processes that brains use to process information.

base rate The overall *likelihood* of the *outcome* in reasonably unselected samples. Contrasts with *conditional probability.*

Bayesian A statistical model that privileges *subjective probabilities.* Named after Thomas Bayes (1702–1761).

Bernoulli trial A *stochastic* process for which there are only two possible outcomes and the *likelihood* of the *outcome* is the same for each trial. Named after Jacob Bernoulli (1654–1705; also called James and Jacques Bernoulli).

bias Systematic *error* that changes the meaning of risk scores for different groups. For example, poor performance on a measure of verbal skills could be related to low intelligence for most respondents but unrelated to intelligence for recent immigrants.

binomial distribution The *frequency distribution* of the *means* of *dichotomous variables.*

black box predictors *Variables* or risk tools that are associated with the *outcome* but are not intended to advance understanding. Contrasts with *psychologically meaningful risk factors.*

bootstrap estimates A method of estimating *sampling error* by resampling subsets of data from the same data set.

broken legs A term popularized by Paul Meehl (1920–2003) to indicate a powerful *external risk factor* that nullifies an actuarial prediction.

calibration The extent to which the observed values in validation studies are similar to the expected values. One of two fundamental indicators of *predictive accuracy* (the other being *discrimination*).

calibration-in-the-large The extent to which a prediction tool, on average, overpredicts or underpredicts. Contrasted with *perfect calibration.*

calibration plots Graphs indicating the extent to which the observed likelihoods in a replication study are similar to the predicted (expected) likelihoods.

categorical variable A *variable* that classifies cases into discrete groups, which are considered different in kind, not just in degree (e.g., cisgender male, cisgender female, transgender male, transgender female, nonbinary, other). Contrasts with *continuous variables.*

censored In *survival analysis*, a case is censored if it does not have the outcome.

central tendency The middle of a distribution of values. Often indexed by the *mean* or *median*.

chi-square goodness-of-fit test A measure of *calibration* that compares the expected *distribution* of outcomes with the observed distribution of outcomes in a replication study. Chi-square values are typically represented by the following symbol: χ^2.

classical probabilities Numeric *likelihoods* for games of chance defined by the frequency of the outcome of interest (e.g., a pair of aces) divided by all possible outcomes.

Cochran's *Q* A statistic from *meta-analysis* indicating whether the *variability* across studies is more than would be expected by chance. Good *calibration* is indicated by small, nonsignificant *Q* statistics.

coefficients The elements (*parameters*) of a *statistical prediction model* that indicate *absolute likelihoods* as well as the size and direction of the *stochastic* relationship between *predictor* and the *outcome*. *Logistic regression*, for example, has *intercept* and *slope coefficients*.

Cohen's *d* A measure of *discrimination* that describes the extent of the difference between individuals who have the *outcome* from individuals who do not have the outcome. Also called the *standardized mean difference*.

cohort effects Changes in the target population or *sampling frame* over time.

competing risks *Survival analyses* in which there are multiple events that can influence *survival time*. For example, estimating the *likelihood* of sexual recidivism is complicated by some individuals being incarcerated during the *follow-up time* for nonsexual offenses.

conditional probability The *likelihood* of the *outcome* for a subgroup of interest. For example, the *base rate* for substance abuse problems may be 15%, whereas the conditional probability could be 25% if one parent has a history of alcoholism.

confidence interval The plausible range of values for interpreting empirical estimates. Ninety-five percent confidence intervals indicate the range of values that would be observed 19 times out of 20 if the study were endlessly repeated.

construct See *latent construct*.

continuous time survival analysis *Survival analyses* that measures time as a *continuous variable*, such as *Kaplan–Meier* and *Cox regression survival analysis*. Contrasts with *discrete-time survival analysis*.

continuous variable A *variable* that can assume a large number of ordered values (e.g., annual income, height in inches). Sometimes used in the strict sense to indicate that for any two observed values, an intermediate value is always possible.

correlation coefficient A measure of association for *continuous variables*, which can range from 1 (perfect positive correlation) to zero (no association) to −1 (perfect inverse correlation). Sometimes used as a measure of *interrater agreement*. The most common form is the *Pearson correlation coefficient*.

covariance A measure of association for *continuous variables*. When standardized, the covariance is a *correlation coefficient*.

covariates *Variables* that are associated with the *outcome*, without implication of a causal relationship.

Cox regression A form of *continuous time survival analysis* used to estimate the extent to which *predictor variables* are associated with the *outcome*.

criterion-reference measure A measure that is interpreted based on the extent to which scores align with a performance standard (e.g., competency in Grade 10 mathematics) or outcome (e.g., graduating from high school). Criterion-referenced prediction tools are those that estimated the *likelihood* of an *outcome*. Contrasts with *norm-referenced* tests.

critical value In *null hypothesis significance testing*, the critical value is the threshold (magnitude of the statistic) required to reject the null hypothesis (i.e., the observed pattern is unlikely to appear based on chance alone).

cumulative stochastic model A theoretical model of prediction in which each *risk factor* contributes *incrementally* to the overall *likelihood* of the *outcome*, and the relationship between the predictors and the outcome is probabilistic (*stochastic*). It assumes that there is relatively little information provided by *interactions* between predictors.

curvilinear relationship A relationship between variables that is well represented by one or more curves, such as a *logistic curve*. Contrasts with *linear relationships*.

Daubert A set of criteria for determining the admissibility of scientific evidence in certain U.S. states. Building on the *Frye* rule, the *Daubert* ruling adds additional criteria, such as whether the theory has been tested, whether there is a known error rate, and whether the information has been published and peer reviewed.

deciles Ten equal-sized groups.

decision trees A statistical approach to creating *prediction algorithms* in which the results of previous classifications influence subsequent classifications. For example, a decision threshold (e.g., less than 10%) could be set in advance, and the sample is divided into groups until there is a group identified for which the *likelihood* of the *outcome* is less than 10%.

degrees of freedom The number of separate *variables* that can vary (are not constrained) in a statistical analysis. For example, the *mean* value of a *dichotomous* variable includes the *proportion* with the *outcome* and the proportion without the outcome; however, if the proportion with the outcome is known, then the proportion without the outcome is also known. Consequently, the mean of a dichotomous variables is fully determined by only one variable, which can be defined as either the proportion with the outcome or the proportion without the outcome. Degrees of freedom are used to select *critical values* in *null hypothesis statistical testing*.

diagnosis Identifying whether a specific condition is currently present.

dichotomous variable A *categorical variable* with only two categories (e.g., has the outcome; does not have the outcome).

dimensions Constructs that exist in nature as a matter of degree. Contrasted with *categorical constructs* that are either present or absent (*taxons*).

discrete-time survival analysis A method for estimating the *likelihood* of the *outcome* when not all cases are followed for the complete *follow-up period*. The complete follow-up period is divided into discrete time intervals, and the *probabilities* (*hazards*) in each of these time intervals are used to estimate the overall probability at the end of the follow-up period.

discrimination The extent to which cases that have the *outcome* are different from cases that do not have the outcome. One of two fundamental properties of risk *prediction tools* (the other being *calibration*).

dynamic risk factors *Risk factors* that can be changed through deliberate intervention (e.g., treating poor emotional self-regulation for an individual at risk for substance abuse relapse).

e An *irrational constant* used as the base for *natural logarithms*. Approximately equal to 2.71828.

effect size A statistic describing a sample (e.g., *mean*), or the strength of the relationship between *variables*. Some authors equate effect size with *Cohen's d*. Diverse statistics from different studies are transformed into a common effect size for the purpose of *meta-analysis*.

empirical probabilities Stable *frequencies* observed in nature, such as the *proportion* of male to female births or the proportion of individuals who live to age 80. Also called empirical proportions.

E/O index A measure of the similarity (*calibration*) between the rates of the outcome predicted by a risk tool and the observed rates in replication studies.

error *Variability* that is not accounted for by the statistical model. Error can be random or systematic. Systematic error can result in *bias* in psychologically assessment. Random error is also called residual error.

expected values The *likelihoods* for *risk tools* set by norms, previous research, or theory. Expected values are specified in advance in *calibration* studies.

exponent; exponential The number of times a number is multiplied by itself. Usually expressed as a superscript, as in 3^2 or e^x. See the Appendix: Useful Algebra and Notation.

external risk factor A *risk factor* that has been demonstrated to be related to the outcome but is not included in a *prediction tool*. May or may not be *incremental* to the prediction tool.

false negatives The cell in the *fourfold table* containing cases with the outcome but not the predictor.

false positives The cell in the *fourfold table* containing cases with the predictor but not the outcome. Also called *false alarms*.

fitted values Smoothed values from a *statistical prediction tool*.

fixed-effect meta-analysis An approach to *meta-analysis* that assumes that all studies are estimating the same effect. Contrasts with *random-effects meta-analysis*.

follow-up time The length of time that cases are at risk for the outcome. Contrasts with *survival time*. Follow-up time can be fixed (same for all cases) or ragged (different follow-up times for difference cases).

forest plot A graphic used to depict the findings of a *meta-analysis* in which the *effect sizes* of each study and the overall, average effect are presented, along with their *confidence intervals.*

fourfold table The frequencies of all possible outcomes when both the *predictor variable* and the *outcome* can take only one of two values (i.e., the relationship between two *dichotomous variables*). Also called the 2 × 2 table.

frailty The principles in *survival analysis* that cases that are more likely to have the outcome will fail before lower risk cases. Frailty complicates the interpretation of changes in *hazard rates* over time.

frequency distribution The number of cases with each score, or range of scores. Often displayed as the *proportion* with each score.

frequentist A theory of statistics in which each observation is considered an independent trial from an unobserved random process. As the number of trials increases, the average of these values approaches the true value (see *Law of Large Numbers*). True values are defined as the limits of an infinite series.

Frye A rule for determining the admissibility of scientific evidence in certain U.S. states. For scientific evidence to be accepted, the basis for the opinion must be grounded in principles that are generally accepted in the relevant scientific community. Contrasts with *Daubert* rules.

funnel plot A graph that displays *effect sizes* on one axis and their *standard error* on the other axis. Used in *meta-analysis* to detect *publication bias.*

goodness-of-fit The degree of correspondence between expected and observed patterns of data.

H^2 An *effect size* indicator of the amount of between study *variability* in *meta-analysis.* It is the ratio of *Cochran's Q* to its *degrees of freedom,* with large values indicating poor *calibration* and values close to one indicating good calibration.

Harrell's C (concordance) An *effect size* statistic from *Cox regression survival analysis* that is interpreted much like the *area under the curve*: specifically, the probability that of two randomly selected cases, the case who had the outcome first had the higher risk score.

hazard The *likelihood* that the *outcome* will occur in the next time interval if it has not already occurred. A fundamental concept in *survival analysis.*

hazard ratio The ratio of two *hazards.* The numerator and the denominator are typically the hazards associated with different values of a predictor or adjacent scores on a prediction tool.

hits See *true positives.*

Hosmer–Lemeshow test A statistical test of *calibration.* Commonly used to assess the extent to which the observed outcome data fits a *logistic distribution.*

I^2 An *effect size* indicator for the amount of between-study *variability* in *meta-analysis.* Can be used as an overall measure of *calibration.* Good calibration is indicated by small I^2 values.

idiographic An approach to personality assessment that privileges the unique personal histories of each case.

incremental validity A *variable* or risk tool that adds risk relevant information not contained in another measure, thereby increasing overall *predictive accuracy.*

inferential statistics The theory and practice of using statistics derived from a *sample* to make inference about a *population.*

instantaneous hazard The *likelihood* of the outcome in the next, vanishingly small instant given that it has not yet occurred. A fundamental concept in *continuous time survival analysis,* such as *Kaplan–Meier survival analysis* and *Cox regression.*

integers Whole numbers (e.g., −1, 0, 3, 2,021).

interaction The relationship of a *variable* to the outcome changes based on the value of another variable.

intercept When graphing a line, the intercept is where the line crosses the vertical axis (y-axis). In *calibration plots* of prediction tools, the intercept is the expected rate of the outcome when the value of the predictor is zero. In *logistic regression,* the intercept is referred to as B_0 ("bee zero").

interval scale A *continuous variable* where the size of the differences between observations is meaningful. Contrasts with *ordinal scale.*

intraclass correlation coefficient An index of *rater reliability* for *continuous* or *ordinal* scores.

irrational number A number that cannot be expressed as the ratio of two *integers.* Irrational numbers can be expressed using nonrepeating decimals. Examples of irrational numbers are π (pi = 3.14159 . . .) and *e* (2.71828 . . .).

Kaplan–Meier survival analysis A form of *continuous time survival analysis* used to estimate the likelihood of the outcome at each time point throughout the *follow-up period.*

Kappa A measure of *rater reliability* for *categorical* or *dichotomous* variables. Also called Cohen's kappa.

language-game According to Ludwig Wittgenstein (1889–1951), a language-game is a structure involving words and their associated implications for action.

latent construct The underlying attribute assessed by psychological measures. Latent constructs are theoretically defined features of nature that are not directly observed but are inferred from the observed scores. For example, responses to the Beck Depression Inventory (the observed scores) can be used to diagnosis depression (the latent construct). The latent constructs may be *dimensional* or *taxonic.*

law of large numbers As the number of observations increases, the average of the observed values approaches the true value.

life-table survival analysis A form of *discrete-time survival analysis* developed for estimating life expectancies. Partial credit is accorded to cases that are followed for only part of the interval. Also called actuarial survival analysis (not to be confused with *actuarial* prediction tools).

likelihood A generic term to indicate the probability or chance that something will occur. For prediction tools, likelihoods indicate the estimated probability of the outcome (e.g., the likelihood of the outcome for Risk Group B is 40%).

likelihood ratio A measure of diagnostic accuracy that considers both *sensitivity* and *specificity*. Likelihood ratios indicate the relative risk of having a symptom (or score) being present for cases that have the disorder compared with cases without the disorder. Can be combined with *base rates* to estimate the *conditional probability* of having the disorder if the symptoms are present.

linear relationship A relationship between *variables* that can be easily represented by a straight line. Contrasts with *curvilinear* and *logistic* relationships.

LOESS curve A type of smoothed curve that connects points on a graph. LOESS is an acronym for LOcally Estimated Scatterplot Smoothing.

logarithm A way of representing numbers based on how many times a base number (either 10 or *e*) is multiplied by itself. See the Appendix: Useful Algebra and Notation.

logistic curve A curve with a logistic shape (i.e., S-shaped). Also called a logistic distribution. The y-values are bounded between zero and one.

logistic regression A statistical analysis that estimates how a *predictor variable* is associated with a *dichotomous* outcome variable. Logistic regression also estimates the *base rate* and the *likelihood* of the outcome for each value of the predictor variable.

logit A logged *odds ratio*. The metric used to represent *proportions* and *relative risk* in *logistic regression*.

machine learning algorithm approach to developing *statistical prediction tools* in which a program makes decisions based not only on the data but also on its previous decisions.

matrix A set of numbers. Usually used to describe numbers organized into two or more rows and two or more columns.

mean The average value of a *variable* calculated by summing all the values and dividing by the number of cases. A measure of *central tendency*.

measurement invariance Results of an assessment measure support the same inferences over repeated administrations and for different groups.

measurement model The relationship between the (unobserved) *latent construct* and the observed scores on a test or measure. In most cases, the relationship is assumed to be either *linear* or *logistic*.

median The value of a *variable* for which half the cases have higher values and half the cases have lower values. Also called the 50th *percentile*. A measure of *central tendency*.

meta-analysis A quantitative summary of the results of different studies. Used to calculate averaged *effect sizes*, as well as assess the generalizability of findings across samples and settings.

midpoint average A method of calculating *percentiles* when more than one case has the same score or risk level (ties). It is the average of (a) the percentile with lower scores and (b) the percentile with the same or lower scores.

monotonic increase An increasing set of values that never decrease. A desirable property for the expected values of *actuarial risk tools*.

natural language How words are used by those without specialized professional training. The *language-games* of everyday life.

natural logarithm A *logarithm* using base *e*. Also called Napierian logarithms. See the Appendix: Useful Algebra and Notation.

negative predictive value or **negative predictive accuracy** In a *fourfold table*, the proportion of cases without the predictor who also do not have the outcome.

nomothetic An approach to personality research based on patterns in group data.

normal distribution A bell-shaped distribution of scores. Commonly used as the default, expected model in statistical analyses. Contrasts with a *skewed distribution*.

norm-referenced test A measure that is primarily interpreted based on the unusualness of the score in a *reference population*.

norms Statistical inferences of a *prediction tool* asserted by the developers, such as *percentile ranks* and *absolute rates* of the *outcome*. Norms are usually based on a *reference population*.

null hypothesis statistical testing A method for limiting the overinterpretation of chance findings. This approach is based on estimating the likelihood of the observed pattern if the null hypothesis were true—that is, if the data were random. By convention, likelihoods less than one in 20 ($p < .05$) are considered statistically significant (worthy of further study).

numeracy The ability to understand and manipulate numbers.

observed values The *likelihoods* found in a replication study of a *prediction* tool. Also used to indicate the number of cases with the outcome in the *E/O index*.

odds A measure of the *likelihood* of the *outcome*, specifically, the *proportion* (or *probability*) with the outcome divided by proportion without the outcome: odds = probability/(1 − probability).

odds ratio An index of *relative risk*. Specifically, it is the *odds* of the *outcome* for individuals with the predictor divided by the odds of the outcome for individuals without the predictor.

ordinal scale The values of the *variable* indicate only the rank order of cases (e.g., first to last). No information is provided by the size of the gap between adjacent values. Contrasts with *continuous* and *interval* scale.

ordinary least squares regression A common form of statistical analysis for estimating the value of a *continuous outcome variable* using one or more *predictor* variables. With one continuous predictor, standardized regression coefficients equal the *Pearson correlation coefficients*.

outcome A generic term to indicate the state, thing, or event predicted by a prediction tool.

outlier An extreme value. Outliers can have disproportionate effects on descriptive statistics (*mean, standard deviation*) and *meta-analyses*. One solution is to analyze *Winsorized variables*.

overfitting Failing to distinguish between chance features of a data set and features of nature. Overfitting is a particular concern with *statistical prediction tools* that are developed on a single data set.

overrides Decisions by evaluators to assign a different risk level than that indicated by an actuarial prediction tool. See *broken legs.*

parameter The *coefficients* of a *statistical prediction model.* For example, in *logistic regression* with one predictor variable, there are two parameters, one for the *intercept* (B_0) and another for the *slope* (B_1).

parametric A shape or function that can be described by a fitted curve or theoretical distribution. Commonly used in *null hypothesis statistical testing* to generate expected distributions. In contrast, nonparametric statistics are those that do not require strong assumptions concerning the underlying distributions.

Pearson correlation coefficient A measure of the extent to which two *continuous variables* are related to each other. Values range from −1 (perfect negative correlation), to zero (no relationship), to +1 (perfect positive correlation).

percentiles Indicate the extent to which a score is unusually high or unusually low. Percentiles indicate the proportion of cases in a *reference population* that have higher or lower scores. Also called percentile ranks.

perfect calibration Exact correspondence between *observed* and *expected* values for all values of a prediction tool.

Poisson distribution A theoretical distribution for *variables* that involve few outcomes from a very large sample (e.g., the number of hospital admissions for suicide in a major urban center). The *standard deviation* of the Poisson distribution is equal to its *mean.* Closely related to the *binomial distribution.*

pooled, within-group standard deviation A weighted average of the *standard deviations* observed in separate groups. The denominator of *Cohen's d.*

population All cases to which a *prediction* tool or measure is meant to apply (e.g., adult males in the United States). Given the difficulty of obtaining complete population data, almost all psychological research and test development is based on *samples* from a population.

positive predictive value or **positive predictive accuracy** In a *fourfold table,* the proportion of cases with the predictor who also have the outcome.

power The likelihood that a statistical analysis will detect an effect that is really there. Also referred to statistical power and 1 – beta, where beta is the likelihood of a *Type II* error.

prediction tool A generic term to indicate a method, procedure, or scale used to estimate the *likelihood* of an *outcome.*

predictive accuracy The degree to which scores on a *prediction tool* are associated with the outcome. The two fundamental types of predictive accuracy are *discrimination* and *calibration.* For *diagnostic* measures, predictive accuracy can be described by the elements of the *fourfold table.*

probability A synonym for *proportion.* Also used as a general term to describe uncertainty and likelihoods, as in the *propensity theory* of probability.

prognosis Estimating the *likelihood* of some future outcome. In medicine, it often refers to the likelihood of recovery from a disorder. The outcome is not currently present and may never be.

propensity The *likelihood* of something to do something.

propensity model of probability A philosophy of probability advanced by Karl Popper (1902–1994) that considers *propensities* to be features of nature that can be ascribed to individual things. This is a variation on the *frequentist* model of probability. Contrasts with the *subjectivist* model of probability.

proportion The number of cases of interest divided by the total number of cases. A number between zero and one. Often used to estimated *likelihoods*.

proportional hazard assumption In *Cox regression*, the assumption that the relative risk differences are consistent over time.

protective factor A feature of the case that decreases the *likelihood* of the *outcome*. Protective factors can be the opposite of *risk factors*, or they could be drawn from a separate category (e.g., characteristics that are not inherently desirable but mitigate the effects of a risk factors, such as chronic ill health decreasing the risk for violent recidivism).

psychologically meaningful risk factors *Risk factors* that are supported by theory and are intended to inform treatment and case management decisions.

publication bias A distortion in the research literature based on selective non-reporting of nonsignificant results.

***Q* statistic** See *Cochran's Q*.

radian A unit for measuring angles, approximately equal to 57.3 degrees.

random-effects meta-analysis An approach to *meta-analysis* that assumes that the results from each study are based on a common effect plus study specific factors (i.e., the findings across studies are not expected to be identical). Contrasts with *fixed-effect meta-analysis*.

rate The frequency of an *outcome* for a group. A synonym for *proportion*. Also used to indicate the frequency of an outcome over time (e.g., the yearly rate).

rate ratio A measure of *relative risk*, or how much a *variable* is related to the *outcome*. Specifically, it compares the *proportion* with the outcome among those with the predictor to the proportion with the outcome among those without the predictor. Also called relative risk ratio.

rater reliability The degree of similarity between scores assigned to the same case by different evaluators. Often indexed by the *intraclass correlation coefficient* (*continuous* and *ordinal* measures) and Cohen's *kappa* (*categorical* measures).

raw scores *Variables* expressed in their original units of measures, which are specific to the risk tool. Also called *unstandardized* scores. Contrasts with *standardized* scores.

receiver operating characteristic (ROC) curve A curve defined by plotting the *sensitivity* and *false alarms* (1 – *specificity*) for each possible value of an ordered predictor variable. Also called the receiving operating characteristics curve.

reference population The *population* or *sampling frame* used to compare or interpret the results of assessment measures.

regression analysis A class of statistical techniques that model the association between one or more *predictor variables* and an *outcome variable. Logistic regression* is the standard type of regression analysis when the outcome variable is *dichotomous.*

regression coefficients The *parameters* in *regression analysis* that indicate how strongly the predictor is related to the outcome (*slope coefficient*) and the expected value of the outcome for a predictor score of zero (*intercept coefficient*).

relative risk A general term for how much riskier one group is than other. Sometimes used to refer to the *rate ratio*, specifically.

risk Individual differences in the *likelihood* of the *outcome.* Also used to indicate *stochastic,* nondeterministic relationships between conditions and the outcome.

risk factor A feature of the case that increases the *likelihood* of the *outcome.*

risk ratios A general term for ratios that compare the *likelihoods* in two groups, including *rate ratios, hazard ratios,* and *odds ratios.*

sample A set of observations drawn from a *population.*

sampling error The random error associated with chance features of the data. Also called *sampling variance.*

sampling frame The characteristics and boundaries of the group for which a measure is intended to be used. For example, the sampling frame for a relapse assessment measure could be males over the age of 18 with a history of substance abuse.

sampling variance The extent to which scores, observations, or statistics are expected to be different based on chance alone. Also called *sampling error.*

scatterplot A graph in which each case is identified by two variables, one of the variables plotted on the x-axis and the other variable plotted on the y-axis (e.g., recidivism rates [*y*] by risk scores [*x*]).

Schoenfeld residuals A statistic used in *Cox regression survival analysis* to test the *proportional hazard assumption.* The proportional hazard assumption is rejected when Schoenfeld residuals are correlated with time.

sensitivity In *fourfold tables,* the proportion of cases with the outcome who also have the predictor.

significance tests Procedures associated with *null hypothesis significance testing* that indicates whether an observed *effect size* or descriptive statistic (e.g., *mean*) is greater than would be expected by chance.

significant figures The number of digits that convey information. Speaks to the precision of measurement. See the Appendix: Useful Algebra and Notation.

skewed distribution A frequency distribution of scores or observations that is not symmetrical (and not a *normal distribution*). Distributions can be positively skewed (long tail to the right) or negatively skewed (long tail to the left).

slope coefficients The elements of *statistical prediction tools* (e.g., *logistic regression*) that indicate the size and direction of the relationship between the predictor and the outcome.

specificity In *fourfold tables,* the proportion of cases without the outcome who do not have the predictor.

standard deviation (*SD*) An indicator of dispersion, variability, or spread of a distribution. Standard deviations are usually used to describe individual variables.

standard error (*SE*) An indicator of dispersion, variability, or spread of summary statistics, such as a *means* or *regression coefficients.*

standard error of the mean A measure of *variability* of *means.* The larger the sample size, the narrower the standard error.

standardized mean difference See *Cohen's d.*

standardized risk levels Risk levels that are intended to communicate the same information regardless of the risk tool used.

standardized variables *Variables* that have been transformed into a common metric that can be compared across risk tools and samples. The most common approaches to standardization are dividing by a measure of *variability* (e.g., *Z scores*) or by an expected value. Contrasts with *raw scores.*

static risk factor *Risk factors* that cannot be changed through deliberate intervention. For example, age at release and prior criminal offenses are static risk factors for criminal recidivism.

statistical prediction tool A prediction tool developed from and closely tied to statistical models, such as *logistic regression* or *decision trees.*

stochastic processes A pattern that includes random elements, which prevent it from being precisely determined.

structured professional judgment An approach to risk assessment in which the risk factors are specified in advance, but there is no mechanical procedure for computing a total score or assigning cases to risk levels. Overall risk evaluations are typically based on unique case formulations.

subjective probabilities Numeric expressions indicating certainty of belief (e.g., I am 90% certain that he is guilty). Contrasts with *empirical probabilities.*

survival analyses A set of statistical procedures for estimating the *likelihood* of the outcome when not all cases are followed for the same length of time.

survival rate The cumulative *proportion* of cases who have not had the *outcome* after a specific *follow-up period.*

survival time The length of time that cases are at risk before they either fail (have the outcome) or are *censored.* Contrasts with *follow-up time.*

syntax Short for computer programming syntax. The commands that tell statistical software programs what analyses to conduct.

taxon A *latent construct* that exist as a true type in nature (plural: taxa). Contrasts with *dimensions.*

trapezoid A four-sided shape with only two parallel sides. Can be decomposed into squares and triangles for calculating *area under the curve.*

true negatives In *fourfold tables,* cases with neither the predictor nor the outcome.

true positives In *fourfold tables,* cases with both the predictor and the outcome. Also called *hits.*

***t*-test** An *inferential statistic* used in *null hypothesis statistical testing* to estimate whether the difference between two groups is greater than would be expected by chance. Closely related to the *normal distribution.*

2 × 2 table See fourfold table.

Type I error In *null hypothesis statistical testing,* Type I error is confusing *sampling variability* with true effects in nature. Also called *alpha,* as in $p < .05$.

Type II error In *null hypothesis statistical testing,* Type II error is failing to detect an effect that is really there. Also called beta, or 1 – *power.*

unstandardized variables Variables that are expressed in their original units of measurement. Also called *raw scores.* Contrasts with *standardized variables.*

unstructured risk assessment An approach to risk assessment in which the risk factors are not specified in advance. Also called unstructured professional judgment.

validation study A study that examines the *predictive accuracy* of a *prediction tool.*

variability The extent to which values of a *variable* are different across cases, samples, or settings. Also called dispersion.

variable A measure or indicator that can take a range of values (i.e., not a constant). For example, "is the individual currently deceased?" is a *dichotomous* variable with only two values (alive, deceased). Contrasts with constant, such as π (pi), which always equals approximately 3.14159.

variance stabilization transformations Transformations of statistical indicators (e.g., *effect sizes*) designed to minimize the influence of arbitrary features of study design on variability.

Wald method A method for estimating the *standard error* of *proportions.*

Winsorized variables A method for minimizing the distorting effects of *outliers.* A fixed percentage of the lowest and highest values are eliminated prior to data analysis (e.g., 10%, 20%).

x-axis The horizontal line (axis) on graphs (e.g., scatterplots).

y-axis The vertical line (axis) on graphs (e.g., scatterplots).

Z A statistic used to describe the *normal frequency distribution.* Commonly used to set the width of *confidence intervals.*

Z-scores Scores expressed in *standard deviation* units. A Z-score of 1.0 would indicate a score that is one standard deviation above the mean (Z-score of zero). Also called *standardized scores.*

REFERENCES

Aalen, O. O., Borgen, Ø., & Gjessing, H. K. (2008). *Survival and event history analysis: A process point of view*. Springer. https://doi.org/10.1007/978-0-387-68560-1

Agresti, A., & Caffo, B. (2000). Simple and effective confidence intervals for proportions and differences of proportions result from adding two successes and two failures. *The American Statistician, 54*(2), 280–288. 10.2307/2685779

Agresti, A., & Coull, B. A. (1998). Approximate is better than "exact" for interval estimation of binomial proportions. *The American Statistician, 52*(2), 119–126. 10.1080/00031305.1998.10480550

Akobeng, A. K. (2007a). Understanding diagnostic tests 1: Sensitivity, specificity and predictive values. *Acta Paediatrica, 96*(3), 338–341. https://doi.org/10.1111/j.1651-2227.2006.00180.x

Akobeng, A. K. (2007b). Understanding diagnostic tests 2: Likelihood ratios, pre- and post-test probabilities and their use in clinical practice. *Acta Paediatrica, 96*(4), 487–491. https://doi.org/10.1111/j.1651-2227.2006.00179.x

Akobeng, A. K. (2008). Communicating the benefits and harms of treatments. *Archives of Disease in Childhood, 93*(8), 710–713. https://doi.org/10.1136/adc.2008.137083

Alba, A. C., Agoritsas, T., Walsh, M., Hanna, S., Iorio, A., Devereaux, P. J., McGinn, T., & Guyatt, G. (2017). Discrimination and calibration of clinical prediction models. *Journal of the American Medical Association, 318*(14), 1377–1384. https://doi.org/10.1001/jama.2017.12126

Alder, K. (2002). *The measure of all things: The seven-year odyssey that transformed the world*. Little, Brown.

Allison, P. D. (1984). *Event history analysis: Regression for longitudinal event data*. Sage Publications.

Allport, G. W. (1937). *Personality: A psychological interpretation*. Henry Holt.

Altman, D. G. (1991). *Practical statistics for medical research*. Chapman & Hall.

Altman, D. G. (1998). Confidence intervals for the number needed to treat. *BMJ (Clinical Research Ed.), 317*(7168), 1309–1312. https://doi.org/10.1136/bmj.317.7168.1309

Altman, D. G., & De Stavola, B. L. (1994). Practical problems in fitting a proportional hazards model to data with updated measurements of the covariates. *Statistics in Medicine, 13*(4), 301–341. https://doi.org/10.1002/sim.4780130402

Altman, D. G., Vergouwe, Y., Royston, P., & Moons, K. G. M. (2009). Prognosis and prognostic research: Validating a prognostic model. *BMJ, 338*(7708), b605. https://doi.org/10.1136/bmj.b605

American Psychiatric Association. (2013). *Diagnostic and statistical manual of mental disorders* (5th ed.).

Anderson, T. W., & Sclove, S. L. (1978). *An introduction to the statistical analysis of data*. Houghton Mifflin.

Andreski, S. (1972). *Social science as sorcery*. St. Martin's Press.

Andrews, D. A., & Bonta, J. (2010). *The psychology of criminal conduct* (5th ed.). LexisNexis Group.

Andrews, D. A., Bonta, J., & Hoge, R. D. (1990). Classification for effective rehabilitation: Rediscovering psychology. *Criminal Justice and Behavior, 17*(1), 19–52. https://doi.org/10.1177/0093854890017001004

Asparouhov, T., & Muthén, B. (2009). Exploratory structural equation modeling. *Structural Equation Modeling, 16*(3), 397–438. https://doi.org/10.1080/10705510903008204

Babchishin, K. M., & Hanson, R. K. (2020). Monitoring changes in risk of reoffending: A prospective study of 632 men on community supervision. *Journal of Consulting and Clinical Psychology, 88*(10), 886–898. https://doi.org/10.1037/ccp0000601

Babchishin, K. M., Hanson, R. K., & Helmus, L. (2012a). Communicating risk for sex offenders: Risk ratios for Static-2002R. *Sexual Offender Treatment, 12*(2), 1–12. https://pdfs.semanticscholar.org/23ca/d38c0ced03d1c67c99f19788ad4454ddcb38.pdf

Babchishin, K. M., Hanson, R. K., & Helmus, L. (2012b). Even highly correlated measures can add incrementally to predicting recidivism among sex offenders. *Assessment, 19*(4), 442–461. https://doi.org/10.1177/1073191112458312

Babchishin, K. M., & Helmus, L. M. (2016). The influence of base rates on correlations: An evaluation of proposed alternative effect sizes with real-world data. *Behavior Research Methods, 48*(3), 1021–1031. https://doi.org/10.3758/s13428-015-0627-7

Baer, T. (2019). *Understand, manage, and prevent algorithmic bias: A guide for business users and data scientists*. Apress. https://doi.org/10.1007/978-1-4842-4885-0

Banks, S., Robbins, P. C., Silver, E., Vesselinov, R., Steadman, H. J., Monahan, J., Mulvey, E., Appelbaum, P., Grisso, T., & Roth, L. H. (2004). A multiple-models approach to violence risk assessment among people with mental disorder. *Criminal Justice and Behavior, 31*(3), 324–340. https://doi.org/10.1177/0093854804263635

Batastini, A. B., Vitacco, M. J., Coaker, L. C., & Lester, M. E. (2019). Communicating violence risk during testimony: Do different formats lead to different perceptions among jurors? *Psychology, Public Policy, and Law, 25*(2), 92–106. https://doi.org/10.1037/law0000196

Belar, C. D. (2000). Scientist–practitioner ≠ science + practice: Boulder is bolder. *American Psychologist, 55*(2), 249–250. https://doi.org/10.1037/0003-066X.55.2.248

Berk, R., Sherman, L., Barnes, G., Kurtz, E., & Ahlman, L. (2009). Forecasting murder within a population of probationers and parolees: A high stakes application of statistical learning. *Journal of the Royal Statistical Society. Series A (Statistics in Society), 172*(1), 191–211. https://doi.org/10.1111/j.1467-985X.2008.00556.x

Blais, J., Babchishin, K. M., & Hanson, R. K. (in press). Improving risk communication: Standardized risk levels for the BARR-2002R. *Sexual Abuse.*

Boccaccini, M. T., Rice, A. K., Helmus, L. M., Murrie, D. C., & Harris, P. B. (2017). Field validity of Static-99/R scores in a statewide sample of 34,687 convicted sexual offenders. *Psychological Assessment, 29*(6), 611–623. https://doi.org/10.1037/pas0000377

Boer, D. P., Hart, S. D., Kropp, P. R., & Webster, C. D. (1997). *Manual for the Sexual Violence Risk—20.* The British Columbia Institute Against Family Violence.

Bonta, J. (1996). Risk-needs assessment and treatment. In A. T. Harland (Ed.), *Choosing correctional options that work: Defining the demand and evaluating the supply* (pp. 18–32). Sage.

Bonta, J., & Andrews, D. A. (2016). *The psychology of criminal conduct* (6th ed.). Taylor & Francis. https://doi.org/10.4324/9781315677187

Borenstein, M., Hedges, L. V., Higgins, J. P. T., & Rothstein, H. R. (2010). A basic introduction to fixed-effect and random-effects models for meta-analysis. *Research Synthesis Methods, 1*(2), 97–111. https://doi.org/10.1002/jrsm.12

Borenstein, M., Hedges, L. V., Higgins, J. P. T., & Rothstein, H. R. (2021). *Introduction to meta-analysis* (2nd ed.). Wiley.

Bourgon, G., Mugford, R., Hanson, R. K., & Coligado, M. (2018). Offender risk assessment practices vary across Canada. *Canadian Journal of Criminology and Criminal Justice, 60*(2), 167–205. https://doi.org/10.3138/cjccj.2016-0024

Brankley, A. E., Babchishin, K. M., & Hanson, R. K. (2021). STABLE-2007 demonstrates predictive and incremental validity in assessing risk-relevant propensities for sexual offending: A meta-analysis. *Sexual Abuse, 33*(1), 34–62. https://doi.org/10.1177/1079063219871572

Brankley, A. E., Helmus, L. M., & Hanson, R. K. (2017). *STABLE-2007 evaluator workbook: Revised 2017.* Public Safety Canada.

Breiman, L. (2001). Random forests. *Machine Learning, 45*(1), 5–32. https://doi.org/10.1023/A:1010933404324

Brennan, T. (2017). An alternate scientific paradigm for criminological risk assessment: Closed or open systems, or both? In F. S. Taxman (Ed.), *Handbook on risk and need assessment: Theory and practice* (pp. 164–190). Routledge.

Brouillette-Alarie, S., Babchishin, K. M., Hanson, R. K., & Helmus, L. (2016). Latent constructs of static risk scales for the prediction of sexual aggression: A three-factor solution. *Assessment, 23*(1), 96–111. https://doi.org/10.1177/1073191114568114

Brown, G. K., Beck, A. T., Steer, R. A., & Grisham, J. R. (2000). Risk factors for suicide in psychiatric outpatients: A 20-year prospective study. *Journal of Consulting and Clinical Psychology, 68*(3), 371–377. https://doi.org/10.1037/0022-006X.68.3.371

Burnham, K. P., & Anderson, D. R. (2002). *Model selection and multimodel inference: A practical information-theoretic approach* (2nd ed.). Springer.

Burnham, K. P., & Anderson, D. R. (2004). Multimodel inference: Understanding AIC and BIC in model selection. *Sociological Methods & Research, 33*(2), 261–304. https://doi.org/10.1177/0049124104268644

Busemeyer, J. R., & Jones, L. E. (1983). Analysis of multiplicative combination rules when the causal variables are measured with error. *Psychological Bulletin, 93*(3), 549–562. https://doi.org/10.1037/0033-2909.93.3.549

Byrt, T. (1996). How good is that agreement? *Epidemiology, 7*(5), 561. https://doi.org/10.1097/00001648-199609000-00030

Cain, P. (2018, September 13). *One university's secret list to judge applicants by their high schools—not just their marks.* https://globalnews.ca/news/4405495/waterloo-engineering-grade-inflation-list/

Campbell, M. A., French, S., & Gendreau, P. (2009). The prediction of violence in adult offenders: A meta-analytic comparison of instruments and methods of assessment. *Criminal Justice and Behavior, 36*(6), 567–590. https://doi.org/10.1177/0093854809333610

Centers for Disease Control and Prevention. (2020, April 28). *Health effects of cigarette smoking.* https://www.cdc.gov/tobacco/data_statistics/fact_sheets/health_effects/effects_cig_smoking/index.htm

Chalmers, T. C., & Lau, J. (1993). Meta-analytic stimulus for changes in clinical trials. *Statistical Methods in Medical Research, 2*(2), 161–172. https://doi.org/10.1177/096228029300200204

Chen, F. F. (2007). Sensitivity of goodness of fit indexes to lack of measurement invariance. *Structural Equation Modeling, 14*(3), 464–504. https://doi.org/10.1080/10705510701301834

Chouldechova, A. (2017). Fair prediction with disparate impact: A study of bias in recidivism prediction instruments. *Big Data, 5*(2), 153–163. https://doi.org/10.1089/big.2016.0047

Cicchetti, D. V. (1994). Guidelines, criteria, and rules of thumb for evaluating normed and standardized assessment instruments in psychology. *Psychological Assessment, 6*(4), 284–290. https://doi.org/10.1037/1040-3590.6.4.284

Cohen, J. (1960). A coefficient of agreement for nominal scales. *Educational and Psychological Measurement, 20*(1), 37–46. https://doi.org/10.1177/001316446002000104

Cohen, J. (1969). *Statistical power analysis for behavioral sciences.* Academic Press.

Cohen, J. (1983). The cost of dichotomization. *Applied Psychological Measurement, 7*(3), 249–253. https://doi.org/10.1177/014662168300700301

Cohen, J. (1988). *Statistical power analysis for the behavioural sciences* (2nd ed.). Lawrence Erlbaum Associates.

Cohen, J. (1994). The earth is round ($p < .05$). *American Psychologist, 49*(12), 997–1003. https://doi.org/10.1037/0003-066X.49.12.997

Cohen, P., & Cohen, J. (1984). The clinician's illusion. *Archives of General Psychiatry, 41*(12), 1178–1182. https://doi.org/10.1001/archpsyc.1984.01790230064010

Cohen, T. H., Lowenkamp, C. T., Bechtel, K., & Flores, A. W. (2020). Risk assessment overrides: Shuffling the risk deck without any improvements in prediction. *Criminal Justice and Behavior, 47*(12), 1609–1629. https://doi.org/10.1177/0093854820953449

Collaborative Outcome Data Committee. (2007a). *Sex offender treatment outcome research: Guidelines for Evaluation (CODC Guidelines). Part 1: Introduction and overview* (Corrections User Report No 2007-02). Public Safety Canada. https://www.publicsafety.gc.ca/cnt/rsrcs/pblctns/sxl-ffndr-trtmnt/index-en.aspx

Collaborative Outcome Data Committee. (2007b). *The Collaborative Outcome Data Committee's Guidelines for the evaluation of sexual offender treatment outcome research.*

Part 2: CODC Guidelines (Corrections User Report No 2007-03). Public Safety Canada. https://www.publicsafety.gc.ca/cnt/rsrcs/pblctns/cllbrtv-tcmdt-gdlns/index-en.aspx

Collins, G. S., Ogundimu, E. O., & Altman, D. G. (2016). Sample size considerations for the external validation of a multivariable prognostic model: A resampling study. *Statistics in Medicine, 35*(2), 214–226. https://doi.org/10.1002/sim.6787

Cook, R. J., & Sackett, D. L. (1995). The number needed to treat: A clinically useful measure of treatment effect. *BMJ, 310*(6977), 452–454. https://doi.org/10.1136/bmj.310.6977.452

Cooke, D. J., & Michie, C. (2010). Limitations of diagnostic precision and predictive utility in the individual case: A challenge for forensic practice. *Law and Human Behavior, 34*(4), 259–274. https://doi.org/10.1007/s10979-009-9176-x

Cooper, J. (2003). Editorial. *Psychological Bulletin, 129*(1), 3–9. https://doi.org/10.1037/0033-2909.129.1.3

Courgeau, D. (2004). Probabilites, demographie et sciences sociales [Probabilities, demography and the social sciences]. *Mathematical Social Sciences, 42*(167), 27–50. https://doi.org/10.4000/msh.2933

Crawford, J. R., & Garthwaite, P. H. (2009). Percentiles please: The case for expressing neuropsychological test scores and accompanying confidence limits as percentile ranks. *The Clinical Neuropsychologist, 23*(2), 193–204. https://doi.org/10.1080/13854040801968450

Crawford, J. R., Garthwaite, P. H., & Slick, D. J. (2009). On percentile norms in neuropsychology: Proposed reporting standards and methods for quantifying the uncertainty over the percentile ranks of test scores. *The Clinical Neuropsychologist, 23*(7), 1173–1195. https://doi.org/10.1080/13854040902795018

Cronbach, L. J., & Meehl, P. E. (1955). Construct validity in psychological tests. *Psychological Bulletin, 52*(4), 281–302. https://doi.org/10.1037/h0040957

Crowson, C. S., Therneau, T. M., Matteson, E. L., & Gabriel, S. E. (2007). Primer: Demystifying risk—understanding and communicating medical risks. *Nature Clinical Practice Rheumatology, 3*(3), 181–187. https://doi.org/10.1038/ncprheum0397

Cumming, G. (2013). *Understanding the new statistics: Effect sizes, confidence intervals, and meta-analysis*. Routledge. https://doi.org/10.4324/9780203807002

Cumming, G., & Finch, S. (2001). A primer on the understanding, use, and calculation of confidence intervals that are based on central and noncentral distributions. *Educational and Psychological Measurement, 61*(4), 532–574. https://doi.org/10.1177/0013164401614002

Cumming, G., & Finch, S. (2005). Inference by eye: Confidence intervals and how to read pictures of data. *American Psychologist, 60*(2), 170–180. https://doi.org/10.1037/0003-066X.60.2.170

Darwin, C. (1887). *The life and letters of Charles Darwin* (Vol. 1). https://charles-darwin.classic-literature.co.uk/the-life-and-letters-of-charles-darwin-volume-i/ebook-page-36.asp

Davies, S. T., Helmus, L. M., & Quinsey, V. L. (2020). Improving risk communication: Developing risk ratios for the VRAG-R. *Journal of Interpersonal Violence*. Advance online publication. https://doi.org/10.1177/0886260520914555

Davies, S. T., Lloyd, C. D., & Polaschek, D. L. (2021). Does reassessment enhance the prediction of imminent criminal recidivism? Replicating Lloyd et al. (2020) with high-risk parolees. *Assessment*. Advance online publication. https://doi.org/10.1177/1073191121993216

Dawes, R. M. (1979). The robust beauty of improper linear models in decision making. *American Psychologist, 34*(7), 571–582. https://doi.org/10.1037/0003-066X.34.7.571

Dawes, R. M., Faust, D., & Meehl, P. E. (1989). Clinical versus actuarial judgment. *Science, 243*(4899), 1668–1674. https://doi.org/10.1126/science.2648573

DeLong, E. R., DeLong, D. M., & Clarke-Pearson, D. L. (1988). Comparing the areas under two or more correlated receiver operating characteristic curves: A non-parametric approach. *Biometrics, 44*(3), 837–845. https://doi.org/10.2307/2531595

Dennett, D. C. (1995). *Darwin's dangerous idea: Evolution and the meanings of life.* Simon and Schuster.

Desmarais, S. L., & Singh, J. P. (2013). *Risk assessment instruments validated and implemented in correctional settings in the United States.* Justice Center, Council of State Governments. https://csgjusticecenter.org/publications/risk-assessment-instruments-validated-and-implemented-in-correctional-settings-in-the-united-states/

Dickersin, K. (1990). The existence of publication bias and risk factors for its occurrence. *Journal of the American Medical Association, 263*(10), 1385–1389. https://doi.org/10.1001/jama.1990.03440100097014

Doren, D. M. (2004). Stability of the interpretative risk percentages for the RRASOR and Static-99. *Sexual Abuse, 16*(1), 25–36. https://doi.org/10.1177/107906320401600102

Douglas, K. S., Hart, S. D., Webster, C. D., & Belfrage, H. (2013). *HCR-20^{V3}: Assessing risk for violence: User guide*. Mental Health, Law, and Policy Institute, Simon Fraser University.

Douglas, K. S., & Skeem, J. L. (2005). Violence risk assessment: Getting specific about being dynamic. *Psychology, Public Policy, and Law, 11*(3), 347–383. https://doi.org/10.1037/1076-8971.11.3.347

Doyle, A. C. (1890/2000). *The sign of four.* https://sherlock-holm.es/stories/pdf/a4/1-sided/sign.pdf

Duwe, G., & Freske, P. J. (2012). Using logistic regression modeling to predict sexual recidivism: The Minnesota Sex Offender Screening Tool-3 (MnSOST-3). *Sexual Abuse, 24*(4), 350–377. https://doi.org/10.1177/1079063211429470

Duwe, G., & Rocque, M. (2018). The home-field advantage and the perils of professional judgment: Evaluating the performance of the Static-99R and the MnSOST-3 in predicting sexual recidivism. *Law and Human Behavior, 42*(3), 269–279. https://doi.org/10.1037/lhb0000277

Edwards, M. J., & Grace, R. C. (2014). The development of an actuarial model for arson recidivism. *Psychiatry, Psychology and Law, 21*(2), 218–230. https://doi.org/10.1080/13218719.2013.803277

Eisenhart, C. (1947). Inverse sine transformation of proportions. In C. Eisenhart, M. W. Hastay, & W. A. Wallis (Eds.), *Selected techniques of statistical analysis for scientific and industrial research and production and management engineering* (pp. 395–416). McGraw-Hill.

Elwood, R. W., Kelley, S. M., & Mundt, J. C. (2017). The 2015 Static-99R: Alternative recidivism tables for high-risk offenders. *International Journal of Offender Therapy and Comparative Criminology, 61*(14), 1593–1605. https://doi.org/10.1177/0306624X15623803

Epstein, S. (1979). The stability of behavior: I. On predicting most of the people much of the time. *Journal of Personality and Social Psychology, 37*(7), 1097–1126. https://doi.org/10.1037/0022-3514.37.7.1097

Erceg-Hurn, D. M., & Mirosevich, V. M. (2008). Modern robust statistical methods: An easy way to maximize the accuracy and power of your research. *American Psychologist, 63*(7), 591–601. https://doi.org/10.1037/0003-066X.63.7.591

Ewert v. Canada, 2015 FC 1093.

Ewert v. Canada, 2018 SCC 30.

Eysenck, H. J. (1978). An exercise in mega-silliness. *American Psychologist, 33*(5), 517. https://doi.org/10.1037/0003-066X.33.5.517.a

Faigman, D. L., Monahan, J., & Slobogin, C. (2014). Group to individual (G2i) inference in scientific expert testimony. *The University of Chicago Law Review, 81*(2), 417–480. http://www.jstor.org/stable/23762370

Fazel, S., Gulati, G., Linsell, L., Geddes, J. R., & Grann, M. (2009). Schizophrenia and violence: Systematic review and meta-analysis. *PLOS Medicine, 6*(8), e1000120. https://doi.org/10.1371/journal.pmed.1000120

Ferguson, G. A. (1976). *Statistical analysis in psychology and education* (4th ed.). McGraw-Hill.

Fernandez, Y., Gotch, K., Hanson, R. K., & Harris, A. J. R. (2015). *Coding manual for ACUTE-2007: Revised 2015*. Public Safety Canada.

Fernandez, Y., Harris, A. J. R., Hanson, R. K., & Sparks, J. (2014). *STABLE-2007 coding manual: Revised 2014*. Public Safety Canada.

Fernandez, Y., & Helmus, L. M. (2017). A field examination of the inter-rater reliability of the Static-99 and STABLE-2007 scored by Correctional Program Officers. *Sexual Offender Treatment, 12*(2), 1–12. http://www.sexual-offender-treatment.org/181.html

Field, A. (2017). *Discovering statistics using IBM SPSS statistics* (5th ed.). Sage Publications.

Fishbein, M., & Ajzen, I. (2010). *Predicting and changing behavior: The reasoned action approach*. Psychology Press.

Fisher v. The University of Texas at Austin. 579 U.S.___ (2016). https://www.scotusblog.com/case-files/cases/fisher-v-university-of-texas-at-austin-2/

Fleiss, J. L., & Berlin, J. A. (2009). Effect sizes for dichotomous data. In H. Cooper, L. V. Hedges, & J. C. Valentine (Eds.), *The handbook of research synthesis and meta-analysis* (2nd ed., pp. 237–254). Russell Sage Foundation.

Fleiss, J. L., Levin, B., & Paik, M. C. (2003). *Statistical methods for rates and proportions* (3rd ed.). Wiley. https://doi.org/10.1002/0471445428

Flynn, J. R. (2007). *What is intelligence? Beyond the Flynn effect*. Cambridge University Press. https://doi.org/10.1017/CBO9780511605253

Friesen, J. (2019, July 29). In a push for diversity, medical schools overhaul how they select Canada's future doctors. *The Globe and Mail*. https://www.theglobeandmail.com/canada/article-in-a-push-for-diversity-medical-schools-overhaul-how-they-select/

Gail, M. H., & Pfeiffer, R. M. (2005). On criteria for evaluating models of absolute risk. *Biostatistics, 6*(2), 227–239. https://doi.org/10.1093/biostatistics/kxi005

Gigerenzer, G., Gaissmaier, W., Kurz-Milcke, E., Schwartz, L. M., & Woloshin, S. (2007). Helping doctors and patients make sense of health statistics. *Psychological Science in the Public Interest, 8*(2), 53–96. https://doi.org/10.1111/j.1539-6053.2008.00033.x

Gillies, D. (2000). Varieties of propensity. *The British Journal for the Philosophy of Science, 51*(4), 807–835. https://doi.org/10.1093/bjps/51.4.807

Gjerdrum, D., & Peter, M. (2011). The new international standard on the practice of risk management—a comparison of ISO 31000: 2009 and the COSO ERM framework. *Risk Management, 31*(21), 8–13. https://doi.org/10.20982/tqmp.14.4.p242

Glass, G. V. (1976). Primary, secondary, and meta-analysis of research. *Educational Researcher, 5*(10), 3–8. https://doi.org/10.3102/0013189X005010003

Gonçalves, L. C., Gerth, J., Rossegger, A., Noll, T., & Endrass, J. (2020). Predictive validity of the Static-99 and Static-99R in Switzerland. *Sexual Abuse, 32*(2), 203–219. https://doi.org/10.1177/1079063218821117

Gore, K. S. (2007). Adjusted actuarial assessment of sex offenders: The impact of clinical overrides on predictive accuracy (UMI No. 3274898). *Dissertation Abstracts International, 68*(07), 4828.

Goulet-Pelletier, J. C., & Cousineau, D. (2018). A review of effect sizes and their confidence intervals, Part I: The Cohen's d family. *The Quantitative Methods for Psychology, 14*(4), 242–265. https://doi.org/10.20982/tqmp.14.4.p242

Grann, M., & Pallvik, A. (2002). An empirical investigation of written risk communication in forensic psychiatric evaluations. *Psychology, Crime & Law, 8*(1), 113–130. https://doi.org/10.1080/10683160208401812

Grant, R. L. (2014). Converting an odds ratio to a range of plausible relative risks for better communication of research findings. *BMJ, 348*(jan24 1), f7450. https://doi.org/10.1136/bmj.f7450

Greenhouse, J. B., Stangl, D., & Bromberg, J. (1989). An introduction to survival analysis: Statistical methods for analysis of clinical trial data. *Journal of Consulting and Clinical Psychology, 57*(4), 536–544. https://doi.org/10.1037/0022-006X.57.4.536

Greenland, S. (1998). Probability logic and probabilistic induction. *Epidemiology, 9*(3), 322–332. https://doi.org/10.1097/00001648-199805000-00018

Grissom, R. J., & Kim, J. J. (2005). *Effect sizes for research: A broad practical approach*. Lawrence Erlbaum Associates.

Haag, A. M., Boyes, A., Cheng, J., MacNeil, A., & Wirove, R. (2016). An introduction to the issues of cross-cultural assessment inspired by *Ewert v. Canada*. *Journal of Threat Assessment and Management, 3*(2), 65–75. https://doi.org/10.1037/tam0000067

Hacking, I. (1975). *The emergence of probability: A philosophical study of early ideas about probability induction and statistical inference*. Cambridge University Press.

Hacking, I. (1990). *The taming of chance*. Cambridge University Press. https://doi.org/10.1017/CBO9780511819766

Haigh, J. (2012). *Probability: A very short introduction*. Oxford University Press. https://doi.org/10.1093/actrade/9780199588480.001.0001

Hájek, A. (2007). The reference class problem is your problem too. *Synthese, 156*(3), 563–585. https://doi.org/10.1007/s11229-006-9138-5

Hald, A. (2003). *History of probability and statistics and their applications before 1750*. John Wiley & Sons.

Hanley, J. A., & Hajian-Tilaki, K. O. (1997). Sampling variability of nonparametric estimates of the areas under the receiver operating characteristic curves: An update. *Academic Radiology, 4*(1), 49–58. https://doi.org/10.1016/S1076-6332(97)80161-4

Hanson, N. R. (1958). *Patterns of discovery: An inquiry into the conceptual foundations of science*. Cambridge University Press.

Hanson, R. K. (2006). Does Static-99 predict recidivism among older sexual offenders? *Sexual Abuse, 18*(4), 343–355. https://doi.org/10.1177/107906320601800403

Hanson, R. K. (2008). What statistics should we use to report predictive accuracy? *Crime Scene, 14*(1), 15–17. http://www.cpa.ca/sections/criminaljustice/publications/

Hanson, R. K. (2009). The psychological assessment of risk for crime and violence. *Canadian Psychology, 50*(3), 172–182. https://doi.org/10.1037/a0015726

Hanson, R. K. (2017). Assessing the calibration of actuarial risk scales: A primer on the E/O index. *Criminal Justice and Behavior, 44*(1), 26–39. https://doi.org/10.1177/0093854816683956

Hanson, R. K. (2018). Long term recidivism studies show that desistance is the norm. *Criminal Justice and Behavior, 45*(9), 1340–1346. https://doi.org/10.1177/0093854818793382

Hanson, R. K., Babchishin, K. M., Helmus, L., & Thornton, D. (2013). Quantifying the relative risk of sex offenders: Risk ratios for Static-99R. *Sexual Abuse, 25*(5), 482–515. https://doi.org/10.1177/1079063212469060

Hanson, R. K., Babchishin, K. M., Helmus, L. M., Thornton, D., & Phenix, A. (2017). Communicating the results of criterion referenced prediction measures: Risk categories for the Static-99R and Static-2002R sexual offender risk assessment tools. *Psychological Assessment, 29*(5), 582–597. https://doi.org/10.1037/pas0000371

Hanson, R. K., Bourgon, G., McGrath, R., Kroner, D., D'Amora, D. A., Thomas, S. S., & Tavarez, L. P. (2017). *A five-level risk and needs system: Maximizing assessment results in corrections through the development of a common language.* The Council of State Governments Justice Center. https://csgjusticecenter.org/publications/a-five-level-risk-and-needs-system-maximizing-assessment-results-in-corrections-through-the-development-of-a-common-language/

Hanson, R. K., & Broom, I. (2005). The utility of cumulative meta-analysis: Application to programs for reducing sexual violence. *Sexual Abuse, 17*(4), 357–373. https://doi.org/10.1177/107906320501700402

Hanson, R. K., & Bussière, M. T. (1996). *Predictors of sexual offender recidivism: A meta-analysis.* (User Report 96-04). Public Safety Canada. https://www.publicsafety.gc.ca/cnt/rsrcs/pblctns/prdctrs-sxl-ffnd/index-en.aspx

Hanson, R. K., & Bussière, M. T. (1998). Predicting relapse: A meta-analysis of sexual offender recidivism studies. *Journal of Consulting and Clinical Psychology, 66*(2), 348–362. https://doi.org/10.1037/0022-006X.66.2.348

Hanson, R. K., Harris, A. J. R., Helmus, L., & Thornton, D. (2014). High-risk sex offenders may not be high risk forever. *Journal of Interpersonal Violence, 29*(15), 2792–2813. https://doi.org/10.1177/0886260514526062

Hanson, R. K., Harris, A. J. R., Letourneau, E., Helmus, L. M., & Thornton, D. (2018). Reductions in risk based on time offense free in the community: Once a sexual offender, not always a sexual offender. *Psychology, Public Policy, and Law, 24*(1), 48–63. https://doi.org/10.1037/law0000135

Hanson, R. K., Harris, A. J. R., Scott, T., & Helmus, L. (2007). *Assessing the risk of sexual offenders on community supervision: The Dynamic Supervision Project* (Corrections User Report No 2007-05). Public Safety Canada. https://www.publicsafety.gc.ca/cnt/rsrcs/pblctns/ssssng-rsk-sxl-ffndrs/index-en.aspx

Hanson, R. K., Helmus, L., & Harris, A. J. R. (2015). Assessing the risk and needs of supervised sexual offenders: A prospective study using STABLE-2007, Static-99R and Static-2002R. *Criminal Justice and Behavior, 42*(12), 1205–1224. https://doi.org/10.1177/0093854815602094

Hanson, R. K., Helmus, L., & Thornton, D. (2010). Predicting recidivism amongst sexual offenders: A multi-site study of static-2002. *Law and Human Behavior, 34*(3), 198–211. https://doi.org/10.1007/s10979-009-9180-1

Hanson, R. K., & Howard, P. D. (2010). Individual confidence intervals do not inform decision-makers about the accuracy of risk assessment evaluations. *Law and Human Behavior, 34*(4), 275–281. https://doi.org/10.1007/s10979-010-9227-3

Hanson, R. K., Lloyd, C. D., Helmus, L., & Thornton, D. (2012). Developing non-arbitrary metrics for risk communication: Percentile ranks for the Static-99/R and Static-2002/R sexual offender risk scales. *International Journal of Forensic Mental Health, 11*(1), 9–23. https://doi.org/10.1080/14999013.2012.667511

Hanson, R. K., Lunetta, A., Phenix, A., Neeley, J., & Epperson, D. (2014). The field validity of Static-99/R sex offender risk assessment tool in California. *Journal of Threat Assessment and Management, 1*(2), 102–117. https://doi.org/10.1037/tam0000014

Hanson, R. K., & Morton-Bourgon, K. E. (2004). *Predictors of sexual recidivism: An updated meta-analysis* (Corrections User Report No. 2004-02). Public Safety Canada. https://www.publicsafety.gc.ca/cnt/rsrcs/pblctns/2004-02-prdctrs-sxl-rcdvsm-pdtd/index-en.aspx

Hanson, R. K., & Morton-Bourgon, K. E. (2005). The characteristics of persistent sexual offenders: A meta-analysis of recidivism studies. *Journal of Consulting and Clinical Psychology, 73*(6), 1154–1163. https://doi.org/10.1037/0022-006X.73.6.1154

Hanson, R. K., & Morton-Bourgon, K. E. (2009). The accuracy of recidivism risk assessments for sexual offenders: A meta-analysis of 118 prediction studies. *Psychological Assessment, 21*(1), 1–21. https://doi.org/10.1037/a0014421

Hanson, R. K., Newstrom, N., Brouillette-Alarie, S., Thornton, D., Robinson, B. E., & Miner, M. H. (2020). Does reassessment improve prediction? A prospective study of the Sexual Offender Treatment Intervention and Progress Scale (SOTIPS). *International Journal of Offender Therapy and Comparative Criminology.* Advance online publication. https://doi.org/10.1177/0306624X20978204

Hanson, R. K., & Thornton, D. (1999). *Static-99: Improving actuarial risk assessments for sex offenders.* User Report 99-02. Public Safety Canada. https://www.publicsafety.gc.ca/cnt/rsrcs/pblctns/sttc-mprvng-actrl/index-en.aspx

Hanson, R. K., & Thornton, D. (2000). Improving risk assessments for sex offenders: A comparison of three actuarial scales. *Law and Human Behavior, 24*(1), 119–136. https://doi.org/10.1023/A:1005482921333

Hanson, R. K., & Thornton, D. (2003). *Notes on the development of Static-2002* (User Report 2003-01). Department of the Solicitor General of Canada.

Hanson, R. K., Thornton, D., Helmus, L.-M., & Babchishin, K. M. (2016). What sexual recidivism rates should be associated with Static-99R and Static-2002R scores? *Sexual Abuse, 28*(3), 218–252. https://doi.org/10.1177/1079063215574710

Hare, R. D. (2003). *Hare PCL-R technical manual* (2nd ed.). Multi-Health Systems.

Harrell, F. E., Jr., Califf, R. M., Pryor, D. B., Lee, K. L., & Rosati, R. A. (1982). Evaluating the yield of medical tests. *Journal of the American Medical Association, 247*(18), 2543–2546. https://doi.org/10.1001/jama.1982.03320430047030

Harris, G. T., Lowenkamp, C. T., & Hilton, N. Z. (2015). Evidence for risk estimate precision: Implications for individual risk communication. *Behavioral Sciences & the Law, 33*(1), 111–127. https://doi.org/10.1002/bsl.2158

Harris, G. T., Rice, M. E., & Quinsey, V. L. (1993). Violent recidivism of mentally disordered offenders: The development of a statistical prediction instrument. *Criminal Justice and Behavior, 20*(4), 315–335. https://doi.org/10.1177/0093854893020004001

Harris, G. T., Rice, M. E., Quinsey, V. L., & Cormier, C. A. (2015). *Violent offenders: Appraising and managing risk* (3rd ed.). American Psychological Association. https://doi.org/10.1037/14572-000

Hart, S. D., & Cooke, D. J. (2013). Another look at the (im-)precision of individual risk estimates made using actuarial risk assessment instruments. *Behavioral Sciences & the Law, 31*(1), 81–102. https://doi.org/10.1002/bsl.2049

Hart, S. D., Michie, C., & Cooke, D. J. (2007). Precision of actuarial risk assessment instruments: Evaluating the "margins of error" of group v. individual predictions of violence. *The British Journal of Psychiatry, 190*(Suppl. 49), S60–S65. https://doi.org/10.1192/bjp.190.5.s60

Haslam, N., McGrath, M. J., Viechtbauer, W., & Kuppens, P. (2020). Dimensions over categories: A meta-analysis of taxometric research. *Psychological Medicine, 50*(9), 1418–1432. https://doi.org/10.1017/S003329172000183X

Hayes, W. L. (1981). *Statistics* (3rd ed.). Holt, Rinehart and Winston.

Head, M. L., Holman, L., Lanfear, R., Kahn, A. T., & Jennions, M. D. (2015). The extent and consequences of p-hacking in science. *PLOS Biology, 13*(3), e1002106. https://doi.org/10.1371/journal.pbio.1002106

Hedges, L. V., & Olkin, I. (1985). *Statistical methods for meta-analysis*. Academic Press.

Heilbrun, K., O'Neill, M. L., Stevens, T. N., Strohman, L. K., Bowman, Q., & Lo, Y. W. (2004). Assessing normative approaches to communicating violence risk: A national survey of psychologists. *Behavioral Sciences & the Law, 22*(2), 187–196. https://doi.org/10.1002/bsl.570

Heilbrun, K., O'Neill, M. L., Strohman, L. K., Bowman, Q., & Philipson, J. (2000). Expert approaches to communicating violence risk. *Law and Human Behavior, 24*(1), 137–148. https://doi.org/10.1023/A:1005435005404

Heilbrun, K., Yasuhara, K., Shah, S., & Locklair, B. (2021). Approaches to violence risk assessment: Overview, critical analysis, and future directions. In K. S. Douglas & R. K. Otto (Eds.), *Handbook of violence risk assessment* (2nd ed., pp. 3–27). Routledge.

Helmus, L. (2009). *Re-norming Static-99 recidivism estimates: Exploring base rate variability across sex offender samples.* [Master's thesis, Carleton University]. https://doi.org/10.22215/etd/2009-09351

Helmus, L., Hanson, R. K., Babchishin, K. M., & Mann, R. E. (2013). Attitudes supportive of sexual offending predict recidivism: A meta-analysis. *Trauma, Violence & Abuse, 14*(1), 34–53. https://doi.org/10.1177/1524838012462244

Helmus, L., Hanson, R. K., Thornton, D., Babchishin, K. M., & Harris, A. J. R. (2012). Absolute recidivism rates predicted by Static-99R and Static-2002R sex offender risk assessment tools vary across samples: A meta-analysis. *Criminal Justice and Behavior, 39*(9), 1148–1171. https://doi.org/10.1177/0093854812443648

Helmus, L., Thornton, D., Hanson, R. K., & Babchishin, K. M. (2012). Improving the predictive accuracy of Static-99 and Static-2002 with older sex offenders: Revised age weights. *Sexual Abuse, 24*(1), 64–101. https://doi.org/10.1177/1079063211409951

Helmus, L. M. (2015). *Developing and validating a risk assessment scale to predict inmate placements in administrative segregation in the Correctional Service of Canada.*

Doctoral dissertation, Carleton University, Ottawa, Ontario, Canada. https://doi.org/10.22215/etd/2015-10835

Helmus, L. M., & Babchishin, K. M. (2017). Primer on risk assessment and the statistics used to evaluate its accuracy. *Criminal Justice and Behavior, 44*(1), 8–25. https://doi.org/10.1177/0093854816678898

Higgins, J. P., Thompson, S. G., Deeks, J. J., & Altman, D. G. (2003). Measuring inconsistency in meta-analyses. *BMJ, 327*(7414), 557–560. https://doi.org/10.1136/bmj.327.7414.557

Hilton, N. Z. (2021). *Domestic violence risk assessment: Tools for effective prediction and management* (2nd ed.). American Psychological Association.

Hilton, N. Z., Carter, A. M., Harris, G. T., & Sharpe, A. J. (2008). Does using non-numerical terms to describe risk aid violence risk communication? Clinician agreement and decision making. *Journal of Interpersonal Violence, 23*(2), 171–188. https://doi.org/10.1177/0886260507309337

Hilton, N. Z., & Helmus, L. M. (2020). Using graphs in sexual violence risk communication: Benefits may depend on the risk metric. *Sexual Abuse*. Advance online publication. https://doi.org/10.1177/1079063220951191

Hogan, N. R. (2020). Critical considerations in the development and interpretation of common risk language. *Psychiatry, Psychology and Law,* 1–17. Advance online publication. https://doi.org/10.1080/13218719.2020.1767719

Hosmer, D. W., Lemeshow, S., & Sturdivant, R. X. (2013). *Applied logistic regression* (3rd ed.). John Wiley & Sons. https://doi.org/10.1002/9781118548387

Howard, P., Francis, B., Soothill, K., & Humphreys, L. (2009). *OGRS 3: The revised Offender Group Reconviction Scale*. Ministry of Justice, Research Summary 7/09. https://core.ac.uk/download/pdf/1556521.pdf

Howard, P. D. (2017). The effect of sample heterogeneity and risk categorization on area under the curve predictive validity metrics. *Criminal Justice and Behavior, 44*(1), 103–120. https://doi.org/10.1177/0093854816678899

Howard, P. D., & Dixon, L. (2012). The construction and validation of the OASys Violence Predictor: Advancing violence risk assessment in the English and Welsh correctional services. *Criminal Justice and Behavior, 39*(3), 287–307. https://doi.org/10.1177/0093854811431239

Hsieh, F. Y. (1989). Sample size tables for logistic regression. *Statistics in Medicine, 8*(7), 795–802. https://doi.org/10.1002/sim.4780080704

Hughes, J. R., Keely, J., & Naud, S. (2004). Shape of the relapse curve and long-term abstinence among untreated smokers. *Addiction, 99*(1), 29–38. https://doi.org/10.1111/j.1360-0443.2004.00540.x

Humphreys, L. G., & Swets, J. A. (1991). Comparison of predictive validities measured with biserial correlations and ROCs of signal detection theory. *Journal of Applied Psychology, 76*(2), 316–321. https://doi.org/10.1037/0021-9010.76.2.316

Hunt, M. (1997). *How science takes stock: The story of meta-analysis*. Russell Sage Foundation.

IBM Corp. (2017). *IBM SPSS statistics algorithms*. https://www.ibm.com/support/pages/ibm-spss-statistics-25-documentation

IBM Corp. (2020). *IBM SPSS Statistics for Windows* (Version 27.0) [Computer software].

Imrey, P. B., & Dawid, A. P. (2015). A commentary on statistical assessment of violence recidivism risk. *Statistics and Public Policy, 2*(1), 1–18. https://doi.org/10.1080/2330443X.2015.1029338

Ingre, M., Åkerstedt, T., Peters, B., Anund, A., Kecklund, G., & Pickles, A. (2006). Subjective sleepiness and accident risk avoiding the ecological fallacy.

Journal of Sleep Research, 15(2), 142–148. https://doi.org/10.1111/j.1365-2869.2006.00517.x

Ioannidis, J. P. A. (2005). Why most published research findings are false. *PLOS Medicine, 2*(8), e124. https://doi.org/10.1371/journal.pmed.0020124

Jacobson, N. S., Follette, W. C., & Revenstorf, D. (1984). Psychotherapy outcome research: Methods for reporting variability and evaluating clinical significance. *Behavior Therapy, 15*(4), 336–352. https://doi.org/10.1016/S0005-7894(84)80002-7

Janus, E. S., & Meehl, P. E. (1997). Assessing the legal standard for predictions of dangerousness in sex offender commitment proceedings. *Psychology, Public Policy, and Law, 3*(1), 33–64. https://doi.org/10.1037/1076-8971.3.1.33

Joint Committee on the Standards for Educational and Psychological Testing of the American Educational Research Association, the American Psychological Association, and the National Council on Measurement in Education. (1999). *Standards for educational and psychological testing*.

Joint Committee on the Standards for Educational and Psychological Testing of the American Educational Research Association, the American Psychological Association, and the National Council on Measurement in Education. (2014). *Standards for educational and psychological testing*.

Jones, W. T. (1970). *The classical mind: A history of Western philosophy* (2nd ed.). Harcourt Brace Jovanovich.

Jüni, P., Witschi, A., Bloch, R., & Egger, M. (1999). The hazards of scoring the quality of clinical trials for meta-analysis. *Journal of the American Medical Association, 282*(11), 1054–1060. https://doi.org/10.1001/jama.282.11.1054

Kahn, R. E., Ambroziak, G., Hanson, R. K., & Thornton, D. (2017). Release from the sex offender label. *Archives of Sexual Behavior, 46*(4), 861–864. https://doi.org/10.1007/s10508-017-0972-y

Kahneman, D. (1973). *Attention and effort*. Prentice-Hall.

Kahneman, D. (2011). *Thinking, fast and slow*. Farrar, Straus and Giroux.

Kahneman, D., & Klein, G. (2009). Conditions for intuitive expertise: A failure to disagree. *American Psychologist, 64*(6), 515–526. https://doi.org/10.1037/a0016755

Kahneman, D., Sibony, O., & Sunstein, C. R. (2021). *Noise: A flaw in human judgment*. Little, Brown Spark.

Kang, L., Chen, W., Petrick, N. A., & Gallas, B. D. (2015). Comparing two correlated C indices with right-censored survival outcome: A one-shot nonparametric approach. *Statistics in Medicine, 34*(4), 685–703. https://doi.org/10.1002/sim.6370

Kelley, S. M., Ambroziak, G., Thornton, D., & Barahal, R. M. (2020). How do professionals assess sexual recidivism risk? An updated survey of practices. *Sexual Abuse, 32*(1), 3–29. https://doi.org/10.1177/1079063218800474

Kelly, G. A. (1963). *A theory of personality: The psychology of personal constructs*. W. W. Norton and Company.

Kenny, D. A., & Judd, C. M. (1984). Estimating the nonlinear and interactive effects of latent variables. *Psychological Bulletin, 96*(1), 201–210. https://doi.org/10.1037/0033-2909.96.1.201

Kolk, M., & Andersson, G. (2020). Two decades of same-sex marriage in Sweden: A demographic account of developments in marriage, childbearing, and divorce. *Demography, 57*(1), 147–169. https://doi.org/10.1007/s13524-019-00847-6

Kraemer, H. C., Kazdin, A. E., Offord, D. R., Kessler, R. C., Jensen, P. S., & Kupfer, D. J. (1997). Coming to terms with the terms of risk. *Archives of General Psychiatry, 54*(4), 337–343. https://doi.org/10.1001/archpsyc.1997.01830160065009

Kraemer, H. C., Kupfer, D. J., Clarke, D. E., Narrow, W. E., & Regier, D. A. (2012). *DSM-5*: How reliable is reliable enough? *The American Journal of Psychiatry, 169*(1), 13–15. https://doi.org/10.1176/appi.ajp.2011.11010050

Krauss, D. A., Cook, G. I., & Klapatch, L. (2018). Risk assessment communication difficulties: An empirical examination of the effects of categorical versus probabilistic risk communication in sexually violent predator decisions. *Behavioral Sciences & the Law, 36*(5), 532–553. https://doi.org/10.1002/bsl.2379

Kroner, D. G., & Derrick, B. (2020). The Council of State Governments Justice Center approach to increasing risk-level consistency in the application of risk assessment instruments. *Assessment*. Advance online publication. https://doi.org/10.1177/1073191120958066

Kroner, D. G., Mills, J. F., & Reddon, J. R. (2005). A coffee can, factor analysis, and prediction of antisocial behavior: The structure of criminal risk. *International Journal of Law and Psychiatry, 28*(4), 360–374. https://doi.org/10.1016/j.ijlp.2004.01.011

Kroner, D. G., Morrison, M. M., & M Lowder, E. (2020). A principled approach to the construction of risk assessment categories: The Council of State Governments Justice Center Five-Level System. *International Journal of Offender Therapy and Comparative Criminology, 64*(10–11), 1074–1090. https://doi.org/10.1177/0306624X19870374

Kropp, R. P., & Gibas, A. (2010). The Spousal Assault Risk Assessment Guide (SARA). In R. K. Otto & K. S. Douglas (Eds.), *Handbook of violence risk assessment* (pp. 227–250). Taylor & Francis.

Kropp, R. P., & Hart, S. D. (2015). *SARA-V3: User manual for Version 3 of the Spousal Assault Risk Assessment Guide*. Protect International Risk and Safety Services.

Kropp, R. P., Hart, S. D., Webster, C. W., & Eaves, D. (1999). *Spousal Assault Risk Assessment: User's guide*. Multi-Health Systems, Inc.

Kühberger, A., Fritz, A., & Scherndl, T. (2014). Publication bias in psychology: A diagnosis based on the correlation between effect size and sample size. *PLOS ONE, 9*(9), e105825. https://doi.org/10.1371/journal.pone.0105825

Kurlychek, M. C., Bushway, S. D., & Brame, R. (2012). Long-term crime desistance and recidivism patterns—evidence from the Essex County convicted felon study. *Criminology, 50*(1), 71–103. https://doi.org/10.1111/j.1745-9125.2011.00259.x

Lakatos, I. (1970). Falsification and the methodology of scientific research programmes. In I. Lakatos & A. Musgrave (Eds.), *Criticism and the growth of knowledge* (pp. 91–195). Cambridge University Press. https://doi.org/10.1017/CBO9781139171434.009

Långström, N. (2004). Accuracy of actuarial procedures for assessment of sexual offender recidivism risk may vary across ethnicity. *Sexual Abuse, 16*(2), 107–120. https://doi.org/10.1177/107906320401600202

Lasher, M. P., McGrath, R. J., Wilson, D., & Cumming, G. F. (2015). Collaborative treatment planning using the Sex Offender Treatment Intervention and Progress Scale (SOTIPS): Concordance of therapist evaluation and client self-evaluation. *International Journal of Forensic Mental Health, 14*(1), 1–9. https://doi.org/10.1080/14999013.2014.974087

Lee, S. C., & Hanson, R. K. (2015, August 30). There is evidence to support the use of Western developed violent risk assessment in China: Responding to Zhou et al. (2015). *Nextgenforensic*. http://wp.me/p2RS15-bc

Lee, S. C., & Hanson, R. K. (2017). Similar predictive accuracy of the Static-99R risk tool for White, Black, and Hispanic sex offenders in California. *Criminal Justice and Behavior, 44*(9), 1125–1140. https://doi.org/10.1177/0093854817711477

Lee, S. C., & Hanson, R. K. (2021). Updated 5-year and new 10-year sexual recidivism rate norms for Static-99R with routine/complete samples. *Law and Human Behavior, 45*(1), 24–38. https://doi.org/10.1037/lhb0000436

Lee, S. C., Hanson, R. K., & Blais, J. (2020). Predictive accuracy of the Static-99R and Static-2002R risk tools for identifying Indigenous and White individuals at high risk for sexual recidivism in Canada. *Canadian Psychology, 61*(1), 42–57. https://doi.org/10.1037/cap0000182

Lehmann, R. J. B., Hanson, R. K., Babchishin, K. M., Gallasch-Nemitz, F., Biedermann, J., & Dahle, K.-P. (2013). Interpreting multiple risk scales for sex offenders: Evidence for averaging. *Psychological Assessment, 25*(3), 1019–1024. https://doi.org/10.1037/a0033098

Lehmann, R. J. B., Thornton, D., Helmus, L. M., & Hanson, R. K. (2016). Developing non-arbitrary metrics for risk communication: Norms for the Risk Matrix 2000. *Criminal Justice and Behavior, 43*(12), 1661–1687. https://doi.org/10.1177/0093854816651656

Lemon, J. (2006). Plotrix: A package in the red light district of R. *R News, 6*(4), 8–12.

Leonhardt, J. M., & Robin Keller, L. (2018). Do pictographs affect probability comprehension and risk perception of multiple-risk communications? *The Journal of Consumer Affairs, 52*(3), 756–769. https://doi.org/10.1111/joca.12185

Levenson, J. S. (2004). Policy interventions designed to combat sexual violence: Community notification and civil commitment. *Journal of Child Sexual Abuse, 12*(3–4), 17–52. https://doi.org/10.1300/J070v12n03_02

Lewis, M. (2003). *Moneyball: The art of winning an unfair game*. W. W. Norton & Company.

Ley, P. (1972). *Quantitative aspects of psychological assessment: An introduction*. Gerald Duckworth.

Lindsay, D. S., Simons, D. J., & Lilienfeld, S. O. (2016). Research preregistration 101. *APS Observer, 29*(10). https://www.psychologicalscience.org/observer/research-preregistration-101

Liu, Y., Millsap, R. E., West, S. G., Tein, J.-Y., Tanaka, R., & Grimm, K. J. (2017). Testing measurement invariance in longitudinal data with ordered-categorical measures. *Psychological Methods, 22*(3), 486–506. https://doi.org/10.1037/met0000075

Lloyd, C. D., Hanson, R. K., Richards, D. K., & Serin, R. C. (2020). Reassessment improves prediction of criminal recidivism: A prospective study of 3,421 individuals in New Zealand. *Psychological Assessment, 32*(6), 568–581. https://doi.org/10.1037/pas0000813

Mann, R. E., Hanson, R. K., & Thornton, D. (2010). Assessing risk for sexual recidivism: Some proposals on the nature of psychologically meaningful risk factors. *Sexual Abuse, 22*(2), 191–217. https://doi.org/10.1177/1079063210366039

Matheny, M. E., Ohno-Machado, L., & Resnic, F. S. (2005). Discrimination and calibration of mortality risk prediction models in interventional cardiology. *Journal of Biomedical Informatics, 38*(5), 367–375. https://doi.org/10.1016/j.jbi.2005.02.007

Matthew, J. (2019). *generalhoslem: Goodness of fit tests for logistic regression models* (R package version 1.3.4) [Computer software]. https://CRAN.R-project.org/package=generalhoslem

McClelland, G. H., & Judd, C. M. (1993). Statistical difficulties of detecting interactions and moderator effects. *Psychological Bulletin, 114*(2), 376–390. https://doi.org/10.1037/0033-2909.114.2.376

Meehl, P. E. (1954). *Clinical vs. statistical prediction: A theoretical analysis and a review of the evidence*. University of Minnesota Press.

Meehl, P. E. (1986). Causes and effects of my disturbing little book. *Journal of Personality Assessment, 50*(3), 370–375. https://doi.org/10.1207/s15327752jpa5003_6

Menger, V., Spruit, M., van Est, R., Nap, E., & Scheepers, F. (2019). Machine learning approach to inpatient violence risk assessment using routinely collected clinical notes in electronic health records. *JAMA Network Open, 2*(7), e196709. https://doi.org/10.1001/jamanetworkopen.2019.6709

Michell, J. (1990). *An introduction to the logic of psychological measurement*. Lawrence Erlbaum Associates.

Mittlböck, M., & Schemper, M. (1996). Explained variation for logistic regression. *Statistics in Medicine, 15*(19), 1987–1997. https://doi.org/10.1002/(SICI)1097-0258(19961015)15:19<1987::AID-SIM318>3.0.CO;2-9

Moher, D., Jadad, A. R., Nichol, G., Penman, M., Tugwell, P., & Walsh, S. (1995). Assessing the quality of randomized controlled trials: An annotated bibliography of scales and checklists. *Controlled Clinical Trials, 16*(1), 62–73. https://doi.org/10.1016/0197-2456(94)00031-W

Moher, D., Shamseer, L., Clarke, M., Ghersi, D., Liberati, A., Petticrew, M., Shekelle, P., Stewart, L. A., & the PRISMA-P Group. (2015). Preferred reporting items for systematic review and meta-analysis protocols (PRISMA-P) 2015 statement. *Systematic Reviews, 4*(1), 1. https://doi.org/10.1186/2046-4053-4-1

Monahan, J. (2007). Statistical literacy: A prerequisite for evidence-based medicine. *Psychological Science in the Public Interest, 8*(2), i–ii. https://doi.org/10.1111/j.1539-6053.2008.00033_1.x

Monahan, J. (2021). The classification of violence risk. In R. K. Otto & K. S. Douglas (Eds.), *Handbook of violence risk assessment* (2nd ed., pp. 93–105). Routledge/Taylor & Francis Group.

Monahan, J., Steadman, H. J., Appelbaum, P. S., Grisso, T., Mulvey, E. P., Roth, L. H., Robbins, P. C., Banks, S., & Silver, E. (2006). The classification of violence risk. *Behavioral Sciences & the Law, 24*(6), 721–730. https://doi.org/10.1002/bsl.725

Mossman, D. (1994). Assessing predictions of violence: Being accurate about accuracy. *Journal of Consulting and Clinical Psychology, 62*(4), 783–792. https://doi.org/10.1037/0022-006X.62.4.783

Mossman, D., & Sellke, T. (2007). Avoiding errors about "margins of error." *The British Journal of Psychiatry, 191*(6), 561–561. https://doi.org/10.1192/bjp.191.6.561

Neal, T. M. S., & Grisso, T. (2014). Assessment practices and expert judgment methods in forensic psychology and psychiatry: An international snapshot. *Criminal Justice and Behavior, 41*(12), 1406–1421. https://doi.org/10.1177/0093854814548449

Nickerson, R. S. (2000). Null hypothesis significance testing: A review of an old and continuing controversy. *Psychological Methods, 5*(2), 241–301. https://doi.org/10.1037/1082-989X.5.2.241

Olkin, I. (1995). Statistical and theoretical considerations in meta-analysis. *Journal of Clinical Epidemiology, 48*(1), 133–146. https://doi.org/10.1016/0895-4356(94)00136-E

Olver, M. E., Mundt, J. C., Thornton, D., Beggs Christofferson, S. M., Kingston, D. A., Sowden, J. N., Nicholaichuk, T. P., Gordon, A., & Wong, S. C. P. (2018). Using the Violence Risk Scale—Sexual Offense version in sexual violence risk assessments: Updated risk categories and recidivism estimates from a multisite sample of treated sexual offenders. *Psychological Assessment, 30*(7), 941–955. https://doi.org/10.1037/pas0000538

Pencina, M. J., & D'Agostino, R. B. (2004). Overall C as a measure of discrimination in survival analysis: Model specific population value and confidence interval estimation. *Statistics in Medicine, 23*(13), 2109–2123. https://doi.org/10.1002/sim.1802

Phenix, A., Doren, D., Helmus, L., Hanson, R. K., & Thornton, D. (2009). *Coding rules for Static-2002.* Public Safety Canada. https://www.publicsafety.gc.ca/cnt/rsrcs/pblctns/sttc-2002/index-en.aspx

Phenix, A., Fernandez, Y., Harris, A. J. R., Helmus, M., Hanson, R. K., & Thornton, D. (2017). *Static-99R Coding Rules Revised—2016* (Research Report: 2017-R012). Public Safety Canada. https://www.publicsafety.gc.ca/cnt/rsrcs/pblctns/sttc-2016/index-en.aspx

Phenix, A., Helmus, L., & Hanson, R. K. (2016). *Static-99R and Static-2002R evaluator's workbook.*

Pierson, E., Simoiu, C., Overgoor, J., Corbett-Davies, S., Jenson, D., Shoemaker, A., Ramachandran, V., Barghouty, P., Phillips, C., Shroff, R., & Goel, S. (2020). A large-scale analysis of racial disparities in police stops across the United States. *Nature Human Behaviour, 4*(7), 736–745. https://doi.org/10.1038/s41562-020-0858-1

Popper, K. R. (1959). The propensity interpretation of probability. *The British Journal for the Philosophy of Science, 10*(37), 25–42. https://doi.org/10.1093/bjps/X.37.25

Quinsey, V. L., & Ambtman, R. (1979). Variables affecting psychiatrists' and teachers' assessments of the dangerousness of mentally ill offenders. *Journal of Consulting and Clinical Psychology, 47*(2), 353–362. https://doi.org/10.1037/0022-006X.47.2.353

Radick, G. (2015). History of science. Beyond the "Mendel–Fisher controversy." *Science, 350*(6257), 159–160. https://doi.org/10.1126/science.aab3846

Raftery, A. E. (1995). Bayesian model selection in social research. *Sociological Methodology, 25*(1), 111–163. https://doi.org/10.2307/271063

Raudenbush, S. W., & Bryk, A. S. (2002). *Hierarchical linear models: Applications and data analysis methods* (2nd ed.). Sage Publications.

R Core Team. (2020). *The R project for statistical computing.* R Foundation. https://www.R-project.org/

Revelle, W. (2020). *Package 'psych': Procedures for psychological, psychometric, and personality research* [Computer software]. https://personality-project.org/r/psych-manual.pdf

Reynolds, C. R. (1982). Methods for detecting construct and predictive bias. In R. A. Berk (Ed.), *Handbook of methods for detecting test bias* (pp. 199–227). Johns Hopkins University Press.

Reynolds, C. R. (2000). Methods for detecting and evaluating cultural bias in neuropsychological tests. In E. Fletcher-Janzen, T. L. Strickland, & C. R. Reynolds

(Eds.), *Handbook of cross-cultural neuropsychology* (pp. 249–285). Plenum Press. https://doi.org/10.1007/978-1-4615-4219-3_15

Reynolds, C. R., & Suzuki, L. A. (2013). Bias in psychological assessment: An empirical review and recommendations. In J. R. Graham, J. A. Naglieri, & I. B. Weiner (Eds.), *Handbook of psychology: Vol. 10. Assessment psychology* (pp. 82–113). John Wiley & Sons.

Rhodes, W., Gaes, G., Luallen, J., Kling, R., Rich, T., & Shively, M. (2016). Following incarceration, most released offenders never return to prison. *Crime and Delinquency, 62*(8), 1003–1025. https://doi.org/10.1177/0011128714549655

Rice, M. E., & Harris, G. T. (1995). Violent recidivism: Assessing predictive validity. *Journal of Consulting and Clinical Psychology, 63*(5), 737–748. https://doi.org/10.1037/0022-006X.63.5.737

Rice, M. E., & Harris, G. T. (2005). Comparing effect sizes in follow-up studies: ROC Area, Cohen's *d*, and *r*. *Law and Human Behavior, 29*(5), 615–620. https://doi.org/10.1007/s10979-005-6832-7

Robin, X., Turck, N., Hainard, A., Tiberti, N., Lisacek, F., Sanchez, J.-C., & Müller, M. (2011). pROC: An open-source package for R and S+ to analyze and compare ROC curves. *BMC Bioinformatics, 12*(1), 77. https://doi.org/10.1186/1471-2105-12-77

Rockhill, B., Byrne, C., Rosner, B., Louie, M. M., & Colditz, G. (2003). Breast cancer risk prediction with a log-incidence model: Evaluation of accuracy. *Journal of Clinical Epidemiology, 56*(9), 856–861. https://doi.org/10.1016/S0895-4356(03)00124-0

Rosenthal, R. (1979). The file drawer problem and tolerance for null results. *Psychological Bulletin, 86*(3), 638–641. https://doi.org/10.1037/0033-2909.86.3.638

Royston, P., Moons, K. G., Altman, D. G., & Vergouwe, Y. (2009). Prognosis and prognostic research: Developing a prognostic model. *BMJ, 338*(7707), b604. https://doi.org/10.1136/bmj.b604

Ruscio, J. (2008). A probability-based measure of effect size: Robustness to base rates and other factors. *Psychological Methods, 13*(1), 19–30. https://doi.org/10.1037/1082-989X.13.1.19

Ruscio, J., Carney, L. M., Dever, L., Pliskin, M., & Wang, S. B. (2018). Using the comparison curve fix index (CCFI) in taxometric analyses: Averaging curves, standard errors, and CCFI profiles. *Psychological Assessment, 30*(6), 744–754. https://doi.org/10.1037/pas0000522

Ruscio, J., Haslam, N., & Ruscio, A. M. (2006). *Introduction to the taxometric method: A practical guide*. Lawrence Erlbaum Associates.

Sánchez-Meca, J., Marín-Martínez, F., & Chacón-Moscoso, S. (2003). Effect-size indices for dichotomized outcomes in meta-analysis. *Psychological Methods, 8*(4), 448–467. https://doi.org/10.1037/1082-989X.8.4.448

Schalkoff, R. J. (1997). *Artificial neural networks*. McGraw-Hill.

Schmidt, F., Sinclair, S. M., & Thomasdóttir, S. (2016). Predictive validity of the Youth Level of Service/Case Management Inventory with youth who have committed sexual and non-sexual offenses: The utility of professional override. *Criminal Justice and Behavior, 43*(3), 413–430. https://doi.org/10.1177/0093854815603389

Schulze, R. (2007). Current methods for meta-analysis: Approaches, issues, and developments. *Zeitschrift für Psychologie/Journal of Psychology, 215*(2), 90–103. https://doi.org/10.1027/0044-3409.215.2.90

Seto, M. C., Hanson, R. K., & Babchishin, K. M. (2011). Contact sexual offending by men with online sexual offenses. *Sexual Abuse, 23*(1), 124–145. https://doi.org/10.1177/1079063210369013

Shapin, S. (2010). *Never pure: Historical studies of science as if it was produced by people with bodies situated in time, space, culture, and society, and struggling for credibility and authority*. Johns Hopkins University Press.

Shrout, P. E., & Fleiss, J. L. (1979). Intraclass correlations: Uses in assessing rater reliability. *Psychological Bulletin, 86*(2), 420–428. https://doi.org/10.1037/0033-2909.86.2.420

Singer, J. D., & Willett, J. B. (1993). It's about time: Using discrete-time survival analysis to study duration and the timing of events. *Journal of Educational Statistics, 18*(2), 155–195. https://doi.org/10.3102/10769986018002155

Singer, J. D., & Willett, J. B. (2003). *Applied longitudinal data analysis: Modeling change and event occurrence*. Oxford University Press. https://doi.org/10.1093/acprof:oso/9780195152968.001.0001

Sivakumar, H., & Peyton, P. J. (2016). Poor agreement in significant findings between meta-analyses and subsequent large randomized trials in perioperative medicine. *British Journal of Anaesthesia, 117*(4), 431–441. https://doi.org/10.1093/bja/aew170

Sjöstedt, G., & Långström, N. (2001). Actuarial assessment of sex offender recidivism risk: A cross-validation of the RRASOR and the Static-99 in Sweden. *Law and Human Behavior, 25*(6), 629–645. https://doi.org/10.1023/A:1012758307983

Skeem, J. L., & Monahan, J. (2011). Current directions in violence risk assessment. *Current Directions in Psychological Science, 20*(1), 38–42. https://doi.org/10.1177/0963721410397271

Slovic, P., Monahan, J., & MacGregor, D. G. (2000). Violence risk assessment and risk communication: The effects of using actual cases, providing instruction, and employing probability versus frequency formats. *Law and Human Behavior, 24*(3), 271–296. https://doi.org/10.1023/A:1005595519944

Smith, M. L., & Glass, G. V. (1977). Meta-analysis of psychotherapy outcome studies. *American Psychologist, 32*(9), 752–760. https://doi.org/10.1037/0003-066X.32.9.752

Statistics Canada. (2019). *Changes in life expectancy by selected causes of death, 2017*. https://www150.statcan.gc.ca/n1/daily-quotidien/190530/dq190530d-eng.htm

Steadman, H. J., Silver, E., Monahan, J., Appelbaum, P. S., Robbins, P. C., Mulvey, E. P., Grisso, T., Roth, L. H., & Banks, S. (2000). A classification tree approach to the development of actuarial violence risk assessment tools. *Law and Human Behavior, 24*(1), 83–100. https://doi.org/10.1023/A:1005478820425

Steyerberg, E. W. (2009). *Clinical prediction models: A practical approach to development, validation, and updating*. Springer. https://doi.org/10.1007/978-0-387-77244-8

Steyerberg, E. W. (2019). *Clinical prediction models: A practical approach to development, validation, and updating* (2nd ed.). Springer. https://doi.org/10.1007/978-3-030-16399-0

Stine, R. (1989). An introduction to bootstrap methods: Examples and ideas. *Sociological Methods & Research, 18*(2–3), 243–291. https://doi.org/10.1177/0049124189018002003

Storey, J. E., Watt, K. A., Jackson, K. J., & Hart, S. D. (2012). Utilization and implications of the Static-99 in practice. *Sexual Abuse, 24*(3), 289–302. https://doi.org/10.1177/1079063211423943

Sweeting, M. J., Sutton, A. J., & Lambert, P. C. (2004). What to add to nothing? Use and avoidance of continuity corrections in meta-analysis of sparse data. *Statistics in Medicine, 23*(9), 1351–1375. https://doi.org/10.1002/sim.1761

Swets, J. A. (1973). The relative operating characteristic in psychology: A technique for isolating effects of response bias finds wide use in the study of perception and cognition. *Science, 182*(4116), 990–1000. https://doi.org/10.1126/science.182.4116.990

Swets, J. A., Dawes, R. M., & Monahan, J. (2000). Psychological science can improve diagnostic decisions. *Psychological Science in the Public Interest, 1*(1), 1–26. https://doi.org/10.1111/1529-1006.001

Therneau, T. (2020). *A package for survival analysis in R* (R package version 3.2-7) [Computer software]. https://CRAN.R-project.org/package=survival

Thornton, D., Hanson, R. K., Kelley, S. M., & Mundt, J. C. (2021). Estimating lifetime and residual risk for individuals who remain sexual offense free in the community: Practical applications. *Sexual Abuse, 33*(1), 3–33. https://doi.org/10.1177/1079063219871573

Torchiano, M. (2020). *Effsize: Efficient effect size computation* (R package version 0.8.1) [Computer software]. https://doi.org/10.5281/zenodo.1480624

Tufte, E. R. (1990). *Envisioning information*. Graphics Press.

Tufte, E. R. (2001). *The visual display of quantitative information* (2nd ed.). Graphics Press.

Tufte, E. R. (2006). *Beautiful evidence*. Graphis Press.

Tully, R. J., Chou, S., & Browne, K. D. (2013). A systematic review on the effectiveness of sex offender risk assessment tools in predicting sexual recidivism of adult male sex offenders. *Clinical Psychology Review, 33*(2), 287–316. https://doi.org/10.1016/j.cpr.2012.12.002

Vergouwe, Y., Steyerberg, E. W., Eijkemans, M. J., & Habbema, J. D. F. (2005). Substantial effective sample sizes were required for external validation studies of predictive logistic regression models. *Journal of Clinical Epidemiology, 58*(5), 475–483. https://doi.org/10.1016/j.jclinepi.2004.06.017

Viallon, V., Ragusa, S., Clavel-Chapelon, F., & Bénichou, J. (2009). How to evaluate the calibration of a disease risk prediction tool. *Statistics in Medicine, 28*(6), 901–916. https://doi.org/10.1002/sim.3517

Viechtbauer, W. (2010). Conducting meta-analyses in R with the metafor package. *Journal of Statistical Software, 36*(3), 1–48. https://doi.org/10.18637/jss.v036.i03

Visschers, V. H. M., Meertens, R. M., Passchier, W. W., & de Vries, N. N. K. (2009). Probability information in risk communication: A review of the research literature. *Risk Analysis, 29*(2), 267–287. https://doi.org/10.1111/j.1539-6924.2008.01137.x

Wanamaker, K. A., & Brown, S. L. (2021). The relationship between patterns of change in dynamic risk and strength scores and reoffending for men on community supervision. *Criminal Justice and Behavior*. Advance online publication. https://doi.org/10.1177/0093854821993512

Webster, C. (2010, June 3–5). *From flipping coins to looking at both sides of them: Assessing violence risk and strengths over the short-term* [Paper presentation]. Annual Convention of the Canadian Psychological Association, Winnipeg, Canada.

Weinberger, D. M., Harboe, Z. B., Sanders, E. A., Ndiritu, M., Klugman, K. P., Rückinger, S., Dagan, R., Adegbola, R., Cutts, F., Johnson, H. L., O'Brien, K. L., Scott, J. A., & Lipsitch, M. (2010). Association of serotype with risk of death due to pneumococcal pneumonia: A meta-analysis. *Clinical Infectious Diseases, 51*(6), 692–699. https://doi.org/10.1086/655828

Welchowski, T., & Schmid, M. (2019). *discSurv: Discrete time survival analysis* (R package version 1.41) [Computer software]. https://CRAN.R-project.org/package=discSurv

West, G. (2017). *Scale: The universal laws of growth, innovation, sustainability, and the pace of lie in organisms, cities, economies, and companies*. Penguin Press.

Whitaker, D. J., Le, B., Hanson, R. K., Baker, C. K., McMahon, P. M., Ryan, G., Klein, A., & Rice, D. D. (2008). Risk factors for the perpetration of child sexual abuse: A review and meta-analysis. *Child Abuse & Neglect, 32*(5), 529–548. https://doi.org/10.1016/j.chiabu.2007.08.005

Whitehurst, G. J. (1984). Interrater agreement for journal manuscript reviews. *American Psychologist, 39*(1), 22–28. https://doi.org/10.1037/0003-066X.39.1.22

Willett, J. B., & Singer, J. D. (1993). Investigating onset, cessation, relapse, and recovery: Why you should, and how you can, use discrete-time survival analysis to examine event occurrence. *Journal of Consulting and Clinical Psychology, 61*(6), 952–965. https://doi.org/10.1037/0022-006X.61.6.952

Wilson, E. B. (1927). Probable inference, the law of succession, and statistical inference. *Journal of the American Statistical Association, 22*(158), 209–212. https://doi.org/10.1080/01621459.1927.10502953

Wilson, H. A., & Gutierrez, L. (2014). Does one size fit all? A meta-analysis examining the predictive ability of the Level of Service Inventory (LSI) with Indigenous offenders. *Criminal Justice and Behavior, 41*(2), 196–219. https://doi.org/10.1177/0093854813500958

Wittgenstein, L. (1976). *Philosophical investigations* (3rd ed., G. E. M. Anscombe, Trans.). Basil Blackwell.

World Health Organization. (2019). *Sex ratio: Population sex ratio (males per 100 females).* http://www.searo.who.int/entity/health_situation_trends/data/chi/sex-ratio/en/

Wormith, J. S., Hogg, S., & Guzzo, L. (2012). The predictive validity of a general risk/needs assessment inventory on sexual offender recidivism and an exploration of the professional override. *Criminal Justice and Behavior, 39*(12), 1511–1538. https://doi.org/10.1177/0093854812455741

Yamagishi, K. (1997). When a 12.86% mortality is more dangerous than 24.14%: Implications for risk communication. *Applied Cognitive Psychology, 11*(6), 495–506. https://doi.org/10.1002/(SICI)1099-0720(199712)11:6<495::AID-ACP481>3.0.CO;2-J

Yang, M., Wong, S. C., & Coid, J. (2010). The efficacy of violence prediction: A meta-analytic comparison of nine risk assessment tools. *Psychological Bulletin, 136*(5), 740–767. https://doi.org/10.1037/a0020473

Yarkoni, T., & Westfall, J. (2017). Choosing prediction over explanation in psychology: Lessons from machine learning. *Perspectives on Psychological Science, 12*(6), 1100–1122. https://doi.org/10.1177/1745691617693393

Zhou, J., Witt, K., Xiang, Y., Zhu, X., Wang, X., & Fazel, S. (2016). Violence risk assessment in psychiatric patients in China: A systematic review. *The Australian and New Zealand Journal of Psychiatry, 50*(1), 33–45. https://doi.org/10.1177/0004867415585580

INDEX

C

D

G

H

I

J

K

L

P

S

T

ABOUT THE AUTHOR

R. Karl Hanson, PhD, CPsych, is one of the leading researchers in the field of recidivism risk assessment for crime and violence. Originally trained as a clinical psychologist, he was a researcher and research manager in the area of corrections and crime policy for Public Safety Canada between 1991 and 2017. Dr. Hanson has published more than 200 articles, including several highly influential reviews. He is lead author of the most widely used measures for assessing the risk and needs of individuals with a history of sexual offending (Static-99R, Static-2002R, STABLE-2007). Based in Ottawa, Ontario, Canada, he is adjunct faculty in the psychology department of Carleton University (Ottawa) and president of the not-for-profit organization SAARNA (Society for the Advancement of Actuarial Risk Need Assessment).